5th Workshop on Computational Approaches to Subjectivity, Sentiment and Social Media Analysis

(WASSA 2014)

AA005926

Held at ACL 2014

Baltimore, Maryland, USA
27 June 2014

ISBN: 978-1-63439-206-8

Printed from e-media with permission by:

Curran Associates, Inc.
57 Morehouse Lane
Red Hook, NY 12571

Some format issues inherent in the e-media version may also appear in this print version.

Printed by Curran Associates, Inc. (2014)

For permission requests, please contact the Association for Computational Linguistics at the address below.

Association for Computational Linguistics
209 N. Eighth Street
Stroudsburg, Pennsylvania 18360

Phone: 1-570-476-8006
Fax: 1-570-476-0860

acl@aclweb.org

Additional copies of this publication are available from:

Curran Associates, Inc.
57 Morehouse Lane
Red Hook, NY 12571 USA
Phone: 845-758-0400
Fax: 845-758-2634
Email: curran@proceedings.com
Web: www.proceedings.com

Introduction

Research in automatic Subjectivity and Sentiment Analysis (SSA), as subtasks of Affective Computing and Natural Language Processing (NLP), has flourished in the past years. The growth in interest in these tasks was motivated by the birth and rapid expansion of the Social Web that made it possible for people all over the world to share, comment or consult content on any given topic. In this context, opinions, sentiments and emotions expressed in Social Media texts have been shown to have a high influence on the social and economic behavior worldwide. SSA systems are highly relevant to many real-world applications (e.g. marketing, eGovernance, business intelligence, social analysis) and also to many tasks in Natural Language Processing (NLP) - information extraction, question answering, textual entailment, to name just a few. The importance of this field has been proven by the high number of approaches proposed in research in the past decade, as well as by the interest that it raised from other disciplines (Economics, Sociology, Psychology) and the applications that were created using its technology.

Despite the large interest shown by the research community and the development of a set of benchmarking resources and methods to tackle sentiment analysis, SSA remains far from being a solved issue. While systems working for English on customer reviews obtain good results in sentiment classification, systems working for other languages or on Social Media texts are still struggling to surpass the baseline. As such, it is necessary to continue the sentiment analysis community's efforts to develop new resources and methods, as well as to bring knowledge and experience from other disciplines that have been dealing with affect phenomena (e.g. Psychology, Sociology, etc.).

The aim of the 5th Workshop on Computational Approaches to Subjectivity, Sentiment and Social Media Analysis (WASSA 2014) was to continue the line of the previous editions, bringing together researchers in Computational Linguistics working on Subjectivity and Sentiment Analysis and researchers working on interdisciplinary aspects of affect computation from text. Starting with 2013, WASSA has extended its scope and focus to Social Media phenomena and the impact of affect-related phenomena in this context.

WASSA 2014 was organized in conjunction to the 52nd Annual Meeting of the Association for Computational Linguistics (ACL 2014), on June 27, 2014, in Baltimore, Maryland, United States of America.

For this year's edition of WASSA, we received a total of 40 submissions, from universities and research centers all over the world, out of which 8 were accepted as long and another 14 as short papers. Each paper has been thoroughly reviewed by at least 2 members of the Program Committee. The accepted papers were all highly assessed by the reviewers, the best paper receiving an average punctuation (computed as an average of all criteria used to assess the papers) of 4.5 out of 5.

The main topics of the accepted papers are related to computational and cognitive modelling of affect, especially in Social Media - the creation and evaluation of resources for subjectivity, sentiment and emotion resources for Twitter mining, the development of semantic analysis-based methods for sentiment detection, argumentation and inference analysis, cross-lingual and multilingual resource creation and use, the detection of irony and sarcasm.

The invited talks reflected the multimodal nature of affect expressions and the strong connection between human affect-sensing mechanisms. At the same time, the talks drew our attention on the possible misuses of social media platforms that can bias opinion analysis, both to humans, as well as automatic systems. Finally, the talk by the organizers described the difficulties involved in porting research to the real-life application scenario.

This year's edition has again shown that the topics put forward to discussion by WASSA are of high interest to the research community and that the papers chosen to be debated in this forum bring an important development to the SSA research area.

We would like to thank the ACL 2014 Organizers for the help and support at the different stages of the workshop organization process. We are also especially grateful to the Program Committee members and the external reviewers for the time and effort spent assessing the papers. We would like to extend our thanks to our invited speakers – Dr. Saif Mohammad and Dr. Myle Ott - for accepting to deliver the keynote talks.

Secondly, we would like to express our gratitude for the official endorsement we received from SIGNLL, the ACL Special Interest Group on Natural Language Learning, and SIGSEM, ACL's Special Interest Group on Computational Semantics.

We would like to express our gratitude to Yaniv Steiner, who created the WASSA logo and to the entire Europe Media Monitor team at the European Commission Joint Research Centre, for the technical support they provided.

Alexandra Balahur, Erik van der Goot, Ralf Steinberger and Andrés Montoyo
WASSA 2014 Chairs

Organizers:

Alexandra Balahur
European Commission Joint Research Centre
Institute for the Protection and Security of the Citizen

Erik van der Goot
European Commission Joint Research Centre
Institute for the Protection and Security of the Citizen

Ralf Steinberger
European Commission Joint Research Centre
Institute for the Protection and Security of the Citizen

Andrés Montoyo
University of Alicante
Department of Software and Computing Systems

Program Committee:

Taras Zagibalov, Brantwatch (U.K.)

Invited Speakers:

Saif M. Mohammad, National Research Council Canada, Canada
Myle Ott, Facebook, U.S.A.

Table of Contents

Conference Program

Friday June 27, 2014

(8:30) Opening Remarks

(8:35) Invited talk: Dr. Saif Mohammad

Words: Evaluative, Emotional, Colourful, Musical!
Saif Mohammad

(9:10) Session 1: Cross-domain and Multilingual Sentiment Analysis

9:10 *Robust Cross-Domain Sentiment Analysis for Low-Resource Languages*
Jakob Elming, Barbara Plank and Dirk Hovy

9:35 *An Investigation for Implicatures in Chinese : Implicatures in Chinese and in English are similar !*
Lingjia Deng and Janyce Wiebe

10:00 *Inducing Domain-specific Noun Polarity Guided by Domain-independent Polarity Preferences of Adjectives*
Manfred Klenner, Michael Amsler and Nora Hollenstein

10:15 *Aspect-Level Sentiment Analysis in Czech*
Josef Steinberger, Tomáš Brychcín and Michal Konkol

(10:30) Break

(10:50) Invited talk: Dr. Myle Ott

10:50 *Linguistic Models of Deceptive Opinion Spam*
Myle Ott

Friday June 27, 2014 (continued)

(11:25) Session 2: Emotion, Irony and Sarcasm Classification

11:25 *Semantic Role Labeling of Emotions in Tweets*
Saif Mohammad, Xiaodan Zhu and Joel Martin

11:50 *An Impact Analysis of Features in a Classification Approach to Irony Detection in Product Reviews*
Konstantin Buschmeier, Philipp Cimiano and Roman Klinger

12:15 *Modelling Sarcasm in Twitter, a Novel Approach*
Francesco Barbieri, Horacio Saggion and Francesco Ronzano

12:30 *Emotive or Non-emotive: That is The Question*
Michal Ptaszynski, Fumito Masui, Rafal Rzepka and Kenji Araki

(12:45) Lunch Break

(14:00) Demo talk: Dr. Alexandra Balahur

14:00 *Challenges in Creating a Multilingual Sentiment Analysis Application for Social Media Mining*
Alexandra Balahur, Hristo Tanev and Erik van der Goot

(14:30) Session 3: Lexical Acquisition and Feature Weighting for Sentiment Analysis

14:30 *Two-Step Model for Sentiment Lexicon Extraction from Twitter Streams*
Ilia Chetviorkin and Natalia Loukachevitch

14:45 *Linguistically Informed Tweet Categorization for Online Reputation Management*
Gerard Lynch and Pádraig Cunningham

15:00 *Credibility Adjusted Term Frequency: A Supervised Term Weighting Scheme for Sentiment Analysis and Text Classification*
Yoon Kim and Owen Zhang

15:15 *Opinion Mining and Topic Categorization with Novel Term Weighting*
Tatiana Gasanova, Roman Sergienko, Shakhnaz Akhmedova, Eugene Semenkin and Wolfgang Minker

Friday June 27, 2014 (continued)

(15:30) Break

(16:00) Session 4: Sentiment Analysis from Discourse and Dialogues

16:00 *Sentiment classification of online political discussions: a comparison of a word-based and dependency-based method*
Hugo Lewi Hammer, Per Erik Solberg and Lilja Øvrelid

16:25 *Improving Agreement and Disagreement Identification in Online Discussions with A Socially-Tuned Sentiment Lexicon*
Lu Wang and Claire Cardie

16:50 *Lexical Acquisition for Opinion Inference: A Sense-Level Lexicon of Benefactive and Malefactive Events*
Yoonjung Choi, Lingjia Deng and Janyce Wiebe

17:05 *Dive deeper: Deep Semantics for Sentiment Analysis*
Nikhilkumar Jadhav and Pushpak Bhattacharyya

(17:20) Break

(17:30) Session 5: Sentiment Analysis Evaluation. Going Beyond Current Sentiment Analysis Approaches

17:30 *Evaluating Sentiment Analysis Evaluation: A Case Study in Securities Trading*
Siavash Kazemian, Shunan Zhao and Gerald Penn

17:55 *Sentiment Classification on Polarity Reviews: An Empirical Study Using Rating-based Features*
Dai Quoc Nguyen, Dat Quoc Nguyen, Thanh Vu and Son Bao Pham

18:20 *Effect of Using Regression on Class Confidence Scores in Sentiment Analysis of Twitter Data*
Itir Onal, Ali Mert Ertugrul and Ruken Cakici

18:35 *A cognitive study of subjectivity extraction in sentiment annotation*
Abhijit Mishra, Aditya Joshi and Pushpak Bhattacharyya

18:50 *The Use of Text Similarity and Sentiment Analysis to Examine Rationales in the Large-Scale Online Deliberations*
Wanting Mao, Lu Xiao and Robert Mercer

19:05 *A Conceptual Framework for Inferring Implicatures*
Janyce Wiebe and Lingjia Deng

Friday June 27, 2014 (continued)

(19:20) Closing remarks

Words: Evaluative, Emotional, Colourful, Musical!

Saif M. Mohammad
National Research Council Canada
1200 Montreal Road,
Building M-50
Ottawa, Ontario K1A 0R6, Canada
Saif.Mohammad@nrc-cnrc.gc.ca

Abstract of the talk

Beyond literal meaning, words have associations with sentiment, emotion, colour, and even music. Identifying such associations is of substantial benefit for information visualization, data sonification, and sentiment analysis, which in turn have applications in commerce, education, art, and health. I will present methods to generate high-coverage resources that capture such associations. I will show how these resources can be used for analyzing emotions in text, detecting personality from essays, and generating music from novels. Finally, I will show how word-sentiment association lexicons have helped create the top-ranking systems in recent SemEval competitions on the sentiment analysis of social media posts.

Proceedings of the 5th Workshop on Computational Approaches to Subjectivity, Sentiment and Social Media Analysis, page 1,
Baltimore, Maryland, USA. June 27, 2014.

Robust Cross-Domain Sentiment Analysis for Low-Resource Languages

Jakob Elming **Dirk Hovy** **Barbara Plank**
Centre for Language Technology
University of Copenhagen
zmk867@hum.ku.dk,{dirk,bplank}@cst.dk

Abstract

While various approaches to domain adaptation exist, the majority of them requires knowledge of the target domain, and additional data, preferably labeled. For a language like English, it is often feasible to match most of those conditions, but in low-resource languages, it presents a problem. We explore the situation when neither data nor other information about the target domain is available. We use two samples of Danish, a low-resource language, from the consumer review domain (film vs. company reviews) in a sentiment analysis task. We observe dramatic performance drops when moving from one domain to the other. We then introduce a simple offline method that makes models more robust towards unseen domains, and observe relative improvements of more than 50%.

1 Introduction

Sentiment analysis, the task of determining the polarity of a text, is a valuable tool for gathering information from the vast amount of opinionated text produced today. It is actively used in reputation management and consumer assessment (Amigó et al., 2012; Amigó et al., 2013). While supervised approaches achieve reasonable performance (Mohammad et al., 2013), they are typically highly domain-dependent. In fact, moving from one (source) domain to a different (target) domain will often lead to severe performance drops (Blitzer et al., 2007; Daumé et al., 2010). This is mainly due to the models overfitting the source (training) data, both in terms of its label and word distribution. The task of overcoming this tendency is known as domain adaptation (DA) (Blitzer et al., 2007; Daumé et al., 2010).

There are three different approaches to DA: in *Supervised DA*, labeled training data for the target domain exists, in *Unsupervised DA*, data for the target domain exists, but it is unlabeled. A third, less investigated scenario is *Blind DA*: the target domain is not known at all in advance. Supervised DA effectively counteracts domain-bias by including labeled data from the target domain during training, thus preventing overfitting to both the label and the word distribution of the source. Unsupervised methods usually rely either on external data, in the form of gazetteers, dictionaries, or on unlabeled data from the target domain. While they do not prevent overfitting to the source domain's label distribution, the additional data acts as a regularizer by introducing a larger vocabulary.

However, both cases presuppose that we already know the target domain and have data from it. In many real-world settings, these conditions are not met, especially when dealing with low-resource languages. We thus need to regularize our models independent of the possible target domains. Effectively, this means that we need to prevent our models from memorizing the observed label distribution, and from putting too much weight on features that are predictive in the source domain, but might not even be present in the target domain.

In this paper, we investigate sentiment analysis for Danish, a low-resource language, and therefore approach it as a *Blind DA* problem. We perform experiments on two types of domains, namely reviews for movies and companies. The challenge lies in the fact that the label distribution (positive, negative, neutral) changes dramatically when moving from one domain to the other, and many highly predictive words in the company domain (e.g., "reliable") are unlikely to carry over to the movie domain, and vice versa. To the best of our knowledge, this is the first study to perform sentiment analysis for Danish, a low-resource language where relevant resources like polarity dictionaries

Proceedings of the 5th Workshop on Computational Approaches to Subjectivity, Sentiment and Social Media Analysis, pages 2–7,
Baltimore, Maryland, USA. June 27, 2014.

are hard to come by.

We present a simple offline-learning version inspired by previous work on corruptions (Søgaard, 2013), which also addresses the sparsity of available training data. Our method introduces a relative improvement on out-of-domain performance by up to 54%.

2 Robust Learning

The main idea behind robust learning is to steer the model away from overfitting the source domain. Overfitting can occur either by

1. putting too much weight on certain features (which might not be present in the target domain), or

2. over-using certain labels (since the label distribution on the target domain might differ).

One approach that has been proven to reduce overfitting is data corruption, also known as dropout training (Søgaard and Johannsen, 2012; Søgaard, 2013), which is a way of regularizing the model by randomly leaving out features. Intuitively, this approach can be viewed as coercing the learning algorithm to rely on more general, but less consistent features. Rather than learning to mainly trust the features that are highly predictive for the given training data, the algorithm is encouraged to use the less predictive features, since the highly predictive features might be deleted by the corruption. Most prior work on dropout regularization (Søgaard and Johannsen, 2012; Wang and Manning, 2012; Søgaard, 2013) has used online corruptions, i.e., the specific dropout function is integrated into the learning objective and thus tied to the specific learner. Here, we propose a simple approximation, i.e., a wrapper function that corrupts instances in an off-line fashion based on the weights learned from a base model. The advantage is that it can be used for any learning function, thereby abstracting away from the underlying learner.

2.1 Our approach

Our off-line feature corruption algorithm works as follows:

1. train an uncorrupted (base) model,

2. create k copies of the training data instances,

3. corrupt copies based on the feature weights of the base model and an exponential function (described below), and

4. train a new model on the corrupted training data.

The advantages of this algorithm compared to online corruption are

1. it is a wrapper method, so it becomes very easy to move to a different learning algorithm, and

2. corruption is done based on knowledge from a full, uncorrupted model, which provides a better picture of the overfitting.

This comes, however, at the cost of longer training times, but in a low-resource language training time is less of an issue.

Specifically, multiple copies of the training data are used in the corrupted training stage. This results in each data point appearing in different, corrupted versions, as visualized in Figure 1. The copying process retains more of the information in the training data, since it is unlikely that the same feature is deleted in each copy. In our experiments, we used k=5. Larger values of k resulted in longer training times without improving performance.

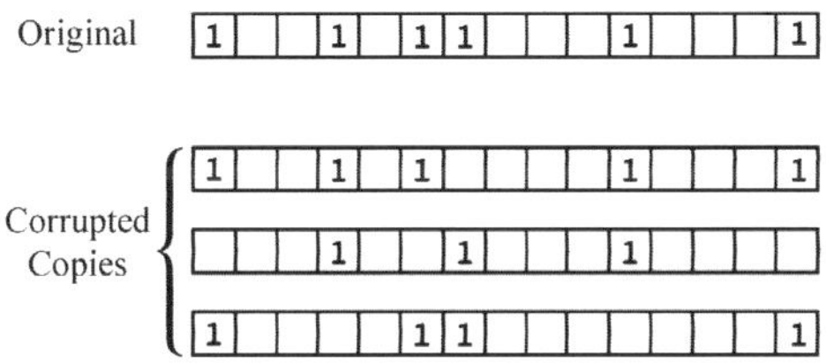

Figure 1: Example of an original feature vector and its multiple corrupted copies.

We experiment with a *random* and a *biased* corruption approach. The first approach (Søgaard and Johannsen, 2012) does not utilize the feature weight information from the base model, but randomly deletes 10% of the features. We use this approach to test whether an effect is merely the result of deleting features.

The biased approach, on the other hand, targets the most predictive features in the base model for deletion. We use a function that increases the probability of deleting a feature exponentially

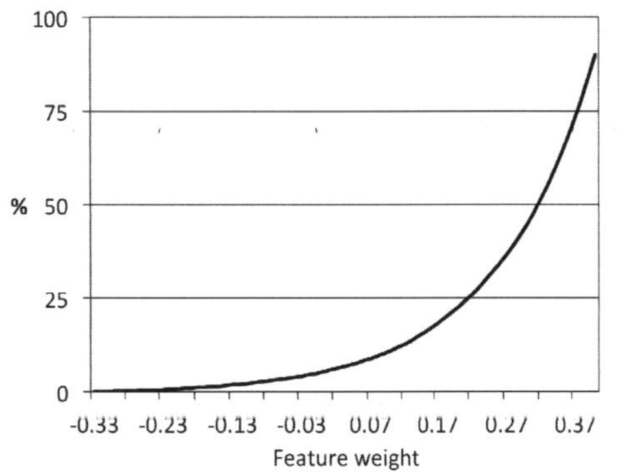

Figure 2: The corruption function conditioning the probability of deleting a feature in a positive instance on its weight in the Scope baseline model.

with its model weight. That is, a highly predictive feature (with a high weight in the model) will be more likely to be deleted. A feature with a low weight, on the other hand, has a much lower chance of being deleted. Figure 2 visualizes the exponential corruption function used. The function assigns the lowest weighted feature of the model zero likelihood of deletion, and the highest weighted feature a 0.9 likelihood of deletion. In order to mainly corrupt the highly predictive features, the exponential function is shifted to an area with a steeper gradient. That is, instead of scaling to the exponential function between 0 and 1, it is scaled to the area between -3 and 2 (parameters set experimentally on the development set). The corruption probability p_{cor} of deleting a feature f given a category c is defined as

$$p_{cor}(f|c) = \frac{exp(\frac{w(f|c)-w_{min}(c)}{w_{max}(c)-w_{min}(c)}*5-3)-exp(-3)}{exp(2)-exp(-3)} * 0.9 \quad (1)$$

with $w(f|c)$ being the weight of f given the instance category c in the model, and $w_{min}(c)$ and $w_{max}(c)$ being the lowest and highest weights of the model respectively for category c.

3 Experiments

Our experiments use Danish reviews from two domains: movies and companies. The specifications of the data sets are listed in Table 1 and Figure 3. The two data sets differ considerably in data size and label distribution.

DOMAIN	SPLIT	REVIEWS	WORDS
Scope	Train	8,718	749,952
	Dev	1,198	107,351
	Test	2,454	210,367
	Total	12,370	1,067,670
Trustpilot	Train	170,137	7,180,160
	Dev	23,958	1,000,443
	Test	48,252	2,040,956
	Total	242,347	10,221,559

Table 1: Overview of data set and split sizes in number of reviews and number of words.

3.1 Data preparation

The movie reviews are downloaded from a Danish movie website, `www.scope.dk`. They contain reviews of 829 movies, each rated on a scale from 1 to 6 stars. The company reviews are downloaded from a Danish consumer review website, `www.trustpilot.dk`. They consist of reviews of 19k companies, each rated between 1 and 5 stars.

Similar to prior work on sentiment analysis (Blitzer et al., 2007), the star ratings are binned into the three standard categories; positive, neutral, and negative. For the Scope data, a 6 star rating is considered positive, a 3 or 4 rating neutral, and a 1 star rating negative. 2 and 5 star ratings are excluded to retain more distinct categories. For the Trustpilot data, 5 star reviews are categorized as positive, 3 stars as neutral, and 1 star as negative. Similar to Scope data, 2 and 4 stars are excluded.

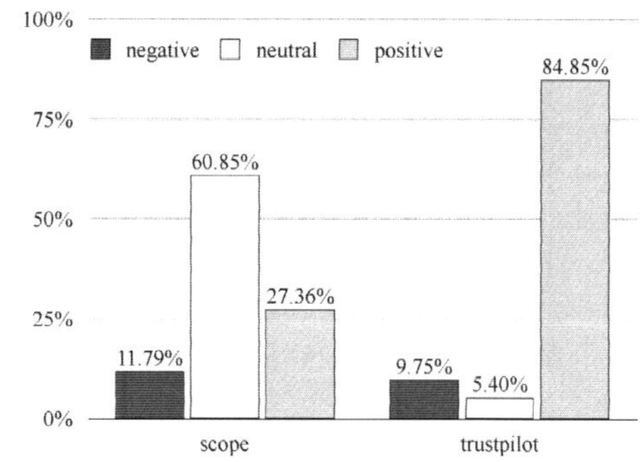

Figure 3: Label distribution in the two data sets.

Apart from the difference in size, the two data sets also differ in the distribution of categories (see Figure 3). This means that a majority label baseline estimated from one would perform horribly on

- N-gram presence for token lengths 1 to 4
- Skip-grams (n-gram with one middle word replaced by *) presence for token lengths 3 to 4
- Character n-gram presence for entire document string for token lengths 1 to 5
- Brown clusters (Brown et al., 1992; Liang, 2005) estimated on the source training data
- Number of words with only upper case characters
- Number of contiguous sequences of question marks, exclamation marks, or both
- Presence of question mark or exclamation mark in last word
- Number of words with characters repeated more than two times e.g. 'sooooo'
- Number of negated contexts using algorithm described in the text
- Most positive, most negative, or same amount of polar words according to a sentiment lexicon

Table 2: Feature set description.

the other domain. For instance, the majority baseline on Scope (assigning $neutral$ to all instances) achieves a 5% accuracy on Trustpilot data. Similarly, the Trustpilot majority baseline obtains an accuracy of 27% on Scope data by always assigning $positive$.

We choose not to balance the data sets, in keeping with the blind DA setup. Knowing the target label distribution can help greatly, but we can assume no prior knowledge about that. In fact, the difference in label distribution is one of the major challenges when predicting on out-of-domain data.

3.2 Features

The features we use (described in Table 2) are inspired by the top performing system from the SemEval-2013 task on Twitter sentiment analysis (Mohammad et al., 2013).

One main difference is that Mohammad et al. (2013) had several high-quality sentiment lexicons at their disposal, shown to be effective. Working with a low-resource language, we only have access to a single lexicon created by an MA student (containing 2248 positive and 4736 negative word forms). Our lexicon features are therefore simpler, i.e., based on whether words are considered positive or negative in the lexicon, as opposed to the score-based features in Mohammad et al. (2013).

We adopted the simple negation scope resolution algorithm directly from Mohammad et al. (2013). Anything appearing in-between a negation token[1] and the first following punctuation mark is considered a negated context. This works well for English, but Danish has different sentence adverbial placement, so the negation may also appear after the negated constituent. This simple algorithm is therefore less likely to be beneficial in a Danish system. We plan to extend the system for better negation handling in future work.

3.3 Corruption

The corruption happens at the feature-instance level. When we refer to the deletion of a feature in the following, it does not mean the deletion of this feature throughout the training data, but the deletion of a single instance in a feature vector (cf. Figure 1).

Corrupting the Scope data deleted 9.24% of all feature instances in the training data. Most features are deleted from $positive$ instances (16.7% of all features) and least from the majority $neutral$ instances (6.5% of all features). Only 9.4% of the minority class $negative$ are deleted.

For Trustpilot, the corruption deleted 11.73% of the feature instances. The pattern is the same here, though more extreme. The majority $positive$ class has the fewest features removed (2.2%), the minority class $neutral$ has 22.8% of its features deleted, and the $negative$ class has an overwhelming 35.6% of its features deleted.

The fact that the corruption function does not take the weight distribution of the individual labels into account, and therefore corrupts the data of some labels much more than others, does prove to be a problem. We will get back to this in the results section.

4 Results

Table 3 shows the results of the experiments. We report both accuracy and the average f-score for positive and negative instances (AF).

AF is the official SemEval-2013 metric (Nakov et al., 2013). It offers a more detailed insight into

[1] We use the following negation markers: *ikke, ingen, intet, ingenting, aldrig, hverken. næppe*.

System	In-domain				Out-of-domain			
	Dev set		Test set		Dev set		Test set	
	Acc.	AF	Acc.	AF	Acc.	AF	Acc.	AF
Scope baseline	**84.2**	**75.6**	82.4	72.1	35.5	43.3	36.0	44.3
Scope random corrupt	83.1	72.9	**82.7**	**72.8**	35.7	43.9	36.2	44.5
Scope biased corrupt	82.7	72.6	81.5	70.6	**55.5**	**48.6**	**55.5**	**44.9**
Trustpilot baseline	**94.8**	**91.8**	94.3	91.2	39.9	45.0	39.9	**46.2**
Trustpilot random corrupt	**94.8**	91.7	**94.4**	**91.4**	39.8	45.6	40.0	46.0
Trustpilot biased corrupt	93.7	89.0	93.4	89.5	**43.6**	**45.7**	**43.4**	44.7

Table 3: Evaluation on development and test sets measured in accuracy (Acc.) and the average f-score for positive and negative instances (AF).

the model's performance on the two "extreme" classes, but it is highly skewed, since it ignores the *neutral* label. As we have seen in our data, this can make up the majority of the instances. Accuracy has the advantage that it provides a clear picture of how often the system makes a correct prediction, but can be harder to interpret when the data sets are highly skewed in favor of one class.

The results show that randomly corrupting the data (cf. Søgaard and Johannsen (2012), Sec. 5) does not have much influence on the model. Performance on in- and out-of-domain data is similar to the baseline system. This indicates that we can not just delete *any* features to help domain adaptation.

The biased corruption model, on the other hand, makes informed choices about deleting features. As expected, this leads to a drop on in-domain data, since we are underfitting the model. Considering that the algorithm is targeting the most important features for this particular domain, the drop is relatively small, though. The percentage of features deleted is roughly the same as the 10% for the random system (see section 3.3).

With the exception of AF on Trustpilot test, our biased corruption approach always increases out-of-domain performance. The increase is especially notable when the model is trained on the small domain, Scope. On both test and development, the corruption approach increases accuracy more than 50%. On the AF measure, the increase is smaller, which indicates that most of the increase stems from the *neutral* category. On the test set, the f-score for *positive* labels increases from 49.1% to 71.2%, *neutral* increases from 13.5% to 18.4%, but *negative* decreases from 39.4% to 27.5%. The fact that f-score decreases on *negative* indicates that the corruption algorithm is too aggressive for this category. We previously saw that this was the category where 35% of the features are deleted.

The lower degree of overfitting in the corrupted model is also reflected in the overall label distribution. For the Scope system, the training data has a negative/neutral/positive distribution (in percentages) of 27/61/12. The baseline predictions on the Trustpilot data has a very similar distribution of 30/63/7, while the corrupted system results in a very different distribution of 52/35/13, which is more similar to the Trustpilot gold distribution of 85/5/10. The KL divergence between the baseline system and the Trustpilot data is 1.26, while for the corrupted system it is 0.46.

5 Related Work

There is a large body of prior work on sentiment analysis (Pang and Lee, 2008), ranging from work on well-edited newswire data using the MPQA corpus (Wilson et al., 2005), to Amazon reviews (Blitzer et al., 2007), blogs (Kessler et al., 2010) and user-generated content such as tweets (Mohammad et al., 2013). All of these studies worked with English, while this study – to the best of our knowledge – is the first to present results for Danish.

As far as we are aware of, the only related work on Danish is Hardt and Wulff (2012). In their exploratory paper, they investigate whether user populations differ systematically in the way they express sentiment, finding that positive ratings are far more common in U.S. reviews than in Danish ones. However, their paper focuses on a quantitative analysis and a single domain (movie reviews), while we build an actual sentiment classification system that performs well *across* domains.

Data corruption has been used for other NLP

tasks (Søgaard and Johannsen, 2012; Søgaard, 2013). Our random removal setup is basically an offline version of the approach presented in (Søgaard and Johannsen, 2012). Their online algorithm removes a random subset of the features in each iteration and was successfully applied to cross-domain experiments on part-of-speech tagging and document classification. Søgaard (2013) presents a follow-up online approach that takes the weights of the current model into consideration, regularizing the most predictive features. Our *biased* approach is inspired by this, but has the advantage that it abstracts away from the underlying learner.

6 Discussion and Future Work

We investigate cross-domain sentiment analysis for a low-resource language, Danish. We observe that performance drops precipitously when training on one domain and evaluating on the other. We presented a robust offline-learning approach that deletes features proportionate to their predictiveness. Applied to blind domain adaptation, this corruption method prevents overfitting to the source domain, and results in relative improvements of more than 50%.

In the future, we plan to experiment with integrating the weight distribution of a label into the corruption function in order to prevent overcorrupting of certain labels.

Acknowledgments

We would like to thank Daniel Hardt for hosting the Copenhagen Sentiment Analysis Workshop and making the data sets available. The last two authors are supported by the ERC Starting Grant LOWLANDS No. 313695.

References

Enrique Amigó, Adolfo Corujo, Julio Gonzalo, Edgar Meij, and Maarten de Rijke. 2012. Overview of RepLab 2012: Evaluating Online Reputation Management Systems. In *CLEF*.

Enrique Amigó, Jorge Carrillo de Albornoz, Irina Chugur, Adolfo Corujo, Julio Gonzalo, Tamara Martín, Edgar Meij, Maarten de Rijke, and Damiano Spina. 2013. Overview of RepLab 2013: Evaluating Online Reputation Monitoring Systems. In *CLEF*.

John Blitzer, Mark Dredze, and Fernando Pereira. 2007. Biographies, bollywood, boom-boxes and blenders: Domain adaptation for sentiment classification. In *ACL*.

P.F. Brown, P.V. Desouza, R.L. Mercer, V.J. DellaPietra, and J.C. Lai. 1992. Class-based n-gram models of natural language. *Computational linguistics*, 18(4):467–479.

Hal Daumé, Abhishek Kumar, and Avishek Saha. 2010. Frustratingly easy semi-supervised domain adaptation. In *ACL Workshop on Domain Adaptation for NLP*.

Daniel Hardt and Julie Wulff. 2012. What is the meaning of 5 *'s? An investigation of the expression and rating of sentiment. In *Proceedings of KONVENS 2012*.

Jason S. Kessler, Miriam Eckert, Lyndsie Clark, and Nicolas Nicolov. 2010. The 2010 ICWSM JDPA sentiment corpus for the automotive domain. In *ICWSM-DWC*.

Percy Liang. 2005. *Semi-supervised learning for natural language*. Ph.D. thesis, Massachusetts Institute of Technology.

Saif Mohammad, Svetlana Kiritchenko, and Xiaodan Zhu. 2013. NRC-Canada: Building the State-of-the-Art in Sentiment Analysis of Tweets. In *SemEval-2013*.

Preslav Nakov, Sara Rosenthal, Zornitsa Kozareva, Veselin Stoyanov, Alan Ritter, and Theresa Wilson. 2013. Semeval-2013 task 2: Sentiment analysis in twitter. In *Second Joint Conference on Lexical and Computational Semantics (*SEM)*.

Bo Pang and Lillian Lee. 2008. Opinion mining and sentiment analysis. *Foundations and trends in information retrieval*, 2(1-2):1–135.

Anders Søgaard and Anders Johannsen. 2012. Robust learning in random subspaces: Equipping nlp for oov effects. In *COLING*.

Anders Søgaard. 2013. Part-of-speech tagging with antagonistic adversaries. In *ACL*.

Sida Wang and Christopher D Manning. 2012. Fast dropout training for logistic regression. In *NIPS workshop on log-linear models*.

Theresa Wilson, Janyce Wiebe, and Paul Hoffmann. 2005. Recognizing contextual polarity in phrase-level sentiment analysis. In *EMNLP*.

An Investigation for Implicatures in Chinese : Implicatures in Chinese and in English are similar !

Lingjia Deng
Intelligent Systems Program
University of Pittsburgh
lid29@pitt.edu

Janyce Wiebe
Department of Computer Science
University of Pittsburgh
wiebe@cs.pitt.edu

Abstract

Implicit opinions are commonly seen in opinion-oriented documents, such as political editorials. Previous work have utilized opinion inference rules to detect implicit opinions evoked by events that positively/negatively affect entities (*goodFor/badFor*) to improve sentiment analysis for English text. Since people in different languages may express implicit opinions in different ways, in this work we investigate implicit opinions expressed via goodFor/badFor events in Chinese. The positive results have provided evidences that such implicit opinions and inference rules are similar in Chinese and in English. Moreover, we have observed cases where the inferences are blocked.

1 Introduction

In the opinion-oriented documents, many opinions are expressed implicitly rather than explicitly. Consider the following example from (Deng and Wiebe, 2014):

> EX(1.1) The reform would **lower** health care costs, which would be *a tremendous positive change* across the entire health-care system.

There is an explicit positive sentiment (*positive*) toward the event of *reform lower costs*. In expressing this sentiment, the writer implies he is negative toward the *costs*, because he's happy to see the costs being decreased. The writer may be positive toward *reform* since it conducts the *lower* event. Such inferences may be seen as opinion-oriented *implicatures* (i.e., defeasible inferences) [1].

We create an annotated corpus (denoted *DCW corpus*) (Deng et al., 2013)[2] and generalizes such events, defining a ***badFor (bf)*** event to be an event that negatively affects the object and a ***goodFor (gf)*** event to be an event that positively affects the object of the event. Here, *lower* is a bf event. According to the annotation scheme, ***goodFor/badFor*** (hereafter ***gfbf***) events have NP agents and objects (though the agent may be implicit), and the polarity of a gf event may be changed to bf by a ***reverser*** (and vice versa). We have developed a set of rules for inferring implicit sentiments, from explicit sentiments and gfbf events (Deng and Wiebe, 2014). We incorporate the rules into a graph-based model, which significantly improves classifying the sentiments toward agents and objects in the gfbf events.

The contribution of this work is investigating implicatures in a second language, specifically in Chinese. People in different languages may express implicit opinions in different ways, so it is better to first assess similarity of implicatures in the two languages, rather than to directly utilize the English resources. In this work we conduct an agreement study for gfbf information in Chinese. The good agreement scores provide evidence for the existence of similar implicature in Chinese. During the analysis of disagreement, we have observed interesting gfbf events triggered by Chinese syntax, which are rare in English but common in Chinese. We should provide additional guidance for such events when developing a Chinese gfbf manual in the future.

We run the graph-based model on the annotated Chinese corpus. The good evaluation results support our hypothesis that the inference rules in English apply for Chinese. Moreover, we have observed gfbf cases where the sentiment inferences are blocked, which are similar to what we have found in English (Wiebe and Deng, 2014).

[1] *Implicatures* "normally accompany the utterances of a given sentence unless special factors exclude that possibility (p. 39)." (Huddleston and Pullum, 2002)

[2] Available at: http://mpqa.cs.pitt.edu/

Proceedings of the 5th Workshop on Computational Approaches to Subjectivity, Sentiment and Social Media Analysis, pages 8–17,
Baltimore, Maryland, USA. June 27, 2014.

Further, we analyze gfbf words and syntax of agents/objects in Chinese. Our analysis shows that it is feasible to extract components of Chinese gfbf events utilizing the existing resources. In the last section we briefly talk bout the Chinese explicit sentiment analysis.

2 Related Work

In addition to researches focusing on explicit sentiments (Wiebe et al., 2005; Johansson and Moschitti, 2013; Yang and Cardie, 2013), recently there are work investigating features that directly indicate implicit sentiments (Zhang and Liu, 2011; Feng et al., 2013), or working on inferring implicit opinions (Choi and Cardie, 2008; Zhang and Liu, 2011; Anand and Reschke, 2010; Reschke and Anand, 2011; Goyal et al., 2013). Different from their work, which do not cover all the inferences of implicit opinions over explicit opinions and gfbf events, we define a generalized set of inference rules and incorporate the rules into a graph-based model to achieve sentiment propagation between the agents and objects of gfbf events (Deng and Wiebe, 2014). The result shows that the graph-based model itself is able to assign the unknown nodes with correct labels 89% of the time.

Many works in Chinese sentiment analysis develop heuristics for adapting methods in English to methods appropriate for Chinese (Tsou et al., 2005; Wang et al., 2007; Li and Sun, 2007). Instead of projecting English methods and resources into Chinese versions, there are also works leveraging Chinese-English parallel corpus to assist Chinese sentiment analysis. Wan (2008) translates Chinese sentiment sentences into English and ensemble the sentiment classification results from both English and Chinese sentiment classifiers. Wan (2009) adopt co-training methods, utilizing labeled English sentences and unlabelled Chinese sentences. Lu et al. (2011) assumes parallel sentences in different languages bear the same sentiment. They utilize unlabelled Chinese-English parallel corpus to jointly improve sentiment classification in both languages. Boyd-Graber and Resnik (2010) present a generative model, jointly modeling topics that are consistent across languages, to improve sentiment rating predictions.

3 Implicature in Chinese

The definition of a gfbf event is from (Deng et al., 2013). A *goodFor (gf)* event is an event that positively affects an entity (similarly, for *badFor (bf)* events). A gfbf triple has the structure of ⟨ agent, gfbf, object⟩, though the agent can be implicit. For example, in the sentence from (Deng et al., 2013), "Repealing the Affordable Care Act (ACA) would hurt our economy.", there are two gfbf triples. One is ⟨Repealing the ACA, hurt, families, our economy⟩, which is a bf. The other is ⟨*implicit*, Repealing, the ACA⟩, which is bf and the agent is implicit. The DCW corpus contains manually annotated gfbf events, the gfbf polarities, the corresponding agents and objects and the writer's attitudes toward the agents and objects.

Because people in different languages may express their opinions in different ways. In this section, we conduct an agreement study for Chinese gfbf information in Section 3.1 and achieve good agreement scores, reported in Section 3.2, which provide supporting evidences for detecting Chinese gfbf events. In the disagreement analysis, we have observed interesting cases which are gfbf events in semantics but are triggered by Chinese own syntax. We explain the cases in Section 3.3.

3.1 Agreement Study Design

Data: We collect 100 political editorials from the Opinion Column in the Chinese version of New York Times[3], where each political editorial has an English version and a Chinese version. The Chinese editorial is a translated and paraphrased version of the corresponding English editorial, written by professional translators. The English version and the Chinese version are paragraph paralleled. In the previous agreement study of (Deng et al., 2013), the annotators are asked to annotate the whole document. Because not all the sentences contain gfbf events and the documents are long, a large proportion of disagreement we find that is due to negligence. In order to reduce negligence and provide a more dense data for annotation, first, we collect a lexicon of English gfbf words in the DCW corpus. Then we find the English sentences containing English gfbf words and select the paragraphs containing those sentences. The parallel Chinese paragraphs are collected. Though a paragraph may contain more than one sentence and some sentences do not have gfbf events, it is much more dense to annotate than the document as a whole. When presenting data to the annotators, we do not provide an isolated paragraph since it may

[3]http://cn.nytimes.com/opinion/

lose the context information. Instead, we present the original Chinese editorials and highlight the selected paragraphs. The annotators are told to read through the whole document but only need to annotate the highlighted paragraphs.

Procedure: We adopt our English manual in (Deng et al., 2013) to train the annotators. The annotators read through the manual and several Chinese gfbf examples. Then, the annotators label several paragraphs and discuss their disagreements to reconcile their differences. For the formal agreement study, we randomly selected 60 paragraphs, which have a total of 253 Chinese sentences. These paragraphs are different from the paragraphs discussed during training. The annotators then independently annotated the 60 selected paragraphs.

3.2 Agreement Study Evaluation and Result

We use the same measurement for agreement for all types of spans. (The type is either gfbf, agent, or object). Suppose A is a set of annotations of a particular type and B is the set of annotations of the same type from the other annotator. For any text span $a \in A$ and $b \in B$, the span coverage c counts the percentage of overlapping Chinese characters between a and b,

$$c(a, b) = \frac{|a \cap b|}{|b|} \quad (1)$$

where $|a|$ is the number of characters in span a, and $\cap$ gives the set of characters that two spans have in common (Johansson and Moschitti, 2013).

Following (Wilson and Wiebe, 2003), we treat each set A and B in turn as the gold-standard and calculate the average F-measure ($agr(A, B)$).

$$agr(A||B) = \frac{\sum_{\substack{a \in A, b \in B, \\ |a \cap b| > 0}} c(a, b)}{|B|} \quad (2)$$

$$agr(A, B) = \frac{agr(A||B) + agr(B||A)}{2} \quad (3)$$

Now that we have the sets of annotations on which the annotators agree, we use κ (Artstein and Poesio, 2008) to measure agreement for the attributes. We report three κ values: one for the polarities of the gfbf events, and the other two for the writer's attitudes toward the agents and objects.

Three annotator participate in the agreement study. All of them are Chinese graduate students studying in US. One of them is the co-author of this work (*Anno 1*), while the other two do not know details of gfbf and implicature before (*Anno2, Anno3*). Since *Anno1* is familiar with this work, we compare the other two's annotations to *Anno1*'s. In Table 1, the upper half is the agreement for span overlapping ($agr(A, B)$), and the lower half is the agreement for attribute (κ).

$agr(A, B)$	gfbf	agent	object
Anno 1& 2	0.7929	0.9091	0.9091
Anno 1 & 3	0.7044	0.9524	1.0
κ	gfbf polarity	agent attitude	object attitude
Anno 1 & 2	0.9385	0.7830	0.7238
Anno 1 & 3	0.8966	0.5913	0.8478

Table 1: Results for Agreement Study Analysis.

The result have shown that the annotators have good agreement scores, though our training period is not long and our training data cover multiple topics. In particular, the annotators agree quite well on recognizing the agents and objects and judging the polarity of gfbf events.

For recognizing gfbf events, we have found two interesting gfbf cases caused by the Chinese syntax that is different from English, elaborated in the next section. Among the spans only one annotator marks, one third is due to the two cases above; one third are borderlines that could be marked; one third are incorrect. For the spans two annotator mark but the third doesn't, we regard it as negligence.

For judging the writer's attitudes toward agents and objects, we can see from Table 1 that *Anno 2* and *Anno 3* behave differently. This is understandable because we are marking the implicit opinions of the writer. Though trained, different annotators have different thresholds for judging whether an opinion is expressed here. Some annotators may be more sensitive than the others. If we don't count the spans that one annotator marks it as *none* (i.e. neutral) but the other doesn't, the κ scores increase a lot, as Row *Polar* shows in Table 2. This indicates that the annotators mainly disagree on whether the sentiment is neutral or not, rather than the polarity of opinions.

To further investigate whether the disagreement is caused by Chinese, or is due to the annotators' inherent different sensitivities of opinions, we randomly select 5 documents from the DCW corpus, delete the writer's attitude toward agents and objects but keep the remaining annotations. The an-

	Anno 1 & 2		Anno 1& 3	
	agent	object	agent	object
Table 1	0.783	0.723	0.591	0.848
Polar	0.875	0.915	1	0.88
Eng	0.738	0.652	0.4633	0.8734

Table 2: κ for Agreement Study Analysis.

notators are then told to mark the attitudes. As Row *Eng* in Table 2 shows, we have got consistent agreement results within the same annotators when they annotate in English and in Chinese. This supports the idea that the differences between the annotators are differences on the underlying task, regardless of the language.

3.3 GoodFor/Badfor Triggered by Chinese Syntax

During the analysis of disagreement, we have found gfbf cases which are triggered by the Chinese syntax that is different from English. Since the annotators are trained by the English manual, some annotators stay consistent with the English syntax, but the others go beyond syntax and identify gfbf according to semantics and pragmatics, which lead to disagreement. In this section we list two major cases due to the Chinese own syntax. This suggests that additional guidance to annotate such cases should be added to the English manual to develop a Chinese gfbf manual.

The first case is due to unclear expression of passive voice in Chinese. In English, the noun phrase that would be the object of an active sentence (Our troops **defeated** the enemy) appears as the subject of a sentence with passive voice (The enemy **was defeated** by our troops)[4]. It is clear that *enemy* is the object and *our troops* is the agent in both sentences. However, this is not intuitive for some Chinese sentences.

A Chinese example is " 经济潜力似乎得以释放 ", whose English translation is: "The economic potential ... appeared to **be unleashed**". A word-to-word translation would be "...appeared to **have got unleashed**". In the two English versions, *potential* is obviously the object of *unleashed* event. However, some annotators analyze this sentence according to syntax[5]. The dependency syntax between the object *potential* (潜力) and the gfbf *unleash* (释放) is **nsubj**(释放-5, 潜力-2) so it is not marked. Some annotators view from pragmatics and read as a passive voice. Since there is no word transformation of Chinese verbs for passive voice (e.g. *unleash* changes to *unleashed* in English), this raises disagreement.

The other case is related to one constraint defined in (Deng et al., 2013). According to the manual, the polarity of a gfbf triple must be determined within the triple. As explained in the manual, in the sentence "Tom has left his cousin a big trouble", the triple ⟨Tom, left, his cousin⟩ is not a gfbf event, since we cannot judge whether this event is good for or bad for his cousin without knowing what Tom leaves to his cousin. While in the sentence "They decrease the manufacturing costs", the event *decrease* is a bf no matter how many or by what means the costs are decreased.

However, a Chinese instance is, "把改革置于死地 ", whose translation is "**put** the reform **to die**". Whether the event *put* (把) is good for or bad for the object *reform* (改革), depends on whether the agent puts the reform to die or puts the reform to revive, for instance. However, in Chinese, 把 is not main verb (Li and Thompson, 1989), the object (改革, reform) of the main verb (置于死地, die) is placed after the function word (把), and the verb is placed after the object, forming a subject–object–verb (SOV) sentence (Chao, 1968)[6], which is defined as *ba structure* (Chao, 1968; Li and Thompson, 1989; Sybesma, 1992). Thus, in Chinese the sentence is read as: "kill the reform", which could be seen as a gfbf event. This structure is very common in Chinese.

In conclusion, there are very similar implicatures in Chinese. However, in order to fully study the gfbf events in Chinese, the manual should be revised to provide guidance for annotating the cases mentioned above.

4 Implicature Inference in Chinese

We propose a set of sentiment inference rules and incorporate them into a graph-based model to conduct sentiment propagation among entities (agents and objects) of gfbf events (Deng and Wiebe, 2014). In Section 4.1, we run this graph-based model on the Chinese annotations. The positive results of sentiment propagation support our hypothesis that the inference rules apply for Chinese as well. Further, we categorize interesting gfbf cases where the inferences are blocked in Section

[4] http://en.wikipedia.org/wiki/English_passive_voice.

[5] We use Stanford's dependency parser in this work.

[6] http://en.wikipedia.org/wiki/B%C7%8E_construction.

4.2. From our observation, the blocking inferences are similar to what we have found in English (Wiebe and Deng, 2014).

4.1 Graph-based Model

In the graph-based model, a node represents an entity (agent, or object), and an edge exists between two nodes if the two entities participate in one or more gfbf events with each other. Scores on the nodes represent the explicit sentiments, if any, expressed by the writer toward the entities. Scores on the edges are based on constraints derived from the rules. Loopy Belief Propagation (Pearl, 1982; Yedidia et al., 2005) is applied to accomplish sentiment propagation in the graph. Given a graph built from manually annotations, an evaluation is carried out to assess the ability to propagate sentiment of the model. In the study, for each subgraph (connected component), we assign one of the nodes in the subgraph with its gold-standard polarity. Then we run LBP on each node in the subgraph. The experiment is run on the subgraph $|S|$ times, where $|S|$ is the number of nodes in the subgraph. Therefore, each node is assigned its gold-standard polarity exactly once, and each node is given a propagated value $|S|-1$ times, as propagated by each of the other nodes in its subgraph. We use Equations (4) and (5) to evaluate the chance of a node given a correct propagated label.

$$correct(a|b) = \begin{cases} 1 & a \text{ is correct} \\ 0 & otherwise \end{cases} \quad (4)$$

$$correctness(a) = \frac{\sum_{b \in S_a, b \neq a} correct(a|b)}{|S_a| - 1} \quad (5)$$

Here we run the graph-based model on the Chinese annotations. The data we use include the training and testing paragraphs in the agreement study, in total 85 paragraphs, 341 sentences and 160 gfbf triples. Later we use this corpus of 160 gfbf triples for analysis (denoted *Chinese gfbf corpus*). Since the edge scores of the model are defined according to the inference rules, if the sentiments are propagated correctly, this is a good evidence that the inference rules apply to Chinese.

The performances of the sentiment propagation are really good, reported in Table 3. The model has an 70%-83% chance of propagating sentiments correctly in Chinese. This gives us confidence that the inference rules apply in Chinese and further we can utilize these rules to assist Chinese sentiment analysis. Compared to the scores of *correctness* reported in (Deng and Wiebe, 2014), which are 0.8874 for all subgraphs and 0.9030 for multi-node subgraphs, our scores are lower. We analyze the reasons for the gap between our scores in Chinese and in English in the next section.

Dataset	# subgraph	correctness
all subgraphs	136	0.7058
multi-node subgraphs	61	0.8251

Table 3: Performance of Graph-Based Model in Chinese.

4.2 Blocking the Inference

A wrong propagation indicates the inferences related to that propagation are blocked. During the error analysis, we have found three interesting categories of cases where the inferences are blocked. Interestingly, we have observed these cases in English as well (Wiebe and Deng, 2014). In other words, we didn't find any blocking case specific to Chinese. The lower scores of *correctness* in Chinese might be due to the smaller amount of experiment data and more blocking cases in this corpus.

Irrealis: This category contains gfbf events that haven't or will not happen. One of the case is when the agent tried to conduct the gfbf event, but failed. In Ex(4.1), the agent and objective are underlined and the gfbf event is boldfaced. By the rules, the writer has the same sentiment toward the agents and objects in gf events and opposite sentiments toward the agents and objects in bf events (Deng and Wiebe, 2014). In Ex(4.1), the writer is negative toward both the agent and the object, though this is a bf event. This is because the event *counter* does not exist due to the failure, which is implied by *intended to*. The inferences for gfbf events in this category are blocked because the writer expresses the sentiments toward entities based on what they have done so far.

> Ex(4.1) ...monetary policy activism intended to **counter** the cyclical bumps and grinds of the free market.

Forced GFBF: This category contains gfbf events whose agents don't intend to do that or being forced to conduct the event. For example, in Ex(4.2), though the triple ⟨Obama, delay, mandate⟩ is an event which does not happen, it is different from Ex(4.1). Here, the agent *Obama* is forced to conduct the *delaying*, though he does not want to and the writer does not blame him if he does so. For the entities involved in forced events, (at least the writer believes the entities are involuntary,) the forced event will not affect the writer's sentiments toward the entities so that the inferences are blocked.

> Ex(4.2) Some of them even seem to think that they can bully Mr. Obama into **delaying** the individual mandate too.

Quoted GFBF: This category contains gfbf events in the quotations. Consider the Ex(4.3), where one of the gfbf triple is ⟨law, reduce, amount of labor ⟩. In the original editorial, the writer supports *the law* and the writer has a positive sentiment toward *the number of jobs* (because he/she expects to see more job opportunities). But merely from the annotated gfbf triple, it is inferred that the law has negative effect since it reduces the number of jobs. This is not contradictory with the writer's stance because the writer regards the event as *a deliberate misreading* he/she doesn't believe. The actual agent of the event should be (misreading, Obama). This example shows that inferences of a triple in the quotation are blocked, or event flipped, based on the writer's sentiment toward the agent saying the quotation. The agent in a quoted gfbf is similar to the notion of *nested source* in sentiment analysis (Wilson and Wiebe, 2003).

> Ex(4.3) Some of the job-killer scare stories are based on *a deliberate misreading* that estimated the law would "**reduce** the amount of labor used in the economy" by about 800,000 jobs.

In conclusion, the good performance in our pilot study gives supporting evidence for our hypothesis. That is, the inference rules apply for Chinese. Moreover, there is no evidence showing that the cases where the inferences are blocked only happen in Chinese.

5 Chinese GoodFor/BadFor Lexicon

Above all we have assessed the similarity of implicatures and inference rules in Chinese and English. In the following sections, we will analyze whether Chinese gfbf components could be captured by similar techniques in English.

Description	Count	(Percentage %)
Parallel Span	122	(76.25%)
Chinese Adding GFBF	10	(6.875%)
Chinese Adding Object	6	(3.75%)
English Out Of Triple	5	(3.125%)
English Neutral	6	(3.125%)
Paraphrase	11	(6.875%)

Table 4: Counts of Chinese-English Corresponds

In this section, we compare the gfbf spans in the Chinese gfbf corpus and the English version, to investigate the possibility of deriving a bilingual gfbf lexicon. Though the Chinese and English editorials are paragraph paralleled, they are not sentence paralleled, because an English sentence may be translated into multiple Chinese sentences and several English sentences may be merged into one Chinese sentence. Therefore, instead of automatic word-alignment, we manually pick up the English parallel spans of the Chinese annotated gfbfs. The correspondences of Chinese and English spans are categorized in Table 4. We present pairs of examples from the Chinese gfbf corpus, beginning with the original English sentence (*Eng*), followed by another English sentence which is the word-by-word translation of the Chinese sentence (*Chi*).

Parallel Span: This category contains instances where the Chinese annotated gfbf spans have the corresponding translations in the English sentences, and the English spans are also gfbf words.

Chinese Adding GFBF: In the original English sentence below, *its own making* is a noun phrase rather than a gfbf verb used as a noun. However, in the Chinese version, there is a clear triple, ⟨itself, makes, a monetary prison⟩. In such case the Chinese version adds a gfbf event into the sentence.

Eng: ...the Fed is domiciled in a monetary prison of **its own making**.

Chi: ...the Fed is domiciled in a monetary prison **which itself makes**.

Chinese Adding Object: As stated in the manual, all gfbf triples should have objects. Thus, in the original sentence below, we will not mark *exclusion* because the object is implicit. However, the Chinese version clearly states the object, *patients*.

Eng: ...no more exclusion based on pre-existing conditions...

Chi: ...no more exclusion **of the patients** based on pre-existing conditions...

English Out Of Triple: Recall from Section 3.3, the gfbf polarity must be sufficient to perceive the gfbf polarity within the triple. The ⟨the Fed, get, unemployment⟩ below cannot be considered as a gfbf, since whether it is good for or bad for the *unemployment* depending on whether it is **below** 6.5% or **up** 6.5%, for instance. On the contrary, the Chinese version uses the word *decrease*, which is a bf word, no matter how many percents are changed.

Eng: If and when the Fed — which now promises to **get** unemployment **below 6.5%**...
Chi: If and when the Fed — which now promises to **decrease** the unemployment to 6.5%...

English Neutral: Sometimes the English word doesn't have a gfbf meaning but the Chinese word has one, based on the translator's interpretation of the whole editorial, though the triple structures are the same in English and Chinese versions.

Eng: We've **had eight decades of** increasingly frenetic monetary policy activism...
Chi: We've been **insisting** increasingly frenetic monetary policy activism for eight decades...

In the original English sentence, *had eight decades of* is hardly regarded as a gfbf word. However, in the translated version, the word *insisting* is a gf word. The change of wording introduces a new gfbf event into the sentence.

Paraphrase: There are other cases where the sentences are paraphrased so largely that we cannot find a corresponding parallel span of the annotated Chinese span in the original English sentence. A majority of cases in this category are gfbf events triggered by the Chinese syntax in Section 3.3.

In conclusion, the percentage of 76.25% in Row *Parallel Span* indicates that it is applicable to derive a bilingual gfbf lexicon from a parallel corpus. However, we need to take into consideration the 23.75% mismatches for higher precision.

5.1 Chinese Reversers

The polarity of a gfbf event could be changed by a reverser (Deng et al., 2013). A common class of reversers is negation. For example, in the sentence, "the bill will not increase the costs", the gf *increase* is changed to be bf via the negation *not*. In this section, we analyze the Chinese reversers.

All of the reversers in the Chinese gfbf corpus happen to be negations. In the English sentences, the negations are easily extracted by *neg* dependency relation. About 50% of the Chinese negations are linked to the gfbf events via *neg* as well. Among this half, there are two negations commonly seen. One is 不 (Not), often labeled as AD (adverb) in terms of Part-Of-Speech, the other is 没有 (do not have), labeled as VV (verb), shown below. The negation is underlined and the gfbf event it negates is boldfaced.

Ex(5.1)<u>不/AD</u> **接受/VV** 同性恋/NN

Ex(5.2)<u>没有/VV</u> **刺激/VV** 贷款/NN

For the other half, the error mostly arises from segmentations. For the sentence below, though 没有 (*doesn't have*), often labeled as VB, could be regarded as a complete token, if we segment the two characters into two independent tokens, the parse is more similar to the English one. Below we only list the most relevant part of the parses.

Eng: He <u>does n't</u> have ability control war budget
Eng dep: neg(have-4, n't-3), root(ROOT-0, have-4), dobj(have-4, ability-6)
Chi: 他 <u>没 有</u> 能力 控制 战争 预算
wrong dep: root(ROOT-0, 没有-2), nsubj(控制-4, 能力-3), dep(没有-2, 控制-4)
correct dep: neg(有-3, 没-2), root(ROOT-0, 有-3), nsubj(控制-5, 能力-4)

In conclusion, it is feasible to recognize reversers in Chinese but it calls for a suitable word segmentation as input.

6 Syntax of Agent/Object in Chinese

According to (Deng et al., 2013), the agent is the entity conducting the gfbf event and the object is the entity that the gfbf event affects. This definition is very similar to subject and (in)direct object in semantic role labeling. Xue and Palmer (2004) investigate the Chinese semantic role labeling. They utilize the PropBank and the constituency parser. However, from a preliminary analysis of constituency parse, we cannot distinguish the agent and object merely from the parse tree, because the sentences in the editorials are usually complicated and it is difficult to classify whether a noun phrase (NP) constituency is agent or object in terms of its position. Kozhevnikov and Titov (2013) adopt a model transfer between different languages using dependency parser. In our case, the dependency parser has labels such as "nsubj" and "dobj", which are strong indications of agents and objects. Thus, we use the Stanford dependency parser, which has both English and Chinese parsers, to analyze the syntax of agents/objects in the gfbf events. We count the types of dependencies on the path in a dependency parse between the tokens of agents/objects and the tokens of gfbf events in the DCW corpus and the Chinese gfbf corpus.

Among all the dependency types, 19.57% of the labels between agents and gfbfs are the ones specially designed for Chinese and 25.82% between objects and gfbf are the ones specially designed for Chinese. This indicates there is a considerable number of differences in dependency types. Chang et al. (2009), who create the Chinese parser, discuss the differences between Chinese and English types, which are similar to our observations.

First, there are more *nsubj* in Chinese for agents (21.53%) and more *dobj* in Chinese for objects (21.59%), compared to English (17.43% and 14.01%), which are easier for the parser to detect.

Second, the most common types specially designed for Chinese are *assm*, *assmod* and *cpm* (in total 12.23% for agents and 16.14% for objects). The relations *assm* is associative marker, *assmod* is associative modifier, and *cpm* is complementizer. These are defined because of the frequent usage of 的 (whose, of) in Chinese. Though there is not a direct mapping between Chinese and English dependency types, they are similar to two common types in English: *prep* and *pobj* (together 23.36% for agents and 31.62% for objects).

Third, there are more *rcmod* in Chinese than those in English. There are 7.05% and 6.5% *rcmod* in Chinese agents and objects, respectively. But there are only 1.7% and 2.16% in English agents and objects. The type *rcomd* is a relative clause modifier. If a verb is used as the modifier of a noun, it will be labelled *rcmod*. Instead, English writers tend to use more adjectives to modify nouns, which will be labeled *amod* (4.04% and 4.48%).

Fourth, there are 7.63% and 6.22% *punct* in Chinese agents and object, compared to both 0% in English. In addition, there are 3.36% and 3.31% *conj* in English agents and objects. Chang et al. (2009) explain that English use conjunctions (*conj*) to link clauses while Chinese tend to use punctuation. Another finding in our corpus is that, translators tend to break down a long English sentence into several Chinese clauses, linked by punctuations.

For the other Chinese types, most of them are modifiers, which may be grouped with similar English modifiers.

7 Chinese Explicit Sentiment Analysis

There are various available resources for Chinese sentiment analysis, such as sentiment lexicon from HowNet[7], NTU Sentiment Dictionary (NTUSD) (Ku and Chen, 2007)[8] and the sentiment lexicon from Tsinghua University (Li and Sun, 2007). The sentiments recognized from lexicon hits are explicit, meaning that the writers use sentiment words to express his/her opinions. These explicit sentiment results are provided to the graph-based model as input. Note that the model plays a role of sentiment inference, instead of directly detecting sentiments from the text. The inferred sentiments are implicit, meaning that the writers express his/her opinions even without using a sentiment lexical clue.

8 Conclusion

In this work we investigate implicit opinions expressed via goodFor/badFor events in Chinese. The positive results have provided evidences that such implicit opinions and inference rules are similar in Chinese and English. There are some gfbf events caused by the Chinese syntax, guidance for which could be added to the current English manual to develop a Chinese manual. Moreover, there is no evidence showing that the blocked inferences only happen in Chinese. We also assess the feasibility of acquiring components of gfbf events from Chinese text using current available resources. In the future, it is promising to utilize gfbf information to assist sentiment analysis in Chinese.

Acknowledgement This work was supported in part by DARPA-BAA-12-47 DEFT grant #12475008 and National Science Foundation grant #IIS-0916046. We would like to thank Changsheng Liu and Fan Zhang for their annotations in the agreement study, and thank anonymous reviewers for their feedback.

[7] Available at: http://www.keenage.com/html/e_index.html

[8] Available at: http://nlg18.csie.ntu.edu.tw:8080/lwku/pub1.html

References

Pranav Anand and Kevin Reschke. 2010. Verb classes as evaluativity functor classes. In *Interdisciplinary Workshop on Verbs. The Identification and Representation of Verb Features*.

Ron Artstein and Massimo Poesio. 2008. Inter-coder agreement for computational linguistics. *Comput. Linguist.*, 34(4):555–596, December.

Jordan Boyd-Graber and Philip Resnik. 2010. Holistic sentiment analysis across languages: Multilingual supervised latent dirichlet allocation. In *Proceedings of the 2010 Conference on Empirical Methods in Natural Language Processing*, pages 45–55, Cambridge, MA, October. Association for Computational Linguistics.

Pi-Chuan Chang, Huihsin Tseng, Dan Jurafsky, and Christopher D Manning. 2009. Discriminative reordering with chinese grammatical relations features. In *Proceedings of the Third Workshop on Syntax and Structure in Statistical Translation*, pages 51–59. Association for Computational Linguistics.

Yuen Ren Chao. 1968. *A grammar of spoken Chinese*. Univ of California Press.

Yejin Choi and Claire Cardie. 2008. Learning with compositional semantics as structural inference for subsentential sentiment analysis. In *Proceedings of the 2008 Conference on Empirical Methods in Natural Language Processing*, pages 793–801, Honolulu, Hawaii, October. Association for Computational Linguistics.

Lingjia Deng and Janyce Wiebe. 2014. Sentiment propagation via implicature constraints. In *Meeting of the European Chapter of the Association for Computational Linguistics (EACL-2014)*.

Lingjia Deng, Yoonjung Choi, and Janyce Wiebe. 2013. Benefactive/malefactive event and writer attitude annotation. In *Proceedings of the 51st Annual Meeting of the Association for Computational Linguistics (Volume 2: Short Papers)*, pages 120–125, Sofia, Bulgaria, August. Association for Computational Linguistics.

Song Feng, Jun Sak Kang, Polina Kuznetsova, and Yejin Choi. 2013. Connotation lexicon: A dash of sentiment beneath the surface meaning. In *Proceedings of the 51th Annual Meeting of the Association for Computational Linguistics (Volume 2: Short Papers)*, Sofia, Bulgaria, Angust. Association for Computational Linguistics.

Amit Goyal, Ellen Riloff, and Hal Daumé III. 2013. A computational model for plot units. *Computational Intelligence*, 29(3):466–488.

Rodney D. Huddleston and Geoffrey K. Pullum. 2002. *The Cambridge Grammar of the English Language*. Cambridge University Press, April.

Richard Johansson and Alessandro Moschitti. 2013. Relational features in fine-grained opinion analysis. *Computational Linguistics*, 39(3).

Mikhail Kozhevnikov and Ivan Titov. 2013. Cross-lingual transfer of semantic role labeling models. In *Proceedings of the 51st Annual Meeting of the Association for Computational Linguistics (Volume 1: Long Papers)*, pages 1190–1200, Sofia, Bulgaria, August. Association for Computational Linguistics.

Lun-Wei Ku and Hsin-Hsi Chen. 2007. Mining opinions from the web: Beyond relevance retrieval. *Journal of the American Society for Information Science and Technology*, 58(12):1838–1850.

Jun Li and Maosong Sun. 2007. Experimental study on sentiment classification of chinese review using machine learning techniques. In *Natural Language Processing and Knowledge Engineering, 2007. NLP-KE 2007. International Conference on*, pages 393–400. IEEE.

Charles N Li and Sandra A Thompson. 1989. *Mandarin Chinese: A functional reference grammar*. Univ of California Press.

Bin Lu, Chenhao Tan, Claire Cardie, and Benjamin K Tsou. 2011. Joint bilingual sentiment classification with unlabeled parallel corpora. In *Proceedings of the 49th Annual Meeting of the Association for Computational Linguistics: Human Language Technologies-Volume 1*, pages 320–330. Association for Computational Linguistics.

J. Pearl. 1982. Reverend bayes on inference engines: A distributed hierarchical approach. In *Proceedings of the American Association of Artificial Intelligence National Conference on AI*, pages 133–136, Pittsburgh, PA.

Kevin Reschke and Pranav Anand. 2011. Extracting contextual evaluativity. In *Proceedings of the Ninth International Conference on Computational Semantics*, IWCS '11, pages 370–374, Stroudsburg, PA, USA. Association for Computational Linguistics.

Rintje Pieter Eelke Sybesma. 1992. *Causatives and accomplishments: The case of Chinese ba*, volume 1. Holland Institute of Generative Linguistics.

Benjamin KY Tsou, Raymond WM Yuen, Oi Yee Kwong, TBY La, and Wei Lung Wong. 2005. Polarity classification of celebrity coverage in the chinese press. In *Proceedings of International Conference on Intelligence Analysis*.

Xiaojun Wan. 2008. Using bilingual knowledge and ensemble techniques for unsupervised Chinese sentiment analysis. In *Proceedings of the 2008 Conference on Empirical Methods in Natural Language Processing*, pages 553–561, Honolulu, Hawaii, October. Association for Computational Linguistics.

Xiaojun Wan. 2009. Co-training for cross-lingual sentiment classification. In *Proceedings of the Joint Conference of the 47th Annual Meeting of the ACL and the 4th International Joint Conference on Natural Language Processing of the AFNLP: Volume 1-Volume 1*, pages 235–243. Association for Computational Linguistics.

Suge Wang, Yingjie Wei, Deyu Li, Wu Zhang, and Wei Li. 2007. A hybrid method of feature selection for chinese text sentiment classification. In *Fuzzy Systems and Knowledge Discovery, 2007. FSKD 2007. Fourth International Conference on*, volume 3, pages 435–439. IEEE.

Janyce Wiebe and Lingjia Deng. 2014. An account of opinion implicatures. arXiv:1404.6491v1 [cs.CL].

Janyce Wiebe, Theresa Wilson, and Claire Cardie. 2005. Annotating expressions of opinions and emotions in language ann. *Language Resources and Evaluation*, 39(2/3):164–210.

Theresa Wilson and Janyce Wiebe. 2003. Annotating opinions in the world press. In *Proceedings of the 4th ACL SIGdial Workshop on Discourse and Dialogue (SIGdial-03)*, pages 13–22.

Nianwen Xue and Martha Palmer. 2004. Calibrating features for semantic role labeling. In *EMNLP*, pages 88–94.

Bishan Yang and Claire Cardie. 2013. Joint Inference for Fine-grained Opinion Extraction. In *Proceedings of ACL*, pages 1640–1649.

Jonathan S Yedidia, William T Freeman, and Yair Weiss. 2005. Constructing free-energy approximations and generalized belief propagation algorithms. *Information Theory, IEEE Transactions on*, 51(7):2282–2312.

Lei Zhang and Bing Liu. 2011. Identifying noun product features that imply opinions. In *Proceedings of the 49th Annual Meeting of the Association for Computational Linguistics: Human Language Technologies*, pages 575–580, Portland, Oregon, USA, June. Association for Computational Linguistics.

Inducing Domain-specific Noun Polarity Guided by Domain-independent Polarity Preferences of Adjectives

Manfred Klenner
Computational Linguistics
University of Zurich
Switzerland
klenner@cl.uzh.ch

Michael Amsler
Computational Linguistics
University of Zurich
Switzerland
mamsler@ifi.uzh.ch

Nora Hollenstein
Computational Linguistics
University of Zurich
Switzerland
hollenstein@ifi.uzh.ch

Abstract

In this paper, we discuss how domain-specific noun polarity lexicons can be induced. We focus on the generation of good candidates and compare two machine learning scenarios in order to establish an approach that produces high precision. Candidates are generated on the basis of polarity preferences of adjectives derived from a large domain-independent corpus. The *polarity preference* of a word, here an adjective, reflects the distribution of positive, negative and neutral arguments the word takes (here: its nominal head). Given a noun modified by some adjectives, a vote among the polarity preferences of these adjectives establishes a good indicator of the polarity of the noun. In our experiments with five domains, we achieved f-measure of 59% up to 88% on the basis of two machine learning approaches carried out on top of the preference votes.

1 Introduction

Polarity lexicons are crucial for fine-grained sentiment analysis. For instance, in approaches carrying out sentiment composition (Moilanen and Pulman, 2007), where phrase-level polarity is composed out of word level polarity (e.g. disappointed$^-$ hope$^+$ $\rightarrow$ NP$^-$). However, often freely available lexicons are domain-independent, which is a problem with domain-specific texts, since lexical gaps reduce composition anchors. But how many domain-specific words do we have to expect? Is it a real or rather a marginal problem? In our experiments, we found that domain-specific nouns do occur quite often - so they do matter. In one of our domains, we identified about 1000 negative nouns, 409 were domain-specific. In that domain, the finance sector, more than 13'000 noun types exist that do not occur at all in the DeWac corpus - a large Web corpus (in German) with over 90 Million sentences. Thus, most of them must be regarded as domain-specific. It would be quite time-consuming to go through all of them in order to identify and annotate the polar ones. Could we, rather, predict good candidates? We would need polarity predictors - words that take other, polar words e.g. as their heads. If they, moreover, had a clear-cut preference, i.e. they mostly took one kind of polar words, say negative, then they were perfect predictors of the polarity of nouns. We found that adjectives (e.g. *acute*) can be used as such polarity predictors (e.g. *acute* mostly takes negative nouns, denoted n$^-$, e.g. *acute pain*)).

Our hypothesis is that the polarity preferences of adjectives are (more or less) domain-independent. We can learn the preferences from domain-independent texts and apply it to domain-specific texts and get good candidates of domain-specific polar nouns. Clearly, if the polarity preferences of an adjective are balanced (0.33 for each polarity), than the predictions could not help at all. But if one polarity clearly prevails, we might even get a good performance by just classifying the polarity of unknown nouns in a domain according to the dominant polarity preference of the adjectives they co-occur with.

In this paper, we show how to generate such a preference model on the basis of a large, domain-independent German corpus and a domain-independent German polarity lexicon. We use this model to generate candidate nouns from five domain-specific text collections - ranging from 3'200 up to 37'000 texts per domain. In order to see how far an automatic induction of a domain-specific noun lexicon could go, we also experimented with machine learning scenarios on the output of the baseline system. We experimented with a distributional feature setting on the basis of unigrams and used the Maximum En-

Proceedings of the 5th Workshop on Computational Approaches to Subjectivity, Sentiment and Social Media Analysis, pages 18–23,
Baltimore, Maryland, USA. June 27, 2014. ©2014 Association for Computational Linguistics

tropy learner, Megam (Daumé III, 2004), to learn a classifier. We also worked with Weka (Frank et al., 2010) and features derived from the German polarity lexicon. Both approaches yield significant gains in terms of precision - so they realize a high-precision scenario.

2 Inducing the Preference Model

We seek to identify adjectives which impose a clear-cut polar preference on their head nouns. The *polarity preference* of an adjective reflects the distribution of positive, negative and neutral nouns the adjective modifies given to some text corpus. We used the domain-independent DeWac corpus (Baroni M., 2009) comprising about 90 million German sentences. We selected those adjectives that frequently co-occurred with polar nouns from PoLex, a freely available German polarity lexicon (Clematide and Klenner, 2010). Since the original polarity lexicon contained no neutral nouns, we first identified 2100 neutral nouns and expanded the lexicon[1]. Altogether 5'500 nouns were available, 2100 neutral, 2100 negative and 1250 positive. For each adjective, we counted how often it took (i.e. modified) positive, negative or neutral nouns in the DeWac corpus and determined their polarity preferences for each class (positive, negative and neutral). This way, 28'500 adjectives got a probability distribution, most of them, however, with a dominating neutral polarity preference. Two lexicons were derived from it: a positive and a negative polarity preference lexicon.

An adjective obeys a polar polarity preference if the sum of its positive and negative polarity preferences is higher than its neutral preference. If the positive preference is higher than the negative, the adjective is a positive polarity predictor, otherwise it is a negative polarity predictor. This procedure leaves us with 506 adjectives, 401 negative polarity predictors and 105 positive polarity predictors. Figure 1 shows some examples of negative polarity predictors. It reveals that, for instance, the adjective *akut* (acute) is mostly coupled with negative nouns (61.50%). Nouns not in PoLex that co-occur with an adjective are not considered. We assume that these unknown nouns of an adjective follow the same distribution that we are sampling from the known co-occurring nouns. Note that polarity predictors not necessarily must have a prior polarity itself. Actually, only 3 of the 12 adjectives from Figure 1 do have a prior polarity (indicated as n^-). For instance, the adjective *plötzlich* (immediate) is not polar but has a negative polarity preference. The polarity preference of a word is not useful in composition, it just reveals the empirical (polar) context of the word. If, however, the polarity of the context word is unknown, the preference might license an informed polarity guess.

adjective	English	POS	NEG	$\#n^-$
arg^-	bad/very	02.65	55.14	301
heftig	intensive	07.73	48.77	814
völlig	total	25.79	42.43	787
akut	acute	06.27	61.50	478
latent	latent	07.96	47.76	402
ziemlich	rather	14.16	52.36	233
$drohend^-$	threatening	35.1	52.54	824
plötzlich	immediate	17.78	41.82	703
gravierend	grave	04.5	48.5	400
chronisch	chronic	03.26	72.11	398
schleichend	subtle	03.76	52.97	319
$hemmunglos^-$	unscrupulous	15.49	43.19	213

Figure 1: Negative Polarity Predictors

Here is the formula for the estimation of the negative polarity preference as given in Figure 1 (n^- denotes a negative noun from PoLex, a_j an adjective modifying an instance of n^-)[2]:

$$prefn^-(a_j) = \frac{\#a_j\, n^-}{\#a_j^{+,-,=}}$$

Note that we count the number of adj-noun types ($\#a_j\, n^-$), not tokens. $\#a_j^{+,-,=}$ is the number of adj-noun types of the adjective a_j for all classes: positive (+), negative(-) and neutral (=).

Figure 2 gives examples of positive polarity predictors with some of their nouns.

German	English	POS
ungetrübt	unclouded	joy
unbeirrbar	unerring	hope
überströmend	overwhelming	happiness
bewunderswert	mirable	competence
falschverstanden	falsely-understood	tolerance
wiedergewonnen	regained	freedom

Figure 2: Positive Polarity Predictors

3 Applying the Preference Model

We applied the preference model to texts from five domains: banks (37'346 texts), transport (3221),

[1]We searched for nouns that frequently co-occurred with the same adjectives the polar nouns from the polarity lexicon did and stopped annotating when we reached 2'100 neutral nouns.

[2]This could be interpreted as the conditional probability of a negative noun given the adjective.

insurance (4768), politics (3208) and pharma (4790). These texts have been manually classified over the last 15 years by an institute carrying out media monitoring[3], not only wrt. their domain, but also wrt. target-specific polarity (we just use the domain annotation, currently).

The polarity of a noun is predicted by the vote of the adjectives it occurred with. The following formula shows the polarity prediction $pol^{+,-,=}$ for the class *negative* (pol^-):

$$pol^-(n_i) = A_i * \prod_{a_j \in PM^- \wedge \exists(a_j,n_i)} prefn^-(a_j)$$

A_i is the number of adjectives that modify the noun n_i in the domain-specific texts. PM^- is the set of adjectives from the polarity model (PM) with a negative polarity preference and (a_j, n_i) is true, if the adjective a_j modifies the noun n_i according to the domain-specific documents.

4 Improving the Predictions

The preference model serves two purposes: it generates a list of candidates for polar nouns and it establishes a baseline. We experimented with two feature settings in order to find out whether we could improve on these results.

In the first setting, the WK setting, we wanted to exploit the fact that for some adjectives that modify a noun, we know their prior polarity (from the polarity lexicon). These adjectives do not necessarily have a clear positive or negative polarity preference. If not, then they are not used in the prediction of the noun polarity.

But could the co-occurrence of a noun with adjectives bearing a prior polarity also be indicative of the noun polarity? For instance, if a noun is coupled frequently and exclusively with negative adjectives. Does this indicate something? Ones intuition might mislead, but a machine learning approach could reveal correlations. We used Simple Logistic Regression (SRL) from Weka and the following features:

1. the number of positive adjectives with a prior polarity that modify the noun
2. the number of negative adjectives with a prior polarity that modify the noun
3. the difference between 1) and 2): absolute and ratio
4. the ratio of positive and negative adjectives
5. two binary features indicating the majority class
6. three features for the output of the preference model: the positive, negative and neutral scores: $pol^-, pol^+, pol^=$, respectively.

In the second setting, the MG setting, we trained Megam, a Maximum Entropy learner, among the following lines: we took all polar nouns from PoLex and extracted from the DeWac corpus all sentences containing these nouns. For each noun, all (context) words (nouns, adjectives, verbs) co-occurring with it in these sentences are used as bag of words training vectors. In other words, we learned a tri-partite classifier to predict the polarity class (positive, negative or neutral) given a target noun and its context, i.e. those nouns co-occurring with it in a text collection.

5 Experiments

The goal of our experiments were the prediction of positive and negative domain-specific nouns in five domains. We used our preference model to generate candidates. Then we manually annotated the results in order to obtain a domain-specific gold standard. We evaluated the output of the preference model relative to the new gold standards and we run our experiments with Megam and Weka's Simple Logistic Regression (SRL). Megam and Weka's SLR were trained on the basis of the positive, negative and neutral nouns from PoLex and the DeWac corpus.

Figure 3 shows the results. #PM gives the number of nouns predicted by the preference model to be negative (e.g. 220 in the politics domain). These are the nouns we annotated for polarity and that formed our gold standard afterwards (e.g. 75.90 out of 110 predicted are true negative nouns and are kept as the gold standard). Since the generation of the gold standard is based on the preference model's output, its recall is 1. We cannot fix the real recall since this would require to manually classify all nouns occurring in those texts (e.g. 13'000 in the banks domain). However, since we wanted to compare the machine learning performance with the preference model, we had to mea-

[3] We would like to thank the *fög* institute (cf. www.foeg.uzh.ch/) for these data (mainly newspaper texts in German).

ID	domain	texts	#PM	prec	f	#WK	prec	rec	f	#MG	prec	rec	f
D1	politics	3208	220	75.90	**86.29**	195	78.97	92.22	83.26	130	*81.54*	63.48	69.13
D2	transport	3221	141	71.63	**83.47**	127	73.22	92.07	80.57	64	*78.12*	49.50	58.54
D3	insurance	4768	255	76.86	**86.91**	238	78.57	95.40	85.13	155	*79.35*	62.75	69.09
D4	pharma	4790	257	71.59	**83.44**	228	76.75	95.11	81.69	137	*87.83*	65.40	68.35
D5	banks	37346	1013	70.38	**88.02**	825	77.84	90.07	79.02	437	*81.23*	49.78	58.32

Figure 3: Prediction of Negative Nouns

sure recall, otherwise we could not determine the overall performance.

From Figure 3 we can see that the preference model (PM) performs best in terms of f-measure (in bold). Of course, recall (i.e. 1, not shown) is idealized, since we took the output of the preference model to generate the gold standard. Note however that this was our premise, that we needed an approach that delivers good candidates, otherwise we were lost given the vast amount of candidate nouns (e.g. remember the 13'000 nouns in the finance sector).

German	English
Wertverminderung	impairment of assets
Stagflation	stagflation
Geldschwemme	money glut
Überhitzungssymptom	overheating symptom
Hyperinflation	hyperinflation
Euroschwäche	weakness of the euro
Werterosion	erosion in value
Nachfrageüberhang	surplus in demand
Margendruck	pressure on margins
Klumpenrisiko	cluster risk
Virus	virus
Handekzem	hand eczema
Schweinegrippe	swine flu
Gebärmutterriss	ruptured uterus
Alzheimer	Alzheimer
Sehstörung	defective eye sight
Tinnitus	tinnitus

Figure 4: Domain-specific Negative Nouns

Figure 4 shows examples of negative nouns from two domains: banks and pharma. But: are all found nouns *domain-specific* negative nouns? In the bank domain, we have manually annotated for domain specificity: out of 1013 nouns predicted to be negative by the model, 409 actually were domain-specific (40.3 %)[4]. The other nouns could also be in a domain-independent polarity lexicon.

Now, we turn to the prediction of positive domain-specific nouns. It is not really surprising that the preference model is unbalanced - that there are far more negative than positive polarity predictors: 401 compared to 105. PoLex, the pool of nouns used for learning of the polarity preferences already is unbalanced (2100 negative compared to 1250 positive nouns). Also, the majority of the texts in our five domains are negative (all texts are annotated for document-level polarity). It is obvious then that our model is better in the prediction of negative than positive polarity. Actually, our base model comprising 105 positive polarity predictors does not trigger often within the whole corpus. For instance, only 10 predictions were made in the banks domain, despite the 37'346 texts. Clearly, newspaper texts often are critical and thus more negative than positive vocabulary is used. This explains the very low recall.

However, what if we relaxed our model? If we, for example, keep those adjectives in our model that have a positive polarity preference > 0.35, at least 35 out of 100 nouns co-occurring with those adjectives should be positive.

ID	#1	prec	#2	prec	#3	prec	#4	prec
D1	18	66.6	25	60.0	25	60.0	8	50
D2	14	85.7	16	75.0	0	0	3	33.3
D3	13	69.2	15	60.0	5	100	1	100
D4	13	84.6	15	80.0	9	55.5	2	100
D5	135	76.2	174	71.2	58	87.9	40	82.5

Figure 5: Prediction of Positive Nouns

We report the results of two runs. The first one, labelled #1, where adjectives are used to predict a positive noun polarity if they have a positive polarity preference > 0.35 and where the negative polarity preference is < 0.1. In the second run, labelled #2, we only require the positive preference to be > 0.35. Table 5 shows the results. We also show the results of Weka (label #3) and Megam (label #4) for the candidates generated by #2.

Compared to the negative settings, the number of found positive nouns is rather low. For instance, in the banks domain, 174 nouns were suggested compared to 1013 negative ones. However, precision has not dropped and it is especially higher than the threshold value of 0.35 seemed to indicate (as discussed previously). Weka (#3) and Megam (#4) again show better precision, however

[4] 51 of the 131 (38.93%) as positive classified nouns actually were domain-specific.

the number of found nouns is too low (in a setting that suffers already from low numbers). Figure 6 shows a couple of found positive nouns.

German	English
Versammlungsfreiheit	freedom of assembly
Ausländerintegration	integration of foreigners
Einlagesicherung	deposit protection
Lohntransparenz	wage transparency
Haushaltsdisziplin	budgetary discipline
Vertriebsstärke	marketing strength
Anlegervertrauen	confidence of investors
Kritikfähigkeit	ability for criticism
Führungskompetenz	leadership competencies

Figure 6: Predicted Positive Nouns

So far, we have discussed a binary approach where each class (positive, negative) was predicted and classified independently and where especially no adjectives with a neutral preference where considered. What happens if we include these adjectives? The results are given in Figure 7.

domain	#neg	prec	#pos	prec
banks	288	80.16	3	66.66
pharma	141	70.92	32	68.75
transport	78	67.94	0	0
politics	115	76.52	0	0
insurance	132	66.66	0	0

Figure 7: Unrestricted Prediction of Noun Polarity

Although precision is good, the results are very conservative, e.g. in the banks domain, only 288 nouns were found compared to 1013 nouns given the binary mode. Recall and f-measure are lower compared to the binary setting. The huge amount of neutral preference adjectives (about 28'000) seems to neutralize polar tendencies. But even then, some predictions survive - so these contexts seem to be strong.

6 Related Work

The expansion or creation of sentiment lexicons has been investigated in many variations from different perspectives and for various goals. Liu and Zhang (2012) subdivide the work in this field into three groups: manual approaches, dictionary-based approaches and corpus-based approaches. While the manual approach is time-consuming, it is still often used to create core lexicons which are not domain-specific, e.g. (Taboada et al., 2011). The dictionary-based approaches which are also called thesaurus-based approaches (Huang et al., 2014) try to make use of existing dictionaries or thesauri like WordNet (e.g. (Esuli and Sebastiani, 2006; Baccianella et al., 2010; Neviarouskaya et al., 2011)) while the corpus-based approaches rely on statistical measures based on different concepts, for example, sentiment consistency (Hatzivassiloglou and McKeown, 1997), pointwise mutual information (Turney, 2002), context coherency (Kanayama and Nasukawa, 2006), double propagation (Qiu et al., 2011) or label propagation (Huang et al., 2014). Our approach is based on the use of an existing dictionary and of an domain-independent corpus. But rather than using the corpus to directly detect new entries for the lexicon, we use it to derive the polarity preference of adjectives which in turn is used to generate candidates from the domain-specific corpus.

The model most similar to our approach is (Klenner and Petrakis, 2014), where the contextual and prior polarity of nouns is learned from the polarity preference of verbs for the verb's direct object. However, no attempt is made to induce domain-specific polarity as we do. We also focus on the polarity preference of adjectives and we also try to improve precision by machine learning.

7 Conclusions

We have introduced a plain model for the induction of domain-specific noun lexicons. First, the polarity preferences of adjectives are learned from domain-independent text and from a general polarity lexicon. A voting approach then predicts noun polarity from adjective noun pairings sampled from domain-specific texts. The predictions based only on adjectives acting as positive or negative polarity predictors perform astonishingly well. Machine Learning can be used to improve precision at the cost of recall. Our approach thus even might be useful for fully automatic generation of a high precision, domain-specific prior noun polarity lexicons.

In future work, we will apply our approach to other languages than German. We then will also have to cope with multiword expressions as well, since compounds not longer - as in German - come as single words. We also would like to carry out an extrinsic evaluation in order to see how big the impact of an induced domain-specific lexicon on polarity text classification actually is.

References

Stefano Baccianella, Andrea Esuli, and Fabrizio Sebastiani. 2010. Sentiwordnet 3.0: An enhanced lexical resource for sentiment analysis and opinion mining. In *Proc. of LREC 2010*, volume 10, pages 2200–2204.

Ferraresi A. Zanchetta E. Baroni M., Bernardini S. 2009. The WaCky Wide Web: A collection of very large linguistically processed Web-crawled corpora. *Language Resources and Evaluation*, 43(3):209–226.

Simon Clematide and Manfred Klenner. 2010. Evaluation and extension of a polarity lexicon for German. In *Proceedings of the First Workshop on Computational Approaches to Subjectivity and Sentiment Analysis*, pages 7–13.

Hal Daumé III. 2004. Notes on CG and LM-BFGS optimization of logistic regression. *Paper available at http://pub.hal3.name#daume04cg-bfgs, implementation available at http://hal3.name/megam.*

Andrea Esuli and Fabrizio Sebastiani. 2006. Sentiwordnet: A publicly available lexical resource for opinion mining. In *Proc. of LREC 2006*, volume 6, pages 417–422.

Eibe Frank, Mark Hall, Geoffrey Holmes, Richard Kirkby, Bernhard Pfahringer, Ian H. Witten, and Len Trigg. 2010. Weka-A Machine Learning Workbench for Data Mining. In Oded Maimon and Lior Rokach, editors, *Data Mining and Knowledge Discovery Handbook*, chapter 66, pages 1269–1277. Springer US, Boston, MA.

Vasileios Hatzivassiloglou and Kathleen R McKeown. 1997. Predicting the semantic orientation of adjectives. In *Proc. of the ACL 1997*, pages 174–181. Association for Computational Linguistics.

Sheng Huang, Zhendong Niu, and Chongyang Shi. 2014. Automatic construction of domain-specific sentiment lexicon based on constrained label propagation. *Knowledge-Based Systems*, 56:191–200.

Hiroshi Kanayama and Tetsuya Nasukawa. 2006. Fully automatic lexicon expansion for domain-oriented sentiment analysis. In *Proc. of EMNLP 2006*, pages 355–363. Association for Computational Linguistics.

Manfred Klenner and Stefanos Petrakis. 2014. Inducing the contextual and prior polarity of nouns from the induced polarity preference of verbs. *Data & Knowledge Engineering*, 90:13–21.

Bing Liu and Lei Zhang. 2012. A survey of opinion mining and sentiment analysis. In *Mining Text Data*, pages 415–463. Springer.

Karo Moilanen and Stephen Pulman. 2007. Sentiment composition. In *Proc. of RANLP 2007*, pages 378–382, Borovets, Bulgaria, September 27-29.

Alena Neviarouskaya, Helmut Prendinger, and Mitsuru Ishizuka. 2011. Sentiful: A lexicon for sentiment analysis. *Affective Computing, IEEE Transactions on*, 2(1):22–36.

Guang Qiu, Bing Liu, Jiajun Bu, and Chun Chen. 2011. Opinion word expansion and target extraction through double propagation. *Computational Linguistics*, 37(1):9–27.

Maite Taboada, Julian Brooke, Milan Tofiloski, Kimberly Voll, and Manfred Stede. 2011. Lexicon-based methods for sentiment analysis. *Computational Linguistics*, 37(2):267–307.

Peter D Turney. 2002. Thumbs up or thumbs down?: semantic orientation applied to unsupervised classification of reviews. In *Proc. of the ACL 2002*, pages 417–424. Association for Computational Linguistics.

Aspect-Level Sentiment Analysis in Czech

Josef Steinberger
Department of Computer Science and Engineering,
Faculty of Applied Sciences,
University of West Bohemia,
Univerzitní 8, 306 14 Plzeň
Czech Republic
jstein@kiv.zcu.cz

Tomáš Brychcín
NTIS – New Technologies for the Information Society,
Faculty of Applied Sciences,
University of West Bohemia,
Univerzitní 8, 306 14 Plzeň
Czech Republic
brychcin@kiv.zcu.cz

Michal Konkol
NTIS – New Technologies for the Information Society,
Faculty of Applied Sciences,
University of West Bohemia,
Univerzitní 8, 306 14 Plzeň
Czech Republic
konkol@kiv.zcu.cz

Abstract

This paper presents a pioneering research on aspect-level sentiment analysis in Czech. The main contribution of the paper is the newly created Czech aspect-level sentiment corpus, based on data from restaurant reviews. We annotated the corpus with two variants of aspect-level sentiment – aspect terms and aspect categories. The corpus consists of 1,244 sentences and 1,824 annotated aspects and is freely available to the research community. Furthermore, we propose a baseline system based on supervised machine learning. Our system detects the aspect terms with F-measure 68.65% and their polarities with accuracy 66.27%. The categories are recognized with F-measure 74.02% and their polarities with accuracy 66.61%.

1 Introduction

The interest in sentiment analysis (SA) is increasing with the amount of easily accessible content on the web, especially from the social media. Sentiment polarity is one of the critical information needed for many analysis of the data. Its use ranges from analysing product reviews (Stepanov and Riccardi, 2011) to predicting sales and stock markets using social media monitoring (Yu et al., 2013).

The majority of current approaches tries to detect the overall polarity of a sentence (or a document) regardless of the target entities (e.g., restaurants, laptops) and their aspects (e.g., food, price, battery, screen). By contrast, the aspect-driven sentiment analysis identifies the aspects of a given target entity and estimates the sentiment polarity for each mentioned aspect. This opens up completely new possibilities how to analyse the data.

The most of the research in automatic sentiment analysis has been devoted to English. There were several attempts in Czech (Steinberger et al., 2011; Veselovská, 2012; Habernal et al., 2013; Brychcín and Habernal, 2013), but all were focused on the global (sentence- or document-level) sentiment. Although Czech is not a widely-spoken language on the global scale, it is in many ways similar to other Slavic languages and their speakers altogether represent an important group. The rich morphology and the free word order also makes it interesting from the linguistic perspective.

Our main goal is the creation of a aspect-level corpus as there is no such resource for Czech. We would like to support the beginning of aspect-level sentiment analysis for Czech and a human-annotated corpus is the first step in this direction. In addition, we want to provide results of a baseline system (based on machine leaning techniques). This creates an easily reproducible starting point and allows anyone to quickly join the research of this task.

The rest of the paper is organised as follows. Section 2 is devoted to related work. It covers the aspect-level SA and sentiment analysis in Czech. Then we introduce the aspect-level architecture (Section 3) used for both the annotation of the corpus (Section 4) and for the automatic supervised approach (Section 5). In Section 6 we sumarize our contribution and reveal our future plans.

2 Related work

The impact of SA can be seen in many practical applications, The users' opinions are mostly extracted either on a certain polarity scale, or binary (positive, negative). From the point of view of the granularity, the polarity has been assigned to a document or to a sentence. However, classifying opinions at the document level or the sentence level is often insufficient for applications because they do not identify opinion targets or assign sentiments to such targets (Liu, 2012). Even if we recognize the target entity (as the entity-centered

Proceedings of the 5th Workshop on Computational Approaches to Subjectivity, Sentiment and Social Media Analysis, pages 24–30,
Baltimore, Maryland, USA. June 27, 2014.

approaches do (e.g. Steinberger et al. (2011)), a positive opinion about the entity does not mean that the author has positive opinions about all aspects of the entity. Aspect-based sentiment analysis, which has been also called 'feature-based' (Hu and Liu, 2004), goes even deeper as it attempts to identify (and assign the polarity to) aspects of the target entity within a sentence (Hajmohammadi et al., 2012). Whenever we talk about an aspect, we must know which entity it belongs to. In the further discussion, we often omit the entity as we analysed restaurant reviews and thus our target entities are the reviewed restaurants.

2.1 Aspect-based sentiment analysis

The aspect scenario can be decomposed into two tasks: aspect extraction and aspect sentiment classification (Liu, 2012).

2.1.1 Aspect extraction

The task of aspect extraction, which can also be seen as an information extraction task, is to detect aspects that have been evaluated. For example, in the sentence, *The voice quality of this phone is amazing*, the aspect is *voice quality* of the entity represented by *this phone*.

The basic approach is finding frequent nouns and noun phrases. In (Liu et al., 2005), a specific method based on a sequential learning method was proposed to extract aspects from pros and cons, Blair-Goldensohn et al. (2008) refined the frequent noun and noun phrase approach by considering mainly those noun phrases that are in sentiment-bearing sentences or in some syntactic patterns which indicate sentiments. Moghaddam and Ester (2010) augmented the frequency-based approach with an additional pattern-based filter to remove some non-aspect terms. Long et al. (2010) extracted aspects (nouns) based on frequency and information distance.

Using supervised learning is another option. Aspect extraction can be seen as a special case of the general information extraction problem. The most dominant methods are based on sequential learning. Since these are supervised techniques, they need manually labeled data for training. One needs to manually annotate aspects and non-aspects in a corpus. The current state-of-the-art sequential learning methods are Hidden Markov Models (HMM) (Rabiner, 2010) and Conditional Random Fields (CRF) (Lafferty et al., 2001).

The last group of methods use topic models (Mei et al., 2007; Titov and McDonald, 2008; Blei et al., 2003). There are two main basic models, pLSA (Probabilistic Latent Semantic Analysis) (Hofmann, 1999) and LDA (Latent Dirichlet allocation) (Blei et al., 2003). In the SA context, one can design a joint model to model both sentiment words and topics at the same time, due to the observation that every opinion has a target.

2.1.2 Aspect sentiment classification

This task is to determine whether the opinions on different aspects are positive, negative, or neutral.

The classification approaches can be divided to supervised learning approaches and lexicon-based approaches. Supervised learning performs better in a particular application domain but it has difficulty to scale up to a large number of domains. Lexicon-based techniques often lose the fight against the learning but they are suitable for open-domain applications (Liu, 2012).

The key issue for learning methods is to determine the scope of each sentiment expression, i.e., whether it covers the aspect of interest in the sentence. In (Jiang et al., 2011), a dependency parser was used to generate a set of aspect dependent features for classification. A related approach was also used in (Boiy and Moens, 2009), which weights each feature based on the position of the feature relative to the target aspect in the parse tree.

Lexicon-based approaches use a list of sentiment phrases as the core resource. The method in (Ding et al., 2008) has four steps to assign a polarity to an aspect: mark sentiment words and phrases, apply sentiment shifters, handle but-clauses and aggregate opinions using an aggregation function (e.g. Hu and Liu (2004)).

2.2 Sentiment analysis for Czech

Pilot study of Czech sentiment analysis was shown in (Steinberger et al., 2012) where sentiment dictionaries for many languages (including Czech) were created using semi-automatic "triangulation" method.

Veselovská (2012) created a small corpus containing polarity categories for 410 news sentences and used the Naive Bayes and lexicon-based classifiers.

Three large labeled corpora (10k Facebook posts, 90k movie reviews, and 130k product reviews) were introduced in (Habernal et al.,

2013).Authors also evaluate three different classifiers, namely Naive Bayes, SVM (Support Vector Machines) and Maximum Entropy on these data.

Recently, Habernal and Brychcín (2013) experimented with building word clusters, obtained from semantic spaces created on unlabeled data, as an additional source of information to tackle the high flection issue in Czech.

These results were later outperformed by another unsupervised extension (Brychcín and Habernal, 2013), where the global target context was shown to be very useful source of information.

3 The task definition

The aspect-level sentiment analysis firstly identifies the aspects of the target entity and then assigns a polarity to each aspect. There are several ways to define aspects and polarities. We use the definition based on the Semeval2014's Aspect-based SA task, which distinguishes two types of aspect-level sentiment – aspect terms and aspect categories.

The task is decomposed into the following 4 subtasks. We briefly describe each subtask and give some examples of source sentences and the expected results of the subtask.

3.1 Subtask 1: Aspect term extraction

Given a set of sentences with pre-identified entities (e.g., restaurants), the task is to identify the aspect terms present in the sentence and return a list containing all the distinct aspect terms. An aspect term names a particular aspect of the target entity.

Examples:

Děti dostaly naprosto krvavé maso.
(They brought a totally bloody meat to the kids.)
→ {*maso (meat)*}

Tlačenka se rozpadla, polévka ušla.
(The porkpie broke down, the soup was ok.)
→ {*Tlačenka (porkpie), polévka (soup)*}

3.2 Subtask 2: Aspect term polarity

For a given set of aspect terms within a sentence, the task is to determine the polarity of each aspect term: positive, negative, neutral or bipolar (i.e., both positive and negative).

Examples:

Děti dostaly naprosto krvavé maso.
(They brought a totally bloody meat to the kids.)
→ {*maso (meat): negative*}

Tlačenka se rozpadla, polévka ušla.
(The porkpie broke down, the soup was ok,)
→ {*Tlačenka (porkpie): negative, polévka (soup): positive*}

3.3 Subtask 3: Aspect category detection

Given a predefined set of aspect categories (e.g., price, food), the task is to identify the aspect categories discussed in a given sentence. Aspect categories are typically coarser than the aspect terms of Subtask 1, and they do not necessarily occur as terms in the given sentence.

For example, given the set of aspect categories food, service, price, ambience:

Přivítala nás velmi příjemná servírka, ale také místnost s ošuntělým nábytkem.
(We found a very nice waitress but also a room with time-worn furniture.)
→ {*service, ambience*}

Tlačenka se rozpadla, polévka ušla.
(The porkpie broke down, the soup was ok.)
→ {*food*}

3.4 Subtask 4: Aspect category polarity

Given a set of pre-identified aspect categories (e.g., {food, price}), the task is to determine the polarity (positive, negative, neutral or bipolar) of each aspect category.

Examples:

Přivítala nás velmi příjemná servírka, ale také místnost s ošuntělým nábytkem.
(We found a very nice waitress but also a room with time-worn furniture.)
→ {*service: positive, ambience: negative*}

Tlačenka se rozpadla, polévka ušla.
(The porkpie broke down, the soup was ok.)
→ {*food: bipolar*}

4 Building the aspect-level corpus

Aspect-level annotations are strictly connected to the analysed domain. As our final goal is going multilingual, we work on the domains selected for the Semeval2014's Aspect-based SA task (restaurants, laptop) which will allow us to compare approaches for both English and Czech on the same domains.

We started with the restaurants and in the future, we would also like to cover the laptops.

We downloaded restaurant reviews from www.nejezto.cz. Ten restaurants with the largest number of reviews were selected. The reviews were splitted into sentences. Average number of sentences per restaurant was 223.

4.1 Guidelines

The purpose of this annotation was to detect aspects and their sentiment polarity within sentences. The target entities were particular restaurants. For a given restaurant, the annotator had following tasks:

1. **Identify irrelevant sentences:** Sentences that do not contain any information relevant to the topic of restaurants. They were later filtered out of the corpus. Example: *Urážet někoho pro jeho názor je nedůstojné dospělého člověka. (Offencing somebody for his opinion is discreditable for an adult.)*

2. **Identify aspect terms:** Single or multiword terms naming particular aspects of the target entity. These are either full nominal phrases (*špíz a restované brambory – skewer with fried potatoes*) or verbs (*stojí – priced*). References, names or pronouns should not be annotated.

3. **Aspect term polarity:** Each aspect term has to be assigned one of the following polarities based on the sentiment that is expressed in the sentence about it: positive, negative, bipolar (both positive and negative sentiment) and neutral (neither positive nor negative sentiment).

4. **Aspect category:** The task of the annotator is to identify the aspect categories discussed in a sentence given the following five aspect categories: food, service, price, ambience, general (sentences mentioning the restaurant as a whole). Example: *Celkově doporučuji a vrátím se tam – Overall I would recommend it and go back again. → general.*

5. **Aspect category polarity:** Each aspect category discussed by a particular sentence has to be assigned one of the following polarities based on the sentiment that is expressed in the sentence about it: positive, negative, bipolar, neutral.

4.2 Annotation statistics

Three native Czech speakers annotated in total 1,532 sentences. 18.8% of the sentences were marked as irrelevant, leaving 1,244 sentences for further analysis. Their average agreement for the task of aspect terms' identification was 82.6% (measured by F-measure). Only strict matches were considered correct. In the case of identifying the categories, their average agreement (F-measure) was 91.8%. The annotators agreed on 85.5% (accuracy) in the task of assigning polarity to terms and on 82.4% (accuracy) in the case of the category polarity assignment. It corresponds to Cohen's of 0.762, resp. 0.711, which represents a substantial agreement level (Pustejovsky and Stubbs, 2013), therefore the task can be considered as well-defined.

There were several reasons of disagreement. The annotators did not always itentify the same terms, mainly in the cases with general meaning. In the case of polarity, the annotators did not agree on the most difficult cases to which bipolar class could be assigned:

Trochu přesolená omáčka, ale jinak luxus.
(Too salted sauce, but luxury otherwise.)
→ {*food: bipolar vs. positive*}

The cases, on which the two annotators did not agree, were judged by the third super-annotator and golden standard data were created. The final dataset[1] contains 1244 sentences. The sentences contain 1824 annotated aspect terms (679 positive, 725 negative, 403 neutral, 17 bipolar) and 1365 categories (521 positive, 569 negative, 246 neutral, 28 bipolar).

5 Results of the supervised approach

5.1 Overview

We use machine learning approach in all subtasks. For aspect term extraction we use Conditional Random Fields (CRF). For the other three tasks we use the Maximum Entropy classifier. We use the Brainy[2] implementation of these algorithms.

During the data preprocessing, we use simple word tokenizer based on regular expressions. All tokens are lowercased for tasks 3 and 4. Due to the complex morphology of Czech we also use the un-

[1] We will provide the dataset at http://liks.fav.zcu.cz/sentiment.

[2] Available at http://home.zcu.cz/~konkol/brainy.php

supervised stemmer called HPS[3], that has already proved to be useful in sentiment analysis (Habernal et al., 2013; Habernal and Brychcín, 2013; Brychcín and Habernal, 2013).

All particular subtasks share following features:

Bag of words: The occurrence of a word.

Bag of bigrams: The occurrence of a bigram.

Bag of stems: The occurrence of a stem.

Bag of stem bigrams: The occurrence of a stem bigram.

5.2 Aspect term extraction

The system for aspect term extraction is based on CRF. The choice of CRF is based on a current state of the art in named entity recognition (see for example (Konkol and Konopík, 2013)) as it is a very similar task. We use the BIO (Ramshaw and Marcus, 1999) model to represent aspect terms. In addition to the previously mentioned features we use affixes and learned dictionaries. Affixes are simply prefixes and suffixes of length 2 to 4. Learned dictionaries are phrases that are aspect terms in the training data.

Our system achieved 58.14 precision, 83.80 recall and 68.65 F-measure.

5.3 Aspect term polarity

During the detection of the aspect term polarities, the words affecting the sentiment of the aspect term are assumed to be close in most of cases. Thus we use a small window (10 words in both directions) around the target aspect term. We assume the further the word or bigram is from the target aspect term, the lower impact it has on sentiment label. To model this assumption we use a weight for each word and bigram feature taken from the Gaussian distribution according to distance from aspect term. The mean is set to 0 and variance is optimized on training data. The classifier uses only the features presented in section 5.1. The results are presented in table 1.

5.4 Aspect category detection

Aspect category detection is based on the Maximum Entropy classifiers. We use one binary classifier for each category. Each classifier then decides whether the sentence has the given category or not. For this task we use only the bag of stems and Tf-Idf features.

Our system achieved 68.71 precision, 80.21 recall and 74.02 F-measure.

Table 1: Aspect term polarity results. , and denote the precision, recall and F-measure. The results are expressed by percentages.

label	[%]	[%]	[%]
negative	76.41	63.31	69.25
neutral	33.75	50.18	40.36
positive	74.78	76.82	75.78
Accuracy: 66.27%			

5.5 Aspect category polarity

For the category polarity detection we use the same features as for aspect term polarity detection. However in this case, we always take the whole sentence into account. We cannot take a limited window as we do not know where exactly the category is mentioned in the sentence. Moreover, it can be at several positions. To distinguish between different categories we use multiple Maximum Entropy classifiers, one for each category. The results are shown in table 2.

Table 2: Aspect category polarity results. , and denote the precision, recall and F-measure. The results are expressed by percentages.

label	[%]	[%]	[%]
negative	74.07	66.04	69.83
neutral	37.80	46.73	41.80
positive	72.12	75.30	73.67
Accuracy: 66.61%			

5.6 Discussion

In section 5 we described our system for aspect-level sentiment analysis and showed the results. We do not use any language-dependent features, everything is learned from the training data. It is thus possible to say that our system is both language and domain independent, i.e. the system is able to work for any domain or language, if the training data are provided.

From another perspective, the already trained model is language and domain dependent (i.e. the model trained on restaurant domain probably will not perform well on laptop domain). The depen-

[3] Available at `http://liks.fav.zcu.cz/HPS`.

dence on the domain has multiple reasons. First, the categories are defined strictly for one domain (e.g. *food, price, etc.*). Second, many words can have different sentiment polarity in different domains.

In general, the sentiment analysis deals with many problems. These problems are much more evident for Czech as a representative of language with rich morphology and also with almost free word order. Here are two examples, where our system wrongly estimate the sentiment label.

Na nic si nejde stěžovat.
(There is nothing to complain about.)
→ {*general: positive*}

The sentence contains words that frequently occur in negative reviews: *nic - nothing*, *stěžovat - complain*; but the sentence is positive.

O těch labužnických a delikatesních zážitcích si člověk pouze přečte, ale realita je jiná.
(One can only read about these gourmand and delicious experiences, but the reality is completely different.)
→ {*food: negative*}

Sentence contains words like *labužnických - gourmand* and *delikatesních - delicious* that are strictly positive, but in this context it is mentioned negatively.

As we already said, this is the pilot study of aspect-level sentiment analysis in Czech. Several studies about sentence-level sentiment analysis of Czech have been already published, and thus it is worth comparing how these two tasks differ in terms of difficulty. Note that the aspect-level sentiment analysis has to deal with multiple aspects and categories in a given sentence, and thus it is apparently a much more difficult task.

We believe the results of (Brychcín and Habernal, 2013) on Czech movie reviews dataset can be a comparable example of sentence-level sentiment analysis as they also distinguish 3 sentiment labels (positive, negative and neutral) and the data are taken from a closed domain (movies). Their best result (given by the model with all extensions) is 81.53%. Our best results are 66.27% and 66.61% for aspect and category polarity detection, respectively.

6 Conclusion

The aspect level sentiment analysis has not been studied for Czech yet. The main reason for this is the lack of annotated data. In this paper, we create a high quality gold data for this task, we describe our approach to their annotation and discuss their properties. Corpus is available for free at `http://liks.fav.zcu.cz/sentiment`.

We also propose a baseline model based on state-of-the-art supervised machine learning techniques. Our system is language and domain independent, i.e. it can be easily trained on data from another domain or language. It achieved 68.65% F-measure in the aspect term detection, 74.02% F-measure in the aspect category assigning, 66.27% accuracy in the aspect term polarity classification, and 66.61% accuracy in the aspect category polarity classification.

In the future, we would like to continue the aspect-level research direction in three ways. We would like to extend the currently created restaurant reviews' corpus, to add the second (laptop's) domain to the corpus, and finally, to experiment with extensions to the baseline system. As the corpus for the Semeval2014 aspect-based SA task contains review sentences from the same domains, we will be able to compare the results of the system cross-lingually.

Acknowledgments

This work was supported by grant no. SGS-2013-029 Advanced computing and information systems, by the European Regional Development Fund (ERDF), by project "NTIS - New Technologies for Information Society", European Centre of Excellence, CZ.1.05/1.1.00/02.0090, and by project MediaGist, EU's FP7 People Programme (Marie Curie Actions), no 630786.

References

Sasha Blair-Goldensohn, Kerry Hannan, Ryan McDonald, Tyler Neylon, George Reis, and Jeff Reynar. 2008. Building a sentiment summarizer for local service reviews. In *Proceedings of WWW-2008 workshop on NLP in the Information Explosion Era*.

David M. Blei, Andrew Y. Ng, and Michael I. Jordan. 2003. Latent dirichlet allocation. *Journal of Machine Learning Research*, 3:993–1022.

Erik Boiy and Marie-Francine Moens. 2009. A machine learning approach to sentiment analysis in multilingual web texts. *Information retrieval*, 12(5):526–558.

Tomáš Brychcín and Ivan Habernal. 2013. Unsupervised improving of sentiment analysis using global target context. In *Proceedings of the International Conference Recent Advances in Natural Language Processing RANLP 2013*, pages 122–128, Hissar, Bulgaria, September. Incoma Ltd. Shoumen, Bulgaria.

Xiaowen Ding, Bing Liu, and Philip S. Yu. 2008. A holistic lexicon-based approach to opinion mining. In *Proceedings of the Conference on Web Search and Web Data Mining*.

Ivan Habernal and Tomáš Brychcín. 2013. Semantic spaces for sentiment analysis. In *Text, Speech and Dialogue*, volume 8082 of *Lecture Notes in Computer Science*, pages 482–489, Berlin Heidelberg. Springer.

Ivan Habernal, Tomáš Ptáček, and Josef Steinberger. 2013. Sentiment analysis in czech social media using supervised machine learning. In *Proceedings of the 4th Workshop on Computational Approaches to Subjectivity, Sentiment and Social Media Analysis*, pages 65–74, Atlanta, Georgia, June. Association for Computational Linguistics.

Mohammad Sadegh Hajmohammadi, Roliana Ibrahim, and Zulaiha Ali Othman. 2012. Opinion mining and sentiment analysis: A survey. *International Journal of Computers & Technology*, 2(3).

Thomas Hofmann. 1999. Probabilistic latent semantic indexing. In *Proceedings of Conference on Uncertainty in Artificial Intelligence*.

Minqing Hu and Bing Liu. 2004. Mining and summarizing customer reviews. In *Proceedings of the tenth ACM SIGKDD international conference on Knowledge discovery and data mining*, KDD '04, pages 168–177, New York, NY, USA. ACM.

Long Jiang, Mo Yu, Ming Zhou, Xiaohua Liu, and Tiejun Zhao. 2011. Target-dependent twitter sentiment classification. In *Proceedings of the 49th Annual Meeting of the Association for Computational Linguistics*.

Michal Konkol and Miloslav Konopík. 2013. Crf-based czech named entity recognizer and consolidation of czech ner research. In Ivan Habernal and Václav Matoušek, editors, *Text, Speech and Dialogue*, volume 8082 of *Lecture Notes in Computer Science*, pages 153–160. Springer Berlin Heidelberg.

John Lafferty, Andrew McCallum, and Fernando Pereira. 2001. Conditional random fields: Probabilistic models for segmenting and labeling sequence data. In *Proceedings of International Conference on Machine Learning*.

Bing Liu, Minqing Hu, and Junsheng Cheng. 2005. Opinion observer: Analyzing and comparing opinions on the web. In *Proceedings of International Conference on World Wide Web*.

Bing Liu. 2012. *Sentiment Analysis and Opinion Mining*. Morgan & Claypool Publishers.

Chong Long, Jie Zhang, and Xiaoyan Zhu. 2010. A review selection approach for accurate feature rating estimation. In *Proceedings of Coling 2010: Poster Volume*.

Qiaozhu Mei, Xu Ling, Matthew Wondra, Hang Su, and ChengXiang Zhai. 2007. Topic sentiment mixture: modeling facets and opinions in weblogs. In *Proceedings of International Conference on World Wide Web*.

Samaneh Moghaddam and Martin Ester. 2010. Opinion digger: an unsupervised opinion miner from unstructured product reviews. In *Proceeding of the ACM conference on Information and knowledge management*.

James Pustejovsky and Amber Stubbs. 2013. *Natural Language Annotation for Machine Learning*. OReilly Media, Sebastopol, CA 95472.

Lawrence Rabiner. 2010. A tutorial on hidden markov models and selected applications in speech recognition. In *Proceedings of the IEEE*, pages 257–286.

Lance A Ramshaw and Mitchell P Marcus. 1999. Text chunking using transformation-based learning. In *Natural language processing using very large corpora*, pages 157–176. Springer.

J. Steinberger, P. Lenkova, M. Kabadjov, R. Steinberger, and E. van der Goot. 2011. Multilingual entity-centered sentiment analysis evaluated by parallel corpora. In *Proceedings of the 8th International Conference Recent Advances in Natural Language Processing*, RANLP'11, pages 770–775.

J. Steinberger, M. Ebrahim, Ehrmann M., A. Hurriyetoglu, M. Kabadjov, P. Lenkova, R. Steinberger, H. Tanev, S. Vzquez, and V. Zavarella. 2012. Creating sentiment dictionaries via triangulation. *Decision Support Systems*, 53:689–694.

E.A. Stepanov and G. Riccardi. 2011. Detecting general opinions from customer surveys. In *Data Mining Workshops (ICDMW), 2011 IEEE 11th International Conference on*, pages 115–122.

Ivan Titov and Ryan McDonald. 2008. Modeling online reviews with multi-grain topic models. In *Proceedings of International Conference on World Wide Web*.

Kateřina Veselovská. 2012. Sentence-level sentiment analysis in czech. In *Proceedings of the 2nd International Conference on Web Intelligence, Mining and Semantics*. ACM.

Liang-Chih Yu, Jheng-Long Wu, Pei-Chann Chang, and Hsuan-Shou Chu. 2013. Using a contextual entropy model to expand emotion words and their intensity for the sentiment classification of stock market news. *Knowledge Based Syst*, 41:89–97, March.

Linguistic Models of Deceptive Opinion Spam

Myle Ott
Facebook
myleott@gmail.com

Abstract of the talk

Consumers increasingly inform their purchase decisions with opinions and other information found on the Web. Unfortunately, the ease of posting content online, potentially anonymously, combined with the public's trust and growing reliance on this content, creates opportunities and incentives for abuse. This is especially worrisome in the case of online reviews of products and services, where businesses may feel pressure to post deceptive opinion spam---fictitious reviews disguised to look like authentic customer reviews.

In recent years, several approaches have been proposed to identify deceptive opinion spam based on linguistic cues in a review's text. In this talk I will summarize a few of these approaches. I will additionally discuss some of the challenges researchers face when studying this problem, including the difficulty of obtaining labeled data, uncertainties surrounding the prevalence of deception, and how linguistic cues to deceptive opinion spam vary with the text's sentiment (e.g., 5-star vs 1- and 2-star reviews), domain (e.g., hotel vs. restaurant reviews) and the domain expertise of the author (e.g., crowdsourced vs. employee-written deceptive opinion spam).

Proceedings of the 5th Workshop on Computational Approaches to Subjectivity, Sentiment and Social Media Analysis, page 31,
Baltimore, Maryland, USA. June 27, 2014.

Semantic Role Labeling of Emotions in Tweets

Saif M. Mohammad, Xiaodan Zhu, and Joel Martin
National Research Council Canada
Ottawa, Ontario, Canada K1A 0R6
{saif.mohammad,xiaodan.zhu,joel.martin}@nrc-cnrc.gc.ca

Abstract

Past work on emotion processing has focused solely on detecting emotions, and ignored questions such as 'who is feeling the emotion (the experiencer)?' and 'towards whom is the emotion directed (the stimulus)?'. We automatically compile a large dataset of tweets pertaining to the 2012 US presidential elections, and annotate it not only for emotion but also for the experiencer and the stimulus. We then develop a classifier for detecting emotion that obtains an accuracy of 56.84 on an eight-way classification task. Finally, we show how the stimulus identification task can also be framed as a classification task, obtaining an F-score of 58.30.

1 Introduction

Detecting emotions in text has a number of applications including tracking sentiment towards politicians, movies, and products (Pang and Lee, 2008), identifying what emotion a newspaper headline is trying to evoke (Bellegarda, 2010), developing more natural text-to-speech systems (Francisco and Gervás, 2006), detecting how people use emotion-bearing-words and metaphors to persuade and coerce others (for example, in propaganda) (Kŏvecses, 2003), tracking response to natural disasters (Mandel et al., 2012), and so on. With the rapid proliferation of microblogging, there is growing amount of emotion analysis research on newly available datasets of Twitter posts (Mandel et al., 2012; Purver and Battersby, 2012; Mohammad, 2012b). However, past work has focused solely on detecting emotional state. It has ignored questions such as 'who is feeling the emotion (the experiencer)?' and 'towards whom is the emotion directed (the stimulus)?'.

In this paper, we present a system that analyzes tweets to determine who is feeling what emotion, and towards whom. We use tweets from the 2012 US presidential elections as our dataset, since we expect political tweets to be particularly rich in emotions. Further, the dataset will be useful for applications such as determining political alignment of tweeters (Golbeck and Hansen, 2011; Conover et al., 2011b), identifying contentious issues (Maynard and Funk, 2011), detecting the amount of polarization in the electorate (Conover et al., 2011a), and so on.

Detecting the who, what, and towards whom of emotions is essentially a semantic role-labeling problem (Gildea and Jurafsky, 2002). The semantic frame for 'emotions' in FrameNet (Baker et al., 1998) is shown in Table 1. In this work, we focus on the roles of *Experiencer, State,* and *Stimulus*. Note, however, that the state or emotion is often not explicitly present in text. Other roles such as *Reason, Degree,* and *Event* are also of significance, and remain suitable avenues for future work.

We automatically compile a large dataset of 2012 US presidential elections using a small number of hand-chosen hashtags. Next we annotate the tweets for Experiencer, State, and Stimulus by crowdsourcing to Amazon's Mechanical Turk.[1] We analyze the annotations to determine the distributions of different types of roles, and show that the dataset is rich in emotions. We develop a classifier for emotion detection that obtains an accuracy of 56.84. We find that most of the tweets express emotions of the tweeter, and only a few are indicative of the emotions of someone else. Finally, we show how the stimulus identification task can be framed as a classification task that circumvents more complicated problems of detecting entity mentions and coreferences. Our supervised classifier obtains an F-score of 58.30 on this task.

[1] https://www.mturk.com/mturk/welcome

Proceedings of the 5th Workshop on Computational Approaches to Subjectivity, Sentiment and Social Media Analysis, pages 32–41,
Baltimore, Maryland, USA. June 27, 2014.

Table 1: The FrameNet frame for emotions. The three roles investigated in this paper are shown in bold.

Role	Description
Core:	
Event	The Event is the occasion or happening that Experiencers in a certain emotional state participate in.
Experiencer	The Experiencer is the person or sentient entity that experiences or feels the emotions.
Expressor	The body part, gesture, or other expression of the Experiencer that reflects his or her emotional state.
State	The State is the abstract noun that describes a more lasting experience by the Experiencer.
Stimulus	The Stimulus is the person, event, or state of affairs that evokes the emotional response in the Experiencer.
Topic	The Topic is the general area in which the emotion occurs. It indicates a range of possible Stimulus.
Non-Core:	
Circumstances	The Circumstances is the condition(s) under which the Stimulus evokes its response.
Degree	The extent to which the Experiencer's emotion deviates from the norm for the emotion.
Empathy_target	The Empathy_target is the individual or individuals with which the Experiencer identifies emotionally.
Manner	Any way the Experiencer experiences the Stimulus which is not covered by more specific frame elements.
Parameter	The Parameter is a domain in which the Experiencer experiences the Stimulus.
Reason	The Reason is the explanation for why the Stimulus evokes a certain emotional response.

2 Related Work

Our work here is related to emotion analysis, semantic role labeling (SRL), and information extraction (IE).

Much of the past work on emotion detection focuses on emotions argued to be the most basic. For example, Ekman (1992) proposed six basic emotions—joy, sadness, anger, fear, disgust, and surprise. Plutchik (1980) argued in favor of eight—Ekman's six, surprise, and anticipation. Many of the automatic systems use affect lexicons pertaining to these basic emotions such as the NRC Emotion Lexicon (Mohammad and Turney, 2010), WordNet Affect (Strapparava and Valitutti, 2004), and the Affective Norms for English Words.[2] Affect lexicons are lists of words and associated emotions.

Emotion analysis techniques have been applied to many different kinds of text (Mihalcea and Liu, 2006; Genereux and Evans, 2006; Neviarouskaya et al., 2009; Mohammad, 2012a). More recently there has been work on tweets as well (Bollen et al., 2011; Tumasjan et al., 2010; Mohammad, 2012b). Bollen et al. (2011) measured tension, depression, anger, vigor, fatigue, and confusion in tweets. Tumasjan et al. (2010) study Twitter as a forum for political deliberation. Mohammad (2012b) developed a classifier to identify emotions using tweets with emotion word hashtags as labeled data. However, none of this work explores the many semantic roles of emotion.

Semantic role labeling (SRL) identifies semantic arguments and roles with regard to a predicate in a sentence (Gildea and Jurafsky, 2002; Màrquez et al., 2008; Palmer et al., 2010). More recently, there has also been some work on semantic role labeling of tweets for verb and nominal predicates (Liu et al., 2012; Liu et al., 2011). There exists work on extracting opinions and the topics of opinions, however most of it if focused on opinions about product features (Popescu and Etzioni, 2005; Zhang et al., 2010; Kessler and Nicolov, 2009). For example, (Kessler and Nicolov, 2009) identifies semantic relations between sentiment expressions and their targets for car and digital-camera reviews. However, there is no work on semantic role labeling of emotions in tweets. We use many of the ideas developed in the sentiment analysis work and apply them to detect the stimulus of emotions in the electoral tweets data.

Our work here is also related to template filling in information extraction (IE), for example as defined in MUC (Grishman, 1997), which extracts information (entities) from a document to fill out a pre-defined template, such as the date, location, target, and other information about an event.

3 Challenges of Semantic Role Labeling of Emotions in Tweets

Semantic role labeling of emotions in tweets poses certain unique challenges. Firstly, there are many differences between tweets and linguistically well-formed texts, such as written news (Liu et al., 2012; Ritter et al., 2011). Tweets are often less well-formed—they tend to be colloquial, have misspellings, and have non-standard tokens. Thus, methods depending heavily on deep language understanding such as syntactic parsing (Kim and Hovy, 2006) are less reliable.

[2]http://www.purl.org/net/NRCEmotionLexicon
http://csea.phhp.ufl.edu/media/anewmessage.html

Secondly, in a traditional SRL system, an argument frame is a cohesive structure with strong dependencies between the arguments. Thus it is often beneficial to develop joint models to identify the various elements of a frame (Toutanova et al., 2005). However, these assumptions are less viable when dealing with emotions in tweets. For example, there is no reason to believe that people with a certain name will have the same emotions towards the same entities. On the other hand, if we make use of information beyond the target tweet to independently identify the political leanings of a person, then that information can help determine the person's emotions towards certain entities. However, that is beyond the scope of this paper. Thus we develop independent classifiers for identifying experiencer, state, and stimulus.

Often, the goal in SRL and IE template filling is the labeling of text spans in the original text. However, emotions are often not explicitly stated in text. Thus we develop a system that assigns an emotion to a tweet even though that emotion is not explicitly mentioned. The stimulus of the emotion may also not be mentioned. Consider *Happy to see #4moreyears come into reality*. The stimulus of the emotion joy is *to see #4moreyears come into reality*. However, the tweet essentially conveys the tweeter's joy towards Barack Obama being re-elected as president. One may argue that the true stimulus here is Barack Obama. Thus it is useful to normalize mentions and resolve the coreference, for example, all mentions of *Barack H. Obama*, *Barack*, *Obama*, and *#4moreyears* should be directed to the same entity. Thus, we *ground* (in the same sense as in *language grounding*) the emotional arguments to the predefined entities. Through our experiments we show the target of an emotion in political tweets is often one among a handful of entities. Thus we develop a classifier to identify which of these pre-chosen entities is the stimulus in a given tweet.

4 Data Collection and Annotation

4.1 Identifying Electoral Tweets

We created a corpus of tweets by polling the Twitter Search API, during August and September 2012, for tweets that contained commonly known hashtags pertaining to the 2012 US presidential elections. Table 2 shows the query terms we used. Apart from 21 hashtags, we also collected tweets with the words Obama, Barack, or Romney. We used these additional terms because they are names of the two presidential candidates, and the probability that these words were used to refer to somebody else in tweets posted in August and September of 2012 was low.

Table 2: Query terms used to collect tweets pertaining to the 2012 US presidential elections.

#4moreyears	#Barack	#campaign2012
#dems2012	#democrats	#election
#election2012	#gop2012	#gop
#joebiden2012	#mitt2012	#Obama
#ObamaBiden2012	#PaulRyan2012	#president
#president2012	#Romney	#republicans
#RomneyRyan2012	#veep2012	#VP2012
Barack	Obama	Romney

The Twitter Search API was polled every four hours to obtain new tweets that matched the query. Close to one million tweets were collected, which we will make freely available to the research community. The query terms which produced the highest number of tweets were those involving the names of the presidential candidates, as well as #election2012, #campaign, #gop, and #president.

We used the metadata tag "iso_language_code" to identify English tweets. Since this tag is not always accurate, we also discarded tweets that did not have at least two valid English words. We used the Roget Thesaurus as the English word inventory.[3] This step also helps discard very short tweets and tweets with a large proportion of misspelled words. Since we were interested in determining the source and target of emotions in tweets, we decided to focus on original tweets as opposed to retweets. We discarded retweets, which can easily be identified through the presence of RT, rt, or Rt in the tweet (usually in the beginning of the post). Finally, there remained close to 170,000 original English tweets.

4.2 Annotating Emotions by Crowdsourcing

We used Amazon's Mechanical Turk service to crowdsource the annotation of the electoral tweets. We randomly selected about 2,000 tweets, each by a different Twitter user. We set up two questionnaires on Mechanical Turk for the tweets. The first questionnaire was used to determine the number of emotions in a tweet and also whether the tweet was truly relevant to the US politics.

[3] www.gutenberg.org/ebooks/10681

Questionnaire 1: Emotions in the US election tweets

Tweet: Mitt Romney is arrogant as hell.

Q1. Which of the following best describes the emotions in this tweet?

- This tweet expresses or suggests an emotional attitude or response to something.
- This tweet expresses or suggests two or more contrasting emotional attitudes or responses.
- This tweet has no emotional content.
- There is some emotion here, but the tweet does not give enough context to determine which emotion it is.
- It is not possible to decide which of the above options is appropriate.

Q2. Is this tweet about US politics and elections?

- Yes, this tweet is about US politics and elections.
- No, this tweet has nothing to do with US politics or anybody involved in it.

These questionnaires are called *HITs* (Human Intelligence Tasks) in Mechanical Turk parlance. We posted 2042 HITs corresponding to 2042 tweets. We requested responses from at least three annotators for each HIT. The response to a HIT by an annotator is called an *assignment*. In Mechanical Turk, an annotator may provide assignments for as many HITs as they wish. Thus, even though only three annotations are requested per HIT, dozens of annotators contribute assignments for the 2,042 tweets.

The tweets that were marked as having one emotion were chosen for annotation by the Questionnaire 2. We requested responses from at least five annotators for each of these HITs. Below is an example:

Questionnaire 2:
Who is feeling what, and towards whom?

Tweet: Mitt Romney is arrogant as hell.

Q1. Who is feeling or who felt an emotion?

Q2. What emotion? Choose one of the options from below that best represents the emotion.

- anger or annoyance or hostility or fury
- anticipation or expectancy or interest
- disgust or dislike
- fear or apprehension or panic or terror
- joy or happiness or elation
- sadness or gloominess or grief or sorrow
- surprise
- trust or like

Table 3: Questionnaire 1: Percentage of tweets in each category of Q1. Only those tweets that were annotated by at least two annotators were included. A tweet belongs to category X if it is annotated with X more often than all other categories combined. There were 1889 such tweets in total.

	Percentage of tweets
suggests an emotional attitude	**87.98**
suggests two contrasting attitudes	2.22
no emotional content	8.21
some emotion; not enough context	1.32
unknown; not enough context	0.26
all	100.0

Q3. Towards whom or what?

After performing a small pilot annotation effort, we realized that the stimulus in most of the electoral tweets was one among a handful of entities. Thus we reformulated question 3 as shown below:

Q3. What best describes the target of the emotion?

- Barack Obama and/or Joe Biden
- Mitt Romney and/or Paul Ryan
- Some other individual
- Democratic party, democrats, or DNC
- Republican party, republicans, or RNC
- Some other institution
- Election campaign, election process, or elections
- The target is not specified in the tweet
- None of the above

4.3 Annotation Analyses

For each annotator and for each question, we calculated the probability with which the annotator agreed with the response chosen by the majority of the annotators. We identified poor annotators as those that had an agreement probability more than two standard deviations away from the mean. All annotations by these annotators were discarded.

We determine whether a tweet is to be assigned a particular category based on strong majority vote. That is, a tweet belongs to category X if it was annotated by at least three annotators and only if at least half of the annotators agreed with each other. Percentage of tweets in each of the five categories of Q1 are shown in Table 3. Observe that the majority category for Q1 is 'suggests an emotion'—87.98% of the tweets were identified as having an emotional attitude.

Table 4: Questionnaire 2: Percentage of tweets in the categories of Q2. Only those tweets that were annotated by at least three annotators were included. A tweet belongs to category X if it is annotated with X more often than all other categories combined. There were 965 such tweets.

Emotion	Percentage of tweets
anger	7.41
anticipation	5.01
disgust	**47.75**
fear	1.98
joy	6.58
sadness	0.83
surprise	6.37
trust	24.03
all	100.00

Responses to Q2 showed that a large majority (95.56%) of the tweets were relevant to US politics and elections. This shows that the hashtags shown earlier in Table 2 were effective in identifying political tweets.

As mentioned earlier, only those tweets that were marked as having an emotion (with high agreement) were annotated further through Questionnaire 2.

Responses to Q1 of Questionnaire 2 revealed that in the vast majority of the cases (99.825%), the tweets contains emotions of the tweeter. The data did include some tweets that referred to emotions of others such as Romney, GOP, and president, but these instances are rare. Tables 4 and 5 give the distributions of the various options for Questions 2, and 3 of Questionnaire 2. Table 4 shows that disgust (49.32%) is by far the most dominant emotion in the tweets of 2012 US presidential elections. The next most prominent emotion is that of trust (23.73%). About 61% of the tweets convey negative emotions towards someone or something. Table 5 shows that the stimulus of emotions was often one of the two presidential candidates (close to 55% of the time)—Obama: 29.90%, Romney: 24.87%.

4.3.1 Inter-Annotator Agreement

We calculated agreement statistics on the full set of annotations, and not just on the annotations with a strong majority as described in the previous section. Table 6 shows *inter-annotator agreement (IAA)* for the questions—the average percentage of times two annotators agree with each other. Another way to gauge agreement is by calculating the average probability with which an annotator picks the majority class. The last column in Table 6 shows the average probability of picking the majority class (APMS) by the annotators (higher numbers indicate higher agreement). Observe that there is high agreement on determining whether a tweet has an emotion or not, and on determining whether the tweet is related to the 2012 US presidential elections or not. The questions in Questionnaire 2 pertaining to the experiencer, state, and stimulus were less straightforward and tend to require more context than just the target tweet for a clear determination, but yet the annotations had moderate agreement.

Table 5: Questionnaire 2: Percentage of tweets in the categories of Q3. A tweet belongs to category X if it is annotated with X more often than all other categories combined. There were 973 such tweets.

Whom	Percentage of tweets
Barack Obama and/or Joe Biden	**29.90**
Mitt Romney and/or Paul Ryan	24.87
Some other individual	5.03
Democratic party, democrats, or DNC	2.46
Republican party, republicans, or RNC	8.42
Some other institution	1.23
Election campaign or process	4.93
The target is not specified in the tweet	1.95
None of the above	21.17
all	100.00

Table 6: Agreement statistics: inter-annotator agreement (IAA) and average probability of choosing the majority class (APMS).

	IAA	APMS
Questionnaire 1:		
Q1	78.02	0.845
Q2	96.76	0.974
Questionnaire 2:		
Q1	52.95	0.731
Q2	59.59	0.736
Q3	44.47	0.641

4.4 Access to the data

All of the data is made freely available through the first author's website:

http://www.purl.org/net/PoliticalTweets2012

It includes: (1) the complete set of tweets collected from the Twitter API with hashtags shown in Table 2, (2) the subset of English tweets, (3) Questionnaires 1 and 2, (4) and tweets annotated as per Questionnaires 1 and 2.

5 Automatically Detecting Semantic Roles of Emotions in Tweets

Since in most instances (99.83%) the experiencer of emotions in a tweet is the tweeter, we focus on automatically detecting the other two semantic roles: the emotional state and the stimulus.

Due to the unique challenges of semantic role labeling of emotions in tweets described earlier in the paper, we treat the detection of emotional state and stimulus as two subtasks for which we train state-of-the-art support vector machine (SVM) classifiers. SVM is a learning algorithm proved to be effective on many classification tasks and robust on large feature spaces. In our experiments, we exploited several different classifiers and found SVM outperforms others such as maximum-entropy models (i.e., logistic regression). We also tested the most popular kernels such as the polynomial and RBF kernels with different parameters in stratified ten-fold cross validation. We found that a simple linear kernel yielded the best performance. We used the LibSVM package (Chang and Lin, 2011).

As mentioned earlier, there is fair amount of work on emotion detection in non-tweet texts (Boucouvalas, 2002; Holzman and Pottenger, 2003; Ma et al., 2005; John et al., 2006; Mihalcea and Liu, 2006; Genereux and Evans, 2006; Aman and Szpakowicz, 2007; Tokuhisa et al., 2008; Neviarouskaya et al., 2009) as well as on tweets (Kim et al., 2009; Tumasjan et al., 2010; Bollen et al., 2011; Mohammad, 2012b; Choudhury et al., 2012; Wang et al., 2012). In the experiments below we draw from various successfully used features described in these papers. More specifically, the system we use builds on the classifier and features used in two previous systems: (1) the system described in (Mohammad, 2012b) which was shown to perform significantly better than some other previous systems on the news paper headlines corpus and the system described in (Mohammad et al., 2013) which ranked first (among 44 participating teams) in a 2013 SemEval competition on detecting sentiment in tweets).

The goal of the experiments in this section is to apply a state-of-the art emotion detection system on the electoral tweets data. We want to set up baseline performance for emotion detection on this new dataset and also validate the data by showing that automatic classifiers can obtain results that are greater than random and majority baselines. In Section 5.2, we apply the SVM classifier and various features for the first time on the task of detecting the stimulus of an emotion in tweets. In each experiment, we report results of ten-fold stratified cross-validation.

5.1 Detecting emotional state

5.1.1 Features

We included the following features for detecting emotional state in tweets.

Word n-grams: We included unigrams (single words) and bigrams (two-word sequences) into our feature set. All words were stemmed with Porter's stemmer (Porter, 1980).

Punctuations: number of contiguous sequences of exclamation marks, question marks, or a combination of them.

Elongated words: the number of words with the final character repeated 3 or more times (*soooo, mannnnnn*, etc). (Elongated words have been used similarly in (Brody and Diakopoulos, 2011).)

Emoticons: presence/absence of positive and negative emoticons. The emoticon and its polarity were determined through a regular expression adopted from Christopher Potts' tokenizing script.[4]

Emotion Lexicons: We used the NRC word–emotion association lexicon (Mohammad and Turney, 2010) to check if a tweet contains emotional words. The lexicon contains human annotations of emotion associations for about 14,200 word types. The annotation includes whether a word is positive or negative (sentiments), and whether it is associated with the eight basic emotions (joy, sadness, anger, fear, surprise, anticipation, trust, and disgust). If a tweet has three words that have associations with emotion joy, then the $LexEmo\_emo\_joy$ feature takes a value of 3. We also counted the number of words with regard to the Osgood's (Osgood et al., 1957) semantic differential categories ($LexOsg$) built for Wordnet ($LexOsg\_wn$) and General Inquirer ($LexOsg\_gi$). To reduce noise, we only considered the words that have an adjective or adverb sense in Wordnet.

Negation features: We examined tweets to determine whether they contained negators such as *no, not,* and *shouldn't*. An additional feature determined whether the negator was located close to an

[4] http://sentiment.christopherpotts.net/tokenizing.html

Table 7: Results for emotion detection.

	Accuracy
random baseline	30.26
majority baseline	47.75
automatic SVM system	56.84
upper bound	69.80

Table 8: The accuracies obtained with one of the feature groups removed. The number in brackets is the difference with the *all features* score. The biggest drop is shown in bold.

Experiment	Accuracy	Difference from all features
all features	56.84	0
all - ngrams	53.35	**-3.49**
all - word ngrams	54.44	-2.40
all - char. ngrams	56.32	-0.52
all - lexicons	54.34	-2.50
all - manual lex.	55.17	-1.67
all - auto lex.	55.38	-1.46
all - negation	55.80	-1.04
all - encodings (elongated words, emoticons, punctns., uppercase)	56.82	-0.02

emotion word (as determined by the emotion lexicon) in the tweet and in the dependency parse of the tweet. The list of negation words was adopted from Christopher Potts' sentiment tutorial.[5]

Position features: We included a set of position features to capture whether the feature terms described above appeared at the beginning or the end of the tweet. For example, if one of the first five terms in a tweet is a joy word, then the feature $LexEmo\_joy\_begin$ was triggered.

Combined features Though non-linear models like SVM (with non-linear kernels) can capture interactions between features, we explicitly combined some of our features. For example, we concatenated all emotion categories found in a given tweet. If the tweet contained both surprise and disgust words, a binary feature "LexEmo_surprise_disgust" was triggered. Also, if a tweet contained more than one joy word and no other emotion words, then the feature $LexEmo\_joy\_only$ was triggered.

5.1.2 Results

Table 7 shows the results. We included two baselines here: the random baseline corresponds to a system that randomly guesses the emotion of a tweet, whereas the majority baseline assigns all tweets to the majority category (disgust). Since the data is significantly skewed towards disgust, the majority baseline is relative high.

The automatic system obtained by the classifier in identifying the emotions (56.84), which is significantly higher than the majority baseline. It should be noted that the highest scores in the SemEval 2013 task of detecting sentiment analysis of tweets was around 69% (Mohammad et al., 2013). That task even though related involved only three classes (positive, negative, and neutral). Thus it is not surprising that for an 8-way classification task, the performance is somewhat lower.

The upper bound of the task here is not 100%—human annotators do not always agree with each other. To estimate the upper bound we can expect an automatic system to achieve, for each tweet we randomly sampled an human annotation from its multiple annotations and treated it as a system output. We compare it with the majority category chosen from the remaining human annotations for that tweet. Such sampling is conducted over all tweets and then evaluated. The results table shows this upper bound.

Table 8 shows results of ablation experiments—the accuracies obtained with one of the feature groups removed. The higher the drop in performance, the more useful is that feature. Observe that the ngrams are the most useful features, followed by the emotion lexicons. Most of the gain from ngrams come through word ngrams, but character ngrams provide small gains as well. Both the manual and automatic sentiment lexicons were found to be useful to a similar degree. Paying attention to negation was also beneficial, whereas emotional encodings such as elongated words, emoticons, and punctuations did not help much. It is possible that much of the discriminating information they might have is already provided by unigram and character ngram features.

5.2 Detecting emotion stimulus

As discussed earlier, instead of detecting and labeling the original text spans, we ground the emotion stimulus directly to the predefined entities. This allows us to circumvent mention detection and co-reference resolution on linguistically less well-formed text. We treat the problem as a classification task, in which we classify a tweet into one of the categories defined in Table 5. We believe that a similar approach is also possible in other

[5] http://sentiment.christopherpotts.net/lingstruc.html

Table 9: Results for detecting stimulus.

	P	R	F
random baseline	16.45	20.87	18.39
majority baseline	34.45	38.00	36.14
automatic rule-based system	43.47	55.15	48.62
automatic SVM system	57.30	59.32	58.30
upper bound	82.87	81.36	82.11

domains such as natural disaster tweets and epidemic surveillance tweets. We perform a ten-fold stratified cross-validation.

5.2.1 Features

We used the features below for detecting emotion stimulus:

Word ngrams: Same as described earlier for emotional state.

Lexical features: We collected lexicons that contain a variety of words and phrases describing the categories in Table 5. For example, the Republican party may be called as "gop" or "Grand Old Party"; all such words or phrases are all put into the lexicon called "republican". We counted how many words in a given tweet are from each of these lexicons.

Hashtag features: Hashtags related to the U.S. election were collected. We organized them into different categories and use them to further smooth the sparseness. For example, "#4moreyear" and "#obama" are put into the same hashtag lexicon and any occurrence of such hashtags in a tweet triggers the feature "hashtag_obama_generalized", indicating that this is a general version of hashtag related to president Barack Obama.

Position features: Same as described earlier for emotional state.

Combined features As discussed earlier, we explicitly combined some of the above features. For example, we first concatenate all lexicon and hashtag categories found in a given tweet—if the tweet contains both the general hashtag of "obama" and "romney", a binary feature "Hashtag_general_obama_romney" takes the value of 1.

5.2.2 Results

Table 9 shows the results obtained by the system. Overall, the system obtains an F-measure of 58.30. The table also shows upper-bound and baselines calculated just as described earlier for the emotional state category. We added results for an additional baseline, *rule-based system*, here that chose the stimulus to be: Obama if the tweet had the terms *obama* or *#obama*; Romney if the tweet had the terms *romney* or *#romney*; Republicans if the tweet had the terms *republican, republicans,* or *#republicans*; Democrats if the tweet had the terms *democrats, democrat,* or #democrats; and Campaign if the tweet had the terms *#election* or *#campaign*. If two or more of the above rules are triggered in the same tweet, then a label is chosen at random. This rule-based system based on hand-chosen features obtains an F-score of 48.62, showing that there are sufficiently many tweets where key words alone are not sufficient to disambiguate the true stimulus. Observe that the SVM-based automatic system performs markedly better than the majority baseline and also the rule-based system baseline.

6 Conclusions and Future Work

In this paper, we framed emotion detection as a semantic role labeling problem, focusing not just on emotional state but also on experiencer and stimulus. We chose tweets about the 2012 US presidential elections as our target domain. We automatically compiled a large dataset of these tweets using hashtags, and annotated them first for presence of emotions, and then for the different semantic roles of emotions. All of the data is made freely available.

We found that a large majority of these tweets (88.1%) carry some emotional attitude towards someone or something. Further, tweets that convey disgust are twice as prevalent than those that convey trust. We found that most tweets express emotions of the tweeter themselves, and the stimulus is often one among a few handful of entities. We developed a classifier for emotion detection that obtained an accuracy of 56.84 on an eight-way classification task. Finally, we showed how the stimulus identification task can be framed as a classification task in which our system outperforms competitive baselines.

Our future work involves exploring the use of more tweets from the same user to determine their political leanings, and use that as an additional feature in emotion detection. We are also interested in automatically identifying other semantic roles of emotions such as degree, reason, and empathy target (described in Table 1). We believe that a more sophisticated sentiment analysis applications and a better understanding of affect require the determination of semantic roles of emotion.

References

Saima Aman and Stan Szpakowicz. 2007. Identifying expressions of emotion in text. In Vclav Matoušek and Pavel Mautner, editors, *Text, Speech and Dialogue*, volume 4629 of *Lecture Notes in Computer Science*, pages 196–205. Springer Berlin / Heidelberg.

Collin F. Baker, Charles J. Fillmore, and John B. Lowe. 1998. The berkeley framenet project. In *Proceedings of the 36th Annual Meeting of the Association for Computational Linguistics and 17th International Conference on Computational Linguistics - Volume 1*, ACL '98, pages 86–90, Stroudsburg, PA. Association for Computational Linguistics.

Jerome Bellegarda. 2010. Emotion analysis using latent affective folding and embedding. In *Proceedings of the NAACL-HLT 2010 Workshop on Computational Approaches to Analysis and Generation of Emotion in Text*, Los Angeles, California.

Johan Bollen, Alberto Pepe, and Huina Mao. 2011. Modeling public mood and emotion: Twitter sentiment and socio-economic phenomena. In *The International AAAI Conference on Weblogs and Social Media (ICWSM)*, Barcelona, Spain.

Anthony C. Boucouvalas. 2002. Real time text-to-emotion engine for expressive internet communication. *Emerging Communication: Studies on New Technologies and Practices in Communication*, 5:305–318.

Samuel Brody and Nicholas Diakopoulos. 2011. Cooooooooooooooollllllllllll!!!!!!!!!!!!!!: using word lengthening to detect sentiment in microblogs. In *Proceedings of the Conference on Empirical Methods in Natural Language Processing*, EMNLP '11, pages 562–570, Stroudsburg, PA, USA. Association for Computational Linguistics.

Chih-Chung Chang and Chih-Jen Lin. 2011. LIBSVM: A library for support vector machines. *ACM Transactions on Intelligent Systems and Technology*, 2:27:1–27:27.

Munmun De Choudhury, Scott Counts, and Michael Gamon. 2012. Not all moods are created equal! exploring human emotional states in social media. In *The International AAAI Conference on Weblogs and Social Media (ICWSM)*.

M D Conover, J Ratkiewicz, M Francisco, B Gonc, A Flammini, and F Menczer. 2011a. Political polarization on Twitter. *Networks*, 133(26):89–96.

Michael D Conover, Bruno Goncalves, Jacob Ratkiewicz, Alessandro Flammini, and Filippo Menczer. 2011b. Predicting the political alignment of Twitter users. In *IEEE Third International Conference on Privacy Security Risk and Trust and IEEE Third International Conference on Social Computing*, pages 192–199. IEEE.

Paul Ekman. 1992. An argument for basic emotions. *Cognition and Emotion*, 6(3):169–200.

Virginia Francisco and Pablo Gervás. 2006. Automated mark up of affective information in english texts. In Petr Sojka, Ivan Kopecek, and Karel Pala, editors, *Text, Speech and Dialogue*, volume 4188 of *Lecture Notes in Computer Science*, pages 375–382. Springer Berlin / Heidelberg.

Michel Genereux and Roger Evans. 2006. Distinguishing affective states in weblogs. In *AAAI-2006 Spring Symposium on Computational Approaches to Analysing Weblogs*, pages 27–29, Stanford, USA.

Daniel Gildea and Daniel Jurafsky. 2002. Automatic labeling of semantic roles. *Computational Linguistics*, 28(3):245–288.

Jennifer Golbeck and Derek Hansen. 2011. Computing political preference among twitter followers. In *Proceedings of the SIGCHI Conference on Human Factors in Computing Systems*, CHI '11, pages 1105–1108, New York, NY. ACM.

Ralph Grishman. 1997. Information extraction: Techniques and challenges. In *SCIE*, pages 10–27.

Lars E. Holzman and William M. Pottenger. 2003. Classification of emotions in internet chat: An application of machine learning using speech phonemes. Technical report, Leigh University.

David John, Anthony C. Boucouvalas, and Zhe Xu. 2006. Representing emotional momentum within expressive internet communication. In *Proceedings of the 24th IASTED international conference on Internet and multimedia systems and applications*, pages 183–188, Anaheim, CA. ACTA Press.

Jason S. Kessler and Nicolas Nicolov. 2009. Targeting sentiment expressions through supervised ranking of linguistic configurations. In *3rd Int'l AAAI Conference on Weblogs and Social Media (ICWSM 2009)*.

S. Kim and E. Hovy. 2006. Extracting opinions, opinion holders, and topics expressed in online news media text. In *Proceedings of the Workshop on Sentiment and Subjectivity in Text*, pages 1–8.

Elsa Kim, Sam Gilbert, Michael J. Edwards, and Erhardt Graeff. 2009. Detecting sadness in 140 characters: Sentiment analysis of mourning Michael Jackson on twitter.

Zoltán Kövecses. 2003. *Metaphor and Emotion: Language, Culture, and Body in Human Feeling (Studies in Emotion and Social Interaction)*. Cambridge University Press.

X. Liu, K. Li, M. Zhou, and Z. Xiong. 2011. Enhancing semantic role labeling for tweets using self-training. In *AAAI*.

X. Liu, Z. Fu, F. Wei, and M. Zhou. 2012. Collective nominal semantic role labeling for tweets. In *AAAI*.

Chunling Ma, Helmut Prendinger, and Mitsuru Ishizuka. 2005. Emotion estimation and reasoning based on affective textual interaction. In J. Tao and R. W. Picard, editors, *First International Conference on Affective Computing and Intelligent Interaction (ACII-2005)*, pages 622–628, Beijing, China.

Benjamin Mandel, Aron Culotta, John Boulahanis, Danielle Stark, Bonnie Lewis, and Jeremy Rodrigue. 2012. A demographic analysis of online sentiment during Hurricane Irene. In *Proceedings of the Second Workshop on Language in Social Media*, LSM '12, pages 27–36, Stroudsburg, PA. Association for Computational Linguistics.

Lluís Màrquez, Xavier Carreras, Kenneth C. Litkowski, and Suzanne Stevenson. 2008. Semantic role labeling: an introduction to the special issue. *Computational Linguistics*, 34(2):145–159.

Diana Maynard and Adam Funk. 2011. Automatic detection of political opinions in tweets. *gateacuk*, 7117:81–92.

Rada Mihalcea and Hugo Liu. 2006. A corpus-based approach to finding happiness. In *AAAI-2006 Spring Symposium on Computational Approaches to Analysing Weblogs*, pages 139–144. AAAI Press.

Saif M. Mohammad and Peter D. Turney. 2010. Emotions evoked by common words and phrases: Using mechanical turk to create an emotion lexicon. In *Proceedings of the NAACL-HLT 2010 Workshop on Computational Approaches to Analysis and Generation of Emotion in Text*, LA, California.

Saif Mohammad, Svetlana Kiritchenko, and Xiaodan Zhu. 2013. Nrc-canada: Building the state-of-the-art in sentiment analysis of tweets. In *Proceedings of the seventh international workshop on Semantic Evaluation Exercises (SemEval-2013)*, Atlanta, Georgia, USA.

Saif Mohammad. 2012a. Portable features for classifying emotional text. In *Proceedings of the 2012 Conference of the North American Chapter of the Association for Computational Linguistics: Human Language Technologies*, pages 587–591, Montréal, Canada.

Saif M. Mohammad. 2012b. #Emotional tweets. In *Proceedings of the First Joint Conference on Lexical and Computational Semantics - Volume 1: Proceedings of the main conference and the shared task, and Volume 2: Proceedings of the Sixth International Workshop on Semantic Evaluation*, SemEval '12, pages 246–255, Stroudsburg, PA.

Alena Neviarouskaya, Helmut Prendinger, and Mitsuru Ishizuka. 2009. Compositionality principle in recognition of fine-grained emotions from text. In *Proceedings of the Third International Conference on Weblogs and Social Media*, pages 278–281, San Jose, California.

C.E. Osgood, Suci G., and P. Tannenbaum. 1957. *The measurement of meaning*. University of Illinois Press.

Martha Palmer, Daniel Gildea, and Nianwen Xue. 2010. Semantic role labeling. *Synthesis Lectures on Human Language Technologies*, 3(1):1–103.

Bo Pang and Lillian Lee. 2008. Opinion mining and sentiment analysis. *Foundations and Trends in Information Retrieval*, 2(1–2):1–135.

Robert Plutchik. 1980. A general psychoevolutionary theory of emotion. *Emotion: Theory, research, and experience*, 1(3):3–33.

Ana-Maria Popescu and Oren Etzioni. 2005. Extracting product features and opinions from reviews. In *Proceedings of the conference on Human Language Technology and Empirical Methods in Natural Language Processing*, pages 339–346, Stroudsburg, PA, USA.

M. Porter. 1980. An algorithm for suffix stripping. *Program*, 14:130–137.

Matthew Purver and Stuart Battersby. 2012. Experimenting with distant supervision for emotion classification. In *Proceedings of the 13th Conference of the European Chapter of the Association for Computational Linguistics*, EACL '12, pages 482–491, Stroudsburg, PA. Association for Computational Linguistics.

A. Ritter, S. Clark, Mausam, and O. Etzioni. 2011. Named entity recognition in tweets: An experimental study. In *Proceedings of the 2010 Conference on Empirical Methods in Natural Language Processing*, pages 1524–1534.

Carlo Strapparava and Alessandro Valitutti. 2004. Wordnet-Affect: An affective extension of WordNet. In *Proceedings of the 4th International Conference on Language Resources and Evaluation (LREC-2004)*, pages 1083–1086, Lisbon, Portugal.

Ryoko Tokuhisa, Kentaro Inui, and Yuji Matsumoto. 2008. Emotion classification using massive examples extracted from the web. In *Proceedings of the 22nd International Conference on Computational Linguistics - Volume 1*, COLING '08, pages 881–888, Stroudsburg, PA, USA. Association for Computational Linguistics.

Kristina Toutanova, Aria Haghighi, and Christopher D. Manning. 2005. Joint learning improves semantic role labeling. In *Proceedings of the 43rd Annual Meeting on Association for Computational Linguistics*, pages 589–596, Stroudsburg, PA. Association for Computational Linguistics.

Andranik Tumasjan, Timm O Sprenger, Philipp G Sandner, and Isabell M Welpe. 2010. Predicting elections with Twitter : What 140 characters reveal about political sentiment. *Word Journal Of The International Linguistic Association*, pages 178–185.

Wenbo Wang, Lu Chen, Krishnaprasad Thirunarayan, and Amit P. Sheth. 2012. Harnessing twitter "big data" for automatic emotion identification. In *Proceedings of the 2012 ASE/IEEE International Conference on Social Computing*, SOCIALCOM-PASSAT '12, pages 587–592, Washington, DC, USA. IEEE Computer Society.

Lei Zhang, Bing Liu, Suk Hwan Lim, and Eamonn O'Brien-Strain. 2010. Extracting and ranking product features in opinion documents. In *Proceedings of the 23rd International Conference on Computational Linguistics: Posters*, COLING '10, pages 1462–1470, Stroudsburg, PA, USA. Association for Computational Linguistics.

An Impact Analysis of Features in a Classification Approach to Irony Detection in Product Reviews

Konstantin Buschmeier, Philipp Cimiano and Roman Klinger
Semantic Computing Group
Cognitive Interaction Technology – Center of Excellence (CIT-EC)
Bielefeld University
33615 Bielefeld, Germany
kbuschme@techfak.uni-bielefeld.de
{rklinger,cimiano}@cit-ec.uni-bielefeld.de

Abstract

Irony is an important device in human communication, both in everyday spoken conversations as well as in written texts including books, websites, chats, reviews, and Twitter messages among others. Specific cases of irony and sarcasm have been studied in different contexts but, to the best of our knowledge, only recently the first publicly available corpus including annotations about whether a text is ironic or not has been published by Filatova (2012). However, no baseline for classification of ironic or sarcastic reviews has been provided. With this paper, we aim at closing this gap. We formulate the problem as a supervised classification task and evaluate different classifiers, reaching an F_1-measure of up to 74 % using logistic regression. We analyze the impact of a number of features which have been proposed in previous research as well as combinations of them.

1 Introduction

Irony is often understood as "the use of words that mean the opposite of what you really think especially in order to be funny" or "a situation that is strange or funny because things happen in a way that seems to be the opposite" of what is expected.[1] Many dictionaries make this difference between verbal irony and situational irony (British Dictionary, 2014; New Oxford American Dictionary, 2014; Merriam Webster Dictionary, 2014). The German Duden (2014) mentions sarcasm as synonym to irony, while the comprehension of sarcasm as a special case of irony might be more common. For instance, the Merriam Webster Dictionary (2014) defines sarcasm as "a sharp and often satirical or ironic utterance designed to cut or give pain".[2]

Irony is a frequent phenomenon within human communication, occurring both in spoken and written discourse including books, websites, fora, chats, Twitter messages, Facebook posts, news articles and product reviews. Even for humans it is sometimes difficult to recognize irony. Irony markers are thus often used in human communication, supporting the correct interpretation (Attardo, 2000). The automatic identification of ironic formulations in written text is a very challenging as well as important task as shown by the comment[3]

> "Read the book!"

which in the context of a movie review could be regarded as ironic and as conveying the fact that the film was far worse compared to the book. Another example is taken from a review for the book "Great Expectations" by Charles Dickens:[4]

> "i would recomend this book to friends who have insomnia or those who i absolutely despise."

The standard approach of recommending X implies that X is worthwhile is clearly not valid in the given context as the author is stating that she disliked the book.

[1] as defined in the Merriam Webster Dictionary (2014), http://www.merriam-webster.com/dictionary/irony

[2] http://www.merriam-webster.com/dictionary/sarcasm, accessed April 28, 2014

[3] Example from Lee (2009).

[4] http://www.amazon.com/review/R86RAMEBZSB11, access date March 10, 2014

Proceedings of the 5th Workshop on Computational Approaches to Subjectivity, Sentiment and Social Media Analysis, pages 42–49, Baltimore, Maryland, USA. June 27, 2014.

In real world applications of sentiment analysis, large data sets are automatically classified into positive statements or negative statements and such output is used to generate summaries of the sentiment about a product. In order to increase the accurateness of such systems, ironic or sarcastic statements need to be identified in order to infer the actual communicative intention of the author.

In this paper, we are concerned with approaches for the automatic detection of irony in texts, which is an important task in a variety of applications, including the automatic interpretation of text-based chats, computer interaction or sentiment analysis and opinion mining. In the latter case, the detection is of outmost importance in order to correctly assign a polarity score to an aspect of a reviewed product or a person mentioned in a Twitter message. In addition, the automatic detection of irony or sarcasm in text requires an operational definition and has therefore the potential to contribute to a deeper understanding of the linguistic properties of irony and sarcasm as linguistic phenomena and their corpus based evaluation and verification.

The rest of this paper is structured as follows: We introduce the background and theories on irony in Section 1.1 and discuss previous work in the area of automatically recognizing irony in Section 1.2. In the methods part in Section 2, we present our set of features (Section 2.1) and the classifiers we take into account (Section 2.2). In Section 3, we discuss the data set used in this work in more detail (Section 3.1), present our experimental setting (Section 3.2) and show the evaluation of our approach (Section 3.3). We conclude with a discussion and summary (Section 4) and with an outlook on possible future work (Section 5).

1.1 Background

Irony is an important and frequent device in human communication that is used to convey an attitude or evaluation towards the propositional content of a message, typically in a humorous fashion (Abrams, 1957, p. 165–168). Between the age of six (Nakassis and Snedeker, 2002) and eight years (Creusere, 2007), children are able to recognize ironic utterances or at least notice that something in the situation is not common (Glenwright and Pexman, 2007). The principle of inferability (Kreuz, 1996) states that figurative language is used if the speaker is confident that the addressee will interpret the utterance and infer the communicative intention of the speaker/author correctly. It has been shown that irony is ubiquitous, with 8 % of the utterances exchanged between interlocutors that are familiar with each other being ironic (Gibbs, 2007).

Utsumi (1996) claim that an ironic utterance can only occur in an *ironic environment*, whose presence the utterance implicitly communicates. Given the formal definition it is possible to computationally resolve if an utterance is ironic using first-order predicate logic and situation calculus. Different theories such as the *echoic account* (Wilson and Sperber, 1992), the *Pretense Theory* (Clark and Gerrig, 1984) or the *Allusional Pretense Theory* (Kumon-Nakamura et al., 1995) have challenged the understanding that an ironic utterance typically conveys the opposite of its literal propositional content. However, in spite of the fact that the attributive nature of irony is widely accepted (see Wilson and Sperber (2012)), no formal or operational definition of irony is available as of today.

1.2 Previous Work

Corpora providing annotations as to whether expressions are ironic or not are scarce. Kreuz and Caucci (2007) have automatically generated such a corpus exploiting Google Book search[5]. They collected excerpts containing the phrase "said sarcastically", removed that phrase and performed a regression analysis on the remaining text, exploiting the number of words as well as the occurrence of adjectives, adverbs, interjections, exclamation and question marks as features.

Tsur et al. (2010) present a system to identify sarcasm in Amazon product reviews exploiting features such as sentence length, punctuation marks, the total number of completely capitalized words and automatically generated patterns which are based on the occurrence frequency of different terms (following the approach by Davidov and Rappoport (2006)). Unfortunately, their corpus is not publicly available. Carvalho et al. (2009) use eight patterns to identify ironic utterances in comments on articles from a Portuguese online newspaper. These patterns contain positive predicates and utilize punctuation, interjections, positive words, emoticons, or onomatopoeia and acronyms for laughing as well as some Portuguese-specific patterns considering the verb-morphology. González-Ibáñez et al. (2011) differentiate between sarcastic and positive or negative Twitter messages. They

[5] `http://books.google.de/`

exploit lexical features like unigrams, punctuation, interjections and dictionary-based as well as pragmatic features including references to other users in addition to emoticons. Reyes et al. (2012) distinguish ironic and non-ironic Twitter messages based on features at different levels of linguistic analysis including quantifiers of sentence complexity, structural, morphosyntactic and semantic ambiguity, polarity, unexpectedness, and emotional activation, imagery, and pleasantness of words. Tepperman et al. (2006) performed experiments to recognize sarcasm in spoken language, specifically in the expression "yeah right", using spectral, contextual and prosodic cues. On the one hand, their results show that it is possible to identify sarcasm based on spectral and contextual features and, on the other hand, they confirm that prosody is insufficient to reliably detect sarcasm (Rockwell, 2005, p. 118).

Very recently, Filatova (2012) published a product review corpus from Amazon, being annotated with Amazon Mechanical Turk. It contains 437 ironic and 817 non-ironic reviews. A more detailed description of this resource can be found in Section 3.1. To our knowledge, no automatic classification approach has been evaluated on this corpus. We therefore contribute a text classification system including the previously mentioned features. Our results serve as a strong baseline on this corpus as well as an "executable review" of previous work.[6]

2 Methods

We model the task of irony detection as a supervised classification problem in which a review is categorized as being ironic or non-ironic. We investigate different classifiers and focus on the impact analysis of different features by investigating what effect their elimination has on the performance of the approach. In the following, we describe the features used and the set of classifiers compared.

2.1 Features

To estimate if a review is ironic or not, we measure a set of features. Following the idea that irony is expressing the opposite of its literal content, we take into account the imbalance between the overall (prior) polarity of words in the review and the star-rating (as proposed by Davidov et al. (2010)). We assume the imbalance to hold if the star-rating is positive (*i. e.*, 4 or 5 stars) but the majority of words is negative, and, vice versa, if the star-rating is negative (*i. e.*, 1 or 2 stars) but occurs with a majority of positive words. We refer to this feature as *Imbalance*. The polarity of words is determined based on a dictionary consisting of about 6,800 words with their polarity (Hu and Liu, 2004).[7]

The feature *Hyperbole* (Gibbs, 2007) indicates the occurrence of a sequence of three positive or negative words in a row. Similarly, the feature *Quotes* indicates that up to two consecutive adjectives or nouns in quotation marks have a positive or negative polarity.

The feature *Pos/Neg&Punctuation* indicates that a span of up to four words contains at least one positive (negative) but no negative (positive) word and ends with at least two exclamation marks or a sequence of a question mark and an exclamation mark (Carvalho et al., 2009). Analogously, the feature *Pos/Neg&Ellipsis* indicates that such a positive or negative span ends with an ellipsis ("…"). *Ellipsis and Punctuation* indicates that an ellipsis is followed by multiple exclamation marks or a combination of an exclamation and a question mark. The *Punctuation* feature conveys the presence of an ellipses as well as multiple question or exclamation marks or a combination of the latter two. The *Interjection* feature indicates the occurrence of terms like "wow" and "huh", and *Laughter* measures onomatopoeia ("haha") as well as acronyms for grin or laughter ("*g*", "lol"). In addition, the feature *Emoticon* indicates the occurrence of an emoticon. In order to capture a range of emotions, it combines a variety of emoticons such as happy, laughing, winking, surprised, dissatisfied, sad, crying, and sticking tongue out. In addition, we use each occurring word as a feature (*bag-of-words*).

All together, we have 21,773 features. The number of specific features (*i. e.*, without bag-of-words) alone is 29.

2.2 Classifiers

In order to perform the classification based on the features mentioned above, we explore a set of standard classifiers typically used in text classification research. We employ the open source machine learning library *scikit-learn* (Pedregosa et al., 2011) for Python.

[6]The system as implemented to perform the described experiments is made available at `https://github.com/kbuschme/irony-detection/`

[7]Note that examples can show that this is not always the case. Funny or odd products ironically receive a positive star-rating. However, this feature may be a strong indicator for irony.

We use a support vector machine (SVM, Cortes and Vapnik (1995)) with a linear kernel in the implementation provided by libSVM (Fan et al., 2005; Chang and Lin, 2011). The naïve Bayes classifier is employed with a multinomial prior (Zhang, 2004; Manning et al., 2008). This classifier might suffer from the issue of over-counting correlated features, such that we compare it to the logistic regression classifier as well (Yu et al., 2011).

Finally, we use a decision tree (Breiman et al., 1984; Hastie et al., 2009) and a random forest classifier (Breiman, 2001).

3 Experiments and Results

3.1 Data Set

The data set by Filatova (2012) consists of 1,254 Amazon reviews, of which 437 are ironic, *i. e.*, contain situational irony or verbal irony, and 817 are non-ironic. It has been acquired using the crowd sourcing platform Amazon Mechanical Turk[8]. Note that Filatova (2012) interprets sarcasm as being verbal irony.

In a first step, the workers were asked to find pairs of reviews on the same product so that one of the reviews is ironic while the other one is not. They were then asked to submit the ID of both reviews, and, in the case of an ironic review, to provide the fragment conveying the irony.

In a second step, each collected review was annotated by five additional workers and remained in the corpus if three of the five new annotators concurred with the initial category, *i. e.*, ironic or non-ironic. The corpus contains 21,744 distinct tokens[9], of which 5,336 occur exclusively in ironic reviews, 9,468 exclusively in non-ironic reviews, and the remaining 6,940 tokens occur in both ironic and non-ironic reviews. Thus, all ironic reviews comprise a total of 12,276 distinct tokens, whereas a total of 16,408 distinct tokens constitute all non-ironic reviews. On average, a single review consists of 271.9 tokens, a single ironic review of an average of 261.4 and a single non-ironic review of an average of 277.5 tokens. The distribution of ironic and non-ironic reviews for the different star-ratings is shown in Table 2. Note that this might be a result of the specific annotation procedure applied by the annotators to search for ironic reviews. Nevertheless, this motivates a simple baseline system which just takes one feature into account: the numbers of stars assigned to the respective review ("Star-rating only").

3.2 Experimental Settings

We run experiments for three baselines: The *star-rating* baseline relies only on the number of stars assigned in the review as a feature. The *bag-of-words* baseline exploits only the unigrams in the text as features. The *sentiment word count* only uses the information whether the number of positive words in the text is larger than the number of negative words.

We emphasize that the first baseline is only of limited applicability as it requires the explicit availability of a star-rating. The second baseline relies on standard text classification features that are not specific for the task. The third baseline relies on a classical feature used in sentiment analysis, but is not specific for irony detection.

We refer to the feature set "All" encompassing all features described in Section 2.1, including bag-of-words and the set "Specific Features".

In order to understand the impact of a specific feature A, we run three sets of experiments:

- Using all features with the exception of A.
- Using all specific features with the exception of A.
- Using A as the only feature.

In addition to evaluating each single feature as described above, we evaluate the set of positive and negative instantiations of features when using the sentiment dictionary. The "Positive set" and "Negative set" take into account the respective subsets of all specific features.

Each experiment is performed in a 10-fold cross-validation setting on document level. We report recall, precision and F_1-measure for each of the classifiers.

3.3 Evaluation

Table 1 shows the results for the three baselines and different feature set combinations, all for the different classifiers. The star-rating as a feature alone is a very strong indicator for irony. However, this result is of limited usefulness as it only regards reviews of a specific rating as ironic, namely results with

[8] `https://www.mturk.com/mturk/`, accessed on March 10, 2014

[9] Using the TreeBankWordTokenizer as implemented in the Natural Language Toolkit (NLTK) (`http://www.nltk.org/`)

	Linear SVM			Logistic Regression			Decision Tree			Random Forest			Naive Bayes		
Feature set	R.	P.	F_1	R.	P.	F_1	R.	P.	F_1	R.	P.	F_1	R.	P.	F_1
Star-rating only	66.7	78.4	71.7	66.7	78.4	71.7	66.7	78.4	71.7	66.7	78.4	71.7	66.7	78.4	71.7
BOW only	61.8	67.2	64.1	63.3	76.0	68.8	53.8	53.4	53.4	21.7	70.4	32.9	48.1	77.4	59.1
Sentiment Word Count	57.3	59.4	58.1	57.3	59.4	58.1	57.3	59.4	58.1	57.3	59.4	58.1	0.0	100.0	0.0
All + Star-rating	69.0	74.4	71.3	68.9	81.7	74.4	71.7	73.2	72.2	34.0	85.0	48.2	55.3	79.7	65.0
All (= Sp. Features + BOW)	61.3	68.0	64.3	62.2	75.2	67.8	55.0	59.8	56.9	24.1	73.2	35.3	50.9	77.3	61.2
All – Imbalance	62.4	67.1	64.4	62.5	75.0	67.9	53.0	54.3	53.3	22.3	75.9	33.8	47.8	75.8	58.4
All – Hyperbole	61.3	68.0	64.3	62.2	75.2	67.8	57.1	61.5	58.9	22.3	79.6	34.4	50.9	77.3	61.2
All – Quotes	61.3	68.0	64.3	62.8	75.1	68.2	57.2	61.7	59.1	25.9	76.8	38.5	50.6	77.0	60.9
All – Pos/Neg&Punctuation	61.5	67.9	64.4	62.4	75.2	68.0	56.7	60.1	58.0	21.8	77.8	33.5	50.9	77.3	61.2
All – Pos/Neg&Ellipsis	61.0	67.4	63.8	63.0	75.1	68.3	57.6	60.5	58.8	29.0	79.2	42.2	50.4	76.6	60.7
All – Ellipsis and Punctuation	61.3	68.0	64.3	62.4	75.2	68.0	55.1	59.7	56.9	24.6	73.6	36.2	50.9	77.3	61.2
All – Punctuation	61.8	67.9	64.5	62.5	74.9	67.8	56.1	61.2	58.3	28.6	78.1	41.5	50.2	76.7	60.6
All – Injections	61.3	68.0	64.3	62.2	75.0	67.8	56.1	61.8	58.5	24.1	75.2	35.6	50.9	77.3	61.2
All – Laughter	61.3	68.2	64.4	62.4	75.3	68.0	56.6	60.9	58.2	24.0	79.3	36.5	50.9	77.3	61.2
All – Emoticons	61.3	68.2	64.4	62.6	75.3	68.1	57.7	60.2	58.6	24.3	76.5	36.7	50.9	77.3	61.2
All – Negative set	61.0	68.0	64.1	62.3	74.7	67.7	59.0	61.1	59.7	25.4	76.8	37.6	50.2	76.6	60.5
All – Positive set	62.6	67.3	64.6	62.5	75.7	68.2	53.7	55.1	54.2	20.5	67.7	31.1	47.8	75.8	58.4
Sp. Features	37.5	77.2	50.2	38.2	77.5	50.8	38.3	76.0	50.6	38.3	74.8	50.2	34.3	80.5	47.7
Sp. Features – Imbalance	9.3	50.4	15.4	11.0	54.1	18.1	11.3	48.5	18.1	12.9	47.4	20.0	5.9	55.8	10.3
Sp. Features – Hyperbole	37.5	77.4	50.3	38.2	77.5	50.8	38.3	76.7	50.7	38.8	76.4	51.2	34.3	80.9	47.8
Sp. Features – Quotes	37.7	76.9	50.3	38.0	78.1	50.7	37.8	75.6	50.1	38.3	73.6	50.0	34.3	80.5	47.7
Sp. Features – Pos/Neg&Punctuation	37.7	77.9	50.5	37.8	77.6	50.5	37.1	74.5	49.2	38.2	73.8	49.9	33.3	80.2	46.7
Sp. Features – Pos/Neg&Ellipsis	37.7	77.3	50.4	38.1	78.2	50.9	37.9	76.2	50.4	39.1	72.3	50.3	34.5	79.7	47.8
Sp. Features – Ellipsis and Punctuation	37.8	76.9	50.3	37.8	76.9	50.3	38.3	75.8	50.6	39.0	72.5	50.5	34.5	80.2	47.9
Sp. Features – Punctuation	37.1	79.7	50.3	37.6	78.7	50.6	37.0	76.7	49.6	38.4	75.4	50.5	32.6	78.9	45.6
Sp. Features – Interjections	37.7	76.9	50.3	37.9	77.5	50.6	38.1	76.1	50.4	38.7	75.2	50.7	34.3	80.5	47.7
Sp. Features – Laughter	37.8	77.3	50.5	38.0	77.7	50.7	37.3	75.5	49.6	37.5	73.4	49.4	34.5	81.2	48.0
Sp. Features – Emoticons	37.3	78.2	50.2	38.2	77.5	50.8	38.0	75.4	50.2	38.7	75.0	50.7	33.4	80.7	46.8
Sp. Features – Positive set	10.5	48.7	17.1	11.0	56.3	18.1	9.9	49.3	16.3	12.3	50.8	19.5	6.3	64.8	11.0
Sp. Features – Negative set	37.7	78.2	50.6	38.0	78.7	50.9	38.2	75.1	50.3	37.6	72.0	48.9	34.9	79.8	48.3
Imbalance only	36.9	81.4	50.4	36.9	81.4	50.4	36.9	81.4	50.4	36.9	81.4	50.4	0.0	100.0	0.0
Hyperbole only	0.0	80.0	0.0	0.0	90.0	0.0	0.0	80.0	0.0	0.2	55.0	0.4	0.0	100.0	0.0
Quotes only	3.9	45.5	7.0	0.9	67.0	1.7	4.0	43.8	7.0	2.5	52.2	4.5	0.0	100.0	0.0
Pos/Neg&Punctuation only	0.9	90.0	1.8	0.5	90.0	0.9	0.0	90.0	0.0	0.4	90.0	0.8	0.9	90.0	1.8
Pos/Neg&Ellipsis only	6.8	59.0	12.1	6.8	59.0	12.1	6.8	59.0	12.1	6.8	59.0	12.1	0.0	100.0	0.0
Ellipsis and Punctuation only	0.9	90.0	1.7	0.4	90.0	0.8	0.9	90.0	1.7	0.9	90.0	1.7	0.0	100.0	0.0
Punctuation only	5.4	64.6	9.8	5.4	64.6	9.8	3.3	60.8	6.2	4.0	60.8	7.5	4.7	64.6	8.6
Interjections only	0.5	75.8	0.9	0.3	82.5	0.5	0.5	75.8	0.9	1.4	74.2	2.7	0.0	100.0	0.0
Laughter only	0.0	100.0	0.0	0.0	100.0	0.0	0.0	100.0	0.0	0.0	80.0	0.0	0.0	100.0	0.0
Emoticons only	0.0	100.0	0.0	0.0	100.0	0.0	0.0	100.0	0.0	0.0	100.0	0.0	0.0	80.0	0.0
Positive set only	36.9	81.4	50.4	36.9	81.1	50.4	37.1	80.5	50.5	37.3	79.3	50.5	32.4	80.7	45.6
Negative set only	8.2	54.5	14.1	7.3	48.8	12.5	8.8	49.4	14.8	9.0	49.9	15.2	0.0	80.0	0.0

Table 1: Comparison of different classification methods using different feature sets. "All" refers to the features described in Section 2 including bag-of-words ("BOW"). "Sp. Features" are "All" without "BOW".

a positive rating by the author, as explained by Table 2, which shows the more real-world compatible result of a rich feature set in addition. Obviously, the depicted distribution is very similar to the distribution of the manually annotated data set, which can obviously not be achieved by the star-rating feature alone.

The best result is achieved by using the star-rating together with bag-of-words and specific features with a logistic regression approach (leading to an F_1-measure of 74 %). The SVM and decision tree have a comparable performance on the task, which is albeit lower compared to the performance of the logistic regression approach.

Using the task-agnostic pure bag-of-words approach leads to a performance of 68.8 % for logistic regression; this classifier has the property of dealing well with correlated features and the additional specific features cannot contribute positively to the result. Similarly, the F_1-measure of 64.1 % produced by the SVM cannot be increased by including additional features. In contrast, a positive impact of additional features can be observed for the decision tree in the case that specific features are combined with bag-of-word-based features, reaching close to 59 % F_1 in comparison to 53.4 % F_1 for bag-of-words alone.

It would be desirable to have a model only or mainly based on the problem-specific features, as this leads to a much more compact and therefore efficient representation than taking all words into account. In addition, the model would be easier to understand. By exploiting task-specific features alone, the performance reaches at most an F_1-measure of 50.9 %, which shows that task-agnostic features such as unigram features are needed. A significant drop in performance when leaving out a feature or feature set can be observed for the *Imbalance* feature and the *Positive set*. Both these feature sets take into account the star-rating.

The task-specific features alone yield high precision results at the expense of a very low recall. This clearly shows that task-specific features should be used with standard, task-independent features (the bag-of-words). The most helpful task-specific features are: Imbalance, Positive set, Quotes and Pos/Neg&Ellipses.

4 Discussion and Summary

The best performance is achieved with very corpus-specific features taking into account meta-data from Amazon, namely the product rating of the reviewer. This leads to an F_1-measure of 74 %. However, we could not show a competitive performance with more problem-specific features (leading to 51 % F_1) or in combination with bag-of-word-based features (leading to 68 % F_1).

The baseline only predicting based on the star-rating itself is highly competitive, however, not applicable to texts without meta-data and of limited use due to its naturally highly biased outcome towards positive reviews being non-ironic and negative reviews being ironic. Our results show that the best results are achieved via meta-data and it remains an open research task to develop comparably good approaches only based on text features.

It should be noted that the corpus used in this work is not a random sample from all reviews available in a specific group of products. We actually assume ironic reviews to be much more sparse when sampling equally distributed. The evaluation should be seen from the angle of the application scenario: For instance, in a discovery setting in which the task is to retrieve examples for ironic reviews, a highly precise system would be desirable. In a setting in which only a small number of reviews should be used for opinion mining, the polarity of a text would be discovered taking the classifier's result into account – therefore a system with high precision and high recall would be needed.

	Distribution			
	Corpus		Predicted	
Rating	ironic	non-ironic	ironic	non-ironic
5	114	605	126	593
4	14	96	17	93
3	20	35	14	41
2	27	17	17	27
1	262	64	192	134
1–5	437	817	366	888

Table 2: Frequencies for the different star-ratings of a review, as annotated, and according to the logistic regression classifier with the feature set "All – Imbalance".

5 Future Work

As discussed at the end of the last section, a study on the distribution of irony in the entirety of available reviews is needed to better shape the structure and characteristics of an irony or sarcasm detection system. This could be approached by performing a random sample from reviews and annotation, though this would lead to a substantial amount of annotation work in comparison to the directed selection procedure used in the corpus by Filatova (2012).

Future research should focus on the development of approaches analyzing the vocabulary used in the review in a deeper fashion. Our impression is that many sarcastic and ironic reviews use words and phrases which are non-typical for the specific domain or product class. Such out-of-domain vocabulary can be detected with text similarity approaches. Preliminary experiments taking into account the average cosine similarity of a review to be classified to a large set of reviews from the same product class have been of limited success. We propose that future research should focus on analyzing the specific vocabulary and develop semantic similarity measures which we assume to be more promising than approaches taking into account lexical approaches only.

Most work has been performed on text sets from one source like Twitter, books, reviews, etc. Some of the proposed features mentioned in this paper or previous publications are probably transferable between text sources. However, this still needs to be proven and further development might be necessary to actually provide automated domain adaption for the area of irony and sarcasm detection. We assume that not only the vocabulary changes (as known in other domain adaptation tasks) but actually the linguistic structure might change.

Finally, it should be noted that the corpus is actually a mixture of ironic and sarcastic reviews. Irony and sarcasm are not fully exchangeable and can be assumed to have different properties. Further investigations and analyses regarding the characteristics that can be transferred are necessary.

Acknowledgements

Roman Klinger has been funded by the "It's OWL" project ("Intelligent Technical Systems Ostwestfalen-Lippe", http://www.its-owl.de/), a leading-edge cluster of the German Ministry of Education and Research. We thank the reviewers for their valuable comments. We thank Christina Unger for proof-reading the manuscript and helpful comments.

References

Meyer Howard Abrams. 1957. *A Glossary of Literary Terms*. Cengage Learning Emea, 9th edition.

Salvatore Attardo. 2000. Irony markers and functions: Towards a goal-oriented theory of irony and its processing. *Rask: Internationalt Tidsskrift for Sprog og Kommunikation*, 12:3–20.

Leo Breiman, Jerome H. Friedman, Richard A. Olshen, and Charles J. Stone. 1984. *Classification and Regression Trees*. Wadsworth, Belmont, California.

Leo Breiman. 2001. Random forests. *Machine Learning*, 45(1):5–32.

British Dictionary. 2014. MacMillan Publishers. Online: http://www.macmillandictionary.com/dictionary/british/irony. accessed April 28, 2014.

Paula Carvalho, Luís Sarmento, Mário J. Silva, and Eugénio de Oliveira. 2009. Clues for detecting irony in user-generated contents: oh...!! it's "so easy" ;-). In *Proceedings of the 1st international CIKM workshop on Topic-sentiment analysis for mass opinion*, TSA '09, pages 53–56, New York, NY, USA. ACM.

Chih-Chung Chang and Chih-Jen Lin. 2011. Libsvm: A library for support vector machines. *ACM Transactions on Intelligent Systems and Technology*, 2(3).

Herbert H. Clark and Richard J. Gerrig. 1984. On the pretense theory of irony. *Journal of Experimental Psychology: General*, 113(1):121–126.

Corinna Cortes and Vladimir Vapnik. 1995. Support-vector networks. *Machine Learning*, 20(3):273–297.

Marlena A. Creusere. 2007. A developmental test of theoretical perspective on the understanding of verbal irony: Children's recognition of allusion and pragmatic insincerity. In Raymond W. Jr. Gibbs and Herbert L. Colston, editors, *Irony in Language and Thought: A Cognitive Science Reader*, chapter 18, pages 409–424. Lawrence Erlbaum Associates, 1st edition.

Dmitry Davidov and Ari Rappoport. 2006. Efficient unsupervised discovery of word categories using symmetric patterns and high frequency words. In *Proceedings of the 21st International Conference on Computational Linguistics and 44th Annual Meeting of the Association for Computational Linguistics*, pages 297–304, Sydney, Australia, July. Association for Computational Linguistics.

Dmitry Davidov, Oren Tsur, and Ari Rappoport. 2010. Semi-supervised recognition of sarcastic sentences in twitter and amazon. In *Proceedings of the Fourteenth Conference on Computational Natural Language Learning*, CoNLL '10, pages 107–116, Stroudsburg, PA, USA. Association for Computational Linguistics.

Duden. 2014. Duden Verlag. Online: http://www.duden.de/rechtschreibung/Ironie. accessed April 28, 2014.

Rong-En Fan, Pai-Hsuen Chen, and Chih-Jen Lin. 2005. Working set selection using second order information for training support vector machines. *Jounral of Machine Learning Reasearch*, 6:1889–1918.

Elena Filatova. 2012. Irony and sarcasm: Corpus generation and analysis using crowdsourcing. In Nicoletta Calzolari, Khalid Choukri, Thierry Declerck, Mehmet Uğur Doğan, Bente Maegaard, Joseph Mariani, Jan Odijk, and Stelios Piperidis, editors, *Proceedings of the Eighth International Conference on Language Resources and Evaluation (LREC-2012)*, pages 392–398, Istanbul, Turkey, May. European Language Resources Association (ELRA).

Raymond W. Jr. Gibbs. 2007. Irony in talk among friends. In Raymond W. Jr. Gibbs and Herbert L. Colston, editors, *Irony in Language and Thought: A Cognitive Science Reader*, chapter 15, pages 339–360. Lawrence Erlbaum Associates, 1st edition, May.

Melanie Harris Glenwright and Penny M. Pexman. 2007. Children's perceptions of the social functions of verbal irony. In Raymond W. Jr. Gibbs and Herbert L. Colston, editors, *Irony in Language and Thought: A Cognitive Science Reader*, chapter 20, pages 447–464. Lawrence Erlbaum Associates, 1st edition.

Roberto González-Ibáñez, Smaranda Muresan, and Nina Wacholder. 2011. Identifying sarcasm in twitter: a closer look. In *Proceedings of the 49th Annual*

Meeting of the Association for Computational Linguistics: Human Language Technologies: short papers - Volume 2, HLT '11, pages 581–586, Stroudsburg, PA, USA. Association for Computational Linguistics.

Trevor Hastie, Robert Tibshirani, and Jerome H. Friedman. 2009. *Elements of Statistical Learning*. Springer, 2nd edition.

Minqing Hu and Bing Liu. 2004. Mining and summarizing customer reviews. In *Proceedings of the tenth ACM SIGKDD international conference on Knowledge discovery and data mining*, KDD '04, pages 168–177, New York, NY, USA. ACM.

Roger J. Kreuz and Gina M. Caucci. 2007. Lexical influences on the perception of sarcasm. In *Proceedings of the Workshop on Computational Approaches to Figurative Language*, pages 1–4, Rochester, New York, April. Association for Computational Linguistics.

Roger J. Kreuz. 1996. The use of verbal irony: Cues and constraints. In Jeffery S. Mio and Albert N. Katz, editors, *Metaphor: Implications and Applications*, pages 23–38, Mahwah, NJ, October. Lawrence Erlbaum Associates.

Sachi Kumon-Nakamura, Sam Glucksberg, and Mary Brown. 1995. How about another piece of pie: The allusional pretense theory of discourse irony. *Journal of Experimental Psychology: General*, 124(1):3–21, Mar 01. Last updated - 2013-02-23.

Lillian Lee. 2009. A tempest or, on the flood of interest in: sentiment analysis, opinion mining, and the computational treatment of subjective language. Tutorial at ICWSM, May.

Christopher D. Manning, Prabhakar Raghavan, and Hinrich Schütze. 2008. *Introduction to Information Retrieval*. Cambridge University Press.

Merriam Webster Dictionary. 2014. Merriam Webster Inc. Online: `www.merriam-webster.com/dictionary/irony`. accessed April 28, 2014.

Constantine Nakassis and Jesse Snedeker. 2002. Beyond sarcasm: Intonation and context as relational cues in children's recognition of irony. In A. Greenhill, M. Hughs, H. Littlefield, and H. Walsh, editors, *Proceedings of the Twenty-sixth Boston University Conference on Language Development*, Somerville, MA, July. Cascadilla Press.

New Oxford American Dictionary. 2014. Oxford University Press. Online: `http://www.oxforddictionaries.com/us/definition/american_english/ironic`. accessed April 28, 2014.

Fabian Pedregosa, Gaël Varoquaux, Alexandre Gramfort, Vincent Michel, Bertrand Thirion, Olivier Grisel, Mathieu Blondel, Peter Prettenhofer, Ron Weiss, Vincent Dubourg, Jake Vanderplas, Alexandre Passos, David Cournapeau, Matthieu Brucher, Matthieu Perrot, and Édouard Duchesnay. 2011. Scikit-learn: Machine learning in Python. *Journal of Machine Learning Research*, 12:2825–2830.

Antonio Reyes, Paolo Rosso, and Davide Buscaldi. 2012. From humor recognition to irony detection: The figurative language of social media. *Data & Knowledge Engineering*, 74:1–12.

Patricia Rockwell. 2005. Sarcasm on television talk shows: Determining speaker intent through verbal and nonverbal cues. In Anita V. Clark, editor, *Psychology of Moods*, chapter 6, pages 109–122. Nova Science Pubishers Inc.

Joseph Tepperman, David Traum, and Shrikanth S. Narayanan. 2006. "yeah right": Sarcasm recognition for spoken dialogue systems. In *Proceedings of InterSpeech*, pages 1838–1841, Pittsburgh, PA, September.

Oren Tsur, Dmitry Davidov, and Ari Rappoport. 2010. ICWSM – A Great Catchy Name: Semi-Supervised Recognition of Sarcastic Sentences in Online Product Reviews. In *Proceedings of the Fourth International AAAI Conference on Weblogs and Social Media*, pages 162–169. The AAAI Press.

Akira Utsumi. 1996. A unified theory of irony and its computational formalization. In *Proceedings of the 16th conference on Computational linguistics - Volume 2*, COLING '96, pages 962–967, Stroudsburg, PA, USA. Association for Computational Linguistics.

Deirdre Wilson and Dan Sperber. 1992. On verbal irony. *Lingua*, 87:53–76.

Deirdre Wilson and Dan Sperber, 2012. *Explaining Irony*, chapter 6, pages 123–145. Cambridge University Press, 1st edition, April.

Hsiang-Fu. Yu, Fang-Lan Huang, and Chih-Jen Lin. 2011. Dual coordinate descent methods for logistic regression and maximum entropy. *Machine Learning*, 85(1–2):41–75, October.

Harry Zhang. 2004. The optimality of naive bayes. In Valerie Barr and Zdravko Markov, editors, *Proceedings of the Seventeenth International Florida Artificial Intelligence Research Society (FLAIRS) Conference*, pages 3–9. AAAI Press.

Modelling Sarcasm in Twitter, a Novel Approach

Francesco Barbieri and **Horacio Saggion** and **Francesco Ronzano**
Pompeu Fabra University, Barcelona, Spain
`<firstName>.<lastName>@upf.edu`

Abstract

Automatic detection of figurative language is a challenging task in computational linguistics. Recognising both literal and figurative meaning is not trivial for a machine and in some cases it is hard even for humans. For this reason novel and accurate systems able to recognise figurative languages are necessary. We present in this paper a novel computational model capable to detect sarcasm in the social network Twitter (a popular microblogging service which allows users to post short messages). Our model is easy to implement and, unlike previous systems, it does not include patterns of words as features. Our seven sets of lexical features aim to detect sarcasm by its inner structure (for example unexpectedness, intensity of the terms or imbalance between registers), abstracting from the use of specific terms.

1 Introduction

Sarcasm is a mode of communication where literal and intended meanings are in opposition. Sarcasm is often used to express a negative message using positive words. Automatic detection of sarcasm is then very important in the sentiment analysis field, as a sarcastic phrase that includes positive words conveys a negative message and can be easily misunderstood by an automatic system.

A number of systems with the objective of detecting sarcasm have been designed in the past years (Davidov et al., 2010; González-Ibáñez et al., 2011; Riloff et al., 2013). All these computational models have in common the use of frequent and typical sarcastic expressions as features. This is of course a good approach as some words are used sarcastically more often than others.

Our research seeks to avoid the use of words as features, for two reasons. Firstly, we want to reduce the complexity of the computational model, decreasing drastically the number of features required for classification. Secondly, typical sarcastic expressions are often culturally specific (an expression that is considered sarcastic in British English is not necessary sarcastic in American English and vice-versa). For these reasons we have designed a system that aims to detect sarcasm without the use of words and patterns of words. We use simple features such as punctuation (Carvalho et al., 2009) and more sophisticated features, that for example detect imbalance between registers (the use of an "out of context" word may suggest sarcastic intentions) or the use of very intense terms.

We study sarcasm detection in the microblogging platform Twitter[1] that allows users to send and read text messages (shorter than 140 characters) called *tweets*, which often do not follow the expected rules of the grammar. The dataset we adopted contains positive examples tagged as sarcastic by the users (using the hashtag #sarcasm) and negative examples (tagged with a different hashtag). This methodology has been previously used in similar studies (Reyes et al., 2013; Lukin and Walker, 2013; Liebrecht et al., 2013).

We presented in Barbieri and Saggion (2014) a model capable of detecting irony, in this paper we add important features to this model and evaluate a new corpus to determine if our system is capable of detecting tweets marked as sarcastic (#sarcasm). The contributions of this paper are the following:

- Novel set of features to improve the performances of our model
- A new set of experiments to test our model's ability to detect sarcasm
- A corpus to study sarcasm in twitter

[1] `https://twitter.com/`

Proceedings of the 5th Workshop on Computational Approaches to Subjectivity, Sentiment and Social Media Analysis, pages 50–58,
Baltimore, Maryland, USA. June 27, 2014.

We will show in the paper that results are positive and the system recognises sarcasm with good accuracy in comparison with the state-of-the-art. The rest of the paper is organised as follows: in the next Section we describe related work. In Section 3 we describes the corpus and text processing tools used and in Section 4 we present our approach to tackle the sarcasm detection problem. Section 5 describes the experiments while Section 6 interprets the results. Finally, we close the paper in Section 7 with conclusions and future work.

2 Related Work

A standard definition for sarcasm seems not to exist. Sarcasm is often identified as irony or verbal irony (?). Irony has been defined in several ways over the years as for example "saying the opposite of what you mean" (Quintilien and Butler, 1953), or by Grice (1975) as a rhetorical figure that violates the maxim of quality: "Do not say what you believe to be false", or as any form of negation with no negation markers (Giora, 1995). Other definitions are the ones of Wilson and Sperber (2002) who states irony is an echoic utterance that shows a negative aspect of someone's else opinion, and as form of pretence by Utsumi (2000) and by Veale and Hao (2010a). Veale states that "ironic speakers usually craft their utterances in spite of what has just happened, not because of it. The pretence alludes to, or echoes, an expectation that has been violated".

Irony and sarcasm has been approached as computation problem recently by Carvalho et al. (2009) who created an automatic system for detecting irony relying on emoticons and special punctuation. They focused on detection of ironic style in newspaper articles. Veale and Hao (2010b) proposed an algorithm for separating ironic from non-ironic similes, detecting common terms used in this ironic comparison. Reyes et al. (2013) and also Barbieri and Saggion (2014) have recently proposed two approaches to detect irony in Twitter. There are also some computational model to detect sarcasm in Twitter. The systems of Gonzalez et al. (2011) and Davidov et al. (2010) detect sarcasm with good accuracy in English tweets (the latter model is also studied in the Amazon review context). Lukin and Walker (2013) used bootstrapping to improve the performance of sarcasm and nastiness classifiers for Online Dialogue, and Liebrecht et al. (2013) designed a model to detect sarcasm in Duch tweets. Finally Riloff (2013) built a model to detect sarcasm with a bootstrapping algorithm that automatically learn lists of positive sentiments phrases and negative situation phrases from sarcastic tweet, in order to detect the characteristic of sarcasm of being a contrast between positive sentiment and negative situation.

One may argue that sarcasm and irony are the same linguistic phenomena, but in our opinion the latter is more similar to mocking or making jokes (sometimes about ourselves) in a sharp and non-offensive manner. On the other hand, sarcasm is a meaner form of irony as it tends to be offensive and directed towards other people (or products like in Amazon reviews). Textual examples of sarcasm lack the sharp tone of an aggressive speaker, so for textual purposes we think irony and sarcasm should be considered as different phenomena and studied separately (Reyes et al., 2013).

Some datasets exist for the study of sarcasm and irony. Filatova (2012) designed a corpus generation experiment where regular and sarcastic Amazon product reviews were collected. Also Bosco et. al (2013) collected and annotate a set of ironic examples (in Italian) for the study of sentiment analysis and opinion mining.

3 Data and Text Processing

We adopted a corpus of 60,000 tweets equally divided into six different topics: *Sarcasm*, *Education*, *Humour*, *Irony*, *Politics* and *Newspaper*. The Newspaper set includes 10,000 tweets from three popular newspapers (New York Times, The Economist and The Guardian). The rest of the tweets (50,000) were automatically selected by looking at Twitter hashtags #education, #humour, #irony, #politics and #sarcasm) added by users in order to link their contribution to a particular subject and community. These hashtags are removed from the tweets for the experiments. According to Reyes et al. (2013), these hashtags were selected for three main reasons: (i) to avoid manual selection of tweets, (ii) to allow irony analysis beyond literary uses, and because (iii) irony hashtag may "reflect a tacit belief about what constitutes irony" (and sarcasm in the case of the hashtag #sarcasm). *Education*, *Humour* and *Politics* tweets were prepared by Reyes et al. (2013), we added *Irony*, *Newspaper* and *Sarcasm* tweets[2]. We obtained these data using the Twitter API.

Examples of tweets tagged with #sarcasm are:

- This script is superb, honestly.
- First run in almost two months. I think I did really well.
- Jeez I just love when I'm trying to eat lunch and someone's blowing smoke in my face. Yum. I love ingesting cigarette smoke.

Another corpora is employed in our approach to measure the frequency of word usage. We adopted the Second Release of the American National Corpus Frequency Data[3] (Ide and Suderman, 2004), which provides the number of occurrences of a word in the written and spoken ANC. From now on, we will mean with "frequency of a term" the absolute frequency the term has in the ANC.

Processing microblog text is not easy because they are noisy, with little context, and often English grammar rules are violated. For these reasons, in order to process the tweets, we use the GATE Plugin TwitIE (Bontcheva et al., 2013) as tokeniser and Part of Speech Tagger. The POS tagger (adapted version of the Stanford tagger (Toutanova et al., 2003)) achieves 90.54% token accuracy, which is a very good results knowing the difficulty of the task in the microblogging context. This POS tagger is more accurate and reliable than the method we used in the previous research, where the POS of a term was defined by the most commonly used (provided by WordNet). TwitIE also includes the best Named Entity Recognitions for Twitter (F1=0.8).

We adopted also Rita WordNet API (Howe, 2009) and Java API for WordNet Searching (Spell, 2009) to perform operations on WordNet synsets.

4 Methodology

We approach the detection of sarcasm as a classification problem applying supervised machine learning methods to the Twitter corpus described in Section 3. When choosing the classifiers we had avoided those requiring features to be independent (e.g. Naive Bayes) as some of our features are not. Since we approach the problem as a binary decision we picked a tree-based classifiers: Decision Tree. We already studied the performance of another classifier (Random Forest) but even if Random Forest performed better in cross validation experiments, Decision Tree resulted better in cross domain experiments, suggesting that it would be more reliable in a real situation (where the negative topics are several). We use the Decision Tree implementation of the Weka toolkit (Witten and Frank, 2005).

Our model uses seven groups of features to represent each tweet. Some of them are designed to detect imbalance and unexpectedness, others to detect common patterns in the structure of the sarcastic tweets (like type of punctuation, length, emoticons), and some others to recognise sentiments and intensity of the terms used. Below is an overview of the group of features in our model:

- Frequency *(gap between rare and common words)*
- Written-Spoken *(written-spoken style uses)*
- Intensity *(intensity of adverbs and adjectives)*
- Structure *(length, punctuation, emoticons)*
- Sentiments *(gap between positive and negative terms)*
- Synonyms *(common vs. rare synonyms use)*
- Ambiguity *(measure of possible ambiguities)*

To the best of our knowledge Frequency, Written Spoken, Intensity and Synonyms groups have not been used before in similar studies. The other groups have been used already (for example by Carvalho et al. (2009) or Reyes et al. (2013)) yet our implementation is different.

In the following sections we quickly describe all the features we used.

4.1 Frequency

Unexpectedness can be a signal of verbal irony, Lucariello (1994) claims that irony is strictly connected to surprise, showing that unexpectedness is the feature most related to situational ironies. In this first group of features we try to detect it. We explore the frequency imbalance between words, i.e. register inconsistencies between terms of the

[2]To make possible comparisons with our system we published the IDs of these tweets at http://sempub.taln.upf.edu/tw/wassa2014/

[3]The American National Corpus (http://www.anc.org/) is, as we read in the web site, a massive electronic collection of American English words (15 million)

same tweet. The idea is that the use of many words commonly used in English (i.e. high frequency in ANC) and only a few terms rarely used in English (i.e. low frequency in ANC) in the same sentence creates imbalance that may cause unexpectedness, since within a single tweet only one kind of register is expected.

Three features belong to this group: **frequency mean**, **rarest word**, **frequency gap**. The first one is the arithmetic average of all the frequencies of the words in a tweet, and it is used to detect the *frequency style* of a tweet. The second one, **rarest word**, is the frequency value of the rarest word, designed to capture the word that may create imbalance. The assumption is that very rare words may be a sign of irony. The third one is the absolute difference between the first two and it is used to measure the imbalance between them, and capture a possible intention of surprise.

4.2 Written-Spoken

Twitter is composed of written text, but an informal spoken English style is often used. We designed this set of features to explore the unexpectedness created by using spoken style words in a mainly written style tweet or vice versa (formal words usually adopted in written text employed in a spoken style context). We can analyse this aspect with ANC written and spoken, as we can see using this corpora whether a word is more often used in written or spoken English. There are three features in this group: **written mean**, **spoken mean**, **written spoken gap**. The first and second ones are the means of the frequency values, respectively, in written and spoken ANC corpora of all the words in the tweet. The third one, **written spoken gap**, is the absolute value of the difference between the first two, designed to see if ironic writers use both styles (creating imbalance) or only one of them. A low difference between written and spoken styles means that both styles are used.

4.3 Structure

With this group of features we want to study the structure of the tweet: if it is long or short (length), if it contains long or short words (mean of word length), and also what kind of punctuation is used (exclamation marks, emoticons, etc.).

The **length** feature consists of the number of characters that compose the tweet, **n. words** is the number of words, and **words length mean** is the mean of the words length. Moreover, we use the number of verbs, nouns, adjectives and adverbs as features, naming them **n. verbs**, **n. nouns**, **n. adjectives** and **n. adverbs**. With these last four features we also computed the ratio of each part of speech to the number of words in the tweet; we called them **verb ratio**, **noun ratio**, **adjective ratio**, and **adverb ratio**. All these features have the purpose of capturing the style of the writer.

The **punctuation** feature is the sum of the number of commas, full stops, ellipsis and exclamation that a tweet presents. We also added a feature called **laughing** which is the sum of all the internet laughs, denoted with *hahah*, *lol*, *rofl*, and *lmao* that we consider as a new form of punctuation: instead of using many exclamation marks internet users may use the sequence *lol* (i.e. laughing out loud) or just type *hahaha*.

Inspired by Davidov et al. (2010) and Carvalho (2009) we designed features related to punctuation. These features are: number of **commas**, **full stops**, **ellipsis**, **exclamation** and **quotation** marks that a tweet contain.

The **emoticon** feature is the sum of the emoticons *:)*, *:D*, *:(* and *;)* in a tweet.

The new features we included are *http* that simply says if a tweet includes or not an Internet link, and the entities features provided by TwitIE (Bontcheva et al., 2013). These features check if a tweet contains the following entities: *n. organisation*, *n. location*, *n. person*, *n. first person*, *n. title*, *n job title*, *n. date*. These last seven features were not available in the previous model, and some of them work very well when distinguishing sarcasm from newspaper tweets.

4.4 Intensity

In order to produce a sarcastic effect some authors might use an expression which is antonymic to what they are trying to describe (saying the opposite of what they mean (Quintilien and Butler, 1953)). In the case the word being an adjective or adverb its intensity (more or less exaggerated) may well play a role in producing the intended effect (Riloff et al., 2013). We adopted the intensity scores of Potts (2011) who uses naturally occurring metadata (star ratings on service and product reviews) to construct adjectives and adverbs scales. An example of adjective scale (and relative scores in brackets) could be the following: horrible (-1.9) → bad (-1.1) → good (0.2) → nice (0.3) → great (0.8).

With these scores we evaluate four features for adjective intensity and four for adverb intensity (implemented in the same way): **adj (adv) tot**, **adj (adv) mean**, **adj (adv) max**, and **adj (adv) gap**. The sum of the AdjScale scores of all the adjectives in the tweet is called **adj tot**. **adj mean** is **adj tot** divided by the number of adjectives in the tweet. The maximum AdjScale score within a single tweet is **adj max**. Finally, **adj gap** is the difference between **adj max** and **adj mean**, designed to see "how much" the most intense adjective is out of context.

4.5 Synonyms

As previously said, sarcasm convey two messages to the audience at the same time. It follows that the choice of a term (rather than one of its synonyms) is very important in order to send the second, not obvious, message.

For each word of a tweet we get its synonyms with WordNet (Miller, 1995), then we calculate their ANC frequencies and sort them into a decreasing ranked list (the actual word is part of this ranking as well). We use these rankings to define the four features which belong to this group. The first one is **syno lower** which is the number of synonyms of the word w_i with frequency lower than the frequency of w_i. It is defined as in Equation 1:

$$sl_{w_i} = |syn_{i,k} \; : \; f(syn_{i,k}) < f(w_i)| \quad (1)$$

where $syn_{i,k}$ is the synonym of w_i with rank k, and $f(x)$ the ANC frequency of x. Then we also defined **syno lower mean** as mean of sl_{w_i} (i.e. the arithmetic average of sl_{w_i} over all the words of a tweet).

We also designed two more features: **syno lower gap** and **syno greater gap**, but to define them we need two more parameters. The first one is *word lowest syno* that is the maximum sl_{w_i} in a tweet. It is formally defined as:

$$wls_t = \max_{w_i}\{|syn_{i,k} \; : \; f(syn_{i,k}) < f(w_i)|\} \quad (2)$$

The second one is *word greatest syno* defined as:

$$wgs_t = \max_{w_i}\{|syn_{i,k} \; : \; f(syn_{i,k}) > f(w_i)|\} \quad (3)$$

We are now able to describe **syno lower gap** which detects the imbalance that creates a common synonym in a context of rare synonyms. It is the difference between *word lowest syno* and **syno lower mean**. Finally, we detect the gap of very rare synonyms in a context of common ones with **syno greater gap**. It is the difference between *word greatest syno* and *syno greater mean*, where *syno greater mean* is the following:

$$sgm_t = \frac{|syn_{i,k} \; : \; f(syn_{i,k}) > f(w_i)|}{n.\, words\, of\, t} \quad (4)$$

The arithmetic averages of **syno greater gap** and of **syno lower gap** in the Sarcasm corpus are higher than in the other topics, suggesting that a very common (or very rare) synonym is often used out of context i.e. a very rare synonym when most of the words are common (have a high rank in our model) and vice versa.

4.6 Ambiguity

Another interesting aspect of sarcasm is ambiguity. We noticed that sarcastic tweets presents words with more meanings (more WordNet synsets). Our assumption is that if a word has many meanings the possibility of "saying something else" with this word is higher than in a term that has only a few meanings, then higher possibility of sending more then one message (literal and intended) at the same time.

There are three features that aim to capture these aspects: **synset mean**, **max synset**, and **synset gap**. The first one is the mean of the number of synsets of each word of the tweet, to see if words with many meanings are often used in the tweet. The second one is the greatest number of synsets that a single word has; we consider this word the one with the highest possibility of being used ironically (as multiple meanings are available to say different things). In addition, we calculate **synset gap** as the difference between the number of synsets of this word (**max synset**) and the average number of synsets (**synset mean**), assuming that if this gap is high the author may have used that inconsistent word intentionally.

4.7 Sentiments

We also evaluate the sentiment of the sarcastic tweets. The SentiWordNet sentiment lexicon (Esuli and Sebastiani, 2006) assigns to each synset of WordNet sentiment scores of positivity and negativity. We used these scores to examine what kind of sentiments characterises sarcasm. We explore ironic sentiments with two different views: the first one is the simple analysis of sentiments (to

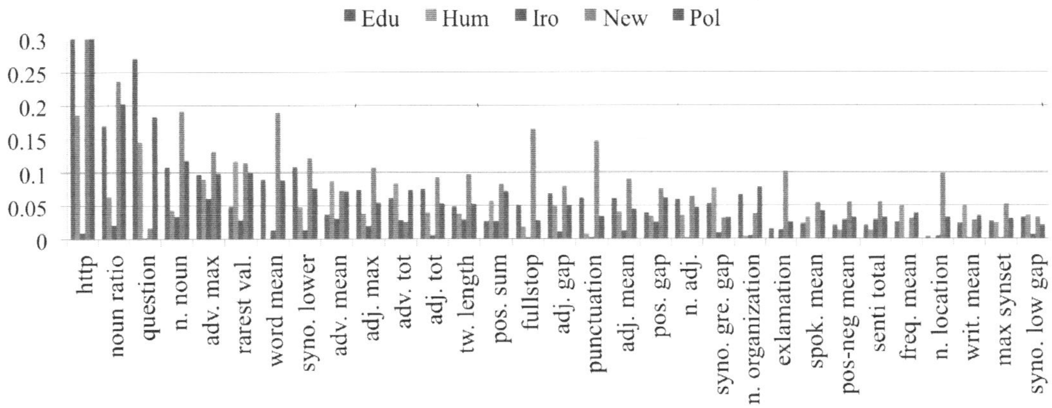

Figure 1: Information gain of each feature of the model. Sarcasm is compared to Education, Humor, Irony, Newspaper and Politics. High values of information gain help to better discriminate sarcastic from non-sarcastic tweets.

identify the main sentiment of a tweet) and the second one concerns sentiment imbalances between words.

There are six features in the **Sentiments** group. The first one is named **positive sum** and it is the sum of all the positive scores in a tweet, the second one is **negative sum**, defined as sum of all the negative scores. The arithmetic average of the previous ones is another feature, named **positive negative mean**, designed to reveal the sentiment that better describe the whole tweet. Moreover, there is **positive-negative gap** that is the difference between the first two features, as we wanted also to detect the positive/negative imbalance within the same tweet.

The imbalance may be created using only one single very positive (or negative) word in the tweet, and the previous features will not be able to detect it, thus we needed to add two more. For this purpose the model includes **positive single gap** defined as the difference between most positive word and the mean of all the sentiment scores of all the words of the tweet and **negative single gap** defined in the same way, but with the most negative one.

5 Experiments and Results

In order to evaluate our system we use five datasets, subsets of the corpus in Section 3: Sarcasm vs Education, Sarcasm vs Humour, Sarcasm vs Irony, Sarcasm vs Newspaper and Sarcasm vs Politics. Each combination is balanced with 10.000 sarcastic and 10.000 of non-sarcastic examples. We run the following two types of experiments:

1. We run in each datasets a 10-fold cross-validation classification experiment.

2. We train the classifier on 75% of positive examples and 75% of negative examples of the same dataset, then we use as test set the rest 25% positive and 25% negative. We perform this experiment for the five datasets.

In Figure 1 and Figure 2 we show the values of information gain of the five combinations of topics (Sarcasm versus each not-sarcastic topic). Note that, in the first figure the scale we chose to better visualise all the features truncates the scores of the feature **http** of Education, Newspaper, and Politics. These three values are respectively 0.4, 0.7 and 0.4. Table 1 and Table 2 includes Precision, Recall, and F-Measure results of Experiment 1 and Experiment 2.

6 Discussion

The best results are obtained when our model has to distinguish Sarcasm from Newspaper tweets. This was expected as the task was simpler than the others. In Newspaper tweets nine out of ten times present an internet link, and this aspect can be used to well distinguish sarcasm as internet links are not used often. Moreover the Newspaper tweets use a formal language easily distinguishable from sarcasm. In Newspaper tweets there are more nouns (average ratio of 0.5) than in sarcastic tweets (ratio

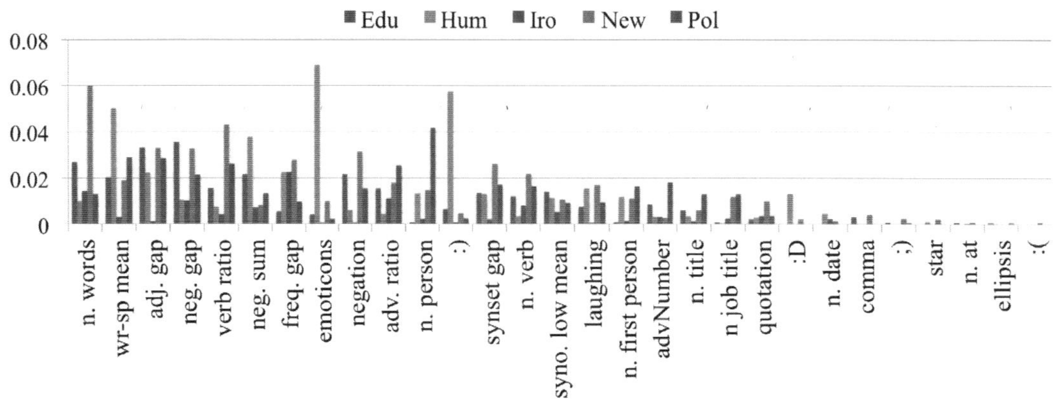

Figure 2: Information gain of each feature of the model. Sarcasm is compared to Education, Humor, Irony, Newspaper and Politics. High values of information gain help to better discriminate sarcastic from non-sarcastic tweets.

	Prec.	Recall	F1
Education	.87	.90	.88
Humour	.88	.87	.88
Irony	.62	.62	.62
Newspaper	.98	.96	.97
Politics	.90	.90	.90

Table 1: Precision, Recall and F-Measure of each topic combination for Experiment 1 (10 cross validation). Sarcasm corpus is compared to Education, Humour, Irony, Newspaper, and Politics corpora. The classifier used is Decision Tree

0.3), and Newspaper uses less punctuation marks than sarcasm. Overall Newspaper results are very good, the F1 is over 0.95.

Education and Politics results are very good as well, F1 of 0.90 and 0.92. Also in these topics the internet link is a good feature. Other powerful features in these two topics are **noun ratio** (as Newspaper they present more number of nouns than sarcasm), **question**, **rarest val.** (sarcasm includes less frequently used words) and **syno lower**.

Results regarding sarcasm versus Humour are positive, F-Measure is above 0.87. The most marked differences between Humour and sarcasm are the following. Humour includes more links (**http**), more question marks are used to mark jokes like: "Do you know the difference between...?", "What is an elephant doing...?" (**question**), sarcasm includes rarer terms and more intense adverbs than Humour (**rarest val., adv. max**).

Our model struggles to detect tweets marked as sarcastic from the ones marked as ironic. Even if not very powerful, relevant features to detect sarcasm against irony are two: use of adverbs (sarcasm uses less but more intense adverbs) and sentiment scores (as expected sarcastic tweets are denoted by more positive sentiments than irony). Poor results in this topic indicate that irony and sarcasm have similar structures in our model, and that new features are necessary to distinguish them.

	Prec.	Recall	F1
Education	.87	.88	.87
Humour	.87	.86	.86
Irony	.60	.61	.60
Newspaper	.95	.96	.95
Politics	.89	.89	.89

Table 2: Precision, Recall and F-Measure of each topic combination for Experiment 2 (Test set). Sarcasm corpus is compared to Education, Humour, Irony, Newspaper, and Politics corpora.The classifier used is Decision Tree

The comparison with other similar systems is not easy. We obtain better results than Reyes et al. (2013) and than Barbieri and Saggion (2014), but the positive class in their experiments is irony. The system of Davidov et al. (2010) to detect sarcasm seems to be powerful as well, and their results can compete with ours, but in the mentioned study there is no negative topic distinction, the not-sarcastic topic is not a fixed domain (and our controlled experiments results show that depending on the negative example the task can be more or less difficult).

7 Conclusion and Future Work

In this study we evaluate our system to detect sarcasm in the social network Twitter. We tackle this problem as binary classification, where the negative topics are Education, Humour, Irony, Newspaper and Politics. The originality of our system is avoiding the use of pattern of words as feature to detect sarcasm. In spite of the good results, there is much space for improvement. We can still enhance our results by including additional features such as language models. We will also run new experiments with different negative topics and different kind of text, for example on Amazon reviews as Davidov et al. (2010). Finally, a very interesting but challenging issue will be distinguishing with better accuracy sarcasm from irony.

Acknowledgments

We are grateful to two anonymous reviewers for their comments and suggestions that help improve our paper. The research described in this paper is partially funded by fellowship RYC-2009-04291 from Programa Ramón y Cajal 2009 and project number TIN2012-38584-C06-03 (SKATER-UPF-TALN) from Ministerio de Economía y Competitividad, Secretaría de Estado de Investigación, Desarrollo e Innovación, Spain. We also acknowledge partial support from the EU project Dr. Inventor (FP7-ICT-2013.8.1 project number 611383).

References

Francesco Barbieri and Horacio Saggion. 2014. Modelling Irony in Twitter. In *Proceedings of the Student Research Workshop at the 14th Conference of the European Chapter of the Association for Computational Linguistics*, pages 56–64, Gothenburg, Sweden, April. Association for Computational Linguistics.

Kalina Bontcheva, Leon Derczynski, Adam Funk, Mark A. Greenwood, Diana Maynard, and Niraj Aswani. 2013. TwitIE: An Open-Source Information Extraction Pipeline for Microblog Text. In *Proceedings of the International Conference on Recent Advances in Natural Language Processing*. Association for Computational Linguistics.

Cristina Bosco, Viviana Patti, and Andrea Bolioli. 2013. Developing corpora for sentiment analysis and opinion mining: the case of irony and senti-tut. *Intelligent Systems, IEEE*.

Paula Carvalho, Luís Sarmento, Mário J Silva, and Eugénio de Oliveira. 2009. Clues for detecting irony in user-generated contents: oh...!! it's so easy;-). In *Proceedings of the 1st international CIKM workshop on Topic-sentiment analysis for mass opinion*, pages 53–56. ACM.

Dmitry Davidov, Oren Tsur, and Ari Rappoport. 2010. Semi-supervised recognition of sarcastic sentences in twitter and amazon. In *Proceedings of the Fourteenth Conference on Computational Natural Language Learning*, pages 107–116. Association for Computational Linguistics.

Andrea Esuli and Fabrizio Sebastiani. 2006. Sentiwordnet: A publicly available lexical resource for opinion mining. In *Proceedings of Language Resources and Evaluation Conference*, volume 6, pages 417–422.

Elena Filatova. 2012. Irony and Sarcasm: Corpus Generation and Analysis Using Crowdsourcing. In *Proceedings of Language Resources and Evaluation Conference*, pages 392–398.

Rachel Giora. 1995. On irony and negation. *Discourse processes*, 19(2):239–264.

Roberto González-Ibáñez, Smaranda Muresan, and Nina Wacholder. 2011. Identifying Sarcasm in Twitter: A Closer Look. In *ACL (Short Papers)*, pages 581–586. Citeseer.

H Paul Grice. 1975. Logic and conversation. *1975*, pages 41–58.

Daniel C Howe. 2009. Rita wordnet. Java based API to access Wordnet.

Nancy Ide and Keith Suderman. 2004. The American National Corpus First Release. In *Proceedings of the Language Resources and Evaluation Conference*.

Christine Liebrecht, Florian Kunneman, and Antal van den Bosch. 2013. The perfect solution for detecting sarcasm in tweets# not. *WASSA 2013*, page 29.

Joan Lucariello. 1994. Situational irony: A concept of events gone awry. *Journal of Experimental Psychology: General*, 123(2):129.

Stephanie Lukin and Marilyn Walker. 2013. Really? well. apparently bootstrapping improves the performance of sarcasm and nastiness classifiers for online dialogue. *NAACL 2013*, page 30.

George A Miller. 1995. WordNet: a lexical database for English. *Communications of the ACM*, 38(11):39–41.

Christopher Potts. 2011. Developing adjective scales from user-supplied textual metadata. *NSF Workshop on Restructuring Adjectives in WordNet. Arlington, VA.*

Quintilien and Harold Edgeworth Butler. 1953. *The Institutio Oratoria of Quintilian. With an English Translation by HE Butler.* W. Heinemann.

Antonio Reyes, Paolo Rosso, and Tony Veale. 2013. A multidimensional approach for detecting irony in Twitter. *Language Resources and Evaluation*, pages 1–30.

Ellen Riloff, Ashequl Qadir, Prafulla Surve, Lalindra De Silva, Nathan Gilbert, and Ruihong Huang. 2013. Sarcasm as contrast between a positive sentiment and negative situation.

Brett Spell. 2009. Java API for WordNet Searching (JAWS).

Kristina Toutanova, Dan Klein, Christopher D Manning, and Yoram Singer. 2003. Feature-rich part-of-speech tagging with a cyclic dependency network. In *Proceedings of the 2003 Conference of the North American Chapter of the Association for Computational Linguistics on Human Language Technology-Volume 1*, pages 173–180. Association for Computational Linguistics.

Akira Utsumi. 2000. Verbal irony as implicit display of ironic environment: Distinguishing ironic utterances from nonirony. *Journal of Pragmatics*, 32(12):1777–1806.

Tony Veale and Yanfen Hao. 2010a. An ironic fist in a velvet glove: Creative mis-representation in the construction of ironic similes. *Minds and Machines*, 20(4):635–650.

Tony Veale and Yanfen Hao. 2010b. Detecting Ironic Intent in Creative Comparisons. In *ECAI*, volume 215, pages 765–770.

Deirdre Wilson and Dan Sperber. 2002. Relevance theory. *Handbook of pragmatics*.

Ian H Witten and Eibe Frank. 2005. *Data Mining: Practical machine learning tools and techniques*. Morgan Kaufmann.

Emotive or Non-emotive: That is The Question

Michal Ptaszynski **Fumito Masui**
Department of Computer Science,
Kitami Institute of Technology
{ptaszynski,f-masui}@
cs.kitami-it.ac.jp

Rafal Rzepka **Kenji Araki**
Graduate School of Information Science
and Technology, Hokkaido University
{rzepka,araki}@
ist.hokudai.ac.jp

Abstract

In this research we focus on discriminating between emotive (emotionally loaded) and non-emotive sentences. We define the problem from a linguistic point of view assuming that emotive sentences stand out both lexically and grammatically. We verify this assumption experimentally by comparing two sets of such sentences in Japanese. The comparison is based on words, longer n-grams as well as more sophisticated patterns. In the classification we use a novel unsupervised learning algorithm based on the idea of language combinatorics. The method reached results comparable to the state of the art, while the fact that it is fully automatic makes it more efficient and language independent.

1 Introduction

Recently the field of sentiment analysis has attracted great interest. It has become popular to try different methods to distinguish between sentences loaded with positive and negative sentiments. However, a few research focused on a task more generic, namely, discriminating whether a sentence is even loaded with emotional content or not. The difficulty of the task is indicated by three facts. Firstly, the task has not been widely undertaken. Secondly, in research which addresses the challenge, the definition of the task is usually based on subjective ad hoc assumptions. Thirdly, in research which do tackle the problem in a systematic way, the results are usually unsatisfactory, and satisfactory results can be obtained only with large workload.

We decided to tackle the problem in a standardized and systematic way. We defined emotionally loaded sentences as those which in linguistics are described as fulfilling the emotive function of language. We assumed that there are repetitive patterns which appear uniquely in emotive sentences. We performed experiments using a novel unsupervised clustering algorithm based on the idea of language combinatorics. By using this method we were also able to minimize human effort and achieve F-score comparable to the state of the art with much higher Recall rate.

The outline of the paper is as follows. We present the background for this research in Section 2. Section 3 describes the language combinatorics approach which we used to compare emotive and non-emotive sentences. In section 4 we describe our dataset and experiment settings. The results of the experiment are presented in Section 5. Finally the paper is concluded in Section 6.

2 Background

There are different linguistic means used to inform interlocutors of emotional states in an everyday communication. The emotive meaning is conveyed verbally and lexically through exclamations (Beijer, 2002; Ono, 2002), hypocoristics (endearments) (Kamei et al., 1996), vulgarities (Crystal, 1989) or, for example in Japanese, through mimetic expressions (*gitaigo*) (Baba, 2003). The function of language realized by such elements of language conveying emotive meaning is called the **emotive function of language**. It was first distinguished by Bühler (1934-1990) in his *Sprachtheorie* as one of three basic functions of language[1]. Bühler's theory was picked up later by Jakobson (1960), who by distinguishing three other functions laid the grounds for structural linguistics and communication studies.

2.1 Previous Research

Detecting whether sentences are loaded with emotional content has been undertaken by a number

[1]The other two being *descriptive* and *impressive*.

Proceedings of the 5th Workshop on Computational Approaches to Subjectivity, Sentiment and Social Media Analysis, pages 59–65,
Baltimore, Maryland, USA. June 27, 2014.

of researchers, most often as an additional task in either sentiment analysis (SA) or affect analysis (AA). SA, in great simplification, focuses on determining whether a language entity (sentence, document) was written with positive or negative attitude toward its topic. AA on the other hand focuses on specifying which exactly emotion type (joy, anger, etc.) has been conveyed. The fact, that the task was usually undertaken as a subtask, influences the way it was formulated. Below we present some of the most influential works on the topic, but formulating it in slightly different terms.

Emotional vs. Neutral: Discriminating whether a sentence is emotional or neutral is to answer the question of whether it can be interpreted as produced in an emotional state. This way the task was studied by Minato et al. (2006), Aman and Szpakowicz (2007) or Neviarouskaya et al. (2011).

Subjective vs. Objective: Discriminating between subjective and objective sentences is to say whether the speaker presented the sentence contents from a first-person-centric perspective or from no specific perspective. The research formulating the problem this way include e.g, Wiebe et al. (1999), who classified subjectivity of sentences using naive Bayes classifier, or later Wilson and Wiebe (2005). In other research Yu and Hatzivassiloglou (2003) used supervised learning to detect subjectivity and Hatzivassiloglou and Wiebe (2012) studied the effect of gradable adjectives on sentence subjectivity.

Emotive vs. Non-emotive: Saying that a sentence is emotive means to specify the linguistic features of language which where used to produce a sentence uttered with emphasis. Research that formulated and tackled the problem this way was done by, e.g., Ptaszynski et al. (2009).

Each of the above nomenclature implies similar, though slightly different assumptions. For example, a sentence produced without any emotive characteristics (non-emotive) could still imply emotional state in some situations. Also Bing and Zhang (2012) notice that "not all subjective sentences express opinions and those that do are a subgroup of opinionated sentences." A comparison of the scopes and overlaps of different nomenclature is represented in Figure 1. In this research we formulate the problem similarly to Ptaszynski et al. (2009), therefore we used their system to compare with our method.

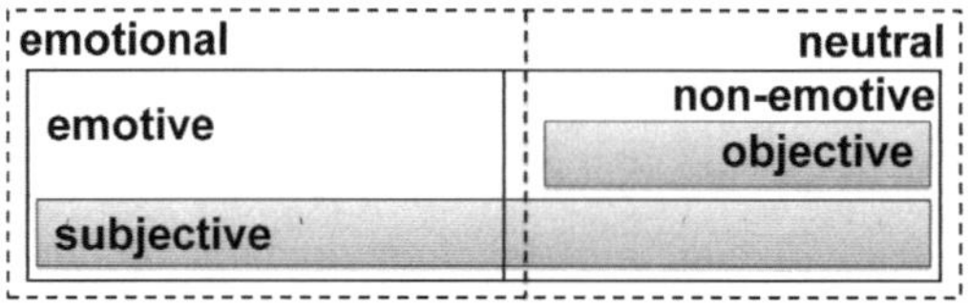

Figure 1: Comparison of between different nomenclature used in sentiment analysis research.

3 Language Combinatorics

The idea of language combinatorics (LC) assumes that patterns with disjoint elements provide better results than the usual bag-of-words or n-gram approach (Ptaszynski et al., 2011). Such patterns are defined as ordered non-repeated combinations of sentence elements. They are automatically extracted by generating all ordered combinations of sentence elements and verifying their occurrences within a corpus.

In particular, in every n-element sentence there is k-number of combination clusters, such as that $1 \leq k \leq n$, where k represents all k-element combinations being a subset of n. The number of combinations generated for one k-element cluster of combinations is equal to binomial coefficient, like in eq. 1. Thus the number of all possible combinations generated for all values of k from the range of $\{1, ..., n\}$ is equal to the sum of all combinations from all k-element clusters, like in eq. 2.

$$\binom{n}{k} = \frac{n!}{k!(n-k)!} \tag{1}$$

$$\sum_{k=1}^{n} \binom{n}{k} = \frac{n!}{1!(n-1)!} + \frac{n!}{2!(n-2)!} + ... + \frac{n!}{n!(n-n)!} = 2^n - 1 \tag{2}$$

One problem with combinatorial approach is the phenomenon of exponential and rapid growth of function values during combinatorial manipulations, called combinatorial explosion (Krippendorff, 1986). Since this phenomenon causes long processing time, combinatorial approaches have been often disregarded. We assumed however, that it could be dealt with when the algorithm is optimized to the requirements of the task. In preliminary experiments Ptaszynski et al. (2011) used a generic sentence pattern extraction architecture SPEC to compare the amounts of generated sophisticated patterns with n-grams, and noticed that it is not necessary to generate patterns of all lengths, since the most useful ones usually appear in the group of 2 to 5 element patterns. Following their experience we limit the pattern length in our research to 6 elements. All non-subsequent el-

Table 1: Some examples from the dataset representing emotive and non-emotive sentences close in content, but differing in emotional load expressed in the sentence (Romanized Japanese / Translation).

emotive	non-emotive
Takasugiru kara ne / 'Cause its just too expensive	*Kōgaku na tame desu.* / Due to high cost.
Un, umai, kangeki da. / Oh, so delicious, I'm impressed.	*Kono karē wa karai.* / This curry is hot.
Nanto ano hito, kekkon suru rashii yo! / Have you heard? She's getting married!	*Ano hito ga kekkon suru rashii desu.* / They say she is gatting married.
Chō ha ga itee / Oh, how my tooth aches!	*Ha ga itai* / A tooth aches
Sugoku kirei na umi da naaa / Oh, what a beautiful sea!	*Kirei na umi desu* / This is a beautiful sea

ements are also separated with an asterisk ("*") to mark disjoint elements.

The weight w_j of each pattern generated this way is calculated, according to equation 3, as a ratio of all occurrences of a pattern in one corpus O_{pos} to the sum of occurrences in two compared corpora $O_{pos}+O_{neg}$. The weights are also normalized to fit in range from +1 (representing purely emotive patterns) to -1 (representing purely non-emotive patterns). The normalization is achieved by subtracting 0.5 from the initial score and multiplying this intermediate product by 2. The score of one sentence is calculated as a sum of weights of patterns found in the sentence, like in eq. 4.

$$w_j = \left(\frac{O_{pos}}{O_{pos}+O_{neg}} - 0.5\right) * 2 \quad (3)$$

$$score = \sum w_j, (1 \geq w_j \geq -1) \quad (4)$$

The weight can be further modified by either

- awarding length k, or
- awarding length k and occurrence O.

The list of generated frequent patterns can also be further modified. When two collections of sentences of opposite features (such as "emotive vs. non-emotive") are compared, a generated list will contain patterns appearing uniquely on only one of the sides (e.g. uniquely emotive patterns and uniquely non-emotive patterns) or in both (ambiguous patterns). Therefore the pattern list can be modified by deleting

- all ambiguous patterns, or
- only ambiguous patterns appearing in the same number on both sides (later called "zero patterns", since their weight is equal 0).

Moreover, since a list of patterns will contain both the sophisticated patterns as well usual n-grams, the experiments were performed separately for all patterns and n-grams only. Also, if the initial collection was biased toward one of the sides (sentences of one kind were longer or more numerous), there will be more patterns of a certain sort. To mitigate this bias, instead of applying a rule of thumb, the threshold was optimized automatically.

4 Experiments

4.1 Dataset Preparation

In the experiments we used a dataset developed by Ptaszynski et al. (2009) for the needs of evaluating their affect analysis system ML-Ask for Japanese language. The dataset contains 50 emotive and 41 non-emotive sentences. It was created as follows.

Thirty people of different age and social groups participated in an anonymous survey. Each participant was to imagine or remember a conversation with any person they know and write three sentences from that conversation: one free, one emotive, and one non-emotive. Additionally, the participants were asked to make the emotive and non-emotive sentences as close in content as possible, so the only difference was whether a sentence was loaded with emotion or not. The participants also annotated on their own free utterances whether or not they were emotive. Some examples from the dataset are represented in Table 1.

In our research the above dataset was further preprocessed to make the sentences separable into elements. We did this in three ways to check how the preprocessing influences the results. We used MeCab[2], a morphological analyzer for Japanese to preprocess the sentences from the dataset in the three following ways:

- **Tokenization:** All words, punctuation marks, etc. are separated by spaces.
- **Parts of speech (POS):** Words are replaced with their representative parts of speech.
- **Tokens with POS:** Both words and POS information is included in one element.

The examples of preprocessing are represented in Table 2. In theory, the more generalized a sentence is, the less unique patterns it will produce, but the produced patterns will be more frequent. This can be explained by comparing tokenized sentence with its POS representation. For example, in the sentence from Table 2 we can see that a simple phrase *kimochi ii* ("feeling good") can be

[2]https://code.google.com/p/mecab/

Table 2: Three kinds of preprocessing of a sentence in Japanese; N = noun, TOP = topic marker, ADV = adverbial particle, ADJ = adjective, COP = copula, EXCL = exclamation mark.

Sentence: 今日はなんて気持ちいい日なんだ！ **Transliteration:** *Kyōwanantekimochiiihinanda!* **Glossing:** Today TOP what pleasant day COP EXCL **Translation:** What a pleasant day it is today!
Preprocessing examples
1. Words: *Kyō wa nante kimochi ii hi nanda !* **2. POS:** `N TOP ADV N ADJ N COP EXCL` **3.Words+POS:** *Kyō*`[N]` *wa*`[TOP]` *nante*`[ADV]` *kimochi*`[N]` *ii*`[ADJ]` *hi*`[N]` *nanda*`[COP]` *!*`[EXCL]`

represented by a POS pattern `N ADJ`. We can easily assume that there will be more `N ADJ` patterns than *kimochi ii*, because many word combinations can be represented as `N ADJ`. Therefore POS patterns will come in less variety but with higher occurrence frequency. By comparing the result of classification using different preprocessing methods we can find out whether it is better to represent sentences as more generalized or as more specific.

4.2 Experiment Setup

The experiment was performed three times, once for each kind of preprocessing. Each time 10-fold cross validation was performed and the results were calculated using Precision (P), Recall (R) and balanced F-score (F) for each threshold. We verified which version of the algorithm achieves the top score within the threshold span. However, an algorithm could achieve the best score for one certain threshold, while for others it could perform poorly. Therefore we also looked at which version achieves high scores for the longest threshold span. This shows which algorithm is more balanced. Finally, we checked the statistical significance of the results. We used paired t-test because the classification results could represent only one of two classes (emotive or non-emotive). We also compared the performance to the state of the art, namely the affect analysis system ML-Ask developed by Ptaszynski et al. (2009).

5 Results and Discussion

The overall F-score results were generally the best for the datasets containing in order: both tokens and POS, tokens only and POS only. The F-scores for POS-preprocessed sentences revealed the least constancy. For many cases n-grams scored higher than all patterns, but almost none of

Table 3: Best results for each version of the method compared with the ML-Ask system.

	ML-Ask	SPEC					
		tokenized		POS		token-POS	
		n-grams	patterns	n-grams	patterns	n-grams	patterns
Precision	0.80	0.61	0.6	0.68	0.59	0.65	0.64
Recall	0.78	1.00	0.96	0.88	1.00	0.95	0.95
F-score	0.79	0.75	0.74	0.77	0.74	0.77	0.76

the results reached statistical significance. The F-score results for the tokenized dataset were also not unequivocal. For higher thresholds patterns scored higher, while for lower thresholds the results were similar. The scores were rarely significant, utmost at 5% level ($p<0.05$), however, in all situations where n-grams visibly scored higher, the differences were not statistically significant. Finally, for the preprocessing including both tokens and POS information, pattern-based approach achieved significantly better results (p-value <0.01 or <0.001). The algorithm reached its plateau at F-score around 0.73–0.74 for tokens and POS separately, and 0.75–0.76 for tokens with POS together. In the POS dataset the elements were more abstracted, while in token-POS dataset the elements were more specific, producing a larger number, but less frequent patterns. Lower scores for POS dataset could suggest that the algorithm works better with less abstracted preprocessing. Examples of F-score comparison between n-grams and patterns for tokenized and token-POS datasets are represented in Figures 2 and 3, respectively.

Results for Precision showed similar tendencies. They were the most ambiguous for POS preprocessing. For the tokenized dataset, although there always was one or two thresholds for which n-grams scored higher, scores for patterns were more balanced, starting with a high score and decreasing slowly. As for the token-POS preprocessing patterns achieved higher Precision for most of the threshold span. The highest Precision of all was achieved in this dataset by patterns with P = 0.87 for R = 0.50.

As for Recall, the scores were consistent for all kinds of preprocessing, with higher scores for patterns within most of the threshold span and equaling while the threshold decreases. The highest scores achieved for each preprocessing for n-grams and patterns are represented in Table 3.

The affect analysis system ML-Ask (Ptaszynski et al., 2009) on the same dataset reached F = 0.79, P = 0.8 and R = 0.78. The results were generally comparable, however slightly higher for ML-Ask when it comes to P and F-score. R was always better for the proposed method. However, ML-Ask is a system requiring handcrafted lexicons, while our method is fully automatic, learning the patterns from data, not needing any particular preparations, which makes it more efficient.

5.1 Detailed Analysis of Learned Patterns

Within some of the most frequently appearing emotive patterns there were for example: *!* (exclamation mark), *n*yo*, *cha* (emotive verb modification), *yo* (exclamative sentence ending particle), *ga*yo*, *n*!* or *naa* (interjection). Some examples of sentences containing those patterns are below (patterns underlined). Interestingly, most elements of those patterns appear in ML-Ask handcrafted databases, which suggests it could be possible to improve ML-Ask performance by extracting additional patterns with SPEC.

Ex. 1. *Megane, soko ni atta nda yo.* (The glasses were over there!)
Ex. 2. *Uuun, butai ga mienai yo.* (Ohh, I cannot see the stage!)
Ex. 3. *Aaa, onaka ga suita yo.* (Ohh, I'm so hungry)

Another advantage of our method is the fact that it can mark both emotive and non-emotive elements in sentence, while ML-Ask is designed to annotate only emotive elements. Some examples of extracted non-emotive patterns were for example: *desu, wa*desu, mashi ta*, or *te*masu*. All of them were patterns described in linguistic literature as typically non-emotive, consisting in copulas (*desu*), verb endings (*masu, mashi ta*). Some sentence examples with those patterns include:

Ex. 4. *Kōgaku na tame desu.* (Due to high cost.)
Ex. 5. *Kirei na umi desu* (This is a beautiful sea)
Ex. 6. *Kyo wa yuki ga futte imasu.* (It is snowing today.)

6 Conclusions and Future Work

We presented a method for automatic extraction of patterns from emotive sentences. We assumed emotive sentences are distinguishable both lexically and grammatically and performed experiments to verify this assumption. In the experiments we used a set of emotive and non-emotive sentences preprocessed in different ways (tokens, POS, token-POS) The patterns extracted from sentences were applied to recognize emotionally loaded sentences.

The algorithm reached its plateau for F-score around 0.75–0.76 for patterns containing both tokens and POS information. Precision for patterns was balanced, while for n-grams, although occasionally achieving high scores, it was quickly decreasing. Recall scores were almost always better for patterns. The generally lower results for POS-represented sentences suggest that the algorithm works better with less abstracted elements.

The results of the proposed method and the affect analysis system ML-Ask were comparable. ML-Ask achieved better Precision, but lower Recall. However, our method is more efficient as it does not require handcrafted lexicons. Moreover, automatically extracted patterns overlap with handcrafted databases of ML-Ask, which suggests it could be possible to improve ML-Ask performance with our method. In the near future we plan to perform experiments on larger datasets, also in other languages, such as English or Chinese.

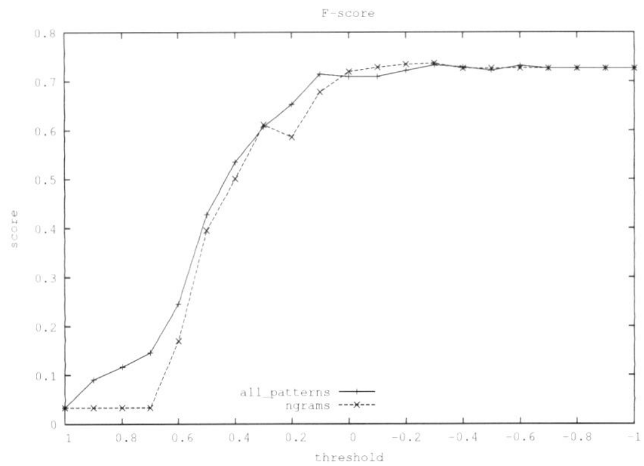

Figure 2: F-score comparison between n-grams and patterns for tokenized detaset (p = 0.0209).

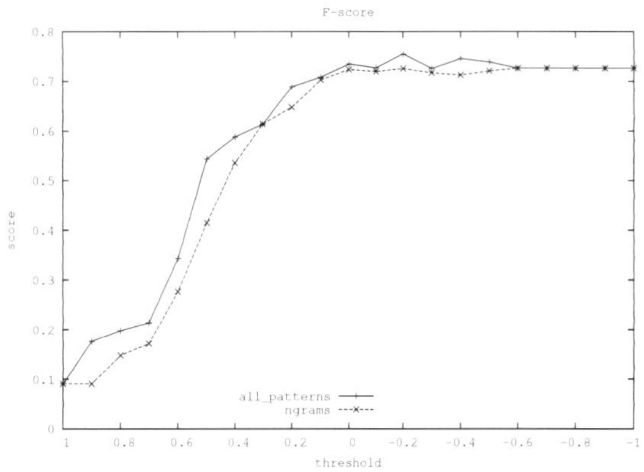

Figure 3: F-score comparison for n-grams and patterns for dataset with tokens and POS (p = 0.001).

References

Saima Aman and Stan Szpakowicz. 2007. Identifying expressions of emotion in text. In *Proceedings of the 10th International Conference on Text, Speech, and Dialogue (TSD-2007)*, Lecture Notes in Computer Science (LNCS), Springer-Verlag.

Junko Baba. 2003. Pragmatic function of Japanese mimetics in the spoken discourse of varying emotive intensity levels. *Journal of Pragmatics*, Vol. 35, No. 12, pp. 1861-1889, Elsevier.

Fabian Beijer. 2002. The syntax and pragmatics of exclamations and other expressive/emotional utterances. *Working Papers in Linguistics 2*, The Dept. of English in Lund.

Bing Liu, Lei Zhang. 2012. A survey of opinion mining and sentiment analysis. In *Mining Text Data*, pp. 415-463. Springer.

Karl Bühler. 1990. *Theory of Language. Representational Function of Language*. John Benjamins Publ. (reprint from Karl Bühler. *Sprachtheorie. Die Darstellungsfunktion der Sprache*, Ullstein, Frankfurt a. M., Berlin, Wien, 1934.)

David Crystal. 1989. *The Cambridge Encyclopedia of Language*. Cambridge University Press.

Vasileios Hatzivassiloglou and Janice Wiebe. Effects of adjective orientation and gradability on sentence subjectivity. In *Proceedings of International Conference on Computational Linguistics (COLING-2000)*, pp. 299-305, 2000.

Roman Jakobson. 1960. Closing Statement: Linguistics and Poetics. *Style in Language*, pp.350-377, The MIT Press.

Takashi Kamei, Rokuro Kouno and Eiichi Chino (eds.). 1996. *The Sanseido Encyclopedia of Linguistics*, Vol. VI, Sanseido.

Klaus Krippendorff. 1986. Combinatorial Explosion, In: Web Dictionary of Cybernetics and Systems. Princia Cybernetica Web.

Junko Minato, David B. Bracewell, Fuji Ren and Shingo Kuroiwa. 2006. Statistical Analysis of a Japanese Emotion Corpus for Natural Language Processing. *LNCS* 4114, pp. 924-929.

Alena Neviarouskaya, Helmut Prendinger and Mitsuru Ishizuka. 2011. Affect analysis model: novel rule-based approach to affect sensing from text. *Natural Language Engineering*, Vol. 17, No. 1 (2011), pp. 95-135.

Hajime Ono. 2002. *An emphatic particle DA and exclamatory sentences in Japanese*. University of California, Irvine.

Christopher Potts and Florian Schwarz. 2008. Exclamatives and heightened emotion: Extracting pragmatic generalizations from large corpora. Ms., UMass Amherst.

Michal Ptaszynski, Pawel Dybala, Rafal Rzepka and Kenji Araki. 2009. Affecting Corpora: Experiments with Automatic Affect Annotation System - A Case Study of the *2channel* Forum -, In *Proceedings of The Conference of the Pacific Association for Computational Linguistics (PACLING-09)*, pp. 223-228.

Michal Ptaszynski, Rafal Rzepka, Kenji Araki and Yoshio Momouchi. 2011. Language combinatorics: A sentence pattern extraction architecture based on combinatorial explosion. *International Journal of Computational Linguistics (IJCL)*, Vol. 2, Issue 1, pp. 24-36.

Kaori Sasai. 2006. The Structure of Modern Japanese Exclamatory Sentences: On the Structure of the *Nanto*-Type Sentence. *Studies in the Japanese Language*, Vol, 2, No. 1, pp. 16-31.

Janyce M. Wiebe, Rebecca F. Bruce and Thomas P. O'Hara. 1999. Development and use of a gold-standard data set for subjectivity classifications. In Proceedings of the Association for Computational Linguistics (ACL-1999), pp. 246-253, 1999.

Theresa Wilson and Janyce Wiebe. 2005. Annotating Attributions and Private States. *Proceedings of the ACL Workshop on Frontiers in Corpus Annotation II*, pp. 53-60.

Hong Yu and Vasileios Hatzivassiloglou. 2003. Towards answering opinion questions: separating facts from opinions and identifying the polarity of opinion sentences. In *Proceedings of Conference on Empirical Methods in Natural Language Processing (EMNLP-2003)*, pp. 129-136, 2003.

Appendix: Comparison of experiment results in all experiment settings for all three ways of dataset preprocessing.

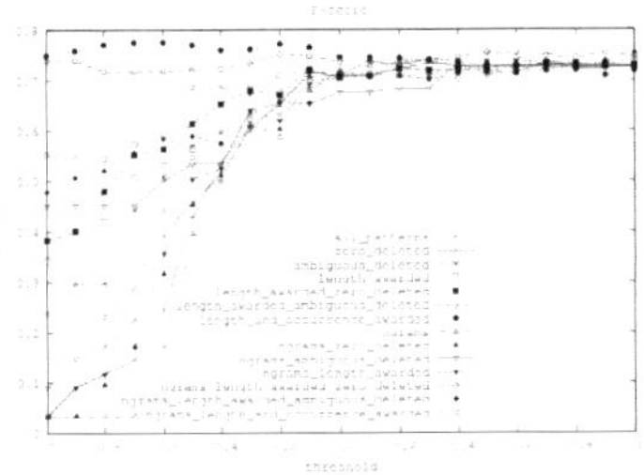

(a) F-score comparison for tokenized dataset.

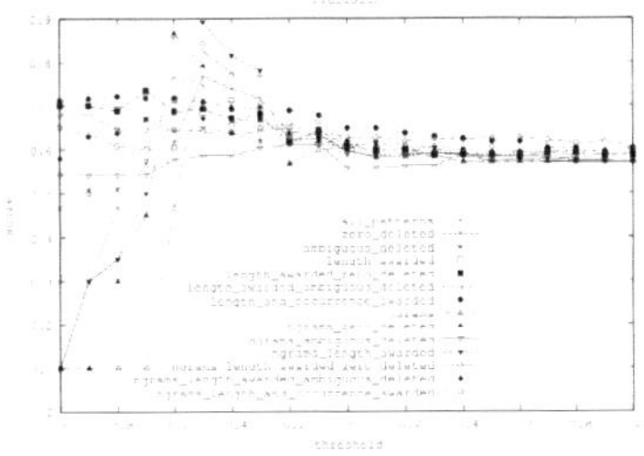

(b) Precision comparison for tokenized dataset.

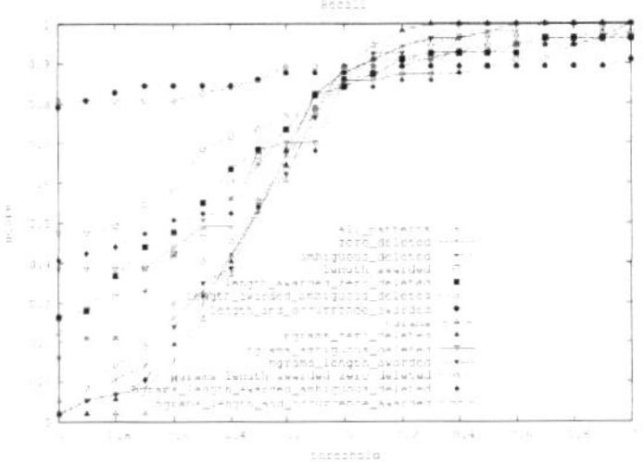

(c) Recall comparison for tokenized dataset.

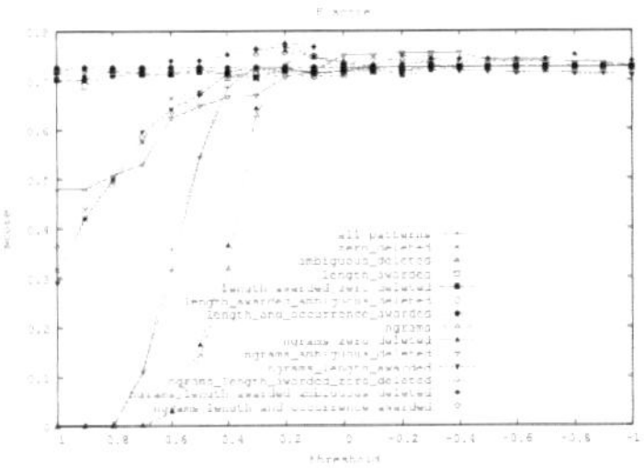

(d) F-score comparison for POS-tagged dataset.

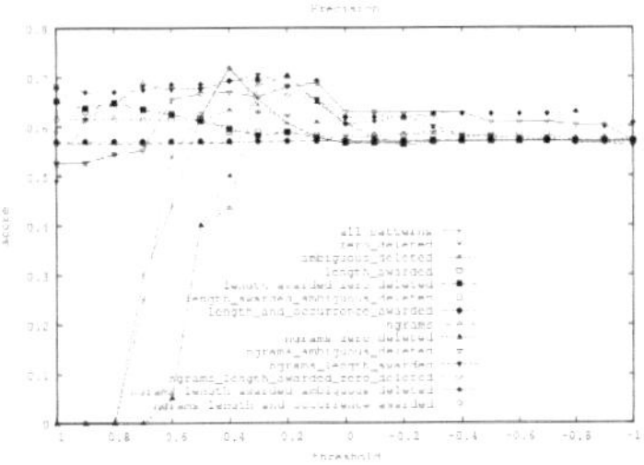

(e) Precision comparison for POS-tagged dataset.

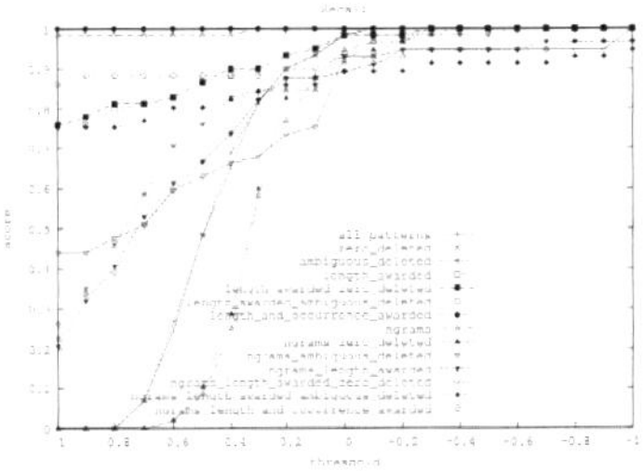

(f) Recall comparison for POS-tagged dataset.

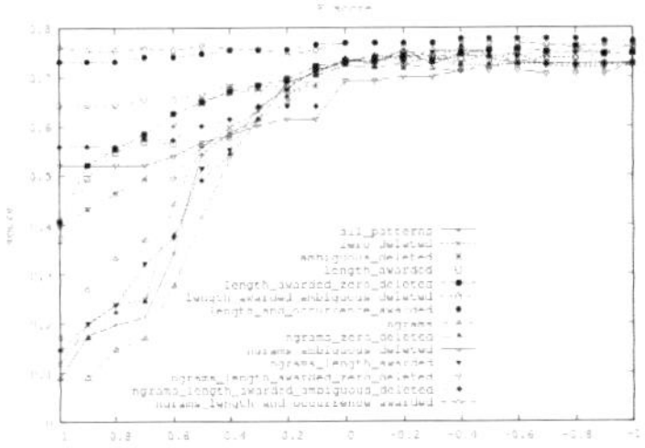

(g) F-score comparison for tokenized dataset with POS tags.

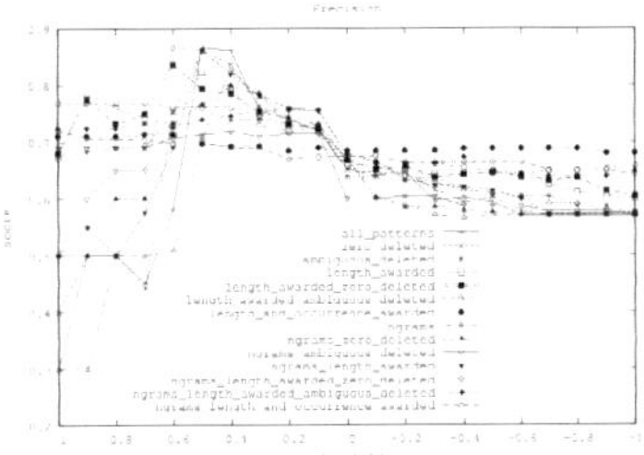

(h) Precision comparison for tokenized dataset with POS tags.

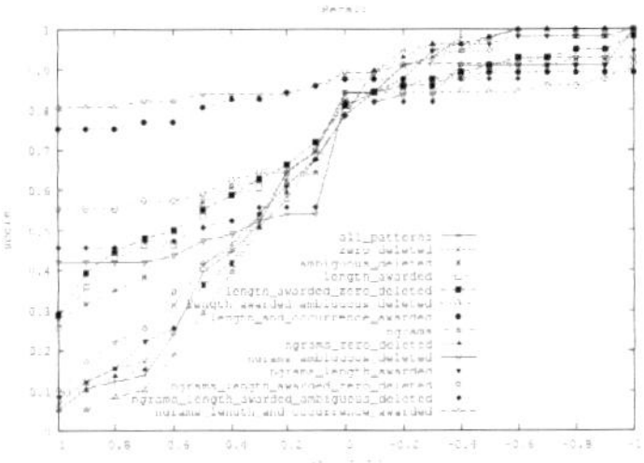

(i) Recall comparison for tokenized dataset with POS tags.

Challenges in Creating a Multilingual Sentiment Analysis Application for Social Media Mining

Alexandra Balahur, Hristo Tanev, Erik van der Goot
European Commission Joint Research Centre
Institute for the Protection and Security of the Citizen
Via E. Fermi 2749, 21027 Ispra (VA), Italy
Firstname.Lastname@jrc.ec.europa.eu

Abstract of the talk

In the past years, there has been an increasing amount of research done in the field of Sentiment Analysis. This was motivated by the growth in the volume of user-generated online data, the information flood in Social Media and the applications Sentiment Analysis has to different fields – Marketing, Business Intelligence, e-Law Making, Decision Support Systems, etc. Although many methods have been proposed to deal with sentiment detection and classification in diverse types of texts and languages, many challenges still arise when passing these methods from the research settings to real-life applications.

In this talk, we will describe the manner in which we employed machine translation together with human-annotated data to extend a sentiment analysis system to various languages. Additionally, we will describe how a joint multilingual model that detects and classifies sentiments expressed in texts from Social Media has been developed (at this point for Twitter and Facebook) and demo its use in a real-life application: a project aimed at detecting the citizens' attitude on Science and Technology.

Proceedings of the 5th Workshop on Computational Approaches to Subjectivity, Sentiment and Social Media Analysis, page 66,
Baltimore, Maryland, USA. June 27, 2014.

Two-Step Model for Sentiment Lexicon Extraction from Twitter Streams

Ilia Chetviorkin
Lomonosov Moscow State University
Moscow, Leninskiye Gory 1
ilia.chetviorkin@gmail.com

Natalia Loukachevitch
Lomonosov Moscow State University
Moscow, Leninskiye Gory 1
louk_nat@mail.ru

Abstract

In this study we explore a novel technique for creation of polarity lexicons from the Twitter streams in Russian and English. With this aim we make preliminary filtering of subjective tweets using general domain-independent lexicons in each language. Then the subjective tweets are used for extraction of domain-specific sentiment words. Relying on co-occurrence statistics of extracted words in a large unlabeled Twitter collections we utilize the Markov random field framework for the word polarity classification. To evaluate the quality of the obtained sentiment lexicons they are used for tweet sentiment classification and outperformed previous results.

1 Introduction

With growing popularity of microblogging services such as Twitter, the amount of subjective information containing user opinions and sentiments is increasing dramatically. People tend to express their opinions about events in the real life and such opinions contain valuable information for market research, brand monitoring and political polls.

The task of automatic processing of such informal resources is challenging because people use a lot of slang, vulgarity and out-of-vocabulary words to state their opinions about various objects and situations. In particular, it is difficult to achieve the high quality of sentiment analysis on such type of short informal texts as tweets are. Standard domain-independent lexicon-based methods suffer from low coverage, and for machine learning methods it is difficult to prepare a representative collection of labeled data because topics of discussion are changing rapidly.

Thus, special methods for processing social media data streams should be developed. We proposed and evaluated our approach for Russian language, where only a limited number of natural language processing tools and resources are available. Then to demonstrate the robustness of the method and to compare the results with the other approaches we used it for English.

The current research can be separated into two steps. We start with a special supervised model based on statistical and linguistic features of sentiment words, which is trained and evaluated in the movie domain. Then this model is utilized for extraction of sentiment words from unlabeled Twitter datasets, which are preliminary filtered using the domain-independent lexicons: ProductSentiRus (Chetviorkin and Loukachevitch, 2012) for Russian and MPQA (Wilson et al., 2005) for English.

In the second step an algorithm for polarity classification of extracted sentiment words is introduced. It is built using the Markov random field framework and uses only information contained in text collections.

To evaluate the quality of the created lexicons extrinsically, we conduct the experiments on the tweet subjectivity and polarity classification tasks using various lexicons.

The key advantage of the proposed two-step algorithm is that once trained it can be utilized to different domains and languages with minor modifications. To demonstrate the ability of the proposed algorithm to extract sentiment words in various domains we took significantly different collections for training and testing: movie review collection for training and large collections of tweets for testing.

2 Related work

There are two major approaches for creation of a sentiment lexicon in a specific language: dictionary-based methods and corpus-based methods.

Proceedings of the 5th Workshop on Computational Approaches to Subjectivity, Sentiment and Social Media Analysis, pages 67–72, Baltimore, Maryland, USA. June 27, 2014.

Dictionary-based methods for various languages have received a lot of attention in the literature (Pérez-Rosas et al., 2012; Mohammad et al., 2009; Clematide and Klenner, 2010), but the main problem of such approaches is that it is difficult to apply them to processing social media. The reason is that short informal texts contain a lot of misspellings and out-of-vocabulary words.

Corpus-based methods are more suitable for processing social media data. In such approaches various statistical and linguistic features are used to discriminate opinion words from all other words (He et al., 2008; Jijkoun et al., 2010).

Another important group of approaches, which can be both dictionary-based and corpus-based are graph-based methods. In (Velikovich et al., 2010) a new method for constructing a lexical network was proposed, which aggregates the huge amount of unlabeled data. Then the graph propagation algorithm was used. Several other researchers utilized the graph or label propagation techniques for solving the problem of opinion word extraction (Rao and Ravichandran, 2009; Speriosu et al., 2011).

In (Takamura et al., 2005) authors describe a probabilistic model for assigning polarity to each word in a collection. This model is based on the Ising spin model of magnetism and is built upon Markov random field framework, using various dictionary-based and linguistic features. In our research, unlike (Takamura et al., 2005) we use only information contained in a text collection without any external dictionary resources (due to the lack of necessary resources for Russian). Our advantage is that we use only potential domain-specific sentiment words during the construction of the network.

A large body of research has been focused on Twitter sentiment analysis during the previous several years (Barbosa and Feng, 2010; Bermingham and Smeaton, 2010; Bifet and Frank, 2010; Davidov et al., 2010; Kouloumpis et al., 2011; Jiang et al., 2011; Agarwal et al., 2011; Wang et al., 2011). In (Chen et al., 2012) authors propose an optimization framework for extraction of opinion expressions from tweets. Using extracted lexicons authors were able to improve the tweet sentiment classification quality. Our approach is based on similar assumptions (like consistency relations), but we do not use any syntactic parsers and dictionary resources. In (Volkova et al., 2013) a new multilingual bootstrapping technique for building tweet sentiment lexicons was introduced. This method is used as a baseline in our work.

3 Data

For the experiments in this paper we use several collections in two domains: movie review collection in Russian for training and fine-tuning of the proposed algorithms and Twitter collections for evaluation and demonstration of robustness in Russian and English languages.

Movie domain. The movie review dataset collected from the online service *imhonet.ru*. There are $28,773$ movie reviews of various genres with numeric scores specified by their authors (DOM).

Additionally, special collections with low concentration of sentiment words are utilized: the contrast collection consists of $17,980$ movie plots (DESC) and a collection of two million news documents (NEWS). Such collections are useful for filtering out of domain-specific and general neutral words, which are very frequent in news and object descriptions.

Twitter collections. We use three datasets for each language: 1M+ of unlabeled tweets (UNL) for extraction of sentiment lexicons, 2K labeled tweets for development data (DEV), and 2K labeled tweets for evaluation (TEST). DEV dataset is used to find the best combination of various lexicons for processing Twitter data and TEST for evaluating the quality of constructed lexicons.

The UNL dataset in Russian was collected during one day using Twitter API. These tweets contain various topics without any filtering. Only strict duplicates and retweets were removed from the dataset. The similar collection for English was downloaded using the links from (Volkova et al., 2013).

All tweets in DEV and TEST collections are manually labeled by subjectivity and polarity using the Mechanical Turk with five workers (majority voting). This data was used for development and evaluation in (Volkova et al., 2013).

4 Method for sentiment word extraction

In this section we introduce an algorithm for sentiment lexicon extraction, which is inspired by the method described in (Chetviorkin and Loukachevitch, 2012), but have more robust features, which allow us to apply it to any unlabeled text collection (e.g. tweets collection). The proposed algorithm is applied to text collections in Russian and English and obtained results are evaluated intrinsically for Russian and extrinsically for both languages.

4.1 An extraction model

Our algorithm is based on several text collections: collection with the high concentration of sentiment words (e.g. DOM collection), contrast domain-specific collection (e.g. DESC collection), contrast domain-independent collection (e.g. NEWS collection). Thus, taking into account statistical distributions of words in such collections we are able to distinguish domain-specific sentiment words.

We experimented with various features to create the robust cross-domain feature representation of sentiment words. As a result the eight most valuable features were used in further experiments:

Linguistic features. Adjective binary indicator, noun binary indicator, feature reflecting part-of-speech ambiguity (for lemma), binary feature of predefined list of prefixes (e.g. *un, im*);

Statistical features. Frequency of capitalized words, frequency of co-occurrence with polarity shifters (e.g. *no, very*), TFIDF feature calculated on the basis of various collection pairs, weirdness feature (the ratio of relative frequencies of certain lexical items in special and general collections) calculated using several pairs of collections.

To train supervised machine learning algorithms all words with frequency greater than three in the Russian movie review collection (DOM) were labeled manually by two assessors. If there was a disagreement about the sentiment of a specific word, the collective judgment after the discussion was used as a final ground truth. As a result of the assessment procedure the list of 4079 sentiment words was obtained.

The best quality of classification using labeled data was shown by the ensemble of three classifiers: Logistic Regression, LogitBoost and Random Forest. The quality according to Precision@n measure can be found in Table 1. This trained model was used in further experiments for extraction of sentiment words both in English and in Russian.

4.2 Extraction of subjective words from Twitter data

To verify the robustness of the model on new unlabeled data it was utilized for sentiment word extraction from multi-topic tweet collection UNL in each language. To apply this model we prepared three collections: domain-specific with high concentration of sentiment words, domain-specific with low concentration of sentiment words and one general collection with low concentration of sentiment words. As the general collection we could take the same NEWS collection (see Section 3) for Russian and British National Corpus[1] for English.

Lexicon	$P@100$	$P@1000$
MovieLex	95.0%	78.3%
TwitterLex	95.0%	79.9%

Table 1: Quality of subjective word extraction in Russian

To prepare domain-specific collections we classified the UNL collections by subjectivity using general purpose sentiment lexicons ProductSentiRus and MPQA in accordance with the language. The subjectivity classifier predicted that a tweet was subjective if it contained at least one subjective term from this lexicon. All subjective tweets constituted a collection with the high concentration of sentiment words and all the other tweets constituted the contrast collection.

Finally, using all specially prepared collections and the trained model (in the movie domain), new lexicons of twitter-specific sentiment words were extracted. The quality of extraction in Russian according to manual labeling of two assessors can be found in Table 1. The resulting quality of extracted Russian lexicon is on the same level as in the initial movie domain, what confirms the robustness of the proposed model.

We took 5000 of the most probable sentiment words from each lexicon for further work.

5 Polarity classification using MRF

In the second part of current research we describe an algorithm for polarity classification of extracted sentiment words. The proposed method relies on several assumptions:

- Each word has the prior sentiment score calculated using the review scores where it appears (simple averaging);
- Words with similar polarity tend to co-occur closely to each other;

[1] http://www.natcorp.ox.ac.uk/

- Negation between sentiment words leads to the opposite polarity labels.

5.1 Algorithm description

To formalize all these assumptions we construct an undirected graphical model using extracted sentiment word co-occurrence statistics. Each extracted word is represented by a vertex in a graph and an edge between two vertexes is established in case if they co-occur together more than once in the collection. We drop all the edges where average distance between words is more than 8 words.

Our model by construction is similar to approach based on the Ising spin model described in (Takamura et al., 2005). Ising model is used to describe ferromagnetism in statistical mechanics. In general, the system is composed of N binary variables (spins), where each variable $x_i \in \{-1, +1\}, i = 1, 2, ..., N$. The energy function of the system is the following:

$$E(x) = -\sum_{ij} s_{ij} x_i x_j - \sum_i h_i x_i \qquad (1)$$

where s_{ij} represents the efficacy of interaction between two spins and h_i stands for external field added to x_i. The probability of each system configuration is provided by Boltzmann distribution:

$$P(X) = \frac{\exp^{-\beta E(X)}}{Z} \qquad (2)$$

where Z is a normalizing factor and $\beta = (T^{-1} > 0)$ is inverse temperature, which is parameter of the model. We calculate values of $P(X)$ with several different values of β and try to find the locally polarized state of the network.

To specify the initial polarity of each word, we assume that each text from the collection has its sentiment score. This condition is not very strict, because there are a lot of internet review services where people assign numerical scores to their reviews. Using such scores we can calculate the deviation from the average score for each word in the collection:

$$h(i) = E(c|w_i) - E(c)$$

where c is the review score random variable, $E(c)$ is the expectation of the score in the collection and $E(c|w_i)$ is the expectation of the score for reviews containing word w_i. Thus we assign the initial weight of each vertex i in the MRF to be equal to $h(i)$.

To specify the weight of each edge in the network we made preliminary experiments to detect the dependency between the probability of the word pair to have similar polarity and average distance between them. The result of such experiment for movie reviews can be found on Figure 1. One can see that if the distance between the words

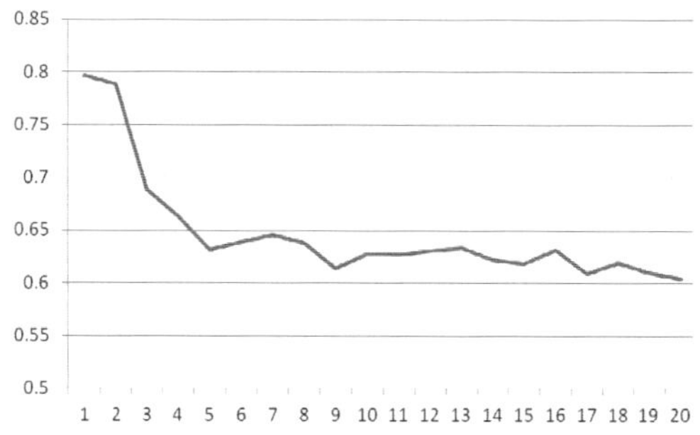

Figure 1: The dependency between the probability to have similar polarity and average distance

is above four, then the probability is remain on the same level which is slightly biased to similar polarity. Relying on this insight and taking into account the frequency of co-occurrence of the words we used the following edge weights:

$$s(i,j) = f(w_i, w_j) \max\Big(0.5 - \frac{d(w_i, w_j)}{d(w_i, w_j) + 4}, 0\Big)$$

where $f(w_i, w_j)$ is the co-occurrence frequency in the collection and $d(w_i, w_j)$ is the average distance between words w_i and w_j.

Finally, we revert the sign of this equation in case of more than half of co-occurrences contains negation (*no, not, but*) between opinion words.

In practice we can find approximate solution using such algorithms as: Loopy Belief Propagation (**BP**), Mean Field (**MF**), Gibbs Sampling (**Gibbs**).

The performance of the methods was evaluated for a lexical network constructed from the first 3000 of the most probable extracted sentiment words in the movie review collection (DOM). We took from them 822 interconnected words with strict polarity labeled by two assessors as a gold standard. Testing was performed by varying β from 0.1 to 1.0. The primary measure in this experiment was accuracy. The best results can be found in Table 2.

The best performance was demonstrated by **MF** algorithm and $\beta = 0.4$. This algorithm and parameter value were used in further experiments on unlabeled tweet collections.

β	**BP**	**MF**	**Gibbs**
0.4	83.8	**85.2**	**83.7**
0.5	83.6	84.5	82.0
0.6	**85.0**	83.1	79.4

Table 2: Dependence between the accuracy of classification and β

5.2 Polarity classification of subjective words from Twitter data

Using the general polarity lexicons we classify all subjective tweets in large UNL collections into positive and negative categories. For the polarity classifier, we predict a tweet to be positive (negative) if it contains at least one positive (negative) term from the lexicon taking into account negation. If a tweet contains both positive and negative terms, we take the majority label. In case if a tweet does not contain any word from the lexicon we predict it to be positive.

These labels ($+1$ for positive and -1 for negative) can be used to compute initial polarity $h(i)$ for all extracted sentiment words from the UNL collections. The weights of the links between words $s(i, j)$ can be also computed using full unlabeled collections.

Thus, we can utilize the algorithm for polarity classification of sentiment words extracted from Twitter. The resulting lexicon for Russian contains 2772 words and 2786 words for English (we take only words that are connected in the network). To evaluate the quality of the obtained lexicons the Russian one was labeled by two assessors. In result of such markup 1734 words with strict positive or negative polarity were taken. The accuracy of the lexicon on the basis of the markup was equal to **72%**, which is 1.5 % better than the simple average score baseline.

6 Lexicon Evaluations

To evaluate all newly created lexicons they were utilized in tweet polarity and subjectivity classification tasks using the TEST collections. The results of the classification for both languages can be found in Table 3 and Table 4.

As one can see, the newly created Twitter-specific sentiment lexicon results outperform the result of (Volkova et al., 2013) in subjectivity classification for Russian but slightly worse than the result for English. On the other hand the results of polarity classification are on par or better

Lexicon	P	R	F_{subj}
Russian			
Volkova, 2013	-	-	61.0
TwitterLex	60.2	79.3	68.5
English			
Volkova, 2013	-	-	75.0
TwitterLex	58.8	95.5	73.0

Table 3: Quality of tweet subjectivity classification

Lexicon	P	R	F_{pol}
Russian			
Volkova, 2013	-	-	73.0
TwitterLex	65.5	82.0	72.8
Combined	65.8	85.5	74.3
English			
Volkova, 2013	-	-	78.0
TwitterLex	72.1	88.1	79.3
Combined	73.2	89.3	80.4

Table 4: Quality of tweet polarity classification

than the results of (Volkova et al., 2013) lexicons bootstrapped from domain-independent sentiment lexicons. Thus, to push the quality of polarity classification forward we combined the domain-independent lexicons and our Twitter-specific lexicons. We experimented with various word counts from general lexicons and found the optimal combination on the DEV collection: all words from TwitterLex and 2000 the most strong sentiment words from ProductSentiRus in Russian and all strong sentiment words from MPQA in English. The lexicon combination outperforms all previous results by F-measure leading to the conclusion that proposed method can capture valuable domain-specific sentiment words.

7 Conclusion

In this paper we proposed a new method for extraction of domain-specific sentiment lexicons and adopted the Ising model for polarity classification of extracted words. This two-stage method was applied to a large unlabeled Twitter dataset and the extracted sentiment lexicons performed on the high level in the tweet sentiment classification task. Our method can be used in a streaming mode for augmentation of sentiment lexicons and supporting the high quality of multilingual sentiment classification.

Acknowledgements This work is partially supported by RFBR grant 14-07-00682.

References

Apoorv Agarwal, Boyi Xie, Ilia Vovsha, Owen Rambow, and Rebecca Passonneau. 2011. Sentiment analysis of twitter data. In *Proceedings of the Workshop on Languages in Social Media*, pages 30–38. Association for Computational Linguistics.

Luciano Barbosa and Junlan Feng. 2010. Robust sentiment detection on twitter from biased and noisy data. In *Proceedings of the 23rd International Conference on Computational Linguistics: Posters*, pages 36–44. Association for Computational Linguistics.

Adam Bermingham and Alan F Smeaton. 2010. Classifying sentiment in microblogs: is brevity an advantage? In *Proceedings of the 19th ACM international conference on Information and knowledge management*, pages 1833–1836. ACM.

Albert Bifet and Eibe Frank. 2010. Sentiment knowledge discovery in twitter streaming data. In *Discovery Science*, pages 1–15. Springer.

Lu Chen, Wenbo Wang, Meenakshi Nagarajan, Shaojun Wang, and Amit P Sheth. 2012. Extracting diverse sentiment expressions with target-dependent polarity from twitter. In *ICWSM*.

Ilia Chetviorkin and Natalia V Loukachevitch. 2012. Extraction of russian sentiment lexicon for product meta-domain. In *COLING*, pages 593–610.

Simon Clematide and Manfred Klenner. 2010. Evaluation and extension of a polarity lexicon for german. In *Proceedings of the First Workshop on Computational Approaches to Subjectivity and Sentiment Analysis*, pages 7–13.

Dmitry Davidov, Oren Tsur, and Ari Rappoport. 2010. Enhanced sentiment learning using twitter hashtags and smileys. In *Proceedings of the 23rd International Conference on Computational Linguistics: Posters*, pages 241–249. Association for Computational Linguistics.

Ben He, Craig Macdonald, Jiyin He, and Iadh Ounis. 2008. An effective statistical approach to blog post opinion retrieval. In *Proceedings of the 17th ACM conference on Information and knowledge management*, pages 1063–1072. ACM.

Long Jiang, Mo Yu, Ming Zhou, Xiaohua Liu, and Tiejun Zhao. 2011. Target-dependent twitter sentiment classification. In *ACL*, pages 151–160.

Valentin Jijkoun, Maarten de Rijke, and Wouter Weerkamp. 2010. Generating focused topic-specific sentiment lexicons. In *Proceedings of the 48th Annual Meeting of the Association for Computational Linguistics*, pages 585–594. Association for Computational Linguistics.

Efthymios Kouloumpis, Theresa Wilson, and Johanna Moore. 2011. Twitter sentiment analysis: The good the bad and the omg! In *ICWSM*.

Saif Mohammad, Cody Dunne, and Bonnie Dorr. 2009. Generating high-coverage semantic orientation lexicons from overtly marked words and a thesaurus. In *Proceedings of the 2009 Conference on Empirical Methods in Natural Language Processing: Volume 2*, pages 599–608. Association for Computational Linguistics.

Verónica Pérez-Rosas, Carmen Banea, and Rada Mihalcea. 2012. Learning sentiment lexicons in spanish. In *LREC*, pages 3077–3081.

Delip Rao and Deepak Ravichandran. 2009. Semi-supervised polarity lexicon induction. In *Proceedings of the 12th Conference of the European Chapter of the Association for Computational Linguistics*, pages 675–682. Association for Computational Linguistics.

Michael Speriosu, Nikita Sudan, Sid Upadhyay, and Jason Baldridge. 2011. Twitter polarity classification with label propagation over lexical links and the follower graph. In *Proceedings of the First workshop on Unsupervised Learning in NLP*, pages 53–63. Association for Computational Linguistics.

H. Takamura, T. Inui, and M. Okumura. 2005. Extracting semantic orientations of words using spin model. In *Proceedings of the 43rd Annual Meeting on Association for Computational Linguistics*, pages 133–140.

Leonid Velikovich, Sasha Blair-Goldensohn, Kerry Hannan, and Ryan McDonald. 2010. The viability of web-derived polarity lexicons. In *Human Language Technologies: The 2010 Annual Conference of the North American Chapter of the Association for Computational Linguistics*, pages 777–785. Association for Computational Linguistics.

Svitlana Volkova, Theresa Wilson, and David Yarowsky. 2013. Exploring sentiment in social media: Bootstrapping subjectivity clues from multilingual twitter streams. In *Proceedings of the 51st Annual Meeting of the Association for Computational Linguistics (ACL13)*, pages 505–510.

Xiaolong Wang, Furu Wei, Xiaohua Liu, Ming Zhou, and Ming Zhang. 2011. Topic sentiment analysis in twitter: a graph-based hashtag sentiment classification approach. In *Proceedings of the 20th ACM international conference on Information and knowledge management*, pages 1031–1040. ACM.

Theresa Wilson, Janyce Wiebe, and Paul Hoffmann. 2005. Recognizing contextual polarity in phrase-level sentiment analysis. In *Proceedings of the conference on human language technology and empirical methods in natural language processing*, pages 347–354. Association for Computational Linguistics.

Linguistically Informed Tweet Categorization for Online Reputation Management

Gerard Lynch and Pádraig Cunningham
Centre for Applied Data Analytics Research
(CeADAR)
University College Dublin
Belfield Office Park
Dublin 4, Ireland
firstname.lastname@ucd.ie

Abstract

Determining relevant content automatically is a challenging task for any aggregation system. In the business intelligence domain, particularly in the application area of Online Reputation Management, it may be desirable to label tweets as either customer comments which deserve rapid attention or tweets from industry experts or sources regarding the higher-level operations of a particular entity. We present an approach using a combination of linguistic and Twitter-specific features to represent tweets and examine the efficacy of these in distinguishing between tweets which have been labelled using Amazon's Mechanical Turk crowdsourcing platform. Features such as part-of-speech tags and function words prove highly effective at discriminating between the two categories of tweet related to several distinct entity types, with Twitter-related metrics such as the presence of hashtags, retweets and user mentions also adding to classification accuracy. Accuracy of 86% is reported using an SVM classifier and a mixed set of the aforementioned features on a corpus of tweets related to seven business entities.

1 Motivation

Online Reputation Management (ORM) is a growing field of interest in the domain of business intelligence. Companies and individuals alike are highly interested in monitoring the opinions of others across social and traditional media and this information can have considerable business value for corporate entities in particular.

1.1 Challenges

There are a number of challenges in creating an end-to-end software solution for such purposes, and several shared tasks have already been established to tackle these issues[1]. The most recent RepLab evaluation was concerned with four tasks related to ORM, *filtering*, *polarity for reputation*, *topic detection* and *priority assignment*. Based on these evaluations, it is clear that although the state of the art of topic-based filtering of tweets is relatively accomplished (Perez-Tellez et al., 2011; Yerva et al., 2011; Spina et al., 2013), other aspects of the task such as sentiment analysis and prioritisation of tweets based on content are less trivial and require further analysis.

Whether Twitter mentions of entities are actual customer comments or in fact represent the views of traditional media or industry experts and sources is an important distinction for ORM systems. With this study we investigate the degree to which this task can be automated using supervised learning methods.

2 Related Work

2.1 Studies on Twitter data

While the majority of research in the computational sciences on Twitter data has focused on issues such as topic detection (Cataldi et al., 2010), event detection, (Weng and Lee, 2011; Sakaki et al., 2010), sentiment analysis, (Kouloumpis et al., 2011), and other tasks based primarily on the topical and/or semantic content of tweets, there is a growing body of work which investigates more subtle forms of information represented in tweets, such as reputation and trustworthiness, (O'Donovan et al., 2012), authorship attribution (Layton et al., 2010; Bhargava et al., 2013) and Twitter spam detection, (Benevenuto et al., 2010).

[1] See (Amigó et al., 2012) and (Amigó et al., 2013) for details of the RepLab series

Proceedings of the 5th Workshop on Computational Approaches to Subjectivity, Sentiment and Social Media Analysis, pages 73–78,
Baltimore, Maryland, USA. June 27, 2014.

These studies combine Twitter-specific and textual features such as retweet counts, tweet lengths and hashtag frequency, together with sentence-length, character n-grams and punctuation counts.

2.2 Studies on non-Twitter data

The textual features used in our work such as n-grams of words and parts-of-speech have been used for gender-based language classification (Koppel et al., 2002), social profiling and personality type detection (Mairesse et al., 2007), native language detection from L2 text, (Brooke and Hirst, 2012) translation source language detection, (van Halteren, 2008; Lynch and Vogel, 2012) and translation quality detection, (Vogel et al., 2013).

3 Experimental setup and corpus

Tweets were gathered between June 2013 and January 2014 using the *twitter4j* Java library. A language detector was used to filter only English-language tweets.[2] The criteria for inclusion were that the entity name was present in the tweet. The entities focused on in this study had relatively unambigious business names, so no complex filtering was necessary.

3.1 Pilot study

A smaller pilot study was carried out before the main study in order to examine response quality and accuracy of instruction. Two hundred sample tweets concerning two airlines[3] were annotated using Amazon's Mechanical Turk system by fourteen Master annotators. After annotation, we selected the subset (72%) of tweets for which both annotators agreed on the category to train the classifier. During the pilot study, the tweets were pre-processed[4] to remove @ and # symbols and punctuation to treat account names and hashtags as words. Hyperlinks representations were maintained within the tweets. The Twitter-specific metrics were not employed in the pilot study.

3.2 Full study

In the full study, 2454 tweets concerning seven business entities[5] were tagged by forty annotators as to whether they corresponded to one of the three categories described in Section 1.1. For 57% of the tweets, annotators agreed on the categories with disagreement in the remaining 43%. The disputed tweets were annotated again by two annotators. From this batch, a similar proportion were agreed on. For the non-agreed tweets in the second round, a majority category vote was reached by combining the four annotations over the first and second rounds. After this process, roughly two hundred tweets remained as ambiguous (each having two annotations for one of two particular categories) and these were removed from the corpus used in the experiments.

3.3 Category breakdown

Table 5 displays the number of tweets for which no majority category agreement was reached. The majority disagreement class across all entities are texts which have been labelled as both business operations and other. For the airline entities, a large proportion of tweets were annotated as both customer comment and other, this appeared to be a categorical issue which may have required clarification in the instructions. The smallest category for tied agreement is customer comment and business operations, it appears that the distinction between these categories was clearer based on the data provided to annotators. 2078 tweets were used in the final experiments. The classes were somewhat imbalanced for the final corpus, the *business operations* category was the largest, with 1184 examples, *customer comments* contained 585 examples and the *other* category contained 309 examples.

3.4 Feature types

The features used for classification purposes can be divided into the following two categories:

1. **Twitter-specific**:
    - Tweet is a retweet or not
    - Tweet contains a mention
    - Tweet contains a hashtag or a link
    - Weight measure (See Fig 3)
    - Retweet account for a tweet.
2. **Linguistic**: The linguistic features are based on the textual content of the tweet represented as word unigrams, word bigrams and part-of-speech bigrams.

[2] A small amount of non-English tweets were found in the dataset, these were assigned to the *Other category*.

[3] Aer Lingus and Ryanair

[4] This was not done in the full study, these symbols were counted and used as features.

[5] Aer Lingus, Ryanair, Bank of Ireland, C & C Group, Permanent TSB, Glanbia, Greencore

We used TagHelperTools, (Rosé et al., 2008) for textual feature creation which utilises the Stanford NLP toolkit for NLP annotation and returns formatted representations of textual features which can be employed in the Weka toolkit which implements various machine learning algorithms. All linguistic feature frequencies were binarised in our representations[6].

4 Results

4.1 Pilot study

Using the Naive Bayes classifier in the Weka toolkit and a feature set consisting of 130 word tokens, 80% classification accuracy was obtained using ten-fold cross validation on the full set of tweets . Table 1 shows the top word features when ranked using 10-fold cross validation and the information gain metric for classification power over the three classes. Using the top 50 ranked POS-bigram features alone, 74% classification accuracy was obtained using the Naive Bayes classifier. Table 2 shows the top twenty features, again ranked by information gain.

Combining the fifty POS-bigrams and the 130 word features, we obtained 84% classification accuracy using the Naive Bayes classifier. Accuracy was improved by removing all noun features from the dataset and using the top seventy five features from the remaining set ranked with information gain, resulting in 86.6% accuracy using the SVM classifier with a linear kernel. Table 3 displays the top twenty combined features.

Rank	Feature	Rank	Feature
1	http	11	investors
2	flight	12	would
3	talks	13	by
4	for	14	says
5	strike	15	profit
6	an	16	cabin
7	you	17	crew
8	I	18	via
9	that	19	at
10	action	20	since

Table 1: Top 20 ranked word features for pilot study

[6]1 if feature is present in a tweet, otherwise 0.

Rank	Feature	Rank	Feature
1	NNP_EOL	11	VB_PRP
2	VBD_JJ	12	NN_NNS
3	NNP_VBD	13	IN_PRP$
4	NNP_NN	14	BOL_CD
5	BOL_PRP	15	BOL_JJS
6	VBD_NNP	16	IN_VBN
7	NNP_CC	17	PRP$_JJ
8	TO_NNP	18	PRP_MD
9	NN_RB	19	PRP$_VBG
10	RB_JJ	20	CC_VBP

Table 2: Top 20 ranked POS bigram features for pilot study

Rank	Feature	Rank	Feature
1	http	11	TO_NNP
2	NNP_EOL	12	RB_JJ
3	NNP_VBD	13	that
4	VBD_JJ	14	tells
5	NNP_NN	15	way
6	BOL_PRP	16	I
7	VBD_NNP	17	would
8	NNP_CC	18	you
9	for	19	NN_RB
10	an	20	BOL_JJS

Table 3: Top 20 ranked combined features for pilot study

4.2 Full study

4.2.1 Results

Using the SMO classifier, Weka's support vector machine implementation using a linear kernel, a hybrid feature set containing linguistic, custom and Twitter-specific features obtained 72% classification accuracy for the three categories. F-measures were highest for the *business operations* class, and lowest for the *other* class, which contained the most diversity. Examining Figure 2, it is clear that f-measures for the *other* class are almost zero. This indicates that tweets given this category may not be homogeneous enough to categorise using the features defined in Table 7.

4.3 Two classes

After the removal of the *other* class from the experiment, the same feature set obtained 86% classification accuracy between the two remaining classes. The distinguishing features consisted predominantly of pronouns (*I, me, my*), part-of-

Entity	BO	CC	Other
Aer Lingus	174	138	44
Ryanair	58	212	52
AIB	69	29	43
BOI	208	85	40
C&C	45	14	15
Glanbia	276	39	46
Greencore	37	4	13
Kerry Group	158	10	36
Permanent TSB	160	54	20

Table 4: Tweets per entity by category: Majority agreement

Entity	CC+BO	O-CC	O-BO
Aer Lingus	4	24	15
Ryanair	7	30	8
AIB	4	5	11
BOI	9	5	16
C&C	0	1	3
Glanbia	7	4	19
Greencore	0	0	2
Kerry Group	5	2	12
Permanent TSB	3	6	10

Table 5: Tweets per entity by category: Tied agreement

speech bigrams including pairs of plural nouns, lines beginning with prepositions and function words (*so, just, new, it*). Business operations tweets were more likely to mention a user account or be a retweet, personal pronouns were more commonplace in customer comments and as observed in the pilot study, customer comments were more likely to begin with a preposition and business operations tweets were more likely to contain noun-noun compounds and pairs of coordinating conjunctions and nouns.

4.4 Features

Hashtags were slightly more common in business operations tweets, however the number of hashtags was not counted, simply whether at least one was present. Hashtags as a proportion of words might be a useful feature for further studies. Function words and POS tags were highly discriminatory, indicating that this classifier may be applicable to different topic areas. Weight (See Figure 3) was a distinguishing feature, with business operations tweets having higher weight scores, reflect-

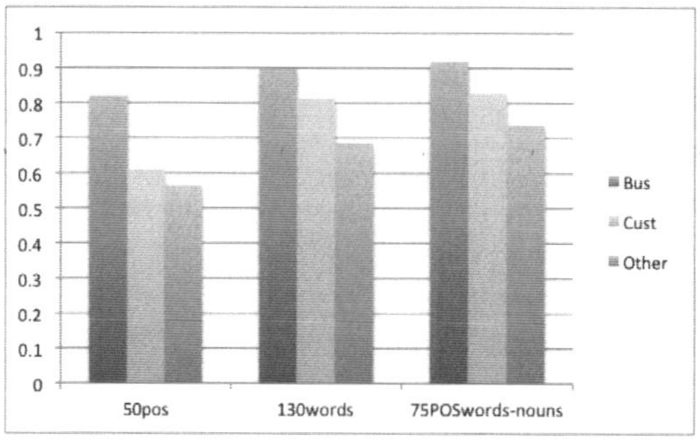

Figure 1: F-scores by category for pilot study

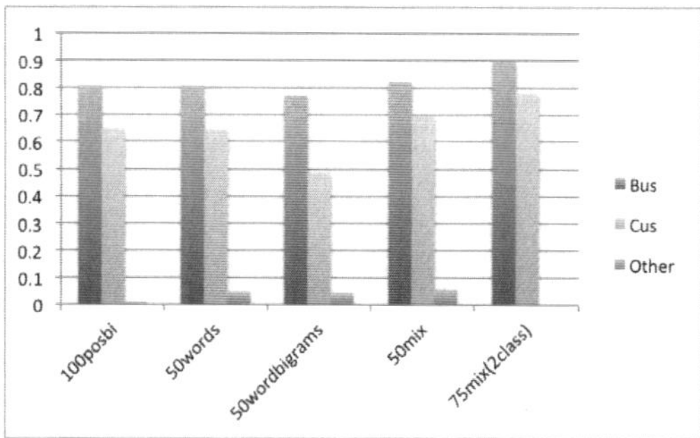

Figure 2: F-scores by category for full study

ing the tendency for these tweets to originate from Twitter accounts linked to news sources or influential industry experts.

5 Results per sub-category

To investigate whether the entity domain had a bearing on the results, we separated the data into three subsets, airlines, banks and food industry concerns. We performed the same feature selection as in previous experiments, calculating each feature type separately, removing proper nouns, hashtags and account names from the word n-grams, then combining and ranking the features using ten-fold cross validation and information gain. The SVM classifier reported similar results to the main study on the three class problem for each sub-domain, and for the two class problem results ranged between 86-87% accuracy, similar

$$\frac{\text{Number of followers}}{\text{Number following}}(\text{retweets})$$

Figure 3: Twitter weight metric

to the results on the mixed set[7]. Thus, we believe that the individual subdomains do not warrant different classifiers for the problem, indeed examining the top 20-ranked features for each subdomain, there is a large degree of overlap, as seen in bold and italics in Table 6.

Banks	Airlines	Food
@	@	@
my	*NNP_NNP*	**PRP_VBP**
i	**i**	**i**
me	**BOL_IN**	**BOL_IN**
PRP_VBP	**PRP_VBP**	VB_PRP
account	*DT_NN*	BOL_PRP
NNP_VBZ	IN_PRP	HASHASH
VB_PRP	the	**you**
IN_PRP	new	**me**
you	PRP_VBD	know
BOL_RB	NNP_VBZ	my
RB_JJ	IN_DT	i_know
NNP_NNP	**you**	PRP_CC
PRP_VBD	BOL_PRP	used
my_bank	*ISRT*	BOL_CC
DT_NN	it	NNP_CD
NN_PRP	**me**	NN_NNP
VBD_PRP	my	CC_PRP
BOL_IN	RB_RB	*ISRT*
i'm	so	CC_NNP

Table 6: Top twenty ranked features by Information Gain for three domains

6 Conclusions and future directions

6.1 Classification results

We found that accurate categorization of our predefined tweet types was possible using shallow linguistic features. This was aided by Twitter specific metrics but these did not add significantly to the classification accuracy[8]. The lower score (72-73%) in the three class categorization problem is due to the linguistic diversity of the *other* tweet category.

6.2 Annotation and Mechanical Turk

We found the definition of categorization criteria to be an important and challenging step when using Mechanical Turk for annotation. The high degree of annotator disagreement reflected this, however it is important to note that in many cases, tweets fit equally into two or more of our defined categories. The use of extra annotations[9] allowed for agreement to be reached in the majority of cases, however employing more evaluations could have also resulted in deadlock. Examples of ambiguous tweets included: *Cheap marketing tactics. Well, if it ain't broke, why fix it! RT @Ryanair's summer '14 schedule is now on sale!* where a Twitter user has retweeted an official announcement and added their own comment.

Another possible pitfall is that as Mechanical Turk is a US-based service and requires workers to have a US bank account in order to perform work, Turkers tend to be US-based, and therefore an annotation task concerning non-US business entities is perhaps more difficult without sufficient background awareness of the entities in question.

Future experiments will apply the methodology developed here to a larger dataset of tweets, one candidate would be the dataset used in the RepLab 2013 evaluation series which contains 2,200 annotated tweets for 61 business entities in four domains.

Acknowledgments

The authors are grateful to Enterprise Ireland and the IDA for funding this research and CeADAR through their Technology Centre Programme.

Rank	Feature	Rank	Feature
1	@	26	NNP_PRP
2	i	27	NN_PRP
3	PRP_VBP	28	VBP_PRP
4	my	29	when
5	BOL_IN	30	if
6	me	31	don't
7	you	32	PRP_MD
8	NNP_NNP	33	they
9	IN_PRP	34	like
10	VB_PRP	35	PRP_VB
11	PRP_VBD	36	got
12	**WEIGHT**	37	CC_NNP
13	so	38	but
14	NNP_VBZ	39	RB_IN
15	BOL_PRP	40	**RT**
16	RB_JJ	41	with
17	DT_NN	42	PRP_IN
18	BOL_RB	43	a
19	it	44	NNS_RB
20	PRP_RB	45	CC_PRP
21	RB_RB	46	VBD_PRP
22	IN_DT	47	VBD_DT
23	i'm	48	no
24	just	49	the
25	get	50	PRP$_NN

Table 7: Top 50 ranked mixed features for main study

[7]The food subset was highly imbalanced however, containing only 43 customer comments and 313 business operations tweets, the other two subsets were relatively balanced.

[8]ca. 2% decrease in accuracy on removal.

[9]over the initial two annotators

References

Enrique Amigó, Adolfo Corujo, Julio Gonzalo, Edgar Meij, and Maarten de Rijke. 2012. Overview of replab 2012: Evaluating online reputation management systems. In *CLEF (Online Working Notes/Labs/Workshop)*.

Enrique Amigó, Jorge Carrillo de Albornoz, Irina Chugur, Adolfo Corujo, Julio Gonzalo, Tamara Martín, Edgar Meij, Maarten de Rijke, and Damiano Spina. 2013. Overview of replab 2013: Evaluating online reputation monitoring systems. In *Information Access Evaluation. Multilinguality, Multimodality, and Visualization*, pages 333–352. Springer.

Fabrıcio Benevenuto, Gabriel Magno, Tiago Rodrigues, and Virgılio Almeida. 2010. Detecting spammers on twitter. In *Collaboration, electronic messaging, anti-abuse and spam conference (CEAS)*, volume 6.

Mudit Bhargava, Pulkit Mehndiratta, and Krishna Asawa. 2013. Stylometric analysis for authorship attribution on twitter. In *Big Data Analytics*, pages 37–47. Springer International Publishing.

Julian Brooke and Graeme Hirst. 2012. Measuring interlanguage: Native language identification with l1-influence metrics. In *LREC*, pages 779–784.

Mario Cataldi, Luigi Di Caro, and Claudio Schifanella. 2010. Emerging topic detection on twitter based on temporal and social terms evaluation. In *Proceedings of the Tenth International Workshop on Multimedia Data Mining*, page 4. ACM.

Moshe Koppel, Shlomo Argamon, and Anat Rachel Shimoni. 2002. Automatically categorizing written texts by author gender. *Literary and Linguistic Computing*, 17(4):401–412.

Efthymios Kouloumpis, Theresa Wilson, and Johanna Moore. 2011. Twitter sentiment analysis: The good the bad and the omg! In *ICWSM*.

Robert Layton, Paul Watters, and Richard Dazeley. 2010. Authorship attribution for twitter in 140 characters or less. In *Cybercrime and Trustworthy Computing Workshop (CTC), 2010 Second*, pages 1–8. IEEE.

Gerard Lynch and Carl Vogel. 2012. Towards the automatic detection of the source language of a literary translation. In *COLING (Posters)*, pages 775–784.

François Mairesse, Marilyn A Walker, Matthias R Mehl, and Roger K Moore. 2007. Using linguistic cues for the automatic recognition of personality in conversation and text. *J. Artif. Intell. Res.(JAIR)*, 30:457–500.

John O'Donovan, Byungkyu Kang, Greg Meyer, Tobias Hollerer, and Sibel Adalii. 2012. Credibility in context: An analysis of feature distributions in twitter. In *Privacy, Security, Risk and Trust (PASSAT), 2012 International Conference on and 2012 International Confernece on Social Computing (SocialCom)*, pages 293–301. IEEE.

Fernando Perez-Tellez, David Pinto, John Cardiff, and Paolo Rosso. 2011. On the difficulty of clustering microblog texts for online reputation management. In *Proceedings of the 2nd Workshop on Computational Approaches to Subjectivity and Sentiment Analysis*, pages 146–152. Association for Computational Linguistics.

Carolyn Rosé, Yi-Chia Wang, Yue Cui, Jaime Arguello, Karsten Stegmann, Armin Weinberger, and Frank Fischer. 2008. Analyzing collaborative learning processes automatically: Exploiting the advances of computational linguistics in computer-supported collaborative learning. *International journal of computer-supported collaborative learning*, 3(3):237–271.

Takeshi Sakaki, Makoto Okazaki, and Yutaka Matsuo. 2010. Earthquake shakes twitter users: real-time event detection by social sensors. In *Proceedings of the 19th international conference on World wide web*, pages 851–860. ACM.

Damiano Spina, Julio Gonzalo, and Enrique Amigó. 2013. Discovering filter keywords for company name disambiguation in twitter. *Expert Systems with Applications*.

Hans van Halteren. 2008. Source language markers in europarl translations. In *Proceedings of the 22nd International Conference on Computational Linguistics-Volume 1*, pages 937–944. Association for Computational Linguistics.

Carl Vogel, Ger Lynch, Erwan Moreau, Liliana Mamani Sanchez, and Phil Ritchie. 2013. Found in translation: Computational discovery of translation effects. *Translation Spaces*, 2(1):81–104.

Jianshu Weng and Bu-Sung Lee. 2011. Event detection in twitter. In *ICWSM*.

Surender Reddy Yerva, Zoltán Miklós, and Karl Aberer. 2011. What have fruits to do with technology?: the case of orange, blackberry and apple. In *Proceedings of the International Conference on Web Intelligence, Mining and Semantics*, page 48. ACM.

Credibility Adjusted Term Frequency: A Supervised Term Weighting Scheme for Sentiment Analysis and Text Classification

Yoon Kim
New York University
yhk255@nyu.edu

Owen Zhang
zhonghua.zhang2006@gmail.com

Abstract

We provide a simple but novel supervised weighting scheme for adjusting term frequency in *tf-idf* for sentiment analysis and text classification. We compare our method to baseline weighting schemes and find that it outperforms them on multiple benchmarks. The method is robust and works well on both snippets and longer documents.

1 Introduction

Baseline discriminative methods for text classification usually involve training a linear classifier over bag-of-words (BoW) representations of documents. In BoW representations (also known as Vector Space Models), a document is represented as a vector where each entry is a count (or binary count) of tokens that occurred in the document. Given that some tokens are more informative than others, a common technique is to apply a weighting scheme to give more weight to discriminative tokens and less weight to non-discriminative ones. Term frequency-inverse document frequency (*tf-idf*) (Salton and McGill, 1983) is an unsupervised weighting technique that is commonly employed. In *tf-idf*, each token i in document d is assigned the following weight,

$$w_{i,d} = tf_{i,d} \cdot \log \frac{N}{df_i} \tag{1}$$

where $tf_{i,d}$ is the number of times token i occurred in document d, N is the number of documents in the corpus, and df_i is the number of documents in which token i occurred.

Many supervised and unsupervised variants of *tf-idf* exist (Debole and Sebastiani (2003); Martineau and Finin (2009); Wang and Zhang (2013)). The purpose of this paper is not to perform an exhaustive comparison of existing weighting schemes, and hence we do not list them here. Interested readers are directed to Paltoglou and Thelwall (2010) and Deng et al. (2014) for comprehensive reviews of the different schemes.

In the present work, we propose a simple but novel supervised method to adjust the term frequency portion in *tf-idf* by assigning a credibility adjusted score to each token. We find that it outperforms the traditional unsupervised *tf-idf* weighting scheme on multiple benchmarks. The benchmarks include both snippets and longer documents. We also compare our method against Wang and Manning (2012)'s Naive-Bayes Support Vector Machine (NBSVM), which has achieved state-of-the-art results (or close to it) on many datasets, and find that it performs competitively against NBSVM. We additionally find that the traditional *tf-idf* performs competitively against other, more sophisticated methods when used with the right scaling and normalization parameters.

2 The Method

Consider a binary classification task. Let $C_{i,k}$ be the count of token i in class k, with $k \in \{-1, 1\}$. Denote C_i to be the count of token i over both classes, and $y^{(d)}$ to be the class of document d. For each occurrence of token i in the training set, we calculate the following,

$$s_i^{(j)} = \begin{cases} \frac{C_{i,1}}{C_i} & \text{, if } y^{(d)} = 1 \\ \frac{C_{i,-1}}{C_i} & \text{, if } y^{(d)} = -1 \end{cases} \tag{2}$$

Here, j is the j-th occurrence of token i. Since there are C_i such occurrences, j indexes from 1 to C_i. We assign a score to token i by,

$$\hat{s}_i = \frac{1}{C_i} \sum_{j=1}^{C_i} s_i^{(j)} \tag{3}$$

Intuitively, $\hat{s}_i$ is the average likelihood of making the correct classification given token i's occurrence in the document, if i was the only token in

Proceedings of the 5th Workshop on Computational Approaches to Subjectivity, Sentiment and Social Media Analysis, pages 79–83,
Baltimore, Maryland, USA. June 27, 2014.

the document. In a binary classification case, this reduces to,

$$\hat{s}_i = \frac{C_{i,1}^2 + C_{i,-1}^2}{C_i^2} \tag{4}$$

Note that by construction, the support of $\hat{s}_i$ is $[0.5, 1]$.

2.1 Credibility Adjustment

Suppose $\hat{s}_i = \hat{s}_j = 0.75$ for two different tokens i and j, but $C_i = 5$ and $C_j = 100$. Intuition suggests that $\hat{s}_j$ is a more credible score than $\hat{s}_i$, and that $\hat{s}_i$ should be shrunk towards the population mean. Let $\hat{s}$ be the (weighted) population mean. That is,

$$\hat{s} = \sum_i \frac{C_i \cdot \hat{s}_i}{C} \tag{5}$$

where C is the count of all tokens in the corpus. We define *credibility adjusted score* for token i to be,

$$\overline{s}_i = \frac{C_{i,1}^2 + C_{i,-1}^2 + \hat{s} \cdot \gamma}{C_i^2 + \gamma} \tag{6}$$

where γ is an additive smoothing parameter. If $C_{i,k}$'s are small, then $\overline{s}_i \approx \hat{s}$ (otherwise, $\overline{s}_i \approx \hat{s}_i$). This is a form of Buhlmann credibility adjustment from the actuarial literature (Buhlmann and Gisler, 2005). We subsequently define $\overline{tf}$, the *credibility adjusted term frequency*, to be,

$$\overline{tf}_{i,d} = (0.5 + \hat{s}_i) \cdot tf_{i,d} \tag{7}$$

and tf is replaced with $\overline{tf}$. That is,

$$w_{i,d} = \overline{tf}_{i,d} \cdot \log \frac{N}{df_i} \tag{8}$$

We refer to above as *cred-tf-idf* hereafter.

2.2 Sublinear Scaling

It is common practice to apply sublinear scaling to tf. A word occurring (say) ten times more in a document is unlikely to be ten times as important. Paltoglou and Thelwall (2010) confirm that sublinear scaling of term frequency results in significant improvements in various text classification tasks. We employ logarithmic scaling, where tf is replaced with $\log(tf) + 1$. For our method, $\overline{tf}$ is simply replaced with $\log(\overline{tf}) + 1$. We found virtually no difference in performance between log scaling and other sublinear scaling methods (such as augmented scaling, where tf is replaced with $0.5 + \frac{0.5+tf}{\max tf}$).

2.3 Normalization

Using normalized features resulted in substantial improvements in performance versus using un-normalized features. We thus use $\hat{\mathbf{x}}^{(d)} = \mathbf{x}^{(d)}/||\mathbf{x}^{(d)}||_2$ in the SVM, where $\mathbf{x}^{(d)}$ is the feature vector obtained from *cred-tf-idf* weights for document d.

2.4 Naive-Bayes SVM (NBSVM)

Wang and Manning (2012) achieve excellent (sometimes state-of-the-art) results on many benchmarks using binary Naive Bayes (NB) log-count ratios as features in an SVM. In their framework,

$$w_{i,d} = \mathbf{1}\{tf_{i,d}\} \log \frac{(df_{i,1} + \alpha)/\sum_i (df_{i,1} + \alpha)}{(df_{i,-1} + \alpha)/\sum_i (df_{i,-1} + \alpha)} \tag{9}$$

where $df_{i,k}$ is the number of documents that contain token i in class k, α is a smoothing parameter, and $\mathbf{1}\{\cdot\}$ is the indicator function equal to one if $tf_{i,d} > 0$ and zero otherwise. As an additional benchmark, we implement NBSVM with $\alpha = 1.0$ and compare against our results.[1]

3 Datasets and Experimental Setup

We test our method on both long and short text classification tasks, all of which were used to establish baselines in Wang and Manning (2012). Table 1 has summary statistics of the datasets. The snippet datasets are:

- **PL-sh**: Short movie reviews with one sentence per review. Classification involves detecting whether a review is positive or negative. (Pang and Lee, 2005).[2]

- **PL-sub**: Dataset with short subjective movie reviews and objective plot summaries. Classification task is to detect whether the sentence is objective or subjective. (Pang and Lee, 2004).

And the longer document datasets are:

[1] Wang and Manning (2012) use the same α but they differ from our NBSVM in two ways. One, they use l_2 hinge loss (as opposed to l_1 loss in this paper). Two, they interpolate NBSVM weights with Multivariable Naive Bayes (MNB) weights to get the final weight vector. Further, their tokenization is slightly different. Hence our NBSVM results are not directly comparable. We list their results in table 2.

[2] https://www.cs.cornell.edu/people/pabo/movie-review-data/. All the PL datasets are available here.

Dataset	Length	Pos	Neg	Test
PL-sh	21	5331	5331	CV
PL-sub	24	5000	5000	CV
PL-2k	746	1000	1000	CV
IMDB	231	12.5k	12.5k	25k
AthR	355	480	377	570
XGraph	276	584	593	784

Table 1: Summary statistics for the datasets. Length is the average number of unigram tokens (including punctuation) per document. Pos/Neg is the number of positive/negative documents in the training set. Test is the number of documents in the test set (CV means that there is no separate test set for this dataset and thus a 10-fold cross-validation was used to calculate errors).

- **PL-2k**: 2000 full-length movie reviews that has become the de facto benchmark for sentiment analysis (Pang and Lee, 2004).
- **IMDB**: 50k full-length movie reviews (25k training, 25k test), from IMDB (Maas et al., 2011).[3]
- **AthR, XGraph**: The 20-Newsgroup dataset, 2nd version with headers removed.[4] Classification task is to classify which topic a document belongs to. AthR: alt.atheism vs religion.misc, XGraph: comp.windows.x vs comp.graphics.

3.1 Support Vector Machine (SVM)

For each document, we construct the feature vector $\mathbf{x}^{(d)}$ using weights obtained from *cred-tf-idf* with log scaling and l_2 normalization. For *cred-tf-idf*, γ is set to 1.0. NBSVM and *tf-idf* (also with log scaling and l_2 normalization) are used to establish baselines. Prediction for a test document is given by

$$y^{(d)} = \text{sign}\,(\mathbf{w}^T\mathbf{x}^{(d)} + b) \quad (10)$$

In all experiments, we use a Support Vector Machine (SVM) with a linear kernel and penalty parameter of $C = 1.0$. For the SVM, $\mathbf{w}$, b are obtained by minimizing,

$$\mathbf{w}^T\mathbf{w} + C\sum_{d=1}^{N} \max(0, 1 - y^{(d)}(\mathbf{w}^T\mathbf{x}^{(d)} + b)) \quad (11)$$

using the LIBLINEAR library (Fan et al., 2008).

[3]http://ai.stanford.edu/ amaas/data/sentiment/index.html
[4]http://people.csail.mit.edu/jrennie/20Newsgroups

3.2 Tokenization

We lower-case all words but do not perform any stemming or lemmatization. We restrict the vocabulary to all tokens that occurred at least twice in the training set.

4 Results and Discussion

For PL datasets, there are no separate test sets and hence we use 10-fold cross validation (as do other published results) to estimate errors. The standard train-test splits are used on IMDB and Newsgroup datasets.

4.1 *cred-tf-idf* outperforms *tf-idf*

Table 2 has the comparison of results for the different datasets. Our method outperforms the traditional *tf-idf* on all benchmarks for both unigrams and bigrams. While some of the differences in performance are significant at the 0.05 level (e.g. IMDB), some are not (e.g. PL-2k). The Wilcoxon signed ranks test is a non-parametric test that is often used in cases where two classifiers are compared over multiple datasets (Demsar, 2006). The Wilcoxon signed ranks test indicates that the overall outperformance is significant at the $<$0.01 level.

4.2 NBSVM outperforms *cred-tf-idf*

cred-tf-idf did not outperform Wang and Manning (2012)'s NBSVM (Wilcoxon signed ranks test p-value = 0.1). But it did outperform our own implementation of NBSVM, implying that the extra modifications by Wang and Manning (2012) (i.e. using squared hinge loss in the SVM and interpolating between NBSVM and MNB weights) are important contributions of their methodology. This was especially true in the case of shorter documents, where our uninterpolated NBSVM performed significantly worse than their interpolated NBSVM.

4.3 *tf-idf* still performs well

We find that *tf-idf* still performs remarkably well with the right scaling and normalization parameters. Indeed, the traditional *tf-idf* outperformed many of the more sophisticated methods that employ distributed representations (Maas et al. (2011); Socher et al. (2011)) or other weighting schemes (Martineau and Finin (2009); Deng et al. (2014)).

	Method	PL-sh	PL-sub	PL-2k	IMDB	AthR	XGraph
Our results	tf-idf-uni	77.1	91.5	88.1	88.6	85.8	88.4
	tf-idf-bi	78.0	92.3	89.2	90.9	86.5	88.0
	cred-tfidf-uni	77.5	91.8	88.7	88.8	86.5	89.8
	cred-tfidf-bi	78.6	**92.8**	**89.7**	**91.3**	**87.4**	88.9
	NBSVM-uni	75.5	89.9	87.0	85.9	86.7	88.5
	NBSVM-bi	76.0	90.5	89.5	90.5	86.7	88.1
Wang & Manning	MNB-uni	77.9	92.6	83.5	83.6	85.0	90.0
	MNB-bi	**79.0**	**93.6**	85.9	86.6	85.1	**91.2**
	NBSVM-uni	78.1	92.4	87.8	88.3	**87.9**	**91.2**
	NBSVM-bi	**79.4**	**93.2**	**89.5**	**91.2**	**87.7**	**90.7**
Other results	Appr. Tax.*	-	-	90.2	-	-	-
	Str. SVM*	-	-	92.4	-	-	-
	aug-tf-mi	-	-	87.8	88.0	-	-
	Disc. Conn.	-	-	-	**91.4**	-	-
	Word Vec.*	-	88.6	88.9	88.9	-	-
	LLR	-	-	**90.4**	-	-	-
	RAE	77.7	-	-	-	-	-
	MV-RNN	**79.0**	-	-	-	-	-

Table 2: Results of our method (*cred-tf-idf*) against baselines (*tf-idf*, NBSVM), using unigrams and bigrams. *cred-tf-idf* and *tf-idf* both use log scaling and l_2 normalization. Best results (that do not use external sources) are underlined, while top three are in bold. Rows 7-11 are MNB and NBSVM results from Wang and Manning (2012). Our NBSVM results are not directly comparable to theirs (see footnote 1). Methods with * use external data or software. **Appr. Tax**: Uses appraisal taxonomies from *WordNet* (Whitelaw et al., 2005). **Str. SVM**: Uses *OpinionFinder* to find objective versus subjective parts of the review (Yessenalina et al., 2010). **aug-tf-mi**: Uses augmented term-frequency with mutual information gain (Deng et al., 2014). **Disc. Conn.**: Uses discourse connectors to generate additional features (Trivedi and Eisenstein, 2013). **Word Vec.**: Learns sentiment-specific word vectors to use as features combined with BoW features (Maas et al., 2011). **LLR**: Uses log-likelihood ratio on features to select features (Aue and Gamon, 2005). **RAE**: Recursive autoencoders (Socher et al., 2011). **MV-RNN**: Matrix-Vector Recursive Neural Networks (Socher et al., 2012).

5 Conclusions and Future Work

In this paper we presented a novel supervised weighting scheme, which we call *credibility adjusted term frequency*, to perform sentiment analysis and text classification. Our method outperforms the traditional *tf-idf* weighting scheme on multiple benchmarks, which include both snippets and longer documents. We also showed that *tf-idf* is competitive against other state-of-the-art methods with the right scaling and normalization parameters.

From a performance standpoint, it would be interesting to see if our method is able to achieve even better results on the above tasks with proper tuning of the γ parameter. Relatedly, our method could potentially be combined with other supervised variants of *tf-idf*, either directly or through ensembling, to improve performance further.

References

A. Aue, M. Gamon. 2005. Customizing sentiment classifiers to new domains: A case study. *Proceedings of the International Conference on Recent Advances in NLP, 2011.*

H. Buhlmann, A. Gisler. 2005. A Course in Credibility Theory and its Applications *Springer-Verlag, Berlin.*

F. Debole, F. Sebastiani. 2003. Supervised Term Weighting for Automated Text Categorization *Proceedings of the 2003 ACM symposium on Applied Computing. 784–788.*

J. Demsar. 2006. Statistical Comparison of classifiers over multiple data sets. *Journal of Machine Learning Research, 7:1-30. 2006.*

Z. Deng, K. Luo, H. Yu. 2014. A study of supervised term weighting scheme for sentiment analysis *Ex-*

pert Systems with Applications. Volume 41, Issue 7, 3506–3513.

R. Fan, K. Chang, J. Hsieh, X. Wang, C. Lin. 2008. LIBLINEAR: A library for large linear classification. *Journal of Machine Learning Research, 9:1871–1874, June.*

A. Maas, R. Daly, P. Pham, D. Huang, A. Ng, C. Potts. 2011. Learning Word Vectors for Sentiment Analysis. *In Proceedings of ACL 2011.*

J. Martineau, T. Finin. 2009. Delta TFIDF: An Improved Feature Space for Sentiment Analysis. *Third AAAI International Conference on Weblogs and Social Media*

G. Paltoglou, M. Thelwall. 2010. A study of Information Retrieval weighting schemes for sentiment analysis. *In Proceedings of ACL 2010.*

B. Pang, L. Lee. 2004. A sentimental education: Sentiment analysis using subjectivity summarization based on minimum cuts. *In Proceedings of ACL 2004.*

B. Pang, L. Lee. 2005. Seeing stars: Exploiting class relationships for sentiment categorization with respect to rating scales. *In Proceedings of ACL 2005.*

R. Socher, J. Pennington, E. Huang, A. Ng, C. Manning. 2011. Semi-Supervised Recursive Autoencoders for Predicting Sentiment Distributions. *In Proceedings of EMNLP 2011.*

R. Socher, B. Huval, C. Manning, A. Ng. 2012. Semantic Compositionality through Recursive Matrix-Vector Spaces. *In Proceedings of EMNLP 2012.*

R. Trivedi, J. Eisenstein. 2013. Discourse Connectors for Latent Subjectivity in Sentiment Analysis. *In Proceedings of NAACL 2011.*

G. Salton, M. McGill. 1983. Introduction to Modern Information Retrieval. *McGraw-Hill.*

S. Wang, C. Manning. 2012. Baselines and Bigrams: Simple, Good Sentiment and Topic Classification. *In proceedings of ACL 2012.*

D. Wang, H. Zhang. 2013. Inverse-Category-Frequency Based Supervised Term Weighting Schemes for Text Categorization. *Journal of Information Science and Engineering 29, 209–225.*

C. Whitelaw, N. Garg, S. Argamon. 2005. Using appraisal taxonomies for sentiment analysis. *In Proceedings of CIKM 2005.*

A. Yessenalina, Y. Yue, C. Cardie. 2010. Multi-level Structured Models for Document-level Sentiment Classification. *In Proceedings of ACL 2010.*

Opinion Mining and Topic Categorization with Novel Term Weighting

Tatiana Gasanova
Institute of Communications Engineering, Ulm University, Germany
tatiana.gasanova@uni-ulm.de

Roman Sergienko
Institute of Communications Engineering, Ulm University, Germany
roman.sergienko@uni-ulm.de

Shakhnaz Akhmedova
Institute of Computer Science and Telecommunications, Siberian State Aerospace University, Russia
shahnaz@inbox.ru

Eugene Semenkin
Institute of Computer Science and Telecommunications, Siberian State Aerospace University, Russia
eugenesemenkin@yandex.com

Wolfgang Minker
Institute of Communications Engineering, Ulm University, Germany
wolfgang.minker@uni-ulm.de

Abstract

In this paper we investigate the efficiency of the novel term weighting algorithm for opinion mining and topic categorization of articles from newspapers and Internet. We compare the novel term weighting technique with existing approaches such as TF-IDF and ConfWeight. The performance on the data from the text-mining campaigns DEFT'07 and DEFT'08 shows that the proposed method can compete with existing information retrieval models in classification quality and that it is computationally faster. The proposed text preprocessing method can be applied in large-scale information retrieval and data mining problems and it can be easily transported to different domains and different languages since it does not require any domain-related or linguistic information.

1 Introduction

Nowadays, Internet and social media generate a huge amount of textual information. It is increasingly important to develop methods of text processing such as text classification. Text classification is very important for such problems as automatic opining mining (sentiment analysis) and topic categorization of different articles from newspapers and Internet.

Text classification can be considered to be a part of natural language understanding, where there is a set of predefined categories and the task is to automatically assign new documents to one of these categories. The method of text preprocessing and text representation influences the results that are obtained even with the same classification algorithms.

The most popular model for text classification is vector space model. In this case text categorization may be considered as a machine learning problem. Complexity of text categorization with vector space model is compounded by the need to extract the numerical data from text information before applying machine learning methods. Therefore text categorization consists of two parts: text preprocessing and classification using obtained numerical data.

All text preprocessing methods are based on the idea that the category of the document depends on the words or phrases from this document. The simplest approach is to take each word of the document as a binary coordinate and the dimension of the feature space will be the number of words in our dictionary.

There exist more advanced approaches for text preprocessing to overcome this problem such as TF-IDF (Salton and Buckley, 1988) and ConfWeight methods (Soucy and Mineau, 2005). A novel term weighting method (Gasanova et al., 2013) is also considered, which has

Proceedings of the 5th Workshop on Computational Approaches to Subjectivity, Sentiment and Social Media Analysis, pages 84–89,
Baltimore, Maryland, USA. June 27, 2014. ©2014 Association for Computational Linguistics

some similarities with the ConfWeight method, but has improved computational efficiency. It is important to notice that we use no morphological or stop-word filtering before text preprocessing. It means that the text preprocessing can be performed without expert or linguistic knowledge and that the text preprocessing is language-independent.

In this paper we have used *k*-nearest neighbors algorithm, Bayes Classifier, support vector machine (SVM) generated and optimized with COBRA (Co-Operation of Biology Related Algorithms) which has been proposed by Akhmedova and Semenkin (2013), Rocchio Classifier or Nearest Centroid Algorithm (Rocchio, 1971) and Neural Network as classification methods. *RapidMiner* and *Microsoft Visual Studio C++ 2010* have been used as implementation software.

For the application of algorithms and comparison of the results we have used the DEFT ("Défi Fouille de Texte") Evaluation Package 2008 (Proceedings of the 4th DEFT Workshop, 2008) which has been provided by ELRA and publically available corpora from DEFT'07 (Proceedings of the 3rd DEFT Workshop, 2007).

The main aim of this work is to evaluate the competitiveness of the novel term weighting (Gasanova et al., 2013) in comparison with the state-of-the-art techniques for opining mining and topic categorization. The criteria using in the evaluation are classification quality and computational efficiency.

This paper is organized as follows: in Section 2, we describe details of the corpora. Section 3 presents text preprocessing methods. In Section 4 we describe the classification algorithms which we have used to compare different text preprocessing techniques. Section 5 reports on the experimental results. Finally, we provide concluding remarks in Section 6.

2 Corpora Description

The focus of DEFT 2007 campaign is the sentiment analysis, also called opinion mining. We have used 3 publically available corpora: reviews on books and movies (*Books*), reviews on video games (*Games*) and political debates about energy project (*Debates*).

The topic of DEFT 2008 edition is related to the text classification by categories and genres. The data consists of two corpora (T1 and T2) containing articles of two genres: articles extracted from French daily newspaper Le Monde and encyclopedic articles from Wikipedia in French language. This paper reports on the results obtained using both tasks of the campaign and focuses on detecting the category.

Corpus	Size	Classes
Books	Train size = 2074 Test size = 1386 Vocabulary = 52507	0: negative, 1: neutral, 2: positive
Games	Train size = 2537 Test size = 1694 Vocabulary = 63144	0: negative, 1: neutral, 2: positive
Debates	Train size = 17299 Test size = 11533 Vocabulary = 59615	0: against, 1: for

Table 1. Corpora description (DEFT'07)

Corpus	Size	Classes
T1	Train size = 15223 Test size = 10596 Vocabulary = 202979	0: Sport, 1: Economy, 2: Art, 3: Television
T2	Train size = 23550 Test size = 15693 Vocabulary = 262400	0: France, 1: International, 2: Literature, 3: Science, 4: Society

Table 2. Corpora description (DEFT'08)

All databases are divided into a training (60% of the whole number of articles) and a test set (40%). To apply our algorithms we extracted all words which appear in the training set regardless of the letter case and we also excluded dots, commas and other punctual signs. We have not used any additional filtering as excluding the stop or ignore words.

3 Text Preprocessing Methods

3.1 Binary preprocessing

We take each word of the document as a binary coordinate and the size of the feature space will be the size of our vocabulary ("bag of words").

3.2 TF-IDF

TF-IDF is a well-known approach for text preprocessing based on multiplication of term frequency tf_{ij} (ratio between the number of times the ith word occurs in the jth document and the document size) and inverse document frequency idf_i.

$$tf_{ij} = \frac{t_{ij}}{T_j}, \tag{1}$$

where t_{ij} is the number of times the ith word occurs in the jth document. T_j is the document size (number of the words in the document).

There are different ways to calculate the weight of each word. In this paper we run classification algorithms with the following variants.

1) TF-IDF 1

$$idf_i = log\frac{|D|}{n_i}, \quad (2)$$

where $|D|$ is the number of document in the training set and n_i is the number of documents that have the ith word.

2) TF-IDF 2

The formula is given by equation (2) except n_i is calculated as the number of times i^{th} word appears in all documents from the training set.

3) TF-IDF 3

$$idf_i = \left(\frac{|D|}{n_i}\right)^{\alpha}, \alpha \in (0,1), \quad (3)$$

where n_i is calculated as in TF-IDF 1 and α is the parameter (in this paper we have tested α = 0.1, 0.5, 0.9).

4) TF-IDF 4

The formula is given by equation (3) except n_i is calculated as in TF-IDF 4.

3.3 ConfWeight

Maximum Strength (Maxstr) is an alternative method to find the word weights. This approach has been proposed by Soucy and Mineau (2005). It implicitly does feature selection since all frequent words have zero weights. The main idea of the method is that the feature f has a non-zero weight in class c only if the f frequency in documents of the c class is greater than the f frequency in all other classes.

The ConfWeight method uses Maxstr as an analog of IDF:

$$ConfWeight_{ij} = log(tf_{ij} + 1) * Maxstr(i).$$

Numerical experiments (Soucy and Mineau, 2005) have shown that the ConfWeight method could be more effective than TF-IDF with SVM and *k*-NN as classification methods. The main drawback of the ConfWeight method is computational complexity. This method is more computationally demanding than TF-IDF method because the ConfWeight method requires time-consuming statistical calculations such as Student distribution calculation and confidence interval definition for each word.

3.4 Novel Term Weighting (TW)

The main idea of the method (Gasanova et al., 2013) is similar to ConfWeight but it is not so time-consuming. The idea is that every word that appears in the article has to contribute some value to the certain class and the class with the biggest value we define as a winner for this article.

For each term we assign a real number term relevance that depends on the frequency in utterances. Term weight is calculated using a modified formula of fuzzy rules relevance estimation for fuzzy classifiers (Ishibuchi et al., 1999). Membership function has been replaced by word frequency in the current class. The details of the procedure are the following:

Let L be the number of classes; n_i is the number of articles which belong to the ith class; N_{ij} is the number of the jth word occurrence in all articles from the ith class; $T_{ij} = N_{ij} / n_i$ is the relative frequency of the jth word occurrence in the ith class.

$R_j = \max_i T_{ij}$, $S_j = \arg(\max_i T_{ij})$ is the number of class which we assign to the jth word;

The term relevance, C_j, is given by

$$C_j = \frac{1}{\sum_{i=1}^{L} T_{ji}} (R_j - \frac{1}{L-1} \sum_{\substack{i=1 \\ i \neq S_j}}^{L} T_{ij}). \quad (4)$$

C_j is higher if the word occurs more often in one class than if it appears in many classes. We use novel TW as an analog of IDF for text preprocessing.

The learning phase consists of counting the C values for each term; it means that this algorithm uses the statistical information obtained from the training set.

4 Classification Methods

We have considered 11 different text preprocessing methods (4 modifications of TF-IDF, two of them with three different values of α parameter, binary representation, ConfWeight and the novel TW method) and compared them using different classification algorithms. The methods have been implemented using *RapidMiner* (Shafait, 2010) and *Microsoft Visual Studio C++ 2010* for Rocchio classifier and SVM. The classification methods are:

- *k*-nearest neighbors algorithm with distance weighting (we have varied k from 1 to 15);
- kernel Bayes classifier with Laplace correction;
- neural network with error back propagation (standard setting in *RapidMiner*);
- Rocchio classifier with different metrics and γ parameter;

- support vector machine (SVM) generated and optimized with Co-Operation of Biology Related Algorithms (COBRA).

Rocchio classifier (Rocchio, 1971) is a well-known classifier based on the search of the nearest centroid. For each category we calculate a weighted centroid:

$$g_c = \frac{1}{|v_c|}\sum_{d \in v_c} d - \gamma \frac{1}{|\overline{v_{c,k}}|}\sum_{d \in \overline{v_{c,k}}} d,$$

where v_c is a set of documents which belong to the class c; $\overline{v_{c,k}}$ are k documents which do not belong to the class c and which are close to the centroid $\frac{1}{|v_c|}\sum_{d \in v_c} d$; γ is parameter corresponds to relative importance of negative precedents. The given document is put to the class with the nearest centroid. In this work we have applied Rocchio classifier with $\gamma \in (0.1; 0.9)$ and with three different metrics: taxicab distance, Euclidean metric and cosine similarity.

COBRA is a new meta-heuristic algorithm which has been proposed by Akhmedova and Semenkin (2013). It is based on cooperation of biology inspired algorithms such as Particle Swarm Optimization (Kennedy and Eberhart, 1995), Wolf Pack Search Algorithm (Yang, 2007), Firefly Algorithm (Yang, 2008), Cuckoo Search Algorithm (Yang and Deb, 2009) and Bat Algorithm (Yang, 2010). For generating SVM-machine the original COBRA is used: each individual in all populations represents a set of kernel function's parameters α, β, d. Then for each individual constrained modification of COBRA is applied for finding vector w and shift factor b. And finally individual that showed the best classification rate is chosen as the designed classifier.

5 Experimental Results

The DEFT ("Défi Fouille de Texte") Evaluation Package 2008 and publically available corpora from DEFT'07 (*Books*, *Games* and *Debates*) have been used for algorithms application and results comparison. In order to evaluate obtained results with the campaign participants we have to use the same measure of classification quality: precision, recall and F-score.

Precision for each class i is calculated as the number of correctly classified articles for class i divided by the number of all articles which algorithm assigned for this class. Recall is the number of correctly classified articles for class i divided by the number of articles that should have been in this class. Overall precision and recall are calculated as the arithmetic mean of the precisions and recalls for all classes (macro-average). F-score is calculated as the harmonic mean of precision and recall.

Tables 3-7 present the F-scores obtained on the test corpora. The best values for each problem are shown in bold. Results of the all classification algorithms are presented with the best parameters. We also present for each corpus only the best TF-IDF modification.

Classification algorithm	Binary	TF-IDF	Conf Weight	Novel TW
Bayes	0.489	0.506	0.238	0.437
k-NN	0.488	0.517	0.559	0.488
Rocchio	0.479	0.498	0.557	0.537
SVM (COBRA)	0.558	0.580	0.588	**0.619**
Neural network	0.475	0.505	0.570	0.493

Table 3. Classification results for *Books*

Classification algorithm	Binary	TF-IDF	Conf Weight	Novel TW
Bayes	0.653	0.652	0.210	0.675
k-NN	0.703	0.701	**0.720**	0.700
Rocchio	0.659	0.678	0.717	0.712
SVM (COBRA)	0.682	0.687	0.645	0.696
Neural network	0.701	0.679	0.717	0.691

Table 4. Classification results for *Games*

Classification algorithm	Binary	TF-IDF	Conf Weight	Novel TW
Bayes	0.555	0.645	0.363	0.616
k-NN	0.645	0.648	0.695	0.695
Rocchio	0.636	0.646	0.697	0.696
SVM (COBRA)	0.673	0.669	**0.714**	0.700
Neural network	0.656	0.647	0.705	0.697

Table 5. Classification results for *Debates*

Classification algorithm	Binary	TF-IDF	Conf Weight	Novel TW
Bayes	0.501	0.690	0.837	0.794
k-NN	0.800	0.816	0.855	0.837
Rocchio	0.794	0.825	0.853	0.838
SVM (COBRA)	0.788	0.827	0.840	**0.856**
Neural network	0.783	0.830	0.853	0.854

Table 6. Classification results for *T1*

Classification algorithm	Binary	TF-IDF	Conf Weight	Novel TW
Bayes	0.569	0.728	0.712	0.746
k-NN	0.728	0.786	0.785	0.811
Rocchio	0.765	0.825	0.803	0.834
SVM (COBRA)	0.794	0.837	0.813	**0.851**
Neural network	0.799	0.838	0.820	0.843

Table 7. Classification results for *T2*

We can see from the Tables 3-7 that the best F-scores have been obtained with either ConfWeight or novel Term Weighting preprocessing. The algorithm performances on the *Games* and *Debates* corpora achieved the best results with ConfWeight; however, we can see that the F-scores obtained with novel Term Weighting preprocessing are very similar (0.712 and 0.720 for *Games*; 0.700 and 0.714 for *Debates*). Almost all best results have been obtained with SVM except the *Games* database where we achieved the highest F-score with *k*-NN algorithm.

This paper focuses on the text preprocessing methods which do not require language or domain-related information; therefore, we have not tried to achieve the best possible classification quality. However, the result obtained on *Books* corpus with novel TW preprocessing and SVM (generated using COBRA) as classification algorithm has reached 0.619 F-score which is higher than the best known performance 0.603 (Proceedings of the 3rd DEFT Workshop, 2007). Performances on other corpora have achieved close F-score values to the best submissions of the DEFT'07 and DEFT'08 participants.

We have also measured computational efficiency of each text preprocessing technique. We have run each method 20 times using the Baden-Württemberg Grid (bwGRiD) Cluster Ulm (Every blade comprehends two 4-Core Intel Harpertown CPUs with 2.83 GHz and 16 GByte RAM). After that we calculated average values and checked statistical significance of the results.

Figure 1 and Figure 2 compare average computational time in minutes for different preprocessing methods applied on DEFT'07 and DEFT'08 corpora.

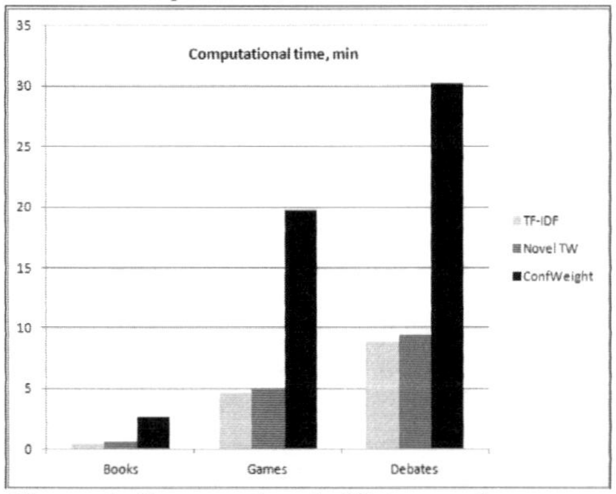

Figure 1. Computational efficiency of text preprocessing methods (DEFT'07)

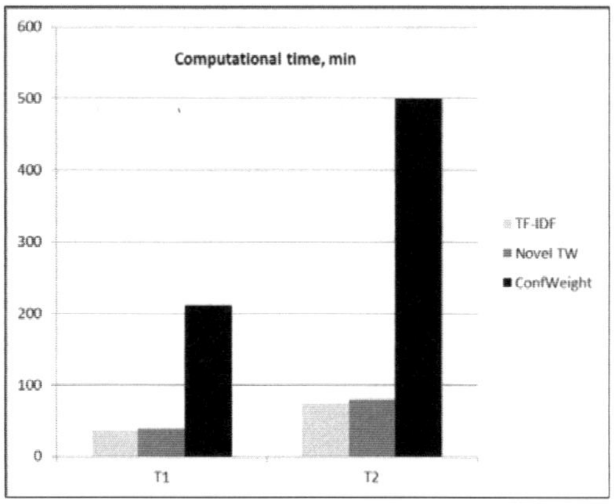

Figure 2. Computational efficiency of text preprocessing methods (DEFT'08)

The average value for all TF-IDF modifications is presented because the time variation for the modifications is not significant.

We can see in Figure 1 and Figure 2 that TF-IDF and novel TW require almost the same computational time. The most time-consuming method is ConfWeight (CW). It requires approximately six times more time than TF-IDF and novel TW for DEFT'08 corpora and about three-four times more time than TF-IDF and novel TW for DEFT'07 databases.

6 Conclusion

This paper reported on text classification experiments on 5 different corpora of opinion mining and topic categorization using several classification methods with different text preprocessing. We have used "bag of words", TF-IDF modifications, ConfWeight and the novel term weighting approach as preprocessing techniques. *K*-nearest neighbors algorithms, Bayes classifier, Rocchio classifier, support vector machine trained by COBRA and Neural Network have been applied as classification algorithms.

The novel term weighting method gives similar or better classification quality than the ConfWeight method but it requires the same amount of time as TF-IDF. Almost all best results have been obtained with SVM generated and optimized with Co-Operation of Biology Related Algorithms (COBRA).

We can conclude that numerical experiments have shown computational and classification efficiency of the proposed method (the novel TW) in comparison with existing text preprocessing techniques for opinion mining and topic categorization.

References

Akhmedova Sh. and Semenkin E. 2013. Co-Operation of Biology Related Algorithms. *Proceedings of the IEEE Congress on Evolutionary Computation (CEC 2013)*:2207-2214.

Association Française d'Intelligence Artificielle. 2007. *Proceedings of the 3rd DEFT Workshop. DEFT '07*. AFIA, Grenoble, France.

Gasanova T., Sergienko R., Minker W., Semenkin E. and Zhukov E. 2013. A Semi-supervised Approach for Natural Language Call Routing. *Proceedings of the SIGDIAL 2013 Conference*:344-348.

Ishibuchi H., Nakashima T., and Murata T. 1999. Performance evaluation of fuzzy classifier systems for multidimensional pattern classification problems. *IEEE Trans. on Systems, Man, and Cybernetics*, 29:601-618.

Kennedy J. and Eberhart R. 1995. Particle Swarm Optimization. *Proceedings of IEEE International Conference on Neural Networks*:1942-1948.

Le traitement automatique du langage naturel ou de la langue naturelle. 2008. *Proceedings of the 4th DEFT Workshop. DEFT '08*. TALN, Avignon, France.

Salton G. and Buckley C. 1988. Term-Weighting Approaches in Automatic Text Retrieval. *Information Processing and Management*:513-523.

Shafait F., Reif M., Kofler C., and Breuel T. M. 2010. Pattern Recognition Engineering. *RapidMiner Community Meeting and Conference*, 9.

Soucy P. and Mineau G.W. 2005. Beyond TFIDF Weighting for Text Categorization in the Vector Space Model. *Proceedings of the 19th International Joint Conference on Artificial Intelligence (IJCAI 2005)*:1130-1135.

Rocchio J. 1971. Relevance Feedback in Information Retrieval. *The SMART Retrieval System-Experiments in Automatic Document Processing*, Prentice-Hall:313-323.

Yang Ch. 2007. Algorithm of Marriage in Honey Bees Optimization Based on the Wolf Pack Search. *Proceedings of International Conference on Intelligent Pervasive Computing*:462-467.

Yang X.S. 2008. *Nature-Inspired Metaheuristic Algorithms*.

Yang X.S. and Deb S. 2009. Cuckoo search via Levy flights. *Proceedings of World Congress on Nature & Biologically Inspired Computing*:210-214.

Yang X.S. 2010. A New Metaheuristic Bat-Inspired Algorithm. *Proceedings of Nature Inspired Cooperative Strategies for Optimization (NISCO 2010)*:65-74.

Sentiment classification of online political discussions: a comparison of a word-based and dependency-based method

Hugo Lewi Hammer
Oslo and Akershus
University College
Department of Computer Science
hugo.hammer@hioa.no

Per Erik Solberg
Språkbanken
The National Library
of Norway
p.e.solberg@ifikk.uio.no

Lilja Øvrelid
Department of Informatics
University of Oslo
liljao@ifi.uio.no

Abstract

Online political discussions have received a lot of attention over the past years. In this paper we compare two sentiment lexicon approaches to classify the sentiment of sentences from political discussions. The first approach is based on applying the number of words between the target and the sentiment words to weight the sentence sentiment score. The second approach is based on using the shortest paths between target and sentiment words in a dependency graph and linguistically motivated syntactic patterns expressed as dependency paths. The methods are tested on a corpus of sentences from online Norwegian political discussions. The results show that the method based on dependency graphs performs significantly better than the word-based approach.

1 Introduction

Over the past years online political discussions have received a lot of attention. E.g. the Obama 2012 election team initiated an extensive use of text analytics and machine learning techniques towards online material to guide advertising campaigns, identifying key voters, and improve fundraising (Issenberg, 2012). There has also been a lot of concern about the alarming growth in hate and racism against minorities like Muslims, Jews and Gypsies in online discussions (Goodwin et al., 2013; Bartlett et al., 2013). Sentiment analysis (SA) is the discipline of automatically determining sentiment in text material and may be one important tool in understanding the diversity of opinions on the Internet.

In this paper we focus on classifying the sentiment towards religious/political topics, say the Quran, in Norwegian political discussion. We use a lexicon-based approach where we classify the sentiment of a sentence based on the polarity of sentiment words in relation to a set of target words in the sentence. We expect that statistically the importance of a sentiment word towards the target word is related to the number of words between the sentiment and target word as suggested by Ding et al. (2008). Information about the syntactic environment of certain words or phrases has in previous work also been shown to be useful for the task of sentiment classification (Wilson et al., 2009; Jiang et al., 2011). In this work we therefore compare the results obtained using a token-based distance measure with a novel syntax-based distance measure obtained using dependency graphs and further augmented with linguistically motivated syntactic patterns expressed as dependency paths. In order to evaluate the proposed methods, we furthermore present a freely available corpus of Norwegian political discussion related to religion and immigration, which has been manually annotated for the sentiment expressed towards a set of target words, as well as a manually translated sentiment lexicon.

2 Previous work

Sentiment classification aims to classify a document or sentence as either positive or negative and sometimes also neutral. There are mainly two approaches, one based on machine learning and one based on using a list of words with given sentiment scores (lexicon-based approach). For machine learning any existing method can be used, e.g. naïve Bayes and support vector machine, (Joachims, 1999; Shawe-Taylor and Cristianini, 2000). One simple lexicon-based approach is to count the number of words with positive and negative sentiment in the document as suggested by Hu and Liu (2004). One may classify the opinion of larger documents like movie or product reviews or smaller documents like tweets, comments

Proceedings of the 5th Workshop on Computational Approaches to Subjectivity, Sentiment and Social Media Analysis, pages 90–96,
Baltimore, Maryland, USA. June 27, 2014. ©2014 Association for Computational Linguistics

or sentences. See Liu (2012), chapters three to five and references therein for the description of several opinion classification methods.

SA has mostly been used to analyze opinions in comments and reviews about commercial products, but there are also examples of SA towards political tweets and discussions, see e.g. Tumasjan et al. (2010); Chen et al. (2010). SA of political discussions is known to be a difficult task since citations, irony and sarcasm is very common (Liu, 2012).

3 Proposed SA methods

In this section we present two methods to classify sentences as either positive, neutral or negative towards a target word. Both methods follow the same general algorithm presented below which is inspired by Ding et al. (2008) and is based on a list of sentiment words each associated with a sentiment score representing the polarity and strength of the sentiment word (sentiment lexicon). Both target words, sentiment words and sentiment shifters can in general appear several times in a sentence. Sentiment shifters are words that potentially shift the sentiment of a sentence from positive to negative or negative to positive. E.g. "not happy" have the opposite polarity than just "happy". Let $tw_i, i \in \{1, 2, \ldots, I\}$ represent appearance number i of the target word in the sentence. Note that we only consider one target word at the time. E.g. if a sentence contains two target words, e.g. Quran and Islam, the sentence is first classified with respect to Quran and then with respect to Islam. Further let $sw_j, j \in \{1, 2, \ldots, J\}$ be appearance number j of a sentiment word in the sentence. Finally let $\mathbf{ss} = (ss_1, ss_2, \ldots, ss_K)$ represent the sentiment shifters in the sentence. We compute a sentiment score, S, for the sentence as follows

$$S = \frac{1}{I}\sum_{i=1}^{I}\sum_{j=1}^{J}\mathbf{imp}(tw_i, sw_j)\mathbf{shift}(sw_j, \mathbf{ss}) \tag{1}$$

where the function **imp** computes the importance of the sentiment word sw_j on the target word appearance tw_i. This will be computed in different ways as described below. Further, the function $\mathbf{shift}(sw_j, \mathbf{ss})$ computes whether the sentiment of sw_j should be shifted based on all the sentiment shifters in the sentence. It returns -1 (sentiment shift) if some of the sentiment shifters are within d_p words in front or d_n words behind sw_j, respectively. Else the function, returns 1 (no sentiment shift). We classify the sentiment towards the target word to be positive, neutral or negative if $S >= t_p$, $t_p > S > t_n$ and $S <= t_n$, respectively. The parameters d_p, d_n, t_p and t_n is tuned using a training set, as described in section 5 below.

3.1 Word distance method

For the word distance method we use the following **imp** function

$$\mathbf{imp}(tw_i, sw_j) = \frac{\mathbf{sentsc}(sw_j)}{\mathbf{worddist}(tw_i, sw_j)} \tag{2}$$

where $\mathbf{sentsc}(sw_j)$ is the sentiment score of sw_j from the sentiment lexicon and $\mathbf{worddist}(tw_i, sw_j)$ is the number of words between tw_i and sw_j in the sentence plus one.

3.2 Parse tree method

When determining the sentiment expressed towards a specific target word, the syntactic environment of this word and how it relates to sentiment-bearing words in the context may clearly be of importance. In the following we present a modification of the scoring function described above to also take into account the syntactic environment of the target words. The function is defined over dependency graphs, i.e. connected, acyclic graphs expressing bilexical relations.

Dependency distance One way of expressing the syntactic environment of a target word with respect to a sentiment word is to determine its distance in the dependency graph. We therefore define a distance function $\mathbf{depdist}(tw_i, sw_j)$ which returns the number of nodes in the shortest dependency path from the target word to the sentiment word in the dependency graph. The shortest path is determined using Dijkstra's shortest path algorithm (Dijkstra, 1959).

Dependency paths A second way of determining the importance of a sentiment word towards a target based on syntactically parsed texts, is to establish a list of grammatical dependency paths between words, and test whether such paths exist between the targets and sentiment words (Jiang et al., 2011). The assumption would be that two words most likely are semantically related to each other if there is a meaningful grammatical relation between them. Furthermore, it is reasonable to expect than some paths are stronger indicators of the overall sentiment of the sentence than others. To test this method, we have manually created a list of 42 grammatical dependency paths, divided into four groups, and given them a score from $0-1$. The higher the score is, the better indicator of sentiment the path is assumed to be. In the following paragraphs, we will briefly present the groups of paths and the maximum score we have assigned in each group. The paths are represented in the following format: postag-target:postag-sentiment word__DEPREL_up/dn(__DEPREL_up/dn etc.). *Up* and *dn* indicate the direction of the traversed arc in the graph.

A first group consists of paths from subject targets to sentiment predicates. Such paths can e.g. go from a subject to a verbal predicate, subst:verb__SUBJ_up, or from a subject to an adjectival or nominal predicate in the context of a copular verb, subst:adj/subst__SUBJ_up__SPRED_dn. Paths in this group can get the maximum score, 1. The combination of a subject and a predicate will result in a proposition, a statement which is evaluated as true or false. We expect that a proposition typically will represent the opinion of the speaker, although e.g. irony and certain kinds of embedding can shift the truth evaluation in some cases. Secondly, if the predicate represents an event brought about by an intentional agent, the subject will typically represent that agent. If the predicate has a positive or negative sentiment, we expect that this sentiment is directed towards this intentional agent.

A second group we have considered, contains paths from subject targets to sentiment words embedded within the predicate, such as from the subject to the nominal direct object of a verb, subst:subst__SUBJ_up__DOBJ_dn. Paths from subjects into different kinds of adverbials are also a part of this group. We consider paths from subjects to objects to be good indicators of sentiment and assign them the highest score, 1 . The reasoning is much the same as for subject predicate paths: The statement is a proposition and the subject will often be the agent of the event. Also, the object and the verb are presumably closely semantically connected, as the former is an argument of the latter. Paths into adverbials get lower values, as adverbials often are less semantically connected to the predicate than objects.

The paths in our third group go from targets to sentiment words within the predicate. These include paths from nominal direct object target to verbal predicates, subst:verb__DOBJ_up, and from various kinds of adverbials to verbal predicates, etc. We assume that predicate-internal paths are less good indicators of sentiment than the above groups, as such paths do not constitute a proposition. Also, arguments within the predicate usually do not represent intentional agents. Such paths will get the score $1/3$.

Our fourth and final group of dependency paths contains paths internal to the nominal phrase, such as from target nouns to attributive adjectives, subst:adj__ATR_dn, and from target complements of attributive prepositions to target nouns, subst:subst__PUTFYLL_up__ATR_up. A positively or negatively qualified noun will probably often represent the sentiment of the speaker. At the same time, a nominal phrase of this kind can be used in many different contexts where the holder of the sentiment is not the speaker. We assign $2/3$ as the maximum score. Table 1 summarizes the groups of dependency paths.

Path group	Number	Score range
Subj. to pred.	9	1
Subj. to pred.-internal	13	$1/3-1$
Pred.-internal	6	$1/3$
NP-internal	14	$1/3-2/3$

Table 1: Grouping of dependency paths with the number of paths and score range for each group.

Modified scoring function Let $\mathcal{D}$ denote the set of all salient dependency paths. The function $\mathbf{gram}(tw_i, sw_j)$ returns the dependency path, and if $\mathbf{gram}(tw_i, sw_j) \in \mathcal{D}$, then the function $W_{\mathbf{dep}}(tw_i, sw_j) \in [0, 1]$, returns the salience score of the path. Further let $\mathbf{depdist}(tw_i, sw_j)$ return the dependency distance, as described above. The **imp** function is computed as follows. If $\mathbf{gram}(tw_i, sw_j) \in \mathcal{D}$ we use

$$\begin{aligned} &\mathbf{imp}(tw_i, sw_j) = \\ &\quad \alpha \cdot \mathbf{sentsc}(sw_j) W_{\mathbf{dep}}(tw_i, sw_j) \\ &\quad +(1-\alpha) \cdot \frac{\mathbf{sentsc}(sw_j)}{\mathbf{depdist}(tw_i, sw_j)} \end{aligned} \tag{3}$$

where $\alpha \in [0, 1]$ is a parameter that weights the score from the salient dependency path and the tree distance and can be tuned using a training set. If $\mathbf{gram}(tw_i, sw_j) \notin \mathcal{D}$ we simply use

$$\mathbf{imp}(tw_i, sw_j) = \frac{\mathbf{sentsc}(sw_j)}{\mathbf{depdist}(tw_i, sw_j)} \quad (4)$$

Note that when $\alpha = 0$, (3) reduces to (4).

4 Linguistic resources

4.1 Sentiment corpus

We did not find any suitable annotated text material related to political discussions in Norwegian and therefore created our own. We manually selected 46 debate articles from the Norwegian online newspapers *NRK Ytring, Dagbladet, Aftenposten, VG and Bergens Tidene*. To each debate article there were attached a discussion thread where readers could express their opinions and feelings towards the content of the debate article. All the text from the debate articles and the subsequent discussions were collected using text scraping (Hammer et al., 2013). The debate articles were related to religion and immigration and we wanted to classify the sentiment towards all forms of the following target words: *islam, muslim, quran, allah, muhammed, imam and mosque*. These represent topics that typically create a lot of active discussions and disagreements.

We automatically divided the material into sentences and all sentences containing at least one target word and one sentiment word were kept for further analysis. If a sentence contained more than one target word, e.g. both Islam and Quran, the sentence was repeated one time for each target word in the final text material. We could then classify the sentiment towards each of the target words in the sentence consecutively. To assure that we do not underestimate the uncertainty in the statistical analysis, we see each repetition of the sentence as the same sentence with respect to the sentence random effect in the regression model in Section 5.1

Each sentence was manually annotated as to whether the commenter was positive, negative or neutral towards the target word in the sentence. Each sentence was evaluated individually. The sentences were annotated based on real-world knowledge, e.g. a sentence like "Muhammed is like Hitler" would be annotated as a negative sentiment towards Muhammed. Further, if a commenter presented a negative fact about the target word, the sentence would be denoted as negative.

	Negative	Neutral	Positive
Training	174 (46%)	162 (42%)	46 (12%)
Test	102 (33%)	182 (59%)	24 (8%)

Table 2: Manual annotation of training and test set.

In order to assess inter-annotator agreement, a random sample of 65 sentences from the original text material was annotated by a second annotator. These sentences were not included in either the training or test set. For these sentences, the two annotators agreed on 58, which is an 89% agreement, with a 95% confidence interval equal to (79%, 95%) assuming that each sentence is independent. Since the sentences are drawn randomly from the population of all sentences this is a fair assumption.

Finally the material was divided into two parts where the first half of the debate articles with subsequent discussions make up the training set and the rest constitutes a held-out test set. In the manual development of the salient dependency paths, only the training set was used. After the division, the training and test set consisted of a total of 382 and 308 sentences, respectively. Table 4.1 summarizes the annotation found in the corpus.

4.2 Corpus postprocessing

The sentiment corpus was PoS-tagged and parsed using the Bohnet&Nivre-parser (Bohnet and Nivre, 2012). This parser is a transition-based dependency parser with joint tagger that implements global learning and a beam search for non-projective labeled dependency parsing. This latter parser has recently outperformed pipeline systems (such as the Malt and MST parsers) both in terms of tagging and parsing accuracy for typologically diverse languages such as Chinese, English, and German. It has been reported to obtain a labeled accuracy of 87.7 for Norwegian (Solberg et al., 2014). The parser is trained on the Norwegian Dependency Treebank (NDT). The NDT is a treebank created at the National Library of Norway in the period 2011-2013, manually annotated with part-of-speech tags, morphological features, syntactic functions and dependency graphs (Solberg et al., 2014; Solberg, 2013). It consists of approximately 600 000 tokens, equally distributed between Norwegian Bokmål and Nynorsk, the two Norwegian written standards. Only the Bokmål subcorpus has been used here. Detailed annotation guidelines in English will be made available in April 2014 (Kinn et al., 2014).

4.3 Sentiment lexicon and sentiment shifters

Unfortunately, no sentiment lexicon existed for the Norwegian language and therefore we developed our own by manually translating the AFINN list (Nielsen, 2011). We also manually added 1590 words relevant to political discussions like 'deport', 'expel', 'extremist' and 'terrorist', ending up with a list of 4067 Norwegian sentiment words. Each word were given a score from -5 to 5 ranging from words with extremely negative sentiment (e.g. 'behead') to highly positive sentiment words (e.g. 'breathtaking').

Several Norwegian sentiment shifters were considered but only the basic shifter 'not' improved the sentiment classification and therefore only this word was used in the method.

5 Experiments

In this study we compare four different methods based on the general algorithm in (1).

- We use the **imp**-function presented in (2). We denote this method WD (word distance).
- For this method and the two below we use the **imp**-function in (3). Further we set $\alpha = 0$ which means that we do not use the salient dependency paths. We denote this method A0 ($\alpha = 0$).
- We set $\alpha = 1$ and for all dependency paths we set $W_{\mathbf{dep}} = 2/3$. We denote this method CW (constant weights).
- We set $\alpha = 1$ and for $W_{\mathbf{dep}}$ we use the weights presented in Table 1. We denote this method OD (optimal use of dependency paths)

For each method we used the training set to manually tune the parameters d_p, d_n, t_p and t_n of the method. The parameters were tuned to optimize the number of correct classifications.

5.1 Statistical analysis of classification performance

We compare the classification performance of a set of M different methods, denoted as $\Pi_1, \Pi_2, \ldots, \Pi_M$, using random effect logistic regression. Let the stochastic variable $Y_{tm} \in \{0, 1\}$ represents whether method Π_m, $m \in \{1, 2, \ldots, M\}$ classified the correct sentiment to sentence number $t \in \{1, 2, \ldots, T\}$, where T is the number of sentences in the test set. We let Y_{tm} be the dependent variable of the regression model. The different methods $\Pi_1, \Pi_2, \ldots, \Pi_M$ is included as a categorical independent variable in the regression model. We also assume that classification performance of the different methods depends on the sentence to be classified, thus the sentence number is included as a random effect. Fitting the model to the observed classification performance of the different methods we are able to see if the probability of classifying correctly significantly vary between the methods.

The statistical analysis is performed using the statistical program R (R Core Team, 2013) and the R package `lme4` (Bates et al., 2013).

	d_p	d_n	t_p	t_n	**Accuracy**	**p-val**
WD	2	0	0.7	0.0	47%	
A0	2	0	2.0	0.3	52%	0.023
CW	2	0	2.0	0.3	52%	0.024
OD	2	0	2.0	0.3	53%	0.016

Table 3: The second to the fifth column show the optimal values of the parameters of the model tuned using the training set. The sixth column show the number of correct classifications and the last column shows p-values testing whether the method performs better than WD.

5.2 Results

Table 3 shows the optimal parameter values of d_p, d_n, t_p and t_n tuned using the training set, and classification performance for the different methods on the test set using the parameter values tuned from the training set. The p-values are computed using the regression model presented in Section 5.1. We see that $d_n = 0$, meaning that the sentiment shifter 'not' only has a positive effect on the classification performance when it is in front of the sentiment word. We see that using dependency distances (method A0) the classification results are significantly improved compared to using word distances in the sentence (method WD) (p-value = 0.023). Also classification based on salient dependency paths (method OD) performs significantly better than WD. We also see that OD performs better than A0 (162 correct compared to 161), but this improvement is not statistically significant.

6 Closing remarks

Classifying sentiment in political discussions is hard because of the frequent use of irony, sarcasm and citations. In this paper we have compared the use of word distance between target word and sentiment word against metrics incorporating syntactic information. Our results show that using dependency tree distances or salient dependency paths, improves the classification performance compared to using word distance.

Manually selecting salient dependency paths for the aim of sentiment analysis is a hard task. A natural further step of our analysis is to expand the training and test material and use machine learning to see if there exists dependency paths that improve results compared to using dependency distance.

References

Jamie Bartlett, Jonathan Birdwell, and Mark Littler. 2013. The rise of populism in Europe can be traced through online behaviour... Demos, `http://www.demos.co.uk/files/Demos_OSIPOP_Book-web_03.pdf?1320601634`. [Online; accessed 21-January-2014].

Douglas Bates, Martin Maechler, and Ben Bolker, 2013. *lme4: Linear mixed-effects models using S4 classes*. R package version 0.999999-2.

Bernd Bohnet and Joakim Nivre. 2012. A transition-based system for joint part-of-speech tagging and labeled non-projective dependency parsing. In *Proceedings of the Conference on Empirical Methods in Natural Language Processing*, pages 1455–1465. Association for Computational Linguistics.

Bi Chen, Leilei Zhu, Daniel Kifer, and Dongwon Lee. 2010. What Is an Opinion About? Exploring Political Standpoints Using Opinion Scoring Model. In *AAAI*.

E. W. Dijkstra. 1959. A note on two problems in connexion with graphs. *Numerische Mathematik*, 1:269–271.

Xiaowen Ding, Bing Liu, and Philip S. Yu. 2008. A Holistic Lexicon-based Approach to Opinion Mining. In *Proceedings of the 2008 International Conference on Web Search and Data Mining*, WSDM '08, pages 231–240, New York, NY, USA. ACM.

Matthew Goodwin, Vidhya Ramalingam, and Rachel Briggs. 2013. The New Radical Right: Violent and Non-Violent Movements in Europe. Institute for Strategic Dialogue, `http://www.strategicdialogue.org/ISD%20Far%20Right%20Feb2012.pdf`. [Online; accessed 21-January-2014].

Hugo Hammer, Alfred Bratterud, and Siri Fagernes. 2013. Crawling Javascript websites using WebKit with application to analysis of hate speech in online discussions. In *Norwegian informatics conference*.

Irene Heim and Angelika Kratzer. 1998. *Semantics in Generative Grammar*. Blackwell.

Joan B. Hooper and Sandra A. Thompson. 1973. On the Applicability of Root Transformations. *Linguistic Inquiry*, 4(4):465–497.

Minqing Hu and Bing Liu. 2004. Mining and Summarizing Customer Reviews. In *Proceedings of the Tenth ACM SIGKDD International Conference on Knowledge Discovery and Data Mining*, KDD '04, pages 168–177, New York, NY, USA. ACM.

Sasha Issenberg. 2012. How President Obamas campaign used big data to rally individual voters. `http://www.technologyreview.com/featuredstory/509026/how-obamas-team-used-big-data-to-rally-voters/` [Online; accessed 21-March-2014].

Long Jiang, Mo Yu, Ming Zhou, Xiaohua Liu, and Tiejun Zhao. 2011. Target-dependent Twitter Sentiment Classification. In *Proceedings of the 49th Annual Meeting of the Association for Computational Linguistics: Human Language Technologies - Volume 1*, HLT '11, pages 151–160, Stroudsburg, PA, USA. Association for Computational Linguistics.

Thorsten Joachims. 1999. Making large-scale SVM Learning Practical. In *Advances in Kernel Methods*.

Kari Kinn, Pl Kristian Eriksen, and Per Erik Solberg. 2014. NDT Guidelines for Morphological and Syntactic Annotation. Technical report, National Library of Norway.

Bing Liu. 2012. *Sentiment Analysis and Opinion Mining*. Synthesis Lectures on Human Language Technologies. Morgan & Claypool Publishers.

Finn Årup Nielsen. 2011. A new ANEW: Evaluation of a word list for sentiment analysis in microblogs. *CoRR*, abs/1103.2903.

R Core Team, 2013. *R: A Language and Environment for Statistical Computing*. R Foundation for Statistical Computing, Vienna, Austria.

John Shawe-Taylor and Nello Cristianini. 2000. *Support Vector Machines*. Cambridge University Press.

Per Erik Solberg, Arne Skjærholt, Lilja Øvrelid, Kristin Hagen, and Janne Bondi Johannessen. 2014. The Norwegian Dependency Treebank. In *Proceedings of LREC 2014*. Accepted.

Per Erik Solberg. 2013. Building Gold-Standard Treebanks for Norwegian. In *Proceedings of NODALIDA 2013*, Linkping Electronic Conference Proceedings no. 85, pages 459–464, Linkping, Sweden. LiU Electronic Press.

Andranik Tumasjan, Timm O Sprenger, Philipp G Sandner, and Isabell M Welpe. 2010. Predicting elections with twitter: What 140 characters reveal about political sentiment. In *Proceedings of the fourth international aaai conference on weblogs and social media*, pages 178–185.

Theresa Wilson, Janyce Wiebe, and Paul Hoffman. 2009. Recognizing contextual polarity: An exploration of features for phrase-level sentiment analysis. *Computational Linguistics*, 35(3):399 – 433.

Improving Agreement and Disagreement Identification in Online Discussions with A Socially-Tuned Sentiment Lexicon

Lu Wang
Department of Computer Science
Cornell University
Ithaca, NY 14853
luwang@cs.cornell.edu

Claire Cardie
Department of Computer Science
Cornell University
Ithaca, NY 14853
cardie@cs.cornell.edu

Abstract

We study the problem of agreement and disagreement detection in online discussions. An isotonic Conditional Random Fields (isotonic CRF) based sequential model is proposed to make predictions on sentence- or segment-level. We automatically construct a socially-tuned lexicon that is bootstrapped from existing general-purpose sentiment lexicons to further improve the performance. We evaluate our agreement and disagreement tagging model on two disparate online discussion corpora – Wikipedia Talk pages and online debates. Our model is shown to outperform the state-of-the-art approaches in both datasets. For example, the isotonic CRF model achieves F1 scores of 0.74 and 0.67 for agreement and disagreement detection, when a linear chain CRF obtains 0.58 and 0.56 for the discussions on Wikipedia Talk pages.

1 Introduction

We are in an era where people can easily voice and exchange their opinions on the internet through forums or social media. Mining public opinion and the social interactions from online discussions is an important task, which has a wide range of applications. For example, by analyzing the users' attitude in forum posts on social and political problems, it is able to identify ideological stance (Somasundaran and Wiebe, 2009) and user relations (Qiu et al., 2013), and thus further discover subgroups (Hassan et al., 2012; Abu-Jbara et al., 2012) with similar ideological viewpoint. Meanwhile, catching the sentiment in the conversation can help detect online disputes, reveal popular or controversial topics, and potentially disclose the public opinion formation process.

In this work, we study the problem of agreement and disagreement identification in online discussions. Sentence-level agreement and disagreement detection for this domain is challenging in its own right due to the dynamic nature of online conversations, and the less formal, and usually very emotional language used. As an example, consider a snippet of discussion from Wikipedia Talk page for article "Iraq War" where editors argue on the correctness of the information in the opening paragraph (Figure 1). *"So what?"* should presumably be tagged as a negative sentence as should the sentence *"If you're going to troll, do us all a favor and stick to the guidelines."*. We hypothesize that these, and other, examples will be difficult for the tagger unless the context surrounding each sentence is considered and in the absence of a sentiment lexicon tuned for conversational text (Ding et al., 2008; Choi and Cardie, 2009).

As a result, we investigate isotonic Conditional Random Fields (isotonic CRF) (Mao and Lebanon, 2007) for the sentiment tagging task since they preserve the advantages of the popular CRF sequential tagging models (Lafferty et al., 2001) while providing an efficient mechanism to encode domain knowledge — in our case, a sentiment lexicon — through isotonic constraints on the model parameters. In particular, we bootstrap the construction of a sentiment lexicon from Wikipedia talk pages using the lexical items in existing general-purpose sentiment lexicons as seeds and in conjunction with an existing label propagation algorithm (Zhu and Ghahramani, 2002).[1]

To summarize, our chief contributions include: (1) We propose an agreement and disagreement identification model based on isotonic Conditional Random Fields (Mao and Lebanon, 2007) to identify users' attitude in online discussion. Our predictions that are made on the sentence-

[1]Our online discussion lexicon (Section 4) will be made publicly available.

Proceedings of the 5th Workshop on Computational Approaches to Subjectivity, Sentiment and Social Media Analysis, pages 97–106, Baltimore, Maryland, USA. June 27, 2014.

Zer0faults: So questions comments feedback welcome. Other views etc. I just hope we can remove the assertations that WMD's were in fact the sole reason for the US invasion, considering that HJ Res 114 covers many many reasons.
>**Mr. Tibbs**: So basically what you want to do is remove all mention of the cassus belli of the Iraq War and try to create the false impression that this military action was as inevitable as the sunrise.$_{[NN]}$ No. Just because things didn't turn out the way the Bush administration wanted doesn't give you license to rewrite history.$_{[NN]}$ ...
>>**MONGO**: Regardless, the article is an antiwar propaganda tool.$_{[NN]}$ ...
>>>**Mr. Tibbs**: So what?$_{[NN]}$ That wasn't the cassus belli and trying to give that impression After the Fact is Untrue.$_{[NN]}$ Hell, the reason it wasn't the cassus belli is because there are dictators in Africa that make Saddam look like a pussycat...
>>**Haizum**: Start using the proper format or it's over for your comments.$_{[N]}$ If you're going to troll, do us all a favor and stick to the guidelines.$_{[N]}$ ...
Tmorton166: Hi, I wonder if, as an outsider to this debate I can put my word in here. I considered mediating this discussion however I'd prefer just to comment and leave it at that :). I agree mostly with what Zer0faults is saying$_{[PP]}$. ...
>**Mr. Tibbs**: Here's the problem with that.$_{[NN]}$ It's not about publicity or press coverage. It's about the fact that the Iraq disarmament crisis set off the 2003 Invasion of Iraq. ... And theres a huge problem with rewriting the intro as if the Iraq disarmament crisis never happened.$_{[NN]}$
>>**Tmorton166**: ... To suggest in the opening paragraph that the ONLY reason for the war was WMD's is wrong - because it simply isn't.$_{[NN]}$ However I agree that the emphasis needs to be on the armaments crisis because it was the reason sold to the public and the major one used to justify the invasion but it needs to acknowledge that there was at least 12 reasons for the war as well.$_{[PP]}$ ...

Figure 1: Example discussion from wikipedia talk page for article "Iraq War", where editors discuss about the correctness of the information in the opening paragraph. We only show some sentences that are relevant for demonstration. Other sentences are omitted by ellipsis. Names of editors are in **bold**. ">" is an indicator for the reply structure, where turns starting with > are response for most previous turn that with one less >. We use "*NN*", "*N*", and "*PP*" to indicate "strongly disagree", "disagree", and "strongly agree". Sentences in blue are examples whose sentiment is hard to detect by an existing lexicon.

or segment-level, are able to discover fine-grained sentiment flow within each turn, which can be further applied in other applications, such as dispute detection or argumentation structure analysis. We employ two existing online discussion data sets: the *Authority and Alignment in Wikipedia Discussions (AAWD)* corpus of Bender et al. (2011) (Wikipedia talk pages) and the *Internet Argument Corpus (IAC)* of Walker et al. (2012a). Experimental results show that our model significantly outperforms state-of-the-art methods on the AAWD data (our F1 scores are 0.74 and 0.67 for agreement and disagreement, vs. 0.58 and 0.56 for the linear chain CRF approach) and IAC data (our F1 scores are 0.61 and 0.78 for agreement and disagreement, vs. 0.28 and 0.73 for SVM).

(2) Furthermore, we construct a new sentiment lexicon for online discussion. We show that the learned lexicon significantly improves performance over systems that use existing general-purpose lexicons (i.e. MPQA lexicon (Wilson et al., 2005), General Inquirer (Stone et al., 1966), and SentiWordNet (Esuli and Sebastiani, 2006)). Our lexicon is constructed from a very large-scale discussion corpus based on Wikipedia talk page, where previous work (Somasundaran and Wiebe, 2010) for constructing online discussion lexicon relies on human annotations derived from limited number of conversations.

In the remainder of the paper, we describe first the related work (Section 2). Then we introduce the sentence-level agreement and disagreement identification model (Section 3) as well as the label propagation algorithm for lexicon construction (Section 4). After explain the experimental setup, we display the results and provide further analysis in Section 6.

2 Related Work

Sentiment analysis has been utilized as a key enabling technique in a number of conversation-based applications. Previous work mainly studies the attitudes in spoken meetings (Galley et al., 2004; Hahn et al., 2006) or broadcast conversations (Wang et al., 2011) using Conditional Random Fields (CRF) (Lafferty et al., 2001). Galley et al. (2004) employ Conditional Markov models to detect if discussants reach at an agreement in spoken meetings. Each state in their model is an individual turn and prediction is made on the turn-level. In the same spirit, Wang et al. (2011) also propose a sequential model based on CRF for detecting agreements and disagreements in broadcast conversations, where they primarily show the efficiency of prosodic features. While we also exploit a sequential model extended from CRFs, our predictions are made for each sentence or segment rather than at the turn-level. Moreover, we experiment with online discussion datasets that exhibit a more realistic distribution of disagreement vs. agreement, where much more disagreement is observed due to its function and the relation between the participants. This renders the detection problem more challenging.

Only recently, agreement and disagreement detection is studied for online discussion, especially for online debate. Abbott et al. (2011) investigate different types of features based on dependency relations as well as *manually*-labeled features, such as if the participants are nice, nasty, or sarcastic, and respect or insult the target participants. Automatically inducing those features from human annotation are challenging itself, so it would be difficult to reproduce their work on new datasets. We use only automatically generated features. Using the same dataset, Misra and Walker (2013) study the effectiveness of topic-independent features, e.g. discourse cues indicating agreement or negative opinion. Those cues, which serve a similar purpose as a sentiment lexicon, are also constructed manually. In our work, we create an online discussion lexicon automatically and construct sentiment features based on the lexicon. Also targeting online debate, Yin et al. (2012) train a logistic regression classifier with features aggregating posts from the same participant to predict the sentiment for each individual post. This approach works only when the speaker has enough posts on each topic, which is not applicable to newcomers. Hassan et al. (2010) focus on predicting the attitude of participants towards each other. They relate the sentiment words to the second person pronoun, which produces strong baselines. We also adopt their baselines in our work. Although there are available datasets with (dis)agreement annotated on Wikipedia talk pages, we are not aware of any published work that utilizes these annotations. Dialogue act recognition on talk pages (Ferschke et al., 2012) might be the most related.

While detecting agreement and disagreement in conversations is useful on its own, it is also a key component for related tasks, such as stance prediction (Thomas et al., 2006; Somasundaran and Wiebe, 2009; Walker et al., 2012b) and subgroup detection (Hassan et al., 2012; Abu-Jbara et al., 2012). For instance, Thomas et al. (2006) train an agreement detection classifier with Support Vector Machines on congressional floor-debate transcripts to determine whether the speeches represent support of or opposition to the proposed legislation. Somasundaran and Wiebe (2009) design various sentiment constraints for inclusion in an integer linear programming framework for stance classification. For subgroup detection, Abu-Jbara et al. (2012) uses the polarity of the expressions in the discussions and partition discussants into subgroups based on the intuition that people in the same group should mostly agree with each other. Though those work highly relies on the component of agreement and disagreement detection, the evaluation is always performed on the ultimate application only.

3 The Model

We first give a brief overview on isotonic Conditional Random Fields (isotonic CRF) (Mao and Lebanon, 2007), which is used as the backbone approach for our sentence- or segment-level agreement and disagreement detection model. We defer the explanation of online discussion lexicon construction in Section 4.

3.1 Problem Description

Consider a discussion comprised of sequential turns uttered by the participants; each turn consists of a sequence of text units, where each unit can be a sentence or a segment of several sentences. Our model takes as input the text units $\mathbf{x} = \{x_1, \cdots, x_n\}$ in the same turn, and outputs a sequence of sentiment labels $\mathbf{y} = \{y_1, \cdots, y_n\}$, where $y_i \in \mathcal{O}, \mathcal{O} = \{\mathrm{NN}, \mathrm{N}, \mathrm{O}, \mathrm{P}, \mathrm{PP}\}$. The labels in $\mathcal{O}$ represent strongly disagree (NN), disagree (N), neutral (O), agree (P), strongly agree (PP), respectively. In addition, elements in the partially ordered set $\mathcal{O}$ possess an ordinal relation $\leq$. Here, we differentiate agreement and disagreement with different intensity, because the output of our classifier can be used for other applications, such as dispute detection, where "strongly disagree" (e.g. NN) plays an important role. Meanwhile, fine-grained sentiment labels potentially provide richer context information for the sequential model employed for this task.

3.2 Isotonic Conditional Random Fields

Conditional Random Fields (CRF) have been successfully applied in numerous sequential labeling tasks (Lafferty et al., 2001). Given a sequence of utterances or segments $\mathbf{x} = \{x_1, \cdots, x_n\}$, according to linear-chain CRF, the probability of the labels $\mathbf{y}$ for $\mathbf{x}$ is given by:

$$p(\mathbf{y}|\mathbf{x}) = \frac{1}{Z(\mathbf{x})} \exp\Big(\sum_i \sum_{\sigma,\tau} \lambda_{\langle \sigma,\tau \rangle} f_{\langle \sigma,\tau \rangle}(y_{i-1}, y_i) + \sum_i \sum_{\sigma,w} \mu_{\langle \sigma,w \rangle} g_{\langle \sigma,w \rangle}(y_i, x_i)\Big) \quad (1)$$

$f_{\langle\sigma,\tau\rangle}(y_{i-1}, y_i)$ and $g_{\langle\sigma,w\rangle}(y_i, x_i)$ are feature functions. Given that y_{i-1}, y_i, x_i take values of σ, τ, w, the functions are indexed by pairs $\langle\sigma, \tau\rangle$ and $\langle\sigma, w\rangle$. $\lambda_{\langle\sigma,\tau\rangle}, \mu_{\langle\sigma,w\rangle}$ are the parameters.

CRF, as defined above, is not appropriate for ordinal data like sentiment, because it ignores the ordinal relation among sentiment labels. Isotonic Conditional Random Fields (isotonic CRF) are proposed by Mao and Lebanon (2007) to enforce a set of monotonicity constraints on the parameters that are consistent with the ordinal structure and domain knowledge (in our case, a sentiment lexicon automatically constructed from online discussions).

Given a lexicon $\mathcal{M} = \mathcal{M}_p \cup \mathcal{M}_n$, where $\mathcal{M}_p$ and $\mathcal{M}_n$ are two sets of features (usually words) identified as strongly associated with positive sentiment and negative sentiment. The constraints are encoded as below. For each feature $w \in \mathcal{M}_p$, isotonic CRF enforces $\sigma \leq \sigma' \Rightarrow \mu_{\langle\sigma,w\rangle} \leq \mu_{\langle\sigma',w\rangle}$. Intuitively, the parameters $\mu_{\langle\sigma,w\rangle}$ are intimately tied to the model probabilities. When a feature such as "totally agree" is observed in the training data, the feature parameter for $\mu_{\langle \text{PP,totally agree} \rangle}$ is likely to increase. Similar constraints are also defined on $\mathcal{M}_n$. In this work, we boostrap the construction of an online discussion sentiment lexicon used as $\mathcal{M}$ in the isotonic CRF (see Section 4).

The parameters can be found by maximizing the likelihood subject to the monotonicity constraints. We adopt the re-parameterization from Mao and Lebanon (2007) for a simpler optimization problem, and refer the readers to Mao and Lebanon (2007) for more details.[2]

3.3 Features

The features used in sentiment prediction are listed in Table 1. Features with numerical values are first normalized by standardization, then binned into 5 categories.

Syntactic/Semantic Features. Dependency relations have been shown to be effective for various sentiment prediction tasks (Joshi and Penstein-Rosé, 2009; Somasundaran and Wiebe, 2009; Hassan et al., 2010; Abu-Jbara et al., 2012). We have two versions of dependency relation as features, one being the original form, another generalizing a word to its POS tag in turn. For instance, "nsubj(wrong, you)" is generlized as the "nsubj(`ADJ`, you)" and "nsubj(wrong, `PRP`)". We use Stanford parser (de Marneffe et al., 2006) to obtain parse trees and dependency relations.

Lexical Features
- unigram/bigram
- num of words all uppercased
- num of words
Discourse Features
- initial uni-/bi-/trigram
- repeated punctuations
- hedging (Farkas et al., 2010)
- number of negators
Syntactic/Semantic Features
- unigram with POS tag
- dependency relation
Conversation Features
- quote overlap with target
- TFIDF similarity with target (remove quote first)
Sentiment Features
- connective + sentiment words
- sentiment dependency relation
- sentiment words

Table 1: Features used in sentiment prediction.

Discourse Features. Previous work (Hirschberg and Litman, 1993; Abbott et al., 2011) suggests that discourse markers, such as *what?*, *actually*, may have their use for expressing opinions. We extract the initial unigram, bigram, and trigram of each utterance as discourse features (Hirschberg and Litman, 1993). Hedge words are collected from the CoNLL-2012 shared task (Farkas et al., 2010).

Conversation Features. Conversation features encode some useful information regarding the similarity between the current utterance(s) and the sentences uttered by the target participant. TFIDF similarity is computed. We also check if the current utterance(s) quotes target sentences and compute its length.

Sentiment Features. We gather connectives from Penn Discourse TreeBank (Rashmi Prasad and Webber, 2008) and combine them with any sentiment word that precedes or follows it as new features. Sentiment dependency relations are the subset of dependency relations with sentiment words. We replace those words with their polarity equivalents. For example, relation "nsubj(wrong, you)" becomes "nsubj($\texttt{SentiWord}_{neg}$, you)".

[2]The full implementation is based on MALLET (McCallum, 2002). We thank Yi Mao for sharing the implementation of the core learning algorithm.

POSITIVE
please elaborate, nod, await response, from experiences, anti-war, profits, promises of, is undisputed, royalty, sunlight, conclusively, badges, prophecies, in vivo, tesla, pioneer, published material, from god, plea for, lend itself, geek, intuition, morning, anti `SentiWord`$_{neg}$, connected closely, Rel(undertake, to), intelligibility, Rel(articles, detailed), of noting, for brevity, Rel(believer, am), endorsements, testable, source carefully
NEGATIVE
: (, TOT, ?!!, in contrast, ought to, whatever, Rel(nothing, you), anyway, Rel(crap, your), by facts, purporting, disproven, Rel(judgement, our), Rel(demonstrating, you), opt for, subdue to, disinformation, tornado, heroin, Rel(newbies, the), Rel (intentional, is), pretext, watergate, folly, perjury, Rel(lock, article), contrast with, poke to, censoring information, partisanship, insurrection, bigot, Rel(informative, less), clowns, Rel(feeling, mixed), never-ending

Table 2: Example terms and relations from our online discussion lexicon. We choose for display terms that do not contain any seed word.

4 Online Discussion Sentiment Lexicon Construction

So far as we know, there is no lexicon available for online discussions. Thus, we create from a large-scale corpus via *label propagation*. The label propagation algorithm, proposed by Zhu and Ghahramani (2002), is a semi-supervised learning method. In general, it takes as input a set of seed samples (e.g. sentiment words in our case), and the similarity between pairwise samples, then iteratively assigns values to the unlabeled samples (see Algorithm 1). The construction of graph G is discussed in Section 4.1. Sample sentiment words in the new lexicon are listed in Table 2.

Input : $G = (V, E), w_{ij} \in [0, 1]$, positive seed words P, negative seed words N, number of iterations T

Output: $\{y_i\}_{i=0}^{|V|-1}$

$y_i = 1.0, \forall v_i \in P$
$y_i = -1.0, \forall v_i \in N$
$y_i = 0.0, \forall v_i \notin P \cup N$

for $t = 1 \cdots T$ **do**

$$y_i = \frac{\sum_{(v_i,v_j)\in E} w_{ij} \times y_j}{\sum_{(v_i,v_j)\in E} w_{ij}}, \forall v_i \in V$$

$y_i = 1.0, \forall v_i \in P$
$y_i = -1.0, \forall v_i \in N$

end

Algorithm 1: The label propagation algorithm (Zhu and Ghahramani, 2002) used for constructing online discussion lexicon.

4.1 Graph Construction

Node Set V. Traditional lexicons, like General Inquirer (Stone et al., 1966), usually consist of polarized unigrams. As we mentioned in Section 1, unigrams lack the capability of capturing the sentiment conveyed in online discussions. Instead, bigrams, dependency relations, and even punctuation can serve as supplement to the unigrams. Therefore, we consider four types of *text units* as nodes in the graph: unigrams, bigrams, dependency relations, sentiment dependency relations. Sentiment dependency relations are described in Section 3.3. We replace all relation names with a general label. Text units that appear in at least 10 discussions are retained as nodes to reduce noise.

Edge Set E. As Velikovich et al. (2010) and Feng et al. (2013) notice, a dense graph with a large number of nodes is susceptible to propagating noise, and will not scale well. We thus adopt the algorithm in Feng et al. (2013) to construct a sparsely connected graph. For each text unit t, we first compute its representation vector $\vec{a}$ using Pairwise Mutual Information scores with respect to the top 50 co-occuring text units. We define "co-occur" as text units appearing in the same sentence. An edge is created between two text units t_0 and t_1 only if they ever co-occur. The similarity between t_0 and t_1 is calculated as the Cosine similarity between $\vec{a}_0$ and $\vec{a}_1$.

Seed Words. The seed sentiment are collected from three existing lexicons: MPQA lexicon, General Inquirer, and SentiWordNet. Each word in SentiWordNet is associated with a positive score and a negative score; words with a polarity score larger than 0.7 are retained. We remove words with conflicting sentiments.

4.2 Data

The graph is constructed based on Wikipedia talk pages. We download the 2013-03-04 Wikipedia data dump, which contains 4,412,582 talk pages. Since we are interested in conversational languages, we filter out talk pages with fewer than 5 participants. This results in a dataset of 20,884 talk pages, from which the graph is constructed.

5 Experimental Setup

5.1 Datasets

Wikipedia Talk pages. The first dataset we use is *Authority and Alignment in Wikipedia Discussions (AAWD)* corpus (Bender et al., 2011). AAWD consists of 221 English Wikipedia discussions with agreement and disagreement annotations.[3]

The annotation of AAWD is made at utterance- or turn-level, where a turn is defined as continuous body of text uttered by the same participant. Annotators either label each utterance as agreement, disagreement or neutral, and select the corresponding spans of text, or label the full turn. Each turn is annotated by two or three people. To induce an utterance-level label for instances that have only a turn-level label, we assume they have the same label as the turn.

To train our sentiment model, we further transform agreement and disagreement labels (i.e. 3-way) into the 5-way labels. For utterances that are annotated as agreement and have the text span specified by at least two annotators, they are treated as "strongly agree" (PP). If an utterance is only selected as agreement by one annotator or it gets the label by turn-level annotation, it is "agree" (P). "Strongly disagree" (NN) and "disagree" (N) are collected in the same way from disagreement label. All others are neutral (O). In total, we have 16,501 utterances. 1,930 and 1,102 utterances are labeled as "NN" and "N". 532 and 99 of them are "PP" and "P". All other 12,648 are neutral samples. [4]

[3]Bender et al. (2011) originally use positive alignment and negative alignment to indicate two types of social moves. They define those alignment moves as "agreeing or disagreeing" with the target. We thus use agreement and disagreement instead of positive and negative alignment in this work.

[4]345 samples with both positive and negative labels are treated as neutral.

Online Debate. The second dataset is the *Internet Argument Corpus (IAC)* (Walker et al., 2012a) collected from an online debate forum. Each discussion in IAC consists of multiple posts, where we treat each post as a turn. Most posts (72.3%) contain quoted content from the posts they target at or other resources. A post can have more than one quote, which naturally break the post into multiple segments. 1,806 discussions are annotated with agreement and disagreement on the segment-level from -5 to 5, with -5 as strongly disagree and 5 as strongly agree. We first compute the average score for each segment among different annotators and transform the score into sentiment label in the following way. We treat $[-5, -3]$ as NN (1595 segments), $(-3, -1]$ as N (4548 segments), $[1, 3)$ as P (911 samples), $[3, 5]$ as PP (199), all others as O (290 segments).

In the test phase, utterances or segments predicted with NN or N are treated as disagreement; the ones predicted as PP or P are agreement; O is neutral.

5.2 Comparison

We compare with two baselines. (1) **Baseline (Polarity)** is based on counting the sentiment words from our lexicon. An utterance or segment is predicted as agreement if it contains more positive words than negative words, or disagreement if more negative words are observed. Otherwise, it is neutral. (2) **Baseline (Distance)** is extended from (Hassan et al., 2010). Each sentiment word is associated with the closest second person pronoun, and a surface distance can be computed between them. A classifier based on Support Vector Machines (Joachims, 1999) (SVM) is trained with the features of sentiment words, minimum/maximum/average of the distances.

We also compare with two state-of-the-art methods that are widely used in sentiment prediction for conversations. The first one is an RBF kernel SVM based approach, which has been used for sentiment prediction (Hassan et al., 2010), and (dis)agreement detection (Yin et al., 2012) in online debates. The second is linear chain CRF, which has been utilized for (dis)agreement identification in broadcast conversations (Wang et al., 2011).

	Strict F1			Soft F1		
	Agree	Disagree	Neutral	Agree	Disagree	Neutral
Baseline (Polarity)	14.56	25.70	64.04	22.53	38.61	66.45
Baseline (Distance)	8.08	20.68	84.87	33.75	55.79	88.97
SVM (3-way)	26.76	35.79	77.39	44.62	52.56	80.84
+ downsampling	21.60	36.32	72.11	31.86	49.58	74.92
CRF (3-way)	20.99	23.85	85.28	56.28	56.37	89.41
CRF (5-way)	20.47	19.42	85.86	58.39	56.30	90.10
+ downsampling	24.26	31.28	77.12	47.30	46.24	80.18
isotonic CRF	24.32	21.95	86.26	68.18	62.53	88.87
+ downsampling	29.62	34.17	80.97	55.38	53.00	84.56
+ new lexicon	**46.01**	***51.49***	*87.40*	***74.47***	***67.02***	*90.56*
+ new lexicon + downsampling	***47.90***	**49.61**	81.60	64.97	58.97	84.04

Table 3: Strict and soft F1 scores for agreement and disagreement detection on Wikipedia talk pages (AAWD). All the numbers are multiplied by 100. In each column, **bold** entries (if any) are statistically significantly higher than all the rest, and the *italic* entry has the highest absolute value. Our model based on the isotonic CRF with the new lexicon produces significantly better results than all the other systems for agreement and disagreement detection. Downsampling, however, is not always helpful.

6 Results

In this section, we first show the experimental results on sentence- and segment-level agreement and disagreement detection in two types of online discussions – *Wikipedia Talk pages* and *online debates*. Then we provide more detailed analysis for the features used in our model. Furthermore, we discuss several types of errors made in the model.

6.1 Wikipedia Talk Pages

We evaluate the systems by standard F1 score on each of the three categories: agreement, disagreement, and neutral. For AAWD, we compute two versions of F1 scores. **Strict F1** is computed against the true labels. For **soft F1**, if a sentence is never labeled by any annotator on the sentence-level and adopts its agreement/disagreement label from the turn-level annotation, then it is treated as a true positive when predicted as neutral.

Table 3 demonstrates our main results on the Wikipedia Talk pages (AAWD dataset). Without downsampling, our isotonic CRF based systems with the new lexicon significantly outperform the compared approaches for agreement and disagreement detection according to the paired-t test ($p < 0.05$). We also perform downsampling by removing the turns only containing neutral utterances. However, it does not always help with performance. We suspect that, with less neutral samples in the training data, the classifier is less likely to make neutral predictions, which thus decreases true positive predictions. For strict F-scores on agreement/disagreement, downsampling has mixed effect, but mostly we get slightly better performance.

	Agree	Disagree	Neu
Baseline (Polarity)	3.33	5.96	65.61
Baseline (Distance)	1.65	5.07	85.41
SVM (3-way)	25.62	69.10	31.47
+ new lexicon features	28.35	72.58	34.53
CRF (3-way)	29.46	74.81	31.93
CRF (5-way)	24.54	69.31	39.60
+ new lexicon features	28.85	71.81	39.14
isotonic CRF	**53.40**	**76.77**	*44.10*
+ new lexicon	***61.49***	***77.80***	*51.43*

Table 4: F1 scores for agreement and disagreement detection on online debate (IAC). All the numbers are multiplied by 100. In each column, **bold** entries (if any) are statistically significantly higher than all the rest, and the *italic* entry has the highest absolute value except baselines. We have two main observations: 1) Both of our models based on isotonic CRF significantly outperform other systems for agreement and disagreement detection. 2) By adding the new lexicon, either as features or constraints in isotonic CRF, all systems achieve better F1 scores.

6.2 Online Debates

Similarly, F1 scores for agreement, disagreement and neutral for online debates (IAC dataset) are displayed in Table 4. Both of our systems based on isotonic CRF achieve significantly better F1 scores than the comparison. Especially, our system with the new lexicon produces the best results. For SVM and linear-chain CRF based systems, we also add new sentiment features constructed from the new lexicon as described in Section 3.3. We can see that those sentiment features also boost the performance for both of the compared approaches.

6.3 Feature Evaluation

Moreover, we evaluate the effectiveness of features by adding one type of features each time. The results are listed in Table 5. As it can be seen, the performance gets improved incrementally with every new set of features.

We also utilize χ^2-test to highlight some of the salient features on the two datasets. We can see from Table 6 that, for online debates (IAC), some features are highly topic related, such as "*the male*" or "*the scientist*". This observation concurs with the conclusion in Misra and Walker (2013) that features with topic information are indicative for agreement and disagreement detection.

AAWD	Agree	Disagree	Neu
Lex	40.77	52.90	79.65
Lex + Syn	68.18	63.91	88.87
Lex + Syn + Disc	70.93	63.69	89.32
Lex + Syn + Disc + Con	71.27	63.72	89.60
Lex + Syn + Disc + Con + Sent	**74.47**	**67.02**	90.56

IAC	Agree	Disagree	Neu
Lex	56.65	75.35	45.72
Lex + Syn	54.16	75.13	46.12
Lex + Syn + Disc	54.27	76.41	47.60
Lex + Syn + Disc + Con	55.31	77.25	48.87
Lex + Syn + Disc + Con + Sent	**61.49**	77.80	**51.43**

Table 5: Results on Wikipedia talk page (AAWD) (with soft F1 score) and online debate (IAC) with different feature sets (i.e **Lex**ical, **Syn**tacitc/Semantic, **Disc**ourse, **Con**versation, and **Sent**iment features) by using isotonic CRF. The numbers in **bold** are statistically significantly higher than the numbers above it (paired-t test, $p < 0.05$).

6.4 Error Analysis

After a closer look at the data, we found two major types of errors. Firstly, people express disagreement not only by using opinionated words, but also by providing contradictory example. This needs a deeper understanding of the semantic information embedded in the text. Techniques like textual entailment can be used in the further work. Secondly, a sequence of sentences with sarcasm is hard to detect. For instance, *"Bravo, my friends! Bravo! Goebbles would be proud of your abilities to whitewash information."* We observe terms like "Bravo", "friends", and "be proud of" that are indicators for positive sentiment; however, they are in sarcastic tone. We believe a model that is able to detect sarcasm would further improve the performance.

AAWD
POSITIVE: agree, nsubj (agree, I), nsubj (right, you), Rel (Sentiment$_{pos}$, I), thanks, amod (idea, good), nsubj(glad, I), good point, concur, happy with, advmod (good, pretty), suggestion$_{Hedge}$
NEGATIVE: you, your, nsubj (negative, you), numberOfNegator, don't, nsubj (disagree, I), actually$_{SentInitial}$, please stop$_{SentInitial}$, what ?$_{SentInitial}$, should$_{Hedge}$
IAC
POSITIVE: amod (conclusion, logical), Rel (agree, on), Rel (have, justified), Rel (work, out), one might$_{SentInitial}$, to confirm$_{Hedge}$, women
NEGATIVE: their kind, the male, the female, the scientist, according to, is stated, poss (understanding, my), hell$_{SentInitial}$, whatever$_{SentInitial}$

Table 6: Relevant features by χ^2 test on AAWD and IAC.

7 Conclusion

We present an agreement and disagreement detection model based on isotonic CRFs that outputs labels at the sentence- or segment-level. We bootstrap the construction of a sentiment lexicon for online discussions, encoding it in the form of domain knowledge for the isotonic CRF learner. Our sentiment-tagging model is shown to outperform the state-of-the-art approaches on both Wikipedia Talk pages and online debates.

Acknowledgments We heartily thank the Cornell NLP Group and the reviewers for helpful comments. This work was supported in part by NSF grants IIS-0968450 and IIS-1314778, and DARPA DEFT Grant FA8750-13-2-0015. The views and conclusions contained herein are those of the authors and should not be interpreted as necessarily representing the official policies or endorsements, either expressed or implied, of NSF, DARPA or the U.S. Government.

References

Rob Abbott, Marilyn Walker, Pranav Anand, Jean E. Fox Tree, Robeson Bowmani, and Joseph King. 2011. How can you say such things?!?: Recognizing disagreement in informal political argument. In *Proceedings of the Workshop on Languages in Social Media*, LSM '11, pages 2–11, Stroudsburg, PA, USA. Association for Computational Linguistics.

Amjad Abu-Jbara, Mona Diab, Pradeep Dasigi, and

Dragomir Radev. 2012. Subgroup detection in ideological discussions. In *Proceedings of the 50th Annual Meeting of the Association for Computational Linguistics: Long Papers - Volume 1*, ACL '12, pages 399–409, Stroudsburg, PA, USA. Association for Computational Linguistics.

Emily M. Bender, Jonathan T. Morgan, Meghan Oxley, Mark Zachry, Brian Hutchinson, Alex Marin, Bin Zhang, and Mari Ostendorf. 2011. Annotating social acts: Authority claims and alignment moves in wikipedia talk pages. In *Proceedings of the Workshop on Languages in Social Media*, LSM '11, pages 48–57, Stroudsburg, PA, USA. Association for Computational Linguistics.

Yejin Choi and Claire Cardie. 2009. Adapting a polarity lexicon using integer linear programming for domain-specific sentiment classification. In *Proceedings of the 2009 Conference on Empirical Methods in Natural Language Processing: Volume 2 - Volume 2*, EMNLP '09, pages 590–598, Stroudsburg, PA, USA. Association for Computational Linguistics.

Marie-Catherine de Marneffe, Bill MacCartney, and Christopher D. Manning. 2006. Generating typed dependency parses from phrase structure trees. In *LREC*.

Xiaowen Ding, Bing Liu, and Philip S. Yu. 2008. A holistic lexicon-based approach to opinion mining. In *Proceedings of the 2008 International Conference on Web Search and Data Mining*, WSDM '08, pages 231–240, New York, NY, USA. ACM.

Andrea Esuli and Fabrizio Sebastiani. 2006. Sentiwordnet: A publicly available lexical resource for opinion mining. In *In Proceedings of the 5th Conference on Language Resources and Evaluation (LREC06*, pages 417–422.

Richárd Farkas, Veronika Vincze, György Móra, János Csirik, and György Szarvas. 2010. The conll-2010 shared task: Learning to detect hedges and their scope in natural language text. In *Proceedings of the Fourteenth Conference on Computational Natural Language Learning — Shared Task*, CoNLL '10: Shared Task, pages 1–12, Stroudsburg, PA, USA. Association for Computational Linguistics.

Song Feng, Jun Seok Kang, Polina Kuznetsova, and Yejin Choi. 2013. Connotation lexicon: A dash of sentiment beneath the surface meaning. In *ACL*, pages 1774–1784. The Association for Computer Linguistics.

Oliver Ferschke, Iryna Gurevych, and Yevgen Chebotar. 2012. Behind the article: Recognizing dialog acts in wikipedia talk pages. In *Proceedings of the 13th Conference of the European Chapter of the Association for Computational Linguistics*, EACL '12, pages 777–786, Stroudsburg, PA, USA. Association for Computational Linguistics.

Michel Galley, Kathleen McKeown, Julia Hirschberg, and Elizabeth Shriberg. 2004. Identifying agreement and disagreement in conversational speech: use of Bayesian networks to model pragmatic dependencies. In *ACL '04: Proceedings of the 42nd Annual Meeting on Association for Computational Linguistics*, pages 669+, Morristown, NJ, USA. Association for Computational Linguistics.

Sangyun Hahn, Richard Ladner, and Mari Ostendorf. 2006. Agreement/disagreement classification: Exploiting unlabeled data using contrast classifiers. In *Proceedings of the Human Language Technology Conference of the NAACL, Companion Volume: Short Papers*, pages 53–56, New York City, USA, June. Association for Computational Linguistics.

Ahmed Hassan, Vahed Qazvinian, and Dragomir Radev. 2010. What's with the attitude?: Identifying sentences with attitude in online discussions. In *Proceedings of the 2010 Conference on Empirical Methods in Natural Language Processing*, EMNLP '10, pages 1245–1255, Stroudsburg, PA, USA. Association for Computational Linguistics.

Ahmed Hassan, Amjad Abu-Jbara, and Dragomir Radev. 2012. Detecting subgroups in online discussions by modeling positive and negative relations among participants. In *Proceedings of the 2012 Joint Conference on Empirical Methods in Natural Language Processing and Computational Natural Language Learning*, EMNLP-CoNLL '12, pages 59–70, Stroudsburg, PA, USA. Association for Computational Linguistics.

Julia Hirschberg and Diane Litman. 1993. Empirical studies on the disambiguation of cue phrases. *Comput. Linguist.*, 19(3):501–530, September.

Thorsten Joachims. 1999. Advances in kernel methods. chapter Making Large-scale Support Vector Machine Learning Practical, pages 169–184. MIT Press, Cambridge, MA, USA.

Mahesh Joshi and Carolyn Penstein-Rosé. 2009. Generalizing dependency features for opinion mining. In *Proceedings of the ACL-IJCNLP 2009 Conference Short Papers*, ACLShort '09, pages 313–316, Stroudsburg, PA, USA. Association for Computational Linguistics.

John D. Lafferty, Andrew McCallum, and Fernando C. N. Pereira. 2001. Conditional random fields: Probabilistic models for segmenting and labeling sequence data. In *Proceedings of the Eighteenth International Conference on Machine Learning*, ICML '01, pages 282–289, San Francisco, CA, USA. Morgan Kaufmann Publishers Inc.

Yi Mao and Guy Lebanon. 2007. Isotonic conditional random fields and local sentiment flow. In *Advances in Neural Information Processing Systems*.

Andrew Kachites McCallum. 2002. Mallet: A machine learning for language toolkit. http://mallet.cs.umass.edu.

Amita Misra and Marilyn Walker. 2013. Topic independent identification of agreement and disagreement in social media dialogue. In *Proceedings of the SIGDIAL 2013 Conference*, pages 41–50, Metz, France, August. Association for Computational Linguistics.

Minghui Qiu, Liu Yang, and Jing Jiang. 2013. Mining user relations from online discussions using sentiment analysis and probabilistic matrix factorization. In *Proceedings of the 2013 Conference of the North American Chapter of the Association for Computational Linguistics: Human Language Technologies*, pages 401–410, Atlanta, Georgia, June. Association for Computational Linguistics.

Alan Lee Eleni Miltsakaki Livio Robaldo Aravind Joshi Rashmi Prasad, Nikhil Dinesh and Bonnie Webber. 2008. The penn discourse treebank 2.0. In Bente Maegaard Joseph Mariani Jan Odijk Stelios Piperidis Daniel Tapias Nicoletta Calzolari (Conference Chair),

Khalid Choukri, editor, *Proceedings of the Sixth International Conference on Language Resources and Evaluation (LREC'08)*, Marrakech, Morocco, may. European Language Resources Association (ELRA). http://www.lrec-conf.org/proceedings/lrec2008/.

Swapna Somasundaran and Janyce Wiebe. 2009. Recognizing stances in online debates. In *Proceedings of the Joint Conference of the 47th Annual Meeting of the ACL and the 4th International Joint Conference on Natural Language Processing of the AFNLP: Volume 1 - Volume 1*, ACL '09, pages 226–234, Stroudsburg, PA, USA. Association for Computational Linguistics.

Swapna Somasundaran and Janyce Wiebe. 2010. Recognizing stances in ideological on-line debates. In *Proceedings of the NAACL HLT 2010 Workshop on Computational Approaches to Analysis and Generation of Emotion in Text*, CAAGET '10, pages 116–124, Stroudsburg, PA, USA. Association for Computational Linguistics.

Philip J. Stone, Dexter C. Dunphy, Marshall S. Smith, and Daniel M. Ogilvie. 1966. *The General Inquirer: A Computer Approach to Content Analysis*. MIT Press, Cambridge, MA.

Matt Thomas, Bo Pang, and Lillian Lee. 2006. Get out the vote: Determining support or opposition from congressional floor-debate transcripts. In *Proceedings of the 2006 Conference on Empirical Methods in Natural Language Processing*, EMNLP '06, pages 327–335, Stroudsburg, PA, USA. Association for Computational Linguistics.

Leonid Velikovich, Sasha Blair-Goldensohn, Kerry Hannan, and Ryan McDonald. 2010. The viability of web-derived polarity lexicons. In *Human Language Technologies: The 2010 Annual Conference of the North American Chapter of the Association for Computational Linguistics*, HLT '10, pages 777–785, Stroudsburg, PA, USA. Association for Computational Linguistics.

Marilyn Walker, Jean Fox Tree, Pranav Anand, Rob Abbott, and Joseph King. 2012a. A corpus for research on deliberation and debate. In *Proceedings of the Eight International Conference on Language Resources and Evaluation (LREC'12)*, Istanbul, Turkey, may. European Language Resources Association (ELRA).

Marilyn A. Walker, Pranav Anand, Rob Abbott, and Ricky Grant. 2012b. Stance classification using dialogic properties of persuasion. In *HLT-NAACL*, pages 592–596. The Association for Computational Linguistics.

Wen Wang, Sibel Yaman, Kristin Precoda, Colleen Richey, and Geoffrey Raymond. 2011. Detection of agreement and disagreement in broadcast conversations. In *Proceedings of the 49th Annual Meeting of the Association for Computational Linguistics: Human Language Technologies: Short Papers - Volume 2*, HLT '11, pages 374–378, Stroudsburg, PA, USA. Association for Computational Linguistics.

Theresa Wilson, Janyce Wiebe, and Paul Hoffmann. 2005. Recognizing contextual polarity in phrase-level sentiment analysis. In *Proceedings of the Conference on Human Language Technology and Empirical Methods in Natural Language Processing*, HLT '05, pages 347–354, Stroudsburg, PA, USA. Association for Computational Linguistics.

Jie Yin, Paul Thomas, Nalin Narang, and Cecile Paris. 2012. Unifying local and global agreement and disagreement classification in online debates. In *Proceedings of the 3rd Workshop in Computational Approaches to Subjectivity and Sentiment Analysis*, WASSA '12, pages 61–69, Stroudsburg, PA, USA. Association for Computational Linguistics.

Xiaojin Zhu and Zoubin Ghahramani. 2002. Learning from labeled and unlabeled data with label propagation. In *Technical Report CMU-CALD-02-107*.

Lexical Acquisition for Opinion Inference: A Sense-Level Lexicon of Benefactive and Malefactive Events

Yoonjung Choi[1], Lingjia Deng[2], and Janyce Wiebe[1,2]
[1]Department of Computer Science
[2]Intelligent Systems Program
University of Pittsburgh
yjchoi@cs.pitt.edu, lid29@pitt.edu, wiebe@cs.pitt.edu

Abstract

Opinion inference arises when opinions are expressed toward states and events which positive or negatively affect entities, i.e., benefactive and malefactive events. This paper addresses creating a lexicon of such events, which would be helpful to infer opinions. Verbs may be ambiguous, in that some meanings may be benefactive and others may be malefactive or neither. Thus, we use WordNet to create a sense-level lexicon. We begin with seed senses culled from FrameNet and expand the lexicon using WordNet relationships. The evaluations show that the accuracy of the approach is well above baseline accuracy.

1 Introduction

Opinions are commonly expressed in many kinds of written and spoken text such as blogs, reviews, new articles, and conversation. Recently, there have been a surge in reserach in *opinion analysis* (*sentiment analysis*) research (Liu, 2012; Pang and Lee, 2008).

While most past researches have mainly addressed explicit opinion expressions, there are a few researches for implicit opinions expressed via *implicatures*. Deng and Wiebe (2014) showed how sentiments toward one entity may be propagated to other entities via opinion implicature rules. Consider *The bill would curb skyrocketing health care costs*. Note that *curb* costs is bad for the object *costs* since the costs are reduced. We can reason that the writer is positive toward the event *curb* since the event is bad for the object *health care costs* which the writer expresses an explicit negative sentiment (*skyrocketing*). We can reason from there that the writer is positive toward *the bill*, since it is the agent of the positive event.

These implicature rules involve events that positively or negatively affect the *object*. Such events are called *malefactive* and *benefactive*, or, for ease of writing, *goodFor* (*gf*) and *badFor* (*bf*) (hereafter *gfbf*). The list of gfbf events and their polarities (gf or bf) are necessary to develop a fully automatic opinion inference system. On first thought, one might think that we only need lists of gfbf *words*. However, it turns out that gfbf terms may be ambiguous – a single word may have both gf and bf meanings.

Thus, in this work, we take a sense-level approach to acquire gfbf lexicon knowledge, leading us to employ lexical resources with fine-grained sense rather than word representations. For that, we adopt an automatic bootstrapping method which disambiguates gfbf polarity at the sense-level utilizing WordNet, a widely-used lexical resource. Starting from the seed set manually generated from FrameNet, a rich lexicon in which words are organized by semantic frames, we explore how gfbf terms are organized in WordNet via semantic relations and expand the seed set based on those semantic relations.

The expanded lexicon is evaluated in two ways. First, the lexicon is evaluated against a corpus that has been annotated with gfbf information at the word level. Second, samples from the expanded lexicon are manually annotated at the sense level, which gives some idea of the prevalence of gfbf lexical ambiguity and provides a basis for sense-level evaluation. Also, we conduct the agreement study. The results show that the expanded lexicon covers more than half of the gfbf instances in the gfbf corpus, and the system's accuracy, as measured against the sense-level gold standard, is substantially higher than baseline. In addition, in the agreement study, the annotators achieve good agreement, providing evidence that the annotation task is feasible and that the concept of gfbf gives us a natural coarse-grained grouping of senses.

Proceedings of the 5th Workshop on Computational Approaches to Subjectivity, Sentiment and Social Media Analysis, pages 107–112,
Baltimore, Maryland, USA. June 27, 2014.

2 The GFBF Corpus

A corpus of blogs and editorials about the *Affordable Care Act*, a controversial topic, was manually annotated with gfbf information by Deng et al. (2013)[1]. This corpus provides annotated gfbf events and the agents and objects of the events. It consists of 134 blog posts and editorials. Because the Affordable Health Care Act is a controversial topic, the data is full of opinions. In this corpus, 1,411 gfbf instances are annotated, each including a gfbf event, its agent, and its object (615 gf instances and 796 bf instances). 196 different words appear in gf instances and 286 different words appear in bf instances; 10 words appear in both.

3 Sense-Level GFBF Ambiguity

A word may have one or more meanings. For that, we use WordNet[2], which is a large lexical database of English (Miller et al., 1990). In WordNet, nouns, verbs, adjectives, and adverbs are organized by semantic relations between meanings (*senses*). We assume that a sense is exactly one of gf, bf, or neither. Since words often have more than one sense, the polarity of a **word** may or may not be consistent, as the following WordNet examples show.

- A word with only gf senses: **encourage**
  S1: (v) promote, advance, boost, further, encourage (contribute to the progress or growth of)
  S2: (v) encourage (inspire with confidence; give hope or courage to)
  S3: (v) encourage (spur on)

- A word with only bf senses: **assault**
  S1: (v) assail, assault, set on, attack (attack someone physically or emotionally)
  S2: (v) rape, ravish, violate, assault, dishonor, dishonour, outrage (force (someone) to have sex against their will)
  S3: (v) attack, round, assail, lash out, snipe, assault (attack in speech or writing)

All senses of *encourage* are good for the object, and all senses of *assault* are bad for the object. The polarity is always same regardless of sense. In such cases, for our purposes, which particular sense is being used does not need to be determined because any instance of the word will be good for (bad for); that is, word-level approaches can work well. However, word-level approaches are not applicable for all the words. Consider the following:

- A word with gf and neutral senses: **inspire**
  S3: (v) prompt, inspire, instigate (serve as the inciting cause of)
  S4: (v) cheer, root on, inspire, urge, barrack, urge on, exhort, pep up (spur on or encourage especially by cheers and shouts)
  S6: (v) inhale, inspire, breathe in (draw in (air))

- A word with bf and neutral senses: **neutralize**
  S2: (v) neutralize, neutralise, nullify, negate (make ineffective by counterbalancing the effect of)
  S6: (v) neutralize, neutralise (make chemically neutral)

The words *inspire* and *neutralize* both have 6 senses (we list a subset due to space limitations). For *inspire*, while S3 and S4 are good for the object, S6 doesn't have any polarity, i.e., it is a neutral (we don't think of inhaling air as good for the air). Also, while S2 of *neutralize* is bad for the object, S6 is neutral (neutralizing a solution just changes its pH). Thus, if word-level approaches are applied using these words, some neutral instances may be incorrectly classified as gf or bf events.

- A word with gf and bf senses: **fight**
  S2: (v) fight, oppose, fight back, fight down, defend (fight against or resist strongly)
  S4: (v) crusade, fight, press, campaign, push, agitate (exert oneself continuously, vigorously, or obtrusively to gain an end or engage in a crusade for a certain cause or person; be an advocate for)

As mentioned in Section 2, 10 words are appeared in both gf and bf instances. Since only words and not senses are annotated in the corpus, such conflicts arise. These 10 words account for 9.07% (128 instances) of all annotated instances. One example is *fight*. In the corpus instance *fight for a piece of legislation*, *fight* is good for the object, *a piece of legislation*. This is S4. However, in the corpus instance *we need to fight this repeal*, the meaning of *fight* here is S2, so *fight* is bad for the object, *this repeal*.

[1]Available at http://mpqa.cs.pitt.edu/corpora/gfbf/
[2]WordNet, http://wordnet.princeton.edu/

Thesefore, approaches for determining the gfbf polarity of an instance that are sense-level instead of word-level promise to have higher precision.

4 Lexicon Acquisition

In this section, we develop a sense-level gfbf lexicon by exploiting WordNet. The method bootstraps from a seed lexicon and iteratively follows WordNet relations. We consider only verbs.

4.1 Seed Lexicon

To preserve the corpus for evaluation, we created a seed set that is independent from the corpus. An annotator who didn't have access to the corpus manually selected gfbf words from FrameNet[3] in the light of semantic frames. The annotator found 592 gf words and 523 bf words. Decomposing each word into its senses in WordNet, there are 1,525 gf senses and 1,154 bf senses. 83 words extracted from FrameNet overlap with gfbf instances in the corpus. For independence, those words were discarded. Among the senses of the remaining words, we randomly choose 200 gf senses and 200 bf senses.

4.2 Expansion Method

In WordNet, verb senses are arranged into hierarchies, that is, verb senses towards the bottom of the trees express increasingly specific manners. Thus, we can follow *hypernym* relations to more general senses and *troponym* relations to more specific verb senses. Since the troponym relation refers to a specific elaboration of a verb sense, we hypothesized that troponyms of a synset tends to have its same polarity (i.e., gf or bf). We only consider the direct troponyms in a single iteration. Although the hypernym is a more general term, we hypothesized that direct hypernyms tend to have the the same or neutral polarity, but not the opposite polarity. Also, the *verb groups* are promising; even though the coverage is incomplete, we expect the verb groups to be the most helpful.

WordNet Similarity[4], is a facility that provides a variety of semantic similarity and relatedness measures based on information found in the WordNet lexical database. We choose Jiang&Conrath (1997) (*jcn*) method which has been found to be effective for such tasks by NLP researchers. When two concetps aren't related at all, it returns 0. The more they are related, the higher the value is retuned. We regarded words with similarity values greater than 1.0 to be similar words.

Beginning with its seed set, each lexicon (gf and bf) is expanded iteratively. On each iteration, for each sense in the current lexicon, all of its direct troponyms, direct hypernyms, and members of the same verb group are extracted and added to the lexicon for the next iteration. Similarity, for each sense, all words with above-threshold *jcn* values are added. For new senses that are extracted for both the gf and bf lexicons, we ignore such senses, since there is conflicting evidence (recall that we assume a sense has only one polarity, even if a word may have senses of different polarities).

4.3 Corpus Evaluation

In this section, we use the gfbf annotations in the corpus as a gold standard. The annotations in the corpus are at the word level. To use the annotations as a sense-level gold standard, all the senses of a word marked gf (bf) in the corpus are considered to be gf (bf). While this is not ideal, this allows us to evaluate the lexicon against the only corpus evidence available.

The 196 words that appear in gf instances in the corpus have a total of 897 senses, and the 286 words that appear in bf instances have a total of 1,154 senses. Among them, 125 senses are conflicted: a sense of a word marked gf in the corpus could be a member of the same synset as a sense of a word marked bf in the corpus. For a more reliable gold-standard set, we ignored these conflicted senses. Thus, the gold-standard set contains 772 gf senses and 1,029 bf senses.

Table 1 shows the results after five iterations of lexicon expansion. In total, the gf lexicon contains 4,157 senses and the bf lexicon contains 5,071 senses. The top half gives the results for the gf lexicon and the bottom half gives the results for the bf lexicon. In the table, *gfOverlap* means the overlap between the senses in the lexicon in that row and the gold-standard **gf** set, while *bfOverlap* is the overlap between the senses in the lexicon in that row and the gold-standard **bf** set. That is, of the 772 senses in the gf gold standard, 449 (58%) are in the gf expanded lexicon while 105 (14%) are in the bf expanded lexicon.

Accuracy (Acc) for gf is calculated as *#gfOverlap / (#gfOverlap + #bfOverlap)* and bf is calculated as *#bfOverlap / (#gfOverlap + #bfOverlap)*.

[3]FrameNet, https://framenet.icsi.berkeley.edu/fndrupal/

[4]WN Similarity, http://wn-similarity.sourceforge.net/

		goodFor		
	#senses	*#gfOverlap*	*#bfOverlap*	Acc
Total	4,157	449	176	0.72
WN Sim	1,073	134	75	0.64
Groups	242	69	24	0.74
Troponym	4,084	226	184	0.55
Hypernym	223	75	33	0.69
		badFor		
	#senses	*#gfOverlap*	*#bfOverlap*	Acc
Total	5,071	105	562	0.84
WN Sim	1,008	34	190	0.85
Groups	255	11	86	0.89
Troponym	4,258	66	375	0.85
Hypernym	286	16	77	0.83

Table 1: Results after lexicon expansion

Overall, accuracy is higher for the bf than the gf lexicon. The results in the table are broken down by semantic relation. Note that the individual counts do not sum to the totals because senses of different words may actually be the same sense in WordNet. The results for the bf lexicon are consistently high over all semantic relations. The results for the gf lexicon are more mixed, but all relations are valuable.

The WordNet Similarity is advantageous because it detects similar senses automatically, so may provide coverage beyond the semantic relations coded in WordNet.

Overall, the verb group is the most informative relation, as we suspected.

Although the gf-lexicon accuracy for the troponym relation is not high, it has the advantage is that it yields the most number of senses. Its lower accuracy doesn't support our original hypothesis. We first thought that verbs lower down in the hierarchy would tend to have the same polarity since they express specific manners characterizing an event. However, this hypothesis is wrong. Even though most troponyms have the same polarity, there are many exceptions. For example, *protect#v#1*, which means the first sense of the verb *protect*, has 18 direct troponyms such as *cover for#v#1*, *overprotect#v#2*, and so on. *protect#v#1* is a gf event because the meaning is *"shielding from danger"* and most troponyms are also gf events. However, *overprotect#v#2*, which is one of troponyms of *protect#v#1*, is a bf event.

For the hypernym relation, the number of detected senses is not large because many were already detected in previous iterations (in general, there are fewer nodes on each level as hypernym links are traversed).

4.4 Sense Annotation Evaluation

For a more direct evaluation, two annotators, who are co-authors, independently annotated a sample of senses. We randomly selected 60 words among the following classes: 10 pure gf words (i.e., all senses of the words are classified by the expansion method, and all senses are put into the gf lexicon), 10 pure bf words, 20 mixed words (i.e., all senses of the words are classified by the expansion method, and some senses are put into the gf lexicon while others are put into the bf lexicon), and 20 incomplete words (i.e., some senses of the words are not classified by the expansion method).

The total number of senses is 151; 64 senses are classified as gf, 56 senses are classified as bf, and 31 senses are not classified. We included more mixed than pure words to make the results of the study more informative. Further, we wanted to included non-classified senses as decoys for the annotators. The annotators only saw the sense entries from WordNet. They didn't know whether the system classified a sense as gf or bf or whether it didn't classify it at all.

Table 2 evaluates the lexicons against the manual annotations, and in comparison to the majority class baseline. The top half of the table shows results when treating Anno1's annotations as the gold standard, and the bottom half shows the results when treating Anno2's as the gold standard. Among 151 senses, Anno1 annotated 56 senses (37%) as gf, 51 senses (34%) as bf, and 44 senses (29%) as neutral. Anno2 annotated 66 senses (44%) as gf, 55 senses (36%) as bf, and 30 (20%) senses as neutral. The incorrect cases are divided into two sets: *incorrect opposite* consists of senses that are classified as the opposite polarity by the expansion method (e.g., the sense is classified into gf, but annotator annotates it as bf), and *incorrect neutral* consists of senses that the expansion method classifies as gf or bf, but the annotator marked it as neutral. We report the accuracy and the percentage of cases for each incorrect case. The accuracies substantially improve over baseline for both annotators and for both classes.

In Table 3, we break down the results into gfbf classes. The *gf accuracy* measures the percentage of correct gf senses out of all senses annotated as gf according to the annotations (same as *bf accuracy*). As we can see, accuracy is higher for the bf than the gf. The conclusion is consistent with what we have discovered in Section 4.3.

By Anno1, 8 words are detected as mixed words, that is, they contain both gf and bf senses. By Anno2, 9 words are mixed words (this set includes the 8 mixed words of Anno1). Among the randomly selected 60 words, the proportion of mixed words range from 13.3% to 15%, according to the two annotators. This shows that gfbf lexical ambiguity does exist.

To measure agreement between the annotators, we calculate two measures: percent agreement and κ (Artstein and Poesio, 2008). κ measures the amount of agreement over what is expected by chance, so it is a stricter measure. Percent agreement is 0.84 and κ is 0.75.

	accuracy	% incorrect opposite	% incorrect neutral	base-line
Anno1	0.53	0.16	0.32	0.37
Anno2	0.57	0.24	0.19	0.44

Table 2: Results against sense-annotated data

	gf accuracy	bf accuracy	baseline
Anno1	0.74	0.83	0.37
Anno2	0.68	0.74	0.44

Table 3: Accuracy broken down for gfbf

5 Related Work

Lexicons are widely used in sentiment analysis and opinion extraction. There are several previous works to acquire or expand sentiment lexicons such as (Kim and Hovy, 2004), (Strapparava and Valitutti, 2004), (Esuli and Sebastiani, 2006), (Gyamfi et al., 2009), (Mohammad and Turney, 2010) and (Peng and Park, 2011). Such sentiment lexicons are helpful for detecting explicitly stated opinions, but are not sufficient for recognizing implicit opinions. Inferred opinions often have opposite polarities from the explicit sentiment expressions in the sentence; explicit sentiments must be combined with benefactive, malefactive state and event information to detect implicit sentiments. There are few previous works closest to ours. (Feng et al., 2011) build *connotation lexicons* that list words with connotative polarity and connotative predicates. Goyal et al. (2010) generate a lexicon of *patient polarity verbs* that imparts positive or negative states on their patients. Riloff et al. (2013) learn a lexicon of negative situation phrases from a corpus of tweets with hashtag "sarcasm".

Our work is complementary to theirs in that their acquisition methods are corpus-based, while we acquire knowledge from lexical resources. Further, all of their lexicons are word level while ours are sense level. Finally, the types of entries among the lexicons are related but not the same. Ours are specifically designed to support the automatic recognition of implicit sentiments in text that are expressed via implicature.

6 Conclusion and Future Work

In this paper, we developed a sense-level gfbf lexicon which was seeded by entries culled from FrameNet and then expanded by exploiting semantic relations in WordNet. Our evaluations show that such lexical resources are promising for expanding such sense-level lexicons. Even though the seed set is completely independent from the corpus, the expanded lexicon's coverage of the corpus is not small. The accuracy of the expanded lexicon is substantially higher than baseline accuracy. Also, the results of the agreement study are positive, providing evidence that the annotation task is feasible and that the concept of gfbf gives us a natural coarse-grained grouping of senses.

However, there is still room for improvement. We believe that gf/bf judgements of word senses could be effectively crowd-sourced; (Akkaya et al., 2010), for example, effectively used Amazon Mechanical Turk (AMT) for similar coarse-grained judgements. The idea would be to use automatic expansion methods to create a sense-level lexicon, and then have AMT workers judge the entries in which we have least confidence. This would be much more time- and cost-effective.

The seed sets we used are small - only 400 total senses. We believe it will be worth the effort to create larger seed sets, with the hope to mine many additional gfbf senses from WordNet.

To exploit the lexicon to recognize sentiments in a corpus, the word-sense ambiguity we discovered needs to be addressed. There is evidence that the performance of word-sense disambiguation systems using a similar coarse-grained sense inventory is much better than when the full sense inventory is used (Akkaya et al., 2009; Akkaya et al., 2011). That, coupled with the fact that our study suggests that many words are unambiguous with respect to the gfbf distinction, makes us hopeful that gfbf information may be practically exploited to improve sentiment analysis in the future.

7 Acknowledgments

This work was supported in part by DARPA-BAA-12-47 DEFT grant #12475008.

References

Cem Akkaya, Janyce Wiebe, and Rada Mihalcea. 2009. Subjectivity word sense disambiguation. In *Proceedings of EMNLP 2009*, pages 190–199.

Cem Akkaya, Alexander Conrad, Janyce Wiebe, and Rada Mihalcea. 2010. Amazon mechanical turk for subjectivity word sense disambiguation. In *Proceedings of the NAACL HLT 2010 Workshop on Creating Speech and Language Data with Amazon's Mechanical Turk*, pages 195–203.

Cem Akkaya, Janyce Wiebe, Alexander Conrad, and Rada Mihalcea. 2011. Improving the impact of subjectivity word sense disambiguation on contextual opinion analysis. In *Proceedings of the Fifteenth Conference on Computational Natural Language Learning*, pages 87–96.

Ron Artstein and Massimo Poesio. 2008. Inter-coder agreement for computational linguistics. *Comput. Linguist.*, 34(4):555–596, December.

Lingjia Deng and Janyce Wiebe. 2014. Sentiment propagation via implicature constraints. In *Proceedings of EACL*.

Lingjia Deng, Yoonjung Choi, and Janyce Wiebe. 2013. Benefactive/malefactive event and writer attitude annotation. In *Proceedings of 51st ACL*, pages 120–125.

Andrea Esuli and Fabrizio Sebastiani. 2006. Sentiwordnet: A publicly available lexical resource for opinion mining. In *Proceedings of 5th LREC*, pages 417–422.

Song Feng, Ritwik Bose, and Yejin Choi. 2011. Learning general connotation of words using graph-based algorithms. In *Proceedings of EMNLP*, pages 1092–1103.

Amit Goyal, Ellen Riloff, and Hal DaumeIII. 2010. Automatically producing plot unit representations for narrative text. In *Proceedings of EMNLP*, pages 77–86.

Yaw Gyamfi, Janyce Wiebe, Rada Mihalcea, and Cem Akkaya. 2009. Integrating knowledge for subjectivity sense labeling. In *Proceedings of NAACL HLT 2009*, pages 10–18.

Jay J. Jiang and David W. Conrath. 1997. Semantic similarity based on corpus statistics and lexical taxonomy. In *Proceedings of COLING*.

Soo-Min Kim and Eduard Hovy. 2004. Determining the sentiment of opinions. In *Proceedings of 20th COLING*, pages 1367–1373.

Bing Liu. 2012. *Sentiment Analysis and Opinion Mining*. Morgan & Claypool.

George A. Miller, Richard Beckwith, Christiane Fellbaum, Derek Gross, and Katherine Miller. 1990. Wordnet: An on-line lexical database. *International Journal of Lexicography*, 13(4):235–312.

Saif M. Mohammad and Peter D. Turney. 2010. Emotions evoked by common words and phrases: Using mechanical turk to create an emotion lexicon. In *Proceedings of the NAACL-HLT 2010 Workshop on Computational Approaches to Analysis and Generation of Emotion in Text*.

Bo Pang and Lillian Lee. 2008. Opinion mining and sentiment analysis. *Found. Trends Inf. Retr.*, 2(1-2):1–135.

Wei Peng and Dae Hoon Park. 2011. Generate adjective sentiment dictionary for social media sentiment analysis using constrained nonnegative matrix factorization. In *Proceedings of ICWSM*.

Ellen Riloff, Ashequl Qadir, Prafulla Surve, Lalindra De Silva, Nathan Gilbert, and Ruihong Huang. 2013. Sarcasm as contrast between a positive sentiment and negative situation. In *Proceedings of EMNLP*, pages 704–714.

Carlo Strapparava and Alessandro Valitutti. 2004. Wordnet-affect: An affective extension of wordnet. In *Proceedings of 4th LREC*, pages 1083–1086.

Dive deeper: Deep Semantics for Sentiment Analysis

Nikhikumar Jadhav
Masters Student
Computer Science & Engineering Dept.
IIT Bombay
nikhilkumar@cse.iitb.ac.in

Pushpak Bhattacharyya
Professor
Computer Science & Engineering Dept.
IIT Bombay
pb@cse.iitb.ac.in

Abstract

This paper illustrates the use of deep semantic processing for sentiment analysis. Existing methods for sentiment analysis use supervised approaches which take into account all the subjective words and or phrases. Due to this, the fact that not all of these words and phrases actually contribute to the overall sentiment of the *text* is ignored. We propose an unsupervised rule-based approach using deep semantic processing to identify only relevant subjective terms. We generate a UNL (Universal Networking Language) graph for the input *text*. Rules are applied on the graph to extract relevant terms. The sentiment expressed in these terms is used to figure out the overall sentiment of the *text*. Results on binary sentiment classification have shown promising results.

1 Introduction

Many works in sentiment analysis try to make use of shallow processing techniques. The common thing in all these works is that they merely try to identify sentiment-bearing expressions as shown by Ruppenhofer and Rehbein (2012). No effort has been made to identify which expression actually contributes to the overall sentiment of the text. In Mukherjee and Bhattacharyya (2012) these expressions are given weight-age according to their position w.r.t. the discourse elements in the *text*. But it still takes into account each expression.

Semantic analysis is essential to understand the exact meaning conveyed in the *text*. Some words tend to mislead the meaning of a given piece of *text* as shown in the previous example. WSD (Word Sense Disambiguation) is a technique which can been used to get the right sense of the word. Balamurali et al., (2012) have made use of WordNet synsets for a supervised sentiment classification task. Tamare (2010) and Rentoumi (2009) have also shown a performance improvement by using WSD as compared to word-based features for a supervised sentiment classification task. In Hasan et al., (2012), semantic concepts have been used as additional features in addition to word-based features to show a performance improvement. Syntagmatic or structural properties of text are used in many NLP applications like machine translation, speech recognition, named entity recognition, etc. A clustering based approach which makes use of syntactic features of text has been shown to improve performance in Kashyap et al., (2013). Another approach can be found in Mukherjee and Bhattacharyya (2012) which makes use of lightweight discourse for sentiment analysis. In general, approaches using semantic analysis are expensive than syntax-based approaches due to the shallow processing involved in the latter. As pointed out earlier, all these works incorporate all the sentiment-bearing expressions to evaluate the overall sentiment of the *text*. The fact that not all expressions contribute to the overall sentiment is completely ignored due to this. Our approach tries to resolve this issue. To do this, we create a UNL graph for each piece of *text* and include only the relevant expressions to predict the sentiment. Relevant expressions are those which satisfy the rules/conditions. After getting these expressions, we use a simple dictionary lookup along with attributes of words in a UNL graph to calculate the sentiment.

The rest of the paper is organized as follows. Section 2 discusses related work. Section 3 explains our approach in detail. The experimental setup is explained in Section 4. Results of the experiments are presented in Section 5. Section 6 discusses these results followed by conclusion in Section 7. Section 8 hints at some future work.

Proceedings of the 5th Workshop on Computational Approaches to Subjectivity, Sentiment and Social Media Analysis, pages 113–118, Baltimore, Maryland, USA. June 27, 2014.

2 Related Work

There has been a lot of work on using semantics in sentiment analysis. Hasan et al., (2012) have made use of semantic concepts as additional features in a word-based supervised sentiment classifier. Each entity is treated as a semantic concept e.g. *iPhone, Apple, Microsoft, MacBook, iPad, etc.*. Using these concepts as features, they try to measure their correlation with positive and negative sentiments. In Verma et al., (2009), effort has been made to construct document feature vectors that are sentiment-sensitive and use world knowledge. This has been achieved by incorporating sentiment-bearing words as features in document vectors. The use of WordNet synsets is found in Balamurali et al., (2012), Rentoumi (2009) and Tamara (2010). The one thing common with these approaches is that they make use of shallow semantics.An argument has been made in Choi and Carde (2008) for determining the polarity of a sentiment-bearing expression that words or constituents within the expression can interact with each other to yield a particular overall polarity. Structural inference motivated by compositional semantics has been used in this work. This work shows use of deep semantic information for the task of sentiment classification. A novel use of semantic frames is found in Ruppenhofer and Rehbein (2012). As a step towards making use of deep semantics, they propose SentiFrameNet which is an extension to FrameNet. A semantic frame can be thought of as a conceptual structure describing an event, relation, or object and the participants in it. It has been shown that potential and relevant sentiment bearing expressions can be easily pulled out from the sentence using the SentiFrameNet. All these works try to bridge the gap between rule-based and machine-learning based approaches but except the work in Ruppenhofer and Rehbein (2012), all the other approaches consider all the sentiment-bearing expressions in the text.

3 Use of Deep Semantics

Before devising any solution to a problem, it is advisable to have a concise definition of the problem. Let us look at the formal definition of the sentiment analysis problem as given in Liu (2010). Before we do that, let us consider the following review for a movie, *"1) I went to watch the new James Bond flick, Skyfall at IMAX which is the best theater in Mumbai with my brother a month ago. 2) I really liked the seating arrangement over there. 3) The screenplay was superb and kept me guessing till the end. 4) My brother doesnt like the hospitality in the theater even now. 5) The movie is really good and the best bond flick ever."* This is a snippet of the review for a movie named Skyfall . There are many entities and opinions expressed in it. 1) is an objective statement. 2) is subjective but is intended for the theater and not the movie. 3) is a positive statement about the screenplay which is an important aspect of the movie. 4) is a subjective statement but is made by the authors brother and also it is about the hospitality in the theater and not the movie or any of its aspects. 5) reflects a positive view of the movie for the author. We can see from this example that not only the opinion but the opinion holder and the entity about which the opinion has been expressed are also very important for sentiment analysis. Also, as can be seen from 1),4) and 5) there is also a notion of time associated with every sentiment expressed. Now, let us define the sentiment analysis problem formally as given in Liu (2010).

A direct opinion about the object is a quintuple $< o_j, f_{jk}, oo_{ijkl}, h_i, t_l >$, *where* o_j *is the the object,* f_{jk} *is the feature of the object* o_j, oo_{ijkl} *is the orientation or polarity of the opinion on feature* f_{jk} *of object* o_j, h_i *is the opinion holder and* t_i *is the time when the opinion is expressed by* h_i.

As can be seen from the formal definition of sentiment analysis and the motivating example, not all sentiment-bearing expressions contribute to the overall sentiment of the *text*. To solve this problem, we can make use of semantic roles in the *text*. Semantic role is the underlying relationship that the underlying participant has with the main verb. To identify the semantic roles, we make use of UNL in our approach.

UNL (Universal Networking Language)

UNL is declarative formal language specifically designed to represent semantic data extracted from natural language texts. In UNL, the information is represented by a semantic network, also called UNL graph. UNL graph is made up of three discrete semantic entities, Universal Words, Universal Relations, and Universal Attributes. Universal Words are nodes in the semantic network, Universal Relations are arcs linking UWs, and Universal attributes are properties of UWs. To understand

UNL better, let us consider an example. UNL graph for *"I like that bad boy"* is as shown in Figure 1

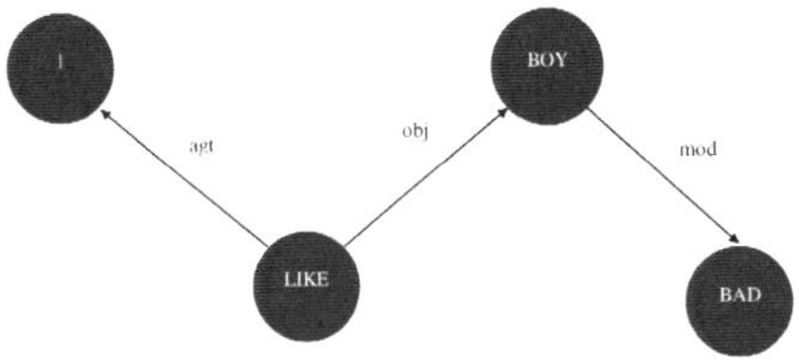

Figure 1: UNL graph for *"I like that bad boy"*

Here, *"I"*, *"like"*, *"bad"*, and *"boy"* are the UWs. *"agt"* (agent), *"obj"* (patient), and *"mod"* (modifier) are the Universal Relations. Universal attributes are the properties associated with UWs which will be explained as and when necessary with the rules of our algorithm.

UNL relations

Syntax of a UNL relation is as shown below,

$$< rel >:< scope >< source >;< target >$$

Where, $< rel >$ is the name of the relation, $< scope >$ is the scope of the relation, $< source >$ is the UW that assigns the relation, and $< target >$ is the UW that receives the relation

We have considered the following Universal relations in our approach,
1) <u>*agt* relation</u> : *agt* stands for agent. An agent is a participant in action that provokes a change of state or location. The *agt* relation for the sentence *"John killed Mary"* is *agt(killed , John).* This means that the action of *killing* was performed by *John*.
2) <u>*obj* relation</u> : *obj* stands for patient. A patient is a participant in action that undergoes a change of state or location. The *obj* relation for the sentence *"John killed Mary"* is *obj(killed , Mary).* This means that the patient/object of *killing* is *Mary*.
3) <u>*aoj* relation</u> : *aoj* stands for object of an attribute. In the sentence *"John is happy"*, the *aoj* relation is *aoj(happy , John).*
4) <u>*mod* relation</u> : *mod* stands for modifier of an object. In the sentence *"a beautiful book"*, the *mod* relation is *mod(book , beautiful).*
5) <u>*man* relation</u> : *man* relation stands for manner. It is used to indicate how the action, experience or process of an event is carried out. In the sentence *"The scenery is beautifully shot"*, the *man* relation is *man(beautifully , shot).*
6) <u>*and* relation</u> : *and* relation is used to state a conjunction between two entities. In the sentence *"Happy and cheerful"*, the *and* relation is *and(Happy,cheerful).*

Architecture

As show in Figure 1, the modifier *"bad"* is associated with the object of the main verb. It shouldn't affect the sentiment of the main agent. Therefore, we can ignore the modifier relation of the main object in such cases. After doing that, the sentiment of this sentence can be inferred to be positive. The approach followed in the project is to first generate a UNL graph for the given input sentence. Then a set of rules is applied and used to infer the sentiment of the sentence. The process is shown in Figure 2. The UNL generator shown in the Figure 2 has been developed at CFILT.[1] Before, the given piece of text is passed on to the UNL generator, it goes through a number of pre-processing stages. Removal of redundant punctuations, special characters, emoticons, etc. are part of this process. This is extremely important because the UNL generator is not able to handle special characters at the moment. We can see that, the performance of the overall system is limited by this. A more robust version of the UNL generator will certainly allow the system to infer the sentiment more accurately.

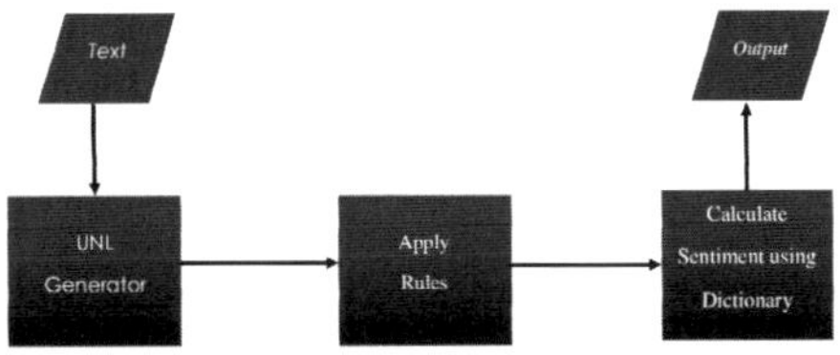

Figure 2: System Architecture

Rules

There is a separate rule for each relation. For each UW (Universal word) considered, if it has a *@not* attribute then its polarity is reversed. Rules used by the system are as follows,
1) If a given UW is source of the *agt* relation, then its polarity is added to the overall polarity of the

[1] `http://www.cfilt.iitb.ac.in/`

text. e.g., *"I like her"*. Here, the agt relation will be *agt (like , I)*. The polarity of like being positive, the overall polarity of the text is positive. e.g, *"I don't like her"*. Here the agt relation will be *agt (like@not , I)*. The polarity of like is positive but it has an attribute *@not* so its polarity is negative. The overall polarity of the text is negative in this case.

2) If a given UW is source or target of the *obj* relation and has the attribute *@entry* then its polarity is added to the overall polarity of the text. This rule merely takes into account the main verb of the sentence into account, and the it's is polarity considered. e.g., *"I like her"*, here the obj relation will be *obj (like@entry , her)*. The polarity of like being positive, the overall polarity of the text is positive

3) If a given UW is the source of the *aoj* relation and has the attribute *@entry* then its polarity is added to the overall polarity of the text. e.g., *"Going downtown tonight it will be amazing on the waterfront with the snow"*. Here, the *aoj* relation is *aoj (amazing@entry , it)*. *amazing* has a positive polarity and therefore overall polarity is positive in this case.

4) If a given UW is the target of the *mod* relation and the source UW has the attribute *@entry* or has the attribute *@indef* then polarity of the target UW is added to the overall polarity of the text. e.g., *"I like that bad boy"*. Here, the aoj relation is *mod (boy , bad)*. *bad* has a negative polarity but the source UW, boy does not have an *@entry* attribute. So, in this case negative polarity of bad is not considered as should be the case. e.g., *"She has a gorgeous face"*. Here, the mod relation is *mod (face@indef , gorgeous)*. *gorgeous* has a positive polarity and face has an attribute *@indef*. So, polarity of gorgeous should be considered.

5) If a given UW is the target of the *man* relation and the source UW has the attribute *@entry* then polarity of the target UW is added to the overall polarity of the text. Or if the target UW has the attribute *@entry* then also we can consider polarity of the target UW. e.g., *"He always runs fast"*. Here, the *aoj* relation is *mod (run@entry , fast)*. *fast* has a positive polarity and the source UW, run has the *@entry* attribute. So, in this case positive polarity of fast is added to the overall polarity of the sentence. Polarities of both the source and target UW of the *and* relation are considered.

6) In *"Happy and Cheerful"*, the *and* relation is *and(Happy, Cheerful)*. *Happy* and *Cheerful*, both have a positive polarity, which gives this sentence an overall positive polarity.

The polarity value of each individual word is looked up in a dictionary of positive of negative words used is Liu (2010) After all the rules are applied, summation of all the calculated polarity values is done. If this sum is greater than 0 then it is considered as positive, and negative otherwise. This system is negative biased due to the fact that people often tend to express negative sentiment indirectly or by comparison with something good. A more detailed discussion on negative texts is provided in section 6.

4 Experimental Setup

Analysis was performed for monolingual binary sentiment classification task. The language used in this case was *English*. The comparison was done between 5 systems viz. System using words as features, WordNet sense based system as given in Balamurali et al., (2012), Clusters based system as described in Kashyap et al., (2013), Discourse rules based system as given in Mukherjee and Bhattacharyya (2012), UNL rule based system. Two polarity datasets were used to perform the experiments.

1. EN-TD: English Tourism corpus as used in Ye et al., (2009). It consists of 594 positive and 593 negative reviews.

2. EN-PD: English Product (music albums) review corpus Blitzer et al., (2007). It consists of 702 positive and 702 negative reviews.

For the WordNet sense, and Clusters based systems, a manually sense tagged version of the (EN-PD) has been used. Also, a automatically sense tagged version of (EN-TD) was used on these systems. The tagging in the later case was using an automated WSD engine, trained on a tourism domain Khapra et al., (2013). The results reported for supervised systems are based on 10-fold cross validation.

5 Results

The results for monolingual binary sentiment classification task are shown in Table 1. The results reported are the best results obtained in case of supervised systems. The cluster based system

System	EN-TD	EN-PD
Bag of Words	85.53	73.24
Synset-based	88.47	71.58
Cluster-based	**95.20**	79.36
Discourse-based	71.52	64.81
UNL rule-based	86.08	**79.55**

Table 1: Classification accuracy (in %) for monolingual sentiment analysis

	EN-TD		EN-PD	
System	Pos	Neg	Pos	Neg
Discourse rules	94.94	48.06	**92.73**	36.89
UNL rules	**95.72**	**76.44**	90.75	**68.35**

Table 2: Classification accuracy (in %) for positive and negative reviews

performs the best in both cases. The UNL rule-based system performs better only than the bag of words and discourse rule based system. For EN-PD (music album reviews) dataset, the UNL based system outperforms every other system . These results are very promising for a rule-based system. The difference between accuracy for positive and negative reviews for the rule-based systems viz. Discourse rules based and UNL rules based is shown in Table 2. It can be seen that the Discourse rules based system performs slightly better than the UNL based system for positive reviews. On the other hand, the UNL rules based system outperforms it in case of negative reviews by a huge margin.

6 Discussion

The UNL generator used in this case is the bottleneck in terms of performance due to it's speed. It can take a long time to generate UNL graphs for large sentences. Also, it makes use of the standard NLP tools viz. parsing, co-reference resolution, etc. to assign the proper semantic roles in the given *text*. It is well known fact that these techniques work properly only on structured data. The language used in the reviews present in both the datasets is unstructured in considerable number of cases. The UNL generator is still in its infancy and cannot handle *text* involving special characters. Due to these reasons, a proper UNL graph is not generated in some cases. Also, it is not able to generator proper UNL graphs for even well structured sentences. As a result of these things, the classification accuracy is low. Negative reviews are difficult to classify due to comparitive statements and presence of positive words. Also there are some sarcastic sentences which are difficult to classify. Sarcasm is a very difficult problem to tackle. Some related works can be found in Carvalho et al., (2009) and Muresan et al., (2011). In some cases, the reviewers make use of their native language and expressions. This is a big problem for the task of monolingual sentiment classification.

7 Conclusion

This paper made use of deep semantics to tackle the the problem of sentiment analysis. A semantic role labeling method through generation of a UNL graph was used to do this. The main motivation behind this research was the fact that not all sentiment bearing expressions contribute to the overall sentiment of the *text*. The approach was evaluated on two datasets and compared with successful previous approaches which don't make use of deep semantics. The system underperformed all the supervised systems but showed promise by yielding better results than the other rule-based approach. Also, in some cases the performance was very close to the other supervised systems. The system works well on sentences where are inherently complex and difficult for sentiment analysis as it makes use of semantic role labeling. Any rule based system can never be exhaustive in terms of rules. We always need to add new rules to improve on it. In some case, adding new rules might cause side-effects. In this case, as the rules are intuitive, adding of new rules will be easy. Also, analysis of the results hints at some ways to tackle specific problems effectively.

8 Future Work

Adding more rules to the system will help to improve the system. Language gets updated almost daily, we plan to update our dictionary with these new words and expressions to increase the accuracy. Also, we plan to replace the UNL system with a dependency parsing system and apply rules similar to the ones described in this work.

References

Ruppenhofer, Josef and Rehbein, Ines. 2012. *Semantic frames as an anchor representation for sentiment analysis*. Proceedings of the 3rd Workshop in Computational Approaches to Subjectivity and Sentiment Analysis

Mukherjee, Subhabrata and Bhattacharyya, Pushpak. 2012. *Sentiment Analysis in Twitter with Lightweight Discourse Analysis*. COLING

Balamuralı, AR and Joshi, Aditya and Bhattacharyya, Pushpak 2011. *Harnessing wordnet senses for supervised sentiment classification*. Proceedings of the Conference on Empirical Methods in Natural Language Processing

Rentoumi, Vassiliki and Giannakopoulos, George and Karkaletsis, Vangelis and Vouros, George A 2009. *Sentiment analysis of figurative language using a word sense disambiguation approach*. Proceedings of the International Conference RANLP

Martın-Wanton, Tamara and Balahur-Dobrescu, Alexandra and Montoyo-Guijarro, Andres and Pons-Porrata, Aurora 2010. *Word sense disambiguation in opinion mining: Pros and cons*. Special issue: Natural Language Processing and its Applications

Kashyap Popat, Balamurali A.R, Pushpak Bhattacharyya and Gholamreza Haffari 2013. *The Haves and the Have-Nots: Leveraging Unlabelled Corpora for Sentiment Analysis*. The Association for Computational Linguistics

Saif, Hassan and He, Yulan and Alani, Harith 2012. *Semantic sentiment analysis of twitter*. The Semantic Web–ISWC 2012

Verma, Shitanshu and Bhattacharyya, Pushpak 2009. *Incorporating semantic knowledge for sentiment analysis*. Proceedings of ICON

Choi, Yejin and Cardie, Claire 2008. *Learning with compositional semantics as structural inference for subsentential sentiment analysis*. Proceedings of the Conference on Empirical Methods in Natural Language Processing

Liu, Bing 2010. *Sentiment analysis and subjectivity*. Handbook of natural language processing

Ye, Qiang and Zhang, Ziqiong and Law, Rob 2009. *Sentiment classification of online reviews to travel destinations by supervised machine learning approaches*. Expert Systems with Applications

Balamurali, AR and Khapra, Mitesh M and Bhattacharyya, Pushpak 2013. *Lost in translation: viability of machine translation for cross language sentiment analysis*. Computational Linguistics and Intelligent Text Processing

Blitzer, John and Dredze, Mark and Pereira, Fernando 2007. *Biographies, bollywood, boom-boxes and blenders: Domain adaptation for sentiment classification*. ACL

González-Ibáñez, Roberto and Muresan, Smaranda and Wacholder, Nina 2011. *Identifying Sarcasm in Twitter: A Closer Look*. ACL

Carvalho, Paula and Sarmento, Luís and Silva, Mário J and de Oliveira, Eugénio 2009. *Clues for detecting irony in user-generated contents: oh...!! it's so easy;-)*. ACM

Evaluating Sentiment Analysis Evaluation: A Case Study in Securities Trading

Siavash Kazemian **Shunan Zhao** **Gerald Penn**
Department of Computer Science
University of Toronto
{kazemian,szhao,gpenn}@cs.toronto.edu

Abstract

There are numerous studies suggesting that published news stories have an important effect on the direction of the stock market, its volatility, the volume of trades, and the value of individual stocks mentioned in the news. There is even some published research suggesting that automated sentiment analysis of news documents, quarterly reports, blogs and/or Twitter data can be productively used as part of a trading strategy. This paper presents just such a family of trading strategies, and then uses this application to re-examine some of the tacit assumptions behind how sentiment analyzers are generally evaluated, in spite of the contexts of their application. This discrepancy comes at a cost.

1 Introduction

Amidst the vast amount of user-generated and professionally-produced textual data, analysts from different fields are turning to the natural language processing community to sift through these large corpora and make sense of them. International collaborative projects such as the Digging into Data Challenge (2012) or the Big Data Conference sponsored by the Marketing Science Institute (2012) are some recent examples of these initiatives.

The proliferation of opinion-rich text on the World Wide Web, which includes anything from product reviews to political blog posts, led to the growth of sentiment analysis as a research field more than a decade ago. The market need to quantify opinions expressed in social media and the blogosphere has provided a great opportunity for sentiment analysis technology to make an impact in many sectors, including the financial industry, in which interest in automatically detecting news sentiment in order to inform trading strategies extends back at least 10 years. In this case, sentiment takes on a slightly different meaning; positive sentiment is not the emotional and subjective use of laudatory language. Rather, a news article that contains positive sentiment is optimistic about the future financial prospects of a company.

Zhang and Skiena (2010) have shown that news sentiment can effectively inform simple market neutral trading algorithms, producing a maximum yearly return of around 30%, and even more when using sentiment from blogs and Twitter data. They did so, however, without an appropriate baseline, making it very difficult to appreciate the significance of this number. Using a very standard sentiment analyzer, we are able to garner annualized returns over twice that percentage (70.1%), and in a manner that highlights some of the better design decisions that Zhang and Skiena (2010) made, viz., their decision to use raw SVM scores rather than discrete positive or negative sentiment classes, and their decision to go long (resp., short) in the n best- (worst-) ranking securities rather than to treat all positive (negative) securities equally. We trade based upon the raw SVM score itself, rather than its relative rank within a basket of other securities, and tune a threshold for that score that determines whether to go long, neutral or short. We sample our stocks for both training and evaluation with and without *survivor bias*, the tendency for long positions in stocks that are publicly traded as of the date of the experiment to pay better using historical trading data than long positions in random stocks sampled on the trading days themselves. Most of the evaluations of sentiment-based trading either unwittingly adopt this bias, or do not need to address it because their returns are computed over historical periods so brief. We also provide appropriate trading baselines as well as Sharpe ratios to attempt to quan-

Proceedings of the 5th Workshop on Computational Approaches to Subjectivity, Sentiment and Social Media Analysis, pages 119–127,
Baltimore, Maryland, USA. June 27, 2014.

tify the relative risk inherent to our experimental strategies. As tacitly assumed by most of the work on this subject, our trading strategy is not portfolio-limited, and our returns are calculated on a percentage basis with theoretical, commission-free trades.

Our motivation for undertaking this study has been to reappraise the evaluation standards for sentiment analyzers. It is not at all uncommon within the sentiment analysis community to evaluate a sentiment analyzer with a variety of classification accuracy or hypothesis testing scores such as F-measures, kappas or Krippendorff alphas derived from human-subject annotations, even when more extensional measures are available. In securities trading, this would of course include actual market returns from historical data. With Hollywood films, another popular domain for automatic sentiment analysis, one might refer to box-office returns or the number of award nominations that a film receives rather than to its star-rankings on review websites where pile-on and confirmation biases are widely known to be rampant. Are the opinions of human judges, paid or unpaid, a sufficient proxy for the business cases that actually drive the demand for sentiment analyzers?

We regret to report that they are not. We have even found a particular modification to our standard financial sentiment analyzer that, when evaluated against an evaluation test set sampled from the same pool of human-subject annotations as the analyzer's training data, returns significantly poorer performance, but when evaluated against actual market returns, yields significantly better performance. This should worry researchers who rely on classification accuracies and hypothesis tests relative to human-subject data, because the improvements that they report, whether based on better feature selection or different pattern recognition algorithms, may in fact not be improvements at all.

The good news, however, is that, based upon our experience within this particular domain, training on human-subject annotations and then tuning on more extensional data, in cases where the latter are less abundant, seems to suffice for bringing the evaluation back to reality. A likely machine-learning explanation for this is that whenever two unbiased estimators are pitted against each other, they often result in an improved combined performance because each acts as a regularizer against the other. If true, this merely attests to the relative independence of task-based and human-annotated knowledge sources. A more HCI-oriented view would argue that direct human-subject annotations are highly problematic unless the annotations have been elicited in manner that is *ecologically valid*. When human subjects are paid to annotate quarterly reports or business news, they are paid regardless of the quality of their annotations, the quality of their training, or even their degree of comprehension of what they are supposed to be doing. When human subjects post film reviews on web-sites, they are participating in a cultural activity in which the quality of the film under consideration is only one factor. These sources of annotation have not been properly controlled.

2 Related Work in Financial Sentiment Analysis

Studies confirming the relationship between media and market performance date back to at least Niederhoffer (1971), who looked at NY Times headlines and determined that large market changes were more likely following world events than on random days. Conversely, Tetlock (2007) looked at media pessimism and concluded that high media pessimism predicts downward prices. Tetlock (2007) also developed a trading strategy, achieving modest annualized returns of 7.3%. Engle and Ng (1993) looked at the effects of news on volatility, showing that bad news introduces more volatility than good news. Chan (2003) claimed that prices are slow to reflect bad news and stocks with news exhibit momentum. Antweiler and Frank (2004) showed that there is a significant, but negative correlation between the number of messages on financial discussion boards about a stock and its returns, but that this trend is economically insignificant. Aside from Tetlock (2007), none of this work evaluated the effectiveness of an actual sentiment-based trading strategy.

There is, of course, a great deal of work on automated sentiment analysis as well; see Pang and Lee (2008) for a survey. More recent developments that are germane to our work include the use of different information retrieval weighting schemes (Paltoglou and Thelwall, 2010) and the utilization of Latent Dirichlet Allocation (LDA) in a joint sentiment/topic framework (Lin and He, 2009).

There has also been some work that analyzes the

sentiment of financial documents without actually using those results in trading strategies (Koppel and Shtrimberg, 2004; Ahmad et al., 2006; Fu et al., 2008; O'Hare et al., 2009; Devitt and Ahmad, 2007; Drury and Almeida, 2011). As to the relationship between sentiment and stock price, Das and Chen (2007) performed sentiment analysis on discussion board posts. Using this analysis, they built a "sentiment index" that computed the time-varying sentiment of the 24 stocks in the Morgan Stanley High-Tech Index (MSH), and tracked how well their index followed the aggregate price of the MSH itself. Their sentiment analyzer was based upon a voting algorithm, although they also discussed a vector distance algorithm that performed better. Their baseline, the Rainbow algorithm, also came within 1 percentage point of their reported accuracy. This is one of the very few studies that has evaluated sentiment analysis itself (as opposed to a sentiment-based trading strategy) against market returns (versus gold-standard sentiment annotations). Das and Chen (2007) focused exclusively on discussion board messages and their evaluation was limited to the stocks on the MSH, whereas we focus on Reuters newswire and evaluate over a wide range of NYSE-listed stocks and market capitalization levels.

Butler and Keselj (2009) try to determine sentiment from corporate annual reports using both character n-gram profiles and readability scores. They also developed a sentiment-based trading strategy with high returns, but do not report how the strategy works or how they computed the returns, making the results difficult to compare to ours. Basing a trading strategy upon annual reports also calls into question the frequency with which the trading strategy could be exercised.

The work that is most similar to ours is that of Zhang and Skiena (2010). They look at both financial blog posts and financial news, forming a market-neutral trading strategy whereby each day, companies are ranked by their reported sentiment. The strategy then goes long and short on equal numbers of positive- and negative-sentiment stocks, respectively. They conduct their trading evaluation over the period from 2005 to 2009, and report a yearly return of roughly 30% when using news data, and yearly returns of up to 80% when they use Twitter and blog data. Furthermore, they trade based upon sentiment ranking rather than pure sentiment analysis, i.e., instead of trading based on the raw sentiment score of the document, they first rank the documents and trade based on this relative ranking.

Zhang and Skiena (2010) compare their strategy to two strategies which they term Worst-sentiment Strategy and Random-selection Strategy. The Worst-sentiment Strategy trades the opposite of their strategy, going short on positive sentiment stocks and going long on negative sentiment stocks. The Random-selection Strategy randomly picks stocks to go long and short in. As trading strategies, these baselines set a very low standard. Our evaluation compares our strategy to standard trading benchmarks such as momentum trading and holding the S&P, as well as to oracle trading strategies over the same trading days.

3 Method and Materials

3.1 News Data

Our dataset consists of a combination of two collections of *Reuters* news documents. The first was obtained for a roughly evenly weighted collection of 22 small-, mid- and large-cap companies, randomly sampled from the list of all companies traded on the NYSE as of 10th March, 1997. The second was obtained for a collection of 20 companies randomly sampled from those companies that were publicly traded in March, 1997 and still listed on 10th March, 2013. For both collections of companies, we collected every chronologically third Reuters news document about them from the period March, 1997 to March, 2013. The news articles prior to 10th March, 2005 were used as training data, and the news articles on or after 10th March, 2005 were reserved as testing data. We chose to split the dataset at a fixed date rather than randomly in order not to incorporate future news into the classifier through lexical choice.

In total, there were 1256 financial news documents. Each was labelled by two human annotators as being one of negative, positive, or neutral sentiment. The annotators were instructed to determine the state of the author's belief about the company, rather than to make a personal assessment of the company's prospects. Of the 1256, only the 991 documents that were labelled twice as negative or positive were used for training and evaluation.

Representation	Accuracy
bm25_freq	81.143%
term_presence	80.164%
bm25_freq_with_sw	79.827%
freq_with_sw	75.564%
freq	79.276%

Table 1: Average 10-fold cross validation accuracy of the sentiment classifier using different term-frequency weighting schemes. The same folds were used in all feature sets.

3.2 Sentiment Analysis and Intrinsic Evaluation

For each selected document, we first filter out all punctuation characters and the most common 429 stop words. Our sentiment analyzer is a support-vector machine with a linear kernel function implemented using SVM^{light} (Joachims, 1999). We have experimented with raw term frequencies, binary term-presence features, and term frequencies weighted by the BM25 scheme, which had the most resilience in the study of information-retrieval weighting schemes for sentiment analysis by Paltoglou and Thelwall (2010). We performed 10 fold cross-validation on the training data, constructing our folds so that each contains an approximately equal number of negative and positive examples. This ensures that we do not accidentally bias a fold.

Pang et al. (2002) use word presence features with no stop list, instead excluding all words with frequencies of 3 or less. Pang et al. (2002) normalize their word presence feature vectors, rather than term weighting with an IR-based scheme like BM25, which also involves a normalization step. Pang et al. (2002) also use an SVM with a linear kernel on their features, but they train and compute sentiment values on film reviews rather than financial texts, and their human judges also classified the training films on a scale from 1 to 5, whereas ours used a scale that can be viewed as being from -1 to 1, with specific qualitative interpretations assigned to each number. Antweiler and Frank (2004) use SVMs with a polynomial kernel (of unstated degree) to train on word frequencies relative to a three-valued classification, but they only count frequencies for the 1000 words with the highest mutual information scores relative to the classification labels. Butler and Keselj (2009) also use an SVM trained upon a very different set of features, and with a polynomial kernel of degree 3.

As a sanity check, we measured the accuracy of our sentiment analyzer on film reviews by training and evaluating on Pang and Lee's (Pang and Lee, 2004) film reviews dataset, which contains 1000 positively and 1000 negatively labelled reviews. Pang and Lee conveniently labelled the folds that they used when they ran their experiments. Using these same folds, we obtain an average accuracy of 86.85%, which is comparable to Pang and Lee's 86.4% score for subjectivity extraction.

Table 1 shows the performance of SVM with BM25 weighting on our Reuters evaluation set versus several baselines. All baselines are identical except for the term weighting schemes used, and whether stop words were removed. As can be observed, SVM-BM25 has the highest sentiment classification accuracy: 80.164% on average over the 10 folds. This compares favourably with previous reports of 70.3% average accuracy over 10 folds on financial news documents (Koppel and Shtrimberg, 2004). We will nevertheless adhere to normalized term presence for now, in order to stay close to Pang and Lee's (Pang and Lee, 2004) implementation.

4 Task-based Evaluation

In our second evaluation protocol, we evaluate the accuracy of the sentiment analyzer by embedding the analyzer inside a simple trading strategy, and then trading with it.

Our trading strategy is simple: going long when the classifier reports positive sentiment in a news article about a company, and short when the classifier reports negative sentiment. In section 4.1, we use the discrete polarity returned by the classifier to decide whether go long/abstain/short a stock. In section 4.2 we instead use the raw SVM score that reports the distance of the current document from the classifier's decision boundary.

In section 4.3, we hold the trading strategy constant, and instead vary the document representation features in the underlying sentiment analyzer. Here, we measure both market return and classifier accuracy to determine whether they agree.

In all three experiments, we compare the per-position returns of trading strategies with the following four standards, where the number of days for which a position is held remains constant:

1. The momentum strategy computes the price

of the stock h days ago, where h is the holding period. Then, it goes long for h days if the previous price is lower than the current price. It goes short otherwise.

2. The S&P strategy simply goes long on the *S&P 500* for the holding period. This strategy completely ignores the stock in question and the news about it.

3. The oracle S&P strategy computes the value of the *S&P 500* index h days into the future. If the future value is greater than the current day's value, then it goes long on the *S&P 500* index. Otherwise, it goes short.

4. The oracle strategy computes the value of the stock h days into the future. If the future value is greater than the current day's value, then it goes long on the stock. Otherwise, it goes short.

The oracle and oracle S&P strategies are included as toplines to determine how close the experimental strategies come to ones with perfect knowledge of the future. "Market-trained" is the same as "experimental" at test time, but trains the sentiment analyzer on the market return of the stock in question for h days following a training article's publication, rather than the article's annotation.

Strategy	Period	Return	S. Ratio
Experimental	30 days	-0.037%	-0.002
	5 days	0.763%	0.094
	3 days	0.742%	0.100
	1 day	0.716%	0.108
Momentum	30 days	1.176%	0.066
	5 days	0.366%	0.045
	3 days	0.713%	0.096
	1 day	0.017%	-0.002
S&P	30 days	0.318%	0.059
	5 days	-0.038%	-0.016
	3 days	-0.035%	-0.017
	1 day	0.046%	0.036
Oracle S&P	30 days	3.765%	0.959
	5 days	1.617%	0.974
	3 days	1.390%	0.949
	1 day	0.860%	0.909
Oracle	30 days	11.680%	0.874
	5 days	5.143%	0.809
	3 days	4.524%	0.761
	1 day	3.542%	0.630
Market-trained	30 days	0.286%	0.016
	5 days	0.447%	0.054
	3 days	0.358%	0.048
	1 day	0.533%	0.080

Table 2: Returns and Sharpe ratios for the Experimental, baseline and topline trading strategies over 30, 5, 3, and 1 day(s) holding periods.

4.1 Experiment One: Utilizing Sentiment Labels in the Trading Strategy

Given a news document for a publicly traded company, the trading agent first computes the sentiment class of the document. If the sentiment is positive, the agent goes long on the stock on the date the news is released. If the sentiment is negative, it goes short. All trades are made based on the adjusted closing price on this date. We evaluate the performance of this strategy using four different holding periods: 30, 5, 3, and 1 day(s).

The returns and Sharpe ratios are presented in Table 2 for the four different holding periods and the five different trading strategies. The Sharpe ratio can be viewed as a return to risk ratio. A high Sharpe ratio indicates good return for relatively low risk. The Sharpe ratio is calculated as follows:

$$S = \frac{E[R_a - R_b]}{\sqrt{\mathrm{var}(R_a - R_b)}},$$

where R_a is the return of a single asset and R_b is the return of a risk-free asset, such as a 10-year U.S. Treasury note.

The returns from this experimental trading system are fairly low, although they do beat the baselines. A one-way ANOVA test between the experimental strategy, momentum strategy, and S&P strategy using the percent returns from the individual trades yields p values of 0.06493, 0.08162, 0.1792, and 0.4164, respectively, thus failing to reject the null hypothesis that the returns are not significantly higher. Furthermore, the means and medians of all three trading strategies are approximately the same and centred around 0. The standard deviations of the experimental strategy and the momentum strategy are nearly identical, differing only in the thousandths digit. The standard deviations for the S&P strategy differ from the other two strategies due to the fact that the strategy buys and sells the entire S&P 500 index and not the individual stocks described in the news articles. There is, in fact, no convincing evidence that discrete sentiment class leads to an improved trading strategy from this or any other study with

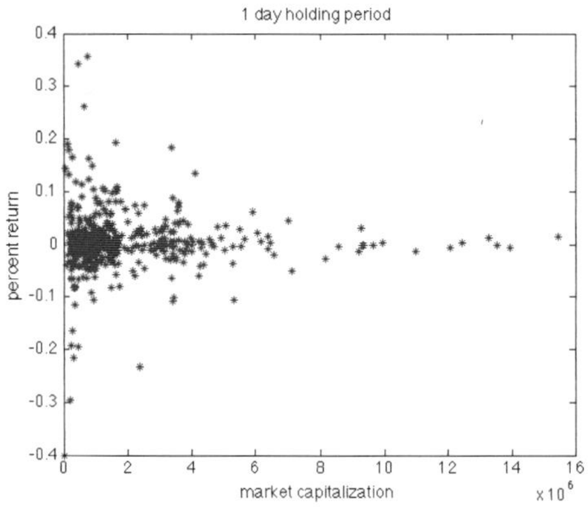

Figure 1: Percent returns for 1 day holding period versus market capitalization of the traded stocks.

which we are familiar, based on the details that they publish. One may note, however, that the returns from the experimental strategy have slightly higher Sharpe ratios than either of the baselines.

One may also note that using a sentiment analyzer mostly beats training directly on market data, which to an extent vindicates the use of sentiment annotation as a separate component.

Figure 1 shows the market capitalizations of the companies for each individual trade plotted against the percent return for the 1 day holding period. The correlation between the two variables is not significant. The graphs for the other holding periods are similar.

Figure 2 shows the percent change in share value plotted against the raw SVM score for the different holding periods. We can see a weak correlation between the two. For the 30 days, 5 days, 3 days, and 1 day holding periods, the correlations are 0.017, 0.16, 0.16, and 0.16, respectively. The line of best fit is shown.

This prompts us to conduct our next experiment.

4.2 Experiment Two: Utilizing SVM scores in Trading Strategy

4.2.1 Variable Single Threshold

Previously, we would label a document as positive (negative) if the score is above (below) 0, because 0 is the decision boundary. However, 0 might not be the best threshold for providing high returns. To examine this hypothesis, we took the evaluation dataset, i.e. the dataset with news articles dated on or after March 10, 2005, and divided it into two folds where each fold has an equal number of documents with positive and negative sentiment. We used the first fold to determine an optimal threshold value θ and trade using the data from the second fold and that threshold. For every news article, if the SVM score for that article is above (below) θ, then we go long (short) on the appropriate stock on the day the article was released. A separate theta was determined for each holding period. We varied θ from -1 to 1 in increments of 0.1.

Using this method, we were able to obtain much higher returns. In order of 30, 5, 3, and 1 day holding periods, the returns were 0.057%, 1.107%, 1.238%, and 0.745%. This is a large improvement over the previous returns, as they are average per-position figures.[1]

4.2.2 Safety Zones

For every news item classified, SVM outputs a score. For a binary SVM with a linear kernel function f, given some feature vector $\mathbf{x}$, $f(\mathbf{x})$ can be viewed as the signed distance of $\mathbf{x}$ from the decision boundary (Boser et al., 1992). It is then possibly justified to interpret raw SVM scores as degrees to which an article is positive or negative.

As in the previous section, we separate the evaluation set into the same two folds, only now we use two thresholds, $\theta > \zeta$. We will go long when the SVM score is above θ, abstain when the SVM score is between θ and ζ, and go short when the SVM score is below ζ. This is a strict generalization of the above experiment, in which $\zeta = \theta$.

For convenience, we will assume in this section that $\zeta = -\theta$, leaving us again with one parameter to estimate. We again vary θ from 0 to 1 in increments of 0.1. Figure 3 shows the returns as a function of θ for each holding period on the development dataset. If we increased the upper bound on θ to be greater than 1, then there would be too few trading examples (less than 10) to reliably calculate the Sharpe ratio. Using this method with $\theta = 1$, we were able to obtain even higher returns: 3.843%, 1.851%, 1.691, and 2.251% for the 30, 5, 3, and 1 day holding periods, versus 0.057%, 1.107%, 1.238%, and 0.745% in the second task-based experiment.

4.3 Experiment Three: Feature Selection

Let us now hold the trading strategy fixed (at the final one, with safety zones) and turn to the underlying sentiment analyzer. With a good trading

[1]Training directly on market data, by comparison, yields -0.258%, -0.282%, -0.036% and -0.388%, respectively.

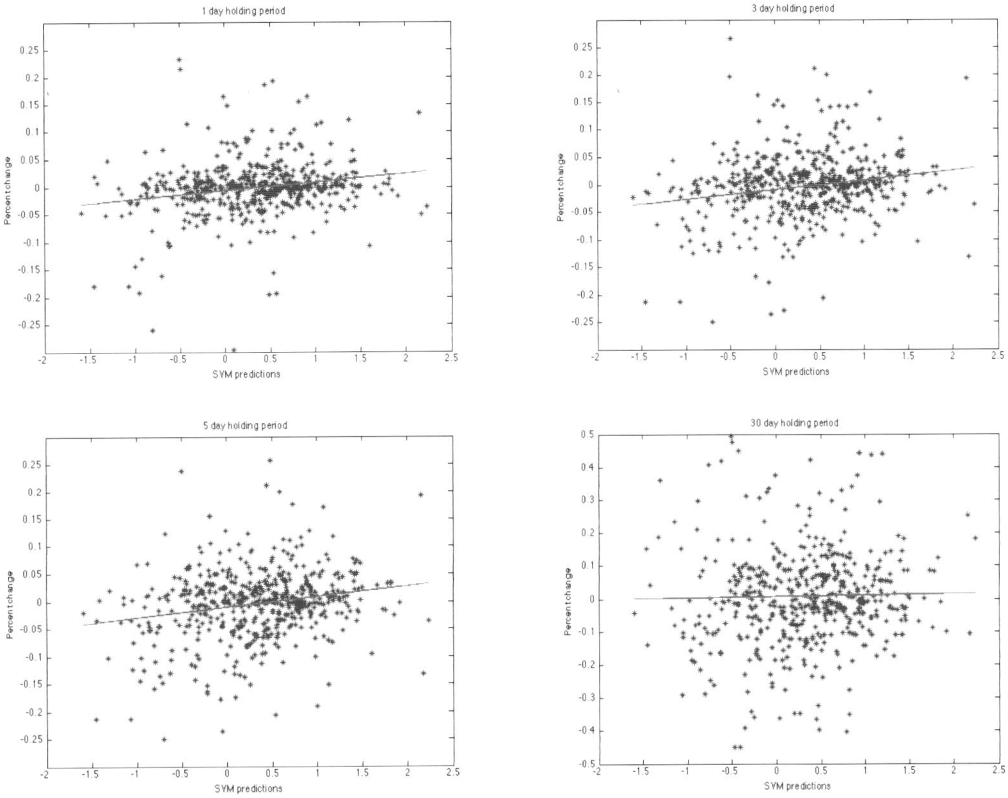

Figure 2: Percent change of trade returns plotted against SVM values for the 1, 3, 5, and 30 day holding periods in Exp. 1. Graphs are cropped to zoom in.

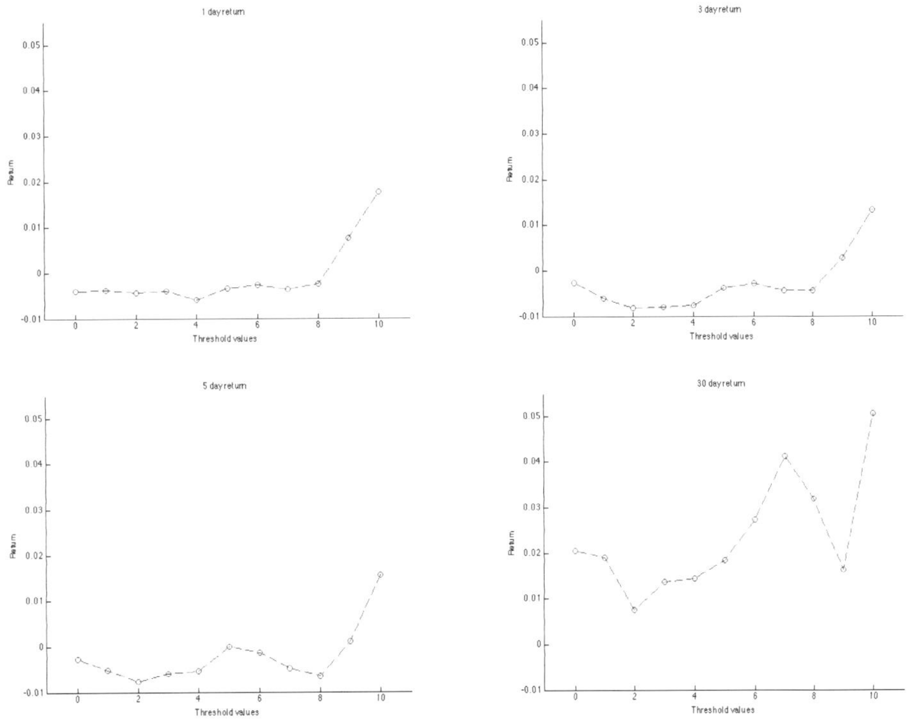

Figure 3: Returns for the different thresholds on the development dataset for 30, 5, 3, and 1 day holding periods in Exp. 2 with safety zone.

Representation	Accuracy	π	κ	α	30 days	5 days	3 days	1 day
term_presence	80.164%	0.589	0.59	0.589	3.843%	1.851%	1.691%	2.251%
bm25_freq	81.143%	0.609	0.61	0.609	1.110%	1.770%	1.781%	0.814%
bm25_freq_d_n_copular	62.094%	0.012	0.153	0.013	3.458%	2.834%	2.813%	2.586%
bm25_freq_with_sw	79.827%	0.581	0.583	0.581	0.390%	1.685%	1.581%	1.250%
freq	79.276%	0.56	0.566	0.561	1.596%	1.221%	1.344%	1.330%
freq_with_sw	75.564%	0.47	0.482	0.47	1.752%	0.638%	1.056%	2.205%

Table 3: Sentiment classification accuracy (average 10-fold cross-validation), Scott's π, Krippendorff's α, Cohen's κ and trade returns of different feature sets and term frequency weighting schemes in Exp. 3. The same folds were used for the different representations. The non-annualized returns are presented in columns 3-6.

strategy in place, it is clearly possible to vary some aspect of the sentiment analyzer in order to determine its best setting in this context. Is classifier accuracy a suitable proxy for this? Indeed, we may hope that classifier accuracy will be more portable to other possible tasks, but then it must at least correlate well with task-based performance.

We tried another feature representation for documents. In addition to evaluating those attempted earlier, we now hypothesize that the passive voice may be useful to emphasize in our representations, as the existential passive can be used to evade responsibility. So we add to the BM25 weighted vector the counts of word tokens ending in "n" or "d" as well as the total count of every conjugated form of the copular verb: "be", "is", "am", "are", "were", "was", and "been". These three features are superficial indicators of the passive voice.

Table 3 presents the returns obtained from these 6 feature representations. The feature set with BM25-weighted term frequencies plus the number of copulars and tokens ending in "n", "d" (bm25_freq_d_n_copular) yields higher returns than any other representation attempted on the 5, 3, and 1 day holding periods, and the second-highest on the 30 days holding period, But it has the worst classification accuracy by far: a full 18 percentage points below term presence. This is a very compelling illustration of how misleading an intrinsic evaluation can be. Other agreement measures likewise point in the opposite direction.

5 Conclusion

In this paper, we examined the application of sentiment analysis in stock trading strategies. We built a binary sentiment classifier that achieves high accuracy when tested on movie data and financial news data from *Reuters*. In three task-based experiments, we evaluated the usefulness of sentiment analysis in simple trading strategies. Although high annual returns can be achieved by simply utilizing sentiment labels in a trading strategy, they can be improved by incorporating the output of the SVM's decision function. We have observed that classification accuracy alone is not always an accurate predictor of task-based performance. This calls into question the benefit of using intrinsic sentiment classification accuracy, particularly when the relative cost of a task-based evaluation may be comparably low. We have also determined that training on human-annotated sentiment does in fact perform better than training on market returns themselves. So sentiment analysis is an important component, but it must be tuned against task data.

As for future work, we plan to explore other ways of deriving sentiment labels for supervised training. It would be interesting to infer the sentiment of published news from stock price fluctuations instead of the reverse. Given that many factors that affect stock price fluctuations and further considering the drift that is present in stock prices as a result of bad published news (Chan, 2003), this mode of inference is not simple and requires careful consideration and design.

Furthermore, we would like to study how sentiment is defined in the financial world. In particular, we want to examine the relationship between the precise definition of news sentiment and trading strategy returns. This study has used a rather general definition of news sentiment. We are interested in exploring if there is a more precise definition that can improve trading performance.

Our current price data only includes adjusted opening and closing prices. Most of our news data contain only the date of the article, not the specific time. It is possible that a much shorter-term trading strategy than we can currently test would be even more successful.

References

Khurshid Ahmad, David Cheng, and Yousif Almas. 2006. Multi-lingual sentiment analysis of financial news streams. In *Proceedings of the 1st International Conference on Grid in Finance*.

Werner Antweiler and Murray Z Frank. 2004. Is all that talk just noise? the information content of internet stock message boards. *The Journal of Finance*, 59(3):1259–1294.

Bernhard E. Boser, Isabelle M. Guyon, and Vladimir N. Vapnik. 1992. A training algorithm for optimal margin classifiers. In *Proceedings of the fifth annual workshop on Computational learning theory*, COLT '92, pages 144–152, New York, NY, USA. ACM.

Matthew Butler and Vlado Keselj. 2009. Financial forecasting using character n-gram analysis and readability scores of annual reports. In *Proceedings of Canadian AI'2009*, Kelowna, BC, Canada, May.

Wesley S. Chan. 2003. Stock price reaction to news and no-news: Drift and reversal after headlines. *Journal of Financial Economics*, 70(2):223–260.

Sanjiv R. Das and Mike Y. Chen. 2007. Yahoo! for amazon: Sentiment extraction from small talk on the web. *Management Science*, 53(9):1375–1388.

Joseph Davies-Gavin, Clarence Lee, and Lingling Zhang. 2012. Conference summary. In *Marketing Science Institute Conference on Big Data*, December.

Ann Devitt and Khurshid Ahmad. 2007. Sentiment polarity identification in financial news: A cohesion-based approach. In *Proceedings of the ACL*.

Brett Drury and J. J. Almeida. 2011. Identification of fine grained feature based event and sentiment phrases from business news stories. In *Proceedings of the International Conference on Web Intelligence, Mining and Semantics*, WIMS '11, pages 27:1–27:7, New York, NY, USA. ACM.

Robert F. Engle and Victor K. Ng. 1993. Measuring and testing the impact of news on volatility. *The Journal of Finance*, 48(5):1749–1778.

Tak-Chung Fu, Ka ki Lee, Donahue C. M. Sze, Fu-Lai Chung, Chak man Ng, and Chak man Ng. 2008. Discovering the correlation between stock time series and financial news. In *Web Intelligence*, pages 880–883.

Thorsten Joachims. 1999. Making large-scale svm learning practical. advances in kernel methods-support vector learning, b. schölkopf and c. burges and a. smola.

Moshe Koppel and Itai Shtrimberg. 2004. Good news or bad news? let the market decide. In *AAAI Spring Symposium on Exploring Attitude and Affect in Text*, pages 86–88. Press.

Chenghua Lin and Yulan He. 2009. Joint sentiment/topic model for sentiment analysis. In *Proceedings of the 18th ACM conference on Information and knowledge management*, CIKM '09, pages 375–384, New York, NY, USA. ACM.

Victor Niederhoffer. 1971. The analysis of world events and stock prices. *Journal of Business*, pages 193–219.

Neil O'Hare, Michael Davy, Adam Bermingham, Paul Ferguson, Páraic Sheridan, Cathal Gurrin, and Alan F. Smeaton. 2009. Topic dependent sentiment analysis of financial blogs. In *Proceedings of the 1st international CIKM workshop on Topic-sentiment analysis for mass opinion measurement*.

Georgios Paltoglou and Mike Thelwall. 2010. A study of information retrieval weighting schemes for sentiment analysis. In *Proceedings of the ACL*, pages 1386–1395. Association for Computational Linguistics.

Bo Pang and Lillian Lee. 2004. A sentimental education: Sentiment analysis using subjectivity summarization based on minimum cuts. In *Proceedings of the ACL*, pages 271–278.

Bo Pang and Lillian Lee. 2008. Opinion mining and sentiment analysis. *Foundations and trends in information retrieval*, 2(1-2):1–135.

Bo Pang, Lillian Lee, and Shivakumar Vaithyanathan. 2002. Thumbs up?: sentiment classification using machine learning techniques. In *Proceedings of the ACL-02 conference on Empirical methods in natural language processing - Volume 10*, EMNLP '02, pages 79–86, Stroudsburg, PA, USA. Association for Computational Linguistics.

Paul C. Tetlock. 2007. Giving content to investor sentiment: The role of media in the stock market. *The Journal of Finance*, 62(3):1139–1168.

Christa Williford, Charles Henry, and Amy Friedlander. 2012. One culture: Computationally intensive research in the humanities and social sciences. Technical report, Council on Library and Information Resources, June.

Wenbin Zhang and Steven Skiena. 2010. Trading strategies to exploit blog and news sentiment. In *The 4th International AAAI Conference on Weblogs and Social Media*.

Sentiment Classification on Polarity Reviews: An Empirical Study Using Rating-based Features

Dai Quoc Nguyen[⋆] and **Dat Quoc Nguyen**[⋆] and **Thanh Vu**[†] and **Son Bao Pham**[⋆]

[⋆] Faculty of Information Technology
University of Engineering and Technology
Vietnam National University, Hanoi
{dainq, datnq, sonpb}@vnu.edu.vn

[†] Computing and Communications Department
The Open University, Milton Keynes, UK
thanh.vu@open.ac.uk

Abstract

We present a new feature type named *rating-based feature* and evaluate the contribution of this feature to the task of document-level sentiment analysis. We achieve state-of-the-art results on two publicly available standard polarity movie datasets: on the dataset consisting of 2000 reviews produced by Pang and Lee (2004) we obtain an accuracy of 91.6% while it is 89.87% evaluated on the dataset of 50000 reviews created by Maas et al. (2011). We also get a performance at 93.24% on our own dataset consisting of 233600 movie reviews, and we aim to share this dataset for further research in sentiment polarity analysis task.

1 Introduction

This paper focuses on document-level sentiment classification on polarity reviews. Specifically, the document-level sentiment analysis is to identify either a positive or negative opinion in a given opinionated review (Pang and Lee, 2008; Liu, 2010). In early work, Turney (2002) proposed an unsupervised learning algorithm to classify reviews by calculating the mutual information between a given phrase and reference words "excellent" and "poor". Pang et al. (2002) applied supervised learners of Naive Bayes, Maximum Entropy, and Support Vector Machine (SVM) to determine sentiment polarity over movie reviews. Pang and Lee (2004) presented a minimum cut-based approach to detect whether each review' sentence is more likely subjective or not. Then the sentiment of the whole document review is determined by employing a machine learning method on the document's most-subjective sentences.

Recently, most sentiment polarity classification systems (Whitelaw et al., 2005; Kennedy and Inkpen, 2006; Martineau and Finin, 2009; Maas et al., 2011; Tu et al., 2012; Wang and Manning, 2012; Nguyen et al., 2013) have obtained state-of-the-art results by employing machine learning techniques using combination of various features such as N-grams, syntactic and semantic representations as well as exploiting lexicon resources (Wilson et al., 2005; Ng et al., 2006; Baccianella et al., 2010; Taboada et al., 2011).

In this paper, we firstly introduce a novel rating-based feature for the sentiment polarity classification task. Our rating-based feature can be seen by that the scores – *which users employ to rate entities on review websites* – could bring useful information for improving the performance of classifying polarity sentiment. For a review with no associated score, we could predict a score for the review in the use of a regression model learned from an external independent dataset of reviews and their actual corresponding scores. We refer to the

Proceedings of the 5th Workshop on Computational Approaches to Subjectivity, Sentiment and Social Media Analysis, pages 128–135,
Baltimore, Maryland, USA. June 27, 2014.

predicted score as the rating-based feature for learning sentiment categorization.

By combining the rating-based feature with unigrams, bigrams and trigrams, we then present the results from sentiment classification experiments on the benchmark datasets published by Pang and Lee (2004) and Maas et al. (2011).

To sum up, the contributions of our study are:

- Propose a novel rating-based feature and describe regression models learned from the external dataset to predict the feature value for the reviews in the two experimental datasets.
- Achieve state-of-the-art performances in the use of the rating-based feature for the sentiment polarity classification task on the two datasets.
- Analyze comprehensively the proficiency of the rating-based feature to the accuracy performance.
- Report additional experimental results on our own dataset containing 233600 reviews.

The paper is organized as follows: We provide some related works and describe our approach in section 2 and section 3, respectively. We detail our experiments in section 4. Finally, section 5 presents concluding remarks.

2 Related Works

Whitelaw et al. (2005) described an approach using appraisal groups such as "extremely boring", or "not really very good" for sentiment analysis, in which a semi-automatically constructed lexicon is used to return appraisal attribute values for related terms. Kennedy and Inkpen (2006) analyzed the effect of contextual valence shifters on sentiment classification of movie reviews. Martineau and Finin (2009) weighted bag-of-words in employing a delta TF-IDF function for training SVMs to classify the reviews. Maas et al. (2011) introduced a model to catch sentiment information and word meanings. Tu et al. (2012) proposed an approach utilizing high-impact parse features for convolution kernels in document-level sentiment recognition. Meanwhile, Wang and Manning (2012) obtained a strong and robust performance by identifying simple NB and SVM variants. Dahl et al. (2012) applied the restricted Boltzmann machine to learn representations capturing meaningful syntactic and semantic properties of words. In addition, Nguyen et al. (2013) constructed a two-stage sentiment classifier applying reject option, where documents rejected at the first stage are forwarded to be classified at the second stage.

3 Our Approach

We apply a supervised machine learning approach to handle the task of document-level sentiment polarity classification. For machine learning experiments, besides the N-gram features, we employ a new rating-based feature for training models.

3.1 Rating-based Feature

Our proposed rating-based feature can be seen by the fact that, on various review websites, users' reviews of entities such as products, services, events and their properties ordinarily associate to scores which the users utilize to rate the entities: a positive review mostly corresponds with a high score whereas a negative one strongly correlates to a low score. Therefore, the rated score could bring useful information to enhance the sentiment classification performance.

We consider the rated score associated to each document review as a feature named RbF for learning classification model, in which the rating-based feature RbF's value of each document review in training and test sets is estimated based on a regression model learned from an *external independent dataset* of reviews along with their actual associated scores.

3.2 N-gram Features

In most related works, unigrams are considered as the most basic features, in which each document is represented as a collection of unique unigram words where each word is considered as an individual feature.

In addition, we take into account bigrams and trigrams since a combination of unigram, bigram and trigram features (N-grams) could outperform a baseline performance based on unigram features as pointed out in (Ng et al., 2006; Martineau and Finin, 2009; Wang and Manning, 2012).

We calculate the value of the N-gram feature i^{th} by using *term frequency - inverse document frequency (tf*idf)* weighting scheme for the document D as follows:

$$Ngram_{iD} = log(1 + tf_{iD}) * log\frac{|\{D\}|}{df_i}$$

where tf_{iD} is the occurrence frequency of the feature i^{th} in document D, $|\{D\}|$ is the number of documents in the data corpus $\{D\}$, and df_i is the number of documents containing the feature i^{th}. We then normalize N-gram feature vector of the document D as follows:

$$\overrightarrow{\eta Ngram_D} = \frac{\sum_{\delta \in \{D\}} \|\overrightarrow{Ngram_\delta}\|}{|\{D\}| * \|\overrightarrow{Ngram_D}\|} * \overrightarrow{Ngram_D}$$

4 Experimental Results

4.1 Experimental Setup

Benchmark datasets. We conducted experimental evaluations on the polarity dataset PL04[1] of 2000 movie reviews constructed by Pang and Lee (2004). The dataset PL04 consists of 1000 positive and 1000 negative document reviews in which each review was split into sentences with lowercase normalization. In order to compare with other published results, we evaluate our method according to 10-fold cross-validation scheme on the dataset PL04.

In addition, we carry out experiments on a large dataset IMDB11[2] of 50000 movie reviews produced by Maas et al. (2011). The large dataset IMDB11 contains a training set of 25000 labeled reviews and a test set of 25000 labeled reviews, where training and test sets have 12500 positive reviews and 12500 negative reviews in each.

Machine learning algorithm. We utilize SVM implementation in LIBSVM[3] (Chang and Lin, 2011) for learning classification models in all our experiments on the two benchmark datasets.

Preprocess. We did not apply stop-word removal, stemming and lemmatization to the dataset in any process in our system, because such stop-words as negation words might indicate sentiment orientation, and as pointed out by Leopold and Kindermann (2002) stemming and lemmatization processes could be detrimental to accuracy.

In all experiments on PL04, *we kept 30000 most frequent N-grams in the training set for each cross-validation run over each polarity class*. After removing duplication, on an average, there are total 39950 N-gram features including 10280 unigrams, 20505 bigrams and 9165 trigrams.

On the dataset IMDB11, *it was 40000 most frequent N-grams in each polarity class* to be selected for creating feature set of 53724 N-grams consisting of 13038 unigrams, 26907 bigrams and 13779 trigrams.

RbF feature extraction procedure. We aim to create an independent dataset for learning a regression model to predict the feature RbF's value for each document review in experimental datasets. Since Maas et al. (2011) also provided 7091 IMDB movie titles[4], we used those movie titles to extract all user reviews that their associated scores[5] are not equal to either 5 or 6 from the IMDB website.

[1] http://www.cs.cornell.edu/people/pabo/movie-review-data/

[2] http://ai.stanford.edu/~amaas/data/sentiment/

[3] http://www.csie.ntu.edu.tw/~cjlin/libsvm/. Using linear kernel, default parameter settings.

[4] http://www.imdb.com/. It is noted that the 7091 movie titles are completely different from those that were used to produce the datasets PL04 and IMDB11.

[5] The score scale ranges from 1 to 10. As the reviews corresponding to rated scores 5 or 6 are likely to be ambiguous for expressing positive or negative sentiments, we decide to ignore those 5-6 score reviews. We also abandon user reviews having no associated rated scores.

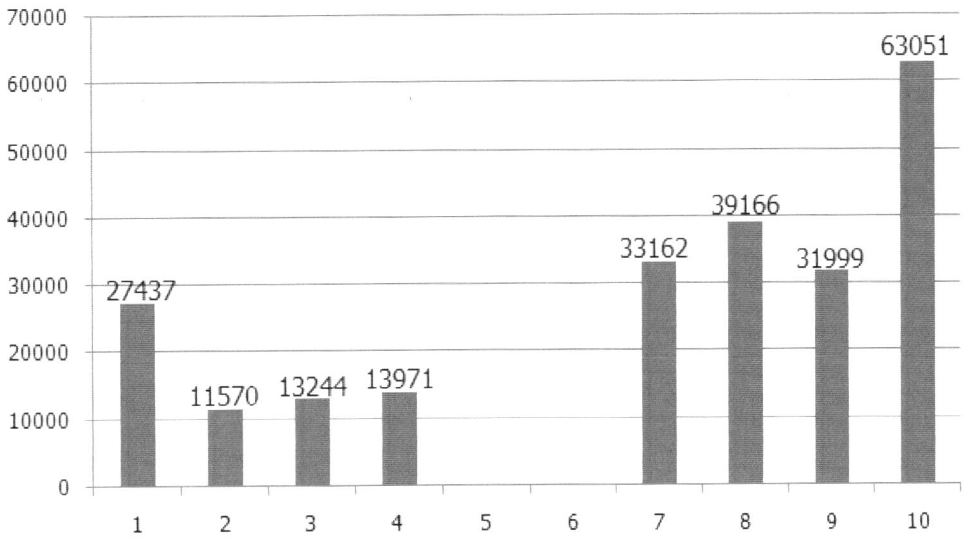

Figure 1: The score distribution of SAR14.

Consequently, we created an independent *s*core-*a*ssociated *r*eview dataset (SAR14)[6] of 233600 movie reviews and their accompanying actual scores. The external dataset SAR14 consists of 167378 user reviews connected to scores valued from 7 to 10, and 66222 reviews linked to 1-4 rated ones (as shown in Figure 1). Using SAR14, we employed Support Vector Regression algorithm implemented in SVM^{light} package[7] (Joachims, 1999) to learn the regression model employing unigram features. We then applied the learned model to predict real score values of reviews in the benchmark datasets, and referred to those values as the values of the feature RbF.

Although using N-gram features (consisting of unigrams, bigrams and trigrams) may give better results, we tend to use only unigrams for learning the regression model because of saving the training time on the large size of SAR14. Furthermore, using unigram features is good enough as presented in section 4.4. To extract the RbF feature's value for each PL04's movie review, the regression model was trained with 20000 most frequent unigrams whilst 35000 most frequent unigrams were employed to learn regression model to estimate the RbF feature for each review in the dataset IMDB11.

4.2 Results on PL04

Table 1 shows the accuracy results of our method in comparison with other state-of-the-art SVM-based performances on the dataset PL04. Our method achieves a baseline accuracy of 87.6% which is higher than baselines obtained by all other compared approaches. The accuracy based on only RbF feature is 88.2% being higher than those published in (Pang and Lee, 2004; Martineau and Finin, 2009; Nguyen et al., 2013). By exploiting a combination of unigram and RbF features, we gain a result at 89.8% which is comparable with the highest performances reached by (Whitelaw et al., 2005; Ng et al., 2006; Wang and Manning, 2012). It is evident that rising from 87.6% to 89.8% proves the effectiveness of using RbF in sentiment polarity classification.

Turning to the use of N-grams, we attain an accuracy of 89.25% which is 1.65% higher than the baseline result of 87.6%. This shows the usefulness of adding bigram and trigram

[6]The SAR14 data set is available to download at https://sites.google.com/site/nquocdai/resources

[7]http://svmlight.joachims.org/. Using with default parameter settings.

Features	PL04	IMDB11
Unigrams (baseline)	87.60	83.69
N-grams	89.25	88.67
RbF	88.20	89.14
Unigrams + RbF	89.80	84.71
N-grams + RbF	**91.60**	**89.87**
Pang and Lee (2004)	87.20	——
Whitelaw et al. (2005)	90.20	——
Ng et al. (2006)	90.50	——
Martineau and Finin (2009)	88.10	——
Maas et al. (2011)	88.90	88.89
Tu et al. (2012)	88.50	——
Dahl et al. (2012)	——	89.23
Wang and Manning (2012)	89.45	91.22
Nguyen et al. (2013)	87.95	——

Table 1: Accuracy results (in %).

features to improve the accuracy. With 91.6%, we reach a new state-of-the-art performance by combining N-gram and RbF features. We also note that our state-of-the-art accuracy is 1.1% impressively higher than the highest accuracy published by Ng et al. (2006).

4.3 Results on IMDB11

Table 1 also shows the performance results of our approach on the dataset IMDB11. Although our method gets a baseline accuracy of 83.69% which is lower than other baseline results of 88.23% and 88.29% reported by Maas et al. (2011) and Wang and Manning (2012) respectively, we achieve a noticeable accuracy of 89.14% based on only RbF feature.

Furthermore, starting at the result of 88.67% with N-gram features, we obtain a significant increase to 89.87% by employing N-gram and RbF features. Particularly, we do better than the performance at 89.23% published by Dahl et al. (2012) with a 0.64% improvement in accuracy on 160 test cases.

From our experimental results in section 4.2 and 4.3, we conclude that there are significant gains in performance results by adding bigrams and trigrams as well as RbF feature for sentiment polarity classification. Our method combining N-grams and RbF feature outperforms most other published results on the two benchmark datasets PL04 and IMDB11.

4.4 Effects of RbF to Accuracy

This section is to give a detail analysis about the effects of using RbF feature to accuracy results of our approach (as shown in Figure 2) using full combination of N-gram and RbF features in which the RbF feature is predicted by regression models learned on the dataset SAR14 in varying number **K** of most frequent unigrams from 5000 to 40000.

On the dataset PL04, the highest accuracy obtained by using only the RbF feature is 88.90% at K's value of 10000, which it is equal to that published by Maas et al. (2011). In most cases of using N-gram and RbF features, we obtain state-of-the-art results which are higher than 91%.

On the IMDB11 dataset, at K's value of 5000, we achieve the lowest accuracy of 89.29% by using N-gram and RbF features, which it is slightly higher than the accuracy of 89.23% given by Dahl et al. (2012). In cases that K's value is higher than 10000, accuracies using only RbF feature are around 89.1%, while using the full combination returns results which are higher than 89.74%.

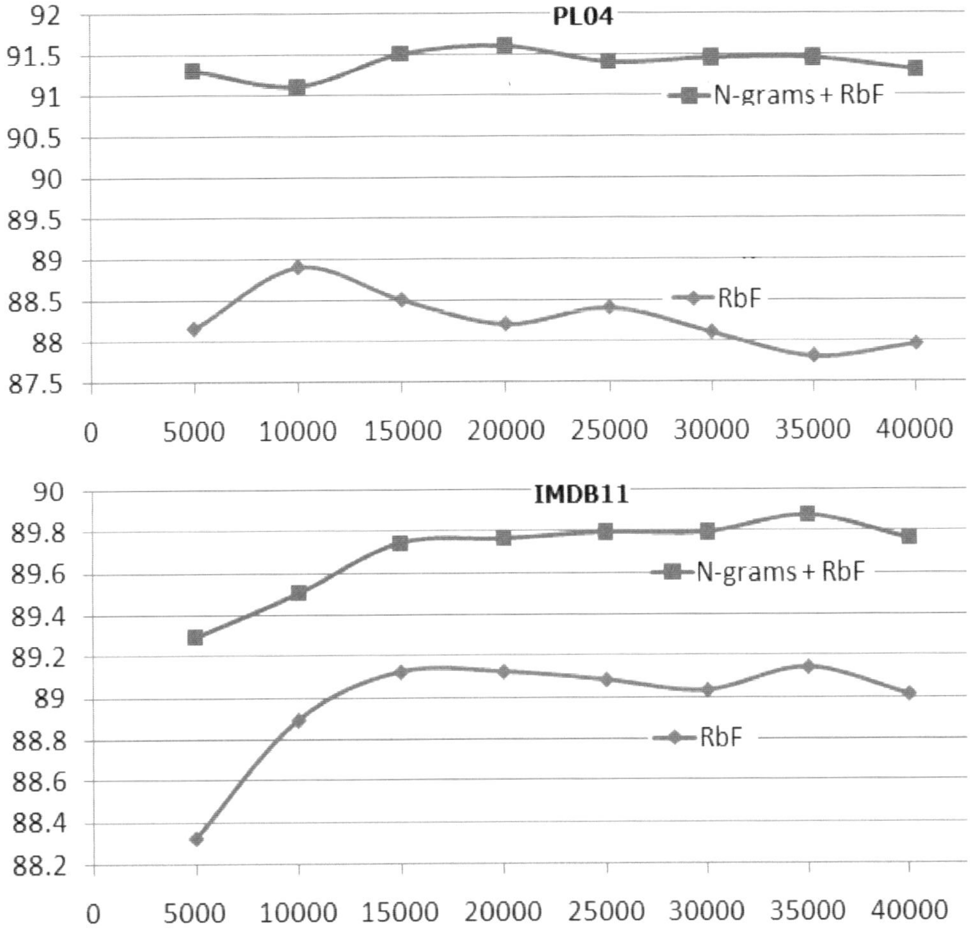

Figure 2: Effects of rating-based feature to our method's performance. The horizontal presents the number of unigram features selected for learning regression models.

4.5 Results on SAR14

As mentioned in section 4.1, our dataset SAR14 contains 233600 movie reviews. We label a review as 'positive' or 'negative' if the review has a score ≥ 7 or ≤ 4 respectively. Therefore, we create a very large dataset of 167378 positive reviews and 66222 negative reviews. Due to the large size of the dataset SAR14 and the training and classification time, we employed LIBLINEAR[8] (Fan et al., 2008) for this experiment under 10 fold cross validation scheme. We kept 50000 N-grams over each polarity class in the training set for each cross-validation run. Finally, we obtained an accuracy of *93.24%* by using N-gram features.

[8]Using L2-regularized logistic regression and setting tolerance of termination criterion to 0.01. http://www.csie.ntu.edu.tw/~cjlin/liblinear/

5 Conclusion

In this paper, we conducted an experimental study on sentiment polarity classification. We firstly described our new rating-based feature, in which the rating-based feature is estimated based on a regression model learned from our external independent dataset SAR14 of 233600 movie reviews. We then examined the contribution of the rating-based feature and N-grams in a machine learning-based approach on two datasets PL04 and IMDB11.

Specifically, we reach state-of-the-art accuracies at 91.6% and 89.87% on the dataset PL04 and IMDB11 respectively. Furthermore, by analyzing the effects of rating-based feature to accuracy performance, we show that the rating-based feature is very efficient to sentiment classification on polarity reviews. And adding bigram and trigram features also enhances accuracy performance. Furthermore, we get an accuracy of 93.24% on the dataset SAR14, and we also share this dataset for further research in sentiment polarity analysis task.

Acknowledgment

This work is partially supported by the Research Grant from Vietnam National University, Hanoi No. QG.14.04.

References

Stefano Baccianella, Andrea Esuli, and Fabrizio Sebastiani. 2010. Sentiwordnet 3.0: An enhanced lexical resource for sentiment analysis and opinion mining. In *Proceedings of the Seventh International Conference on Language Resources and Evaluation (LREC'10)*, pages 2200–2204.

Chih-Chung Chang and Chih-Jen Lin. 2011. LIBSVM: A library for support vector machines. *ACM Transactions on Intelligent Systems and Technology*, 2:27:1–27:27.

George Dahl, Hugo Larochelle, and Ryan P. Adams. 2012. Training restricted boltzmann machines on word observations. In *Proceedings of the 29th International Conference on Machine Learning (ICML-12)*, pages 679–686.

Rong-En Fan, Kai-Wei Chang, Cho-Jui Hsieh, Xiang-Rui Wang, and Chih-Jen Lin. 2008. LIBLINEAR: A Library for Large Linear Classification. *Journal of Machine Learning Research*, 9:1871–1874.

Thorsten Joachims. 1999. Making large-scale support vector machine learning practical. In Bernhard Schölkopf, Christopher J. C. Burges, and Alexander J. Smola, editors, *Advances in Kernel Methods: Support Vector Machines*, pages 169–184.

Alistair Kennedy and Diana Inkpen. 2006. Sentiment Classification of Movie Reviews Using Contextual Valence Shifters. *Computational Intelligence*, 22(2):110–125.

Edda Leopold and Jörg Kindermann. 2002. Text categorization with support vector machines. how to represent texts in input space? *Mach. Learn.*, 46(1-3):423–444.

Bing Liu. 2010. Sentiment analysis and subjectivity. In *Handbook of Natural Language Processing, Second Edition*, pages 1–38.

Andrew L. Maas, Raymond E. Daly, Peter T. Pham, Dan Huang, Andrew Y. Ng, and Christopher Potts. 2011. Learning word vectors for sentiment analysis. In *Proceedings of the 49th Annual Meeting of the Association for Computational Linguistics: Human Language Technologies, Vol 1*, pages 142–150.

Justin Martineau and Tim Finin. 2009. Delta tfidf: an improved feature space for sentiment analysis. In *Proceedings of the Third Annual Conference on Weblogs and Social Media*, pages 258–261.

Vincent Ng, Sajib Dasgupta, and S. M. Niaz Arifin. 2006. Examining the role of linguistic knowledge sources in the automatic identification and classification of reviews. In *Proceedings of the COLING/ACL on Main conference poster sessions*, pages 611–618.

Dai Quoc Nguyen, Dat Quoc Nguyen, and Son Bao Pham. 2013. A Two-Stage Classifier for Sentiment Analysis. In *Proceedings of the 6th International Joint Conference on Natural Language Processing*, pages 897–901.

Bo Pang and Lillian Lee. 2004. A sentimental education: Sentiment analysis using subjectivity summarization based on minimum cuts. In *Proceedings of the 42nd Meeting of the Association for Computational Linguistics (ACL'04)*, pages 271–278.

Bo Pang and Lillian Lee. 2008. Opinion Mining and Sentiment Analysis. *Foundations and Trends in Information Retrieval*, 2(1-2):1–135, January.

Bo Pang, Lillian Lee, and Shivakumar Vaithyanathan. 2002. Thumbs up?: sentiment classification using machine learning techniques. In *Proceedings of the ACL-02 conference on Empirical methods in natural language processing - Volume 10*, pages 79–86.

Maite Taboada, Julian Brooke, Milan Tofiloski, Kimberly Voll, and Manfred Stede. 2011. Lexicon-based methods for sentiment analysis. *Comput. Linguist.*, 37(2):267–307, June.

Zhaopeng Tu, Yifan He, Jennifer Foster, Josef van Genabith, Qun Liu, and Shouxun Lin. 2012. Identifying high-impact sub-structures for convolution kernels in document-level sentiment classification. In *Proceedings of the 50th Annual Meeting of the Association for Computational Linguistics (Volume 2: Short Papers)*, ACL '12, pages 338–343.

Peter D. Turney. 2002. Thumbs up or thumbs down?: semantic orientation applied to unsupervised classification of reviews. In *Proceedings of the 40th Annual Meeting on Association for Computational Linguistics*, ACL '02, pages 417–424.

Sida Wang and Christopher D. Manning. 2012. Baselines and bigrams: simple, good sentiment and topic classification. In *Proceedings of the 50th Annual Meeting of the Association for Computational Linguistics (Volume 2: Short Papers)*, ACL '12, pages 90–94.

Casey Whitelaw, Navendu Garg, and Shlomo Argamon. 2005. Using appraisal groups for sentiment analysis. In *Proceedings of the 14th ACM international conference on Information and knowledge management*, CIKM '05, pages 625–631.

Theresa Wilson, Janyce Wiebe, and Paul Hoffmann. 2005. Recognizing contextual polarity in phrase-level sentiment analysis. In *Proceedings of the conference on Human Language Technology and Empirical Methods in Natural Language Processing*, HLT '05, pages 347–354.

Effect of Using Regression on Class Confidence Scores in Sentiment Analysis of Twitter Data

Itir Onal[*], **Ali Mert Ertugrul**[†], **Ruken Cakici**[*]
[*]Department of Computer Engineering, Middle East Technical University, Ankara, Turkey
itir,ruken@ceng.metu.edu.tr
[†]Department of Information Systems, Middle East Technical University, Ankara, Turkey
alimert@metu.edu.tr

Abstract

In this study, we aim to test our hypothesis that confidence scores of sentiment values of tweets aid in classification of sentiment. We used several feature sets consisting of lexical features, emoticons, features based on sentiment scores and combination of lexical and sentiment features. Since our dataset includes confidence scores of real numbers in [0-1] range, we employ regression analysis on each class of sentiments. We determine the class label of a tweet by looking at the maximum of the confidence scores assigned to it by these regressors. We test the results against classification results obtained by converting the confidence scores into discrete labels. Thus, the strength of sentiment is ignored. Our expectation was that taking the strength of sentiment into consideration would improve the classification results. Contrary to our expectations, our results indicate that using classification on discrete class labels and ignoring sentiment strength perform similar to using regression on continuous confidence scores.

1 Introduction

In the past few years, there has been a growing interest in using microblogging sites such as Twitter. Generally, people tend to share their opinions, ideas about entities, topics and issues via these microblogs. Therefore, companies show interest in these for the sentiment analysis to be used as means of customer satisfaction evaluation about their products.

Although some tweets express direct sentiment, the polarity and intent of some tweets cannot be understood even by humans because of lack of context. Moreover, a tweet may be perceived as positive or negative by some people whereas others may think that the tweet is not polar. Therefore, sometimes it is not easy to assign a sentiment class to a tweet. Instead of assigning a single sentiment to a tweet, confidence scores reflecting the likelihoods of sentiments of the tweet may be provided. Our dataset consists of tweets and their corresponding confidence scores of five sentiments namely *positive, negative, neutral, irrelevant* and *unknown*. An analysis on the dataset reflects that, some tweets get similar confidence scores for many classes. In other words, different people assign different class labels to the same tweet. On the other hand, confidence scores of some tweets for a class are close to or equal to 1, meaning that the sentiment of the tweets are clear. If we have discrete class labels for all tweets, tweets assigned to classes with a low confidence score will have equal effect as the ones whose confidence scores are high during the training phase of sentiment analysis.

In this study, we investigate whether the strength of sentiment plays a role in classification or not. We build regression models to estimate the confidence scores of tweets for each class separately. Then, we assign the sentiment, whose confidence score is maximum among others to the tweet. On the other hand, we also converted the confidence scores to discrete class labels and performed classification directly. The experiments and results are explained in Section 5.

2 Related Work

Sentiment analysis on Twitter has some challenges compared to the classical sentiment analysis methods on formal documents since the tweets may have irregular structure, short length and non-English words. Moreover, they may include elements specific to microblogs such as hashtags, emoticons, etc. Go et al. (2009) used emoticons as features and Barbosa et al. (2010) used

Proceedings of the 5th Workshop on Computational Approaches to Subjectivity, Sentiment and Social Media Analysis, pages 136–141,
Baltimore, Maryland, USA. June 27, 2014. ©2014 Association for Computational Linguistics

retweets, hashtags, emoticons, links, etc. as features to classify the sentiments as positive or negative. Furthermore, Kouloumpis et al. (2011) showed that the features including presence of intensifiers, positive/negative/neutral emoticons and abbreviations are more successful than part-of-speech tags for sentiment analysis on Twitter. Saif et al. (2012) extracted sentiment topics from tweets and then used them to augment the feature space. Agarwal et al. (2011) used tree kernel to determine features and they used SVM, Naïve Bayes, Maximum entropy for classification. In our experiments we used k-Nearest Neighbor (k-NN) and SVM as classifiers.

Due to the rarity of class confidence scores of datasets in the literature, a few studies employ regression. Jain et al. (2012) use Support Vector Regression (SVR) for sentiment analysis in movie reviews but the labels they use are discrete. So, they use SVR directly for classification purpose, not regression. However, we employed SVR on confidence scores with the aim of regression. Moreover, Lu et al. (2011) use SVR in multi-aspect sentiment analysis to detect the ratings of each aspect. Since our approach does not include aspects, our results are not comparable with that of (Lu et al., 2011). The study of Liu (2012) consists of studies employing regression in sentiment analysis. Yet, in most of these studies the regressors are trained using discrete rating scores between 1 and 5. Furthermore, Pang et al. (2008) also mentions regression to classify sentiments using discrete rating scores. Unlike these approaches, we employ regression on real-valued confidence scores between 0 and 1.

3 Data Description and Pre-processing

The data set we use (Kaggle, 2013) consists of 77946 tweets which are obtained with the aim of sentiment classification. Each tweet is rated by multiple raters and as a result, each tweet has confidence scores of five classes namely *positive, negative, neutral, irrelevant* and *unknown*. Among 77946 tweets, only 800 of them has the maximum confidence score of *unknown* class. Therefore, in order to have a balanced dataset in our experiments, we selected 800 tweets from each class. As a result, the dataset used in our experiments is balanced and includes a total of 4000 tweets.

The data set includes tweets both relevant and irrelevant to weather. Tweets are expected to get high confidence score of irrelevant class if the tweet is not related to weather. Moreover, as their name implies, positive and negative confidence values represent the polarity level of each tweet towards weather. If a tweet is not polar, it is expected to be given a high neutral confidence score. Unknown class is expected to have a high score when the tweet is related with weather, but the polarity of tweet cannot be decided.

The tweets in the data set are labeled by multiple raters. Then, the confidence scores for labels are obtained by aggregating labels given to tweets by raters and the individual reliability of each rater. For a tweet, confidence scores of all categories sum to 1 and confidence score values are in range [0,1].

Before feature extraction, we pre-process the data in a few steps. Firstly, we remove *links* and *mentions* that are features specific to tweets. Then, we remove *emoticons* from the text while recording their number for each tweet in order to use them later.

4 Features

Our features can be divided into four main categories which are lexical features, emoticons, features based on sentiment scores and a combination of the lexical and sentiment features.

4.1 Lexical Features

We extracted two different lexical features which are word n-grams, part-of-speech (POS) n-grams. Using all tweets in our training data, we extracted only unigrams of words to be used as baseline. Moreover, after extracting POS tags of sentences in each tweet using the POS tagger given in (Toutanova et al., 2003), we computed unigrams and bigrams of POS tags. We considered the presence of word unigrams, POS unigrams and bigrams. Therefore, those features can get binary values.

4.2 Emoticons

In the preprocessing step, we remove the emoticons from the text. However, since emoticons carry sentiment information, we also record whether the tweet includes positive, negative or neutral emoticons (see Table 1) during the removal of emoticons. Therefore, we extract 3 binary features based on emoticon presence in the tweet.

Table 1: Emoticons and their sentiments

Sentiment	Emoticon
Positive	:) , :-), =), =D, :D
Negative	:(, :-(, =(, :/
Neutral	:|

4.3 Features Based on Sentiment Scores

We extract features based on sentiment scores using two different approaches. In the first one, we use SentiWordNet 3.0 (Baccianella et al., 2010) to obtain the sentiment scores of each word. We used the word and a tag representing the POS tag of the word to output the sentiment score of the word. Since the same word with different senses have different scores, we obtained a single sentiment score by computing the weighted average of SentiWordNet scores for each sense. Furthermore, POS tagging is performed as explained in 4.1. However, since POS tags of Penn TreeBank and SentiWordNet are different, we convert one to other as shown in Table 2. Therefore, the sentiment score for a word is obtained after the Penn TreeBank tags are converted to SentiWordNet tags. Using all the words in a tweet and their corresponding SentiWordNet scores, we compute the following features:

- # of words having positive sentiment
- # of words having negative sentiment
- total sentiment score

As a result, using SentiWordNet, we extract 3 more features. We observe that the acronym *lol* representing *laughing out loud* is used extensively in tweets. In order to keep its meaning, when a *lol* is encountered, its sentiment score is assigned to 1. Moreover, sentiment scores of words having other POS tags than the ones in Table 2 are assigned to 0. When *not* is encountered, we multiply the sentiment score of its successor word by -1 and convert the sentiment score of *not* to 0.

Table 2: Conversion of POS tags to SentiWordNet tags

SentiWordNet Tag	Penn TreeBank tag
a (adjective)	JJ, JJR, JJS
n (noun)	NN, NNS, NNP, NNPS
v (verb)	VB,VBD, VBG, VBN, VBP, VPZ
r (adverb)	RB, RBR, RBS

The second approach is using LabMT word list (Dodds et al., 2011) which includes scores for sentiment analysis. It includes a list of words with their happiness rank, happiness average and happiness standard deviation. In our study, we computed those values for all the words in a tweet and extracted the 6 features namely the minima and the maxima of happiness rank, happiness average and happiness standard deviation.

Note that, if a word is not encountered in either SentiWordNet or labMT dictionary, then the sentiment score of that word is assigned to 0.

4.4 Combination of Lexical and Sentiment Features

We extract features using POS tags and sentiment scores. After the conversion of POS tags in Table 2, we have four main tags namely, ***a** (adjective)*, ***n** (noun)*, ***v** (verb)*, ***r** (adverb)*. For each tweet we compute the number of adjectives, nouns, verbs and adverbs having positive, negative and neutral sentiments. Therefore, we extract 12 features using combination of lexical and sentiment features. Table 3 shows all the features used.

5 Experiments

In our experiments we extract the features using training data set. Then, we formed training and test feature matrices using these features. By using these matrices, we both conduct classification and regression.

We train separate regressors for each class using the training feature matrix and confidence scores of the corresponding class. We use Support Vector Regression (SVR) library of (Chang et al., 2011) in our computations. Recall that, the confidence scores are between 0 and 1 and they carry information about how likely it is that a tweet belongs to a specified class. For instance it is very likely that a positive with a 0.9 confidence score is actually a positive, whereas a positive with a 0.2 confidence score is much less likely to be positive. In order to assign a sentiment label to a test tweet, we separately test that tweet with the regressors trained for each class. Then, each regressor assigns a score between 0 and 1 to that test tweet. Finally, we assign the class label with maximum score to the test tweet.

During classification, we convert confidence scores to discrete class labels by assigning them the class which the majority of the raters agreed upon. Using training feature matrix and their corresponding discrete labels, we train a Support Vec-

Table 3: Features used in our experiments

Lexical	word unigram	f_1
	POS unigram + bigram	f_2
Emoticons	# of pos, neg, neu emoticons	f_3
Sentiment Scores	SentiWordNet (# of pos, neg words, total sentiment score)	f_4
	labMT (min, max of happiness rank, avg and std)	f_5
Sentiment + Lexical	# of pos a, pos n, pos v, pos r # of neg a, neg n, neg v, neg r # of neu a, neu n, neu v, neu r	f_6

tor Machine (SVM) using the method of (Chang et al., 2011) and a k-Nearest Neighbor (k-NN) classifier. SVM and k-NN directly assigns class labels to test tweets.

We employed classification and regression on three types of data having classes:

- positive - negative - neutral - irrelevant - unknown
- positive - negative - neutral
- positive - negative

5.1 Positive vs. Negative vs. Neutral vs. Irrelevant vs. Unknown

In 5-class classification, our dataset consists of 4000 tweets (800 for each class). We used 3000 of them as training data (600 for each class) and 1000 of them as test data (200 for each class). Since our dataset is balanced, chance accuracy is 20% if we assing all the tweets to one class. Using various features to train k-NN, SVM and SVR, we obtained the results in Table 4.

Table 4: k-NN, SVM and SVR Performances for 5-class classification

Features	**k-NN**	**SVM**	**SVR**
Unigram (f_1)	0,3140	0,4430	0,4290
$+f_2$	0,3130	0,4330	0,4300
$+f_3$	0,3350	0,4410	0,4350
$+f_5$	0,3280	0,4460	0,4340
$+f_6$	0,3490	0,4500	0,4260
$+f_3, f_4$	0,3450	**0,4570**	0,4370
$+f_3, f_5$	0,3300	0,4430	0,4340
$+f_4, f_5$	**0,3550**	0,4490	0,4350
$+f_4, f_6$	0,3490	0,4550	0,4260
$+f_3, f_4, f_5$	0,3530	0,4490	**0,4430**
$+f_2, f_3, f_4, f_5$	0,3500	0,4350	0,4420
$+f_2, f_3, f_4, f_5, f_6$	0,3430	0,4250	0,4350

Results in Table 4 show that, classification with SVM performs the best when emoticon features (f_3) and SentiWordNet features (f_4) are combined with unigram baseline. Moreover, using emoticon features (f_3), and sentiment score features (both SentiWordNet (f_4) and labMT (f_5)) together with the word unigram baseline perform the best among others when SVR is used. Notice that using regression performs slightly worse than using SVM for most of the feature combinations. However, the p-value of SVM vs. SVR is 0.06, meaning that the performance improvement of SVM is insignificant. On the other hand, using SVR always performs much better than k-NN with a p-value of 2×10^{-10}.

5.2 Positive vs. Negative vs. Neutral

In 3-class classification, our dataset consists of 2400 tweets (800 for each class). We use 1800 of them as training data (600 for each class) and 600 of them as test data (200 for each class). Since our dataset is balanced, chance accuracy is 33%. Using various features to train k-NN, SVM and SVR, we obtain the results in Table 5.

Table 5: k-NN, SVM and SVR Performances for 3-class classification

Features	**k-NN**	**SVM**	**SVR**
Unigram (f_1)	0,5183	0,6650	0,6467
$+f_2$	0,5017	0,6267	0,6450
$+f_3$	0,5333	**0,6767**	0,6567
$+f_5$	0,5467	0,6617	0,6533
$+f_6$	0,5450	**0,6767**	**0,6700**
$+f_3, f_4$	0,5550	0,6717	0,6583
$+f_3, f_5$	0,5517	0,6700	0,6667
$+f_4, f_5$	0,5533	0,6733	0,6567
$+f_4, f_6$	0,5233	0,6750	**0,6700**
$+f_3, f_4, f_5$	**0,5700**	0,6700	0,6550
$+f_2, f_3, f_4, f_5$	0,5367	0,6583	0,6567
$+f_2, f_3, f_4, f_5, f_6$	0,5450	0,6500	0,6550

Table 5 reflects that, using the combination of sentiment and lexical features (f_6) play an important role in positive - negative - neutral classification using SVR. On the other hand, using emoticon features (f_3) with unigram baseline or labMT features (f_5) with unigram baseline performs the best when SVM is used. It can be seen that SVM performs slightly better than SVR most of the time yet the performance improvemen is again insignificant with a p-value of 0.58. Furthermore, they always perform much better than k-NN with a p-value of 2×10^{-8}.

5.3 Positive vs. Negative

In 2-class classification, since we have 800 positive and 800 negative tweets among 4000 tweets, we used 1600 tweets. We used 1200 of them as training data (600 for each class) and 400 of them as test data (200 for each class). Since our dataset is balanced, chance accuracy is 50%. Using the same set of features to train k-NN, SVM and SVR, we obtained the results in Table 6.

Table 6: k-NN, SVM and SVR Performances for 2-class classification

Features	k-NN	SVM	SVR
Unigram (f_1)	0,6275	0,7700	0,7775
$+f_2$	0,6575	0,7575	0,7375
$+f_3$	**0,7225**	0,7850	0,7775
$+f_5$	0,6900	0,7575	0,7700
$+f_6$	0,6950	**0,7975**	**0,7975**
$+f_3, f_4$	0,6900	0,7825	0,7850
$+f_3, f_5$	0,7125	0,7800	0,7700
$+f_4, f_5$	0,6950	0,7800	0,7800
$+f_4, f_6$	0,6725	0,7950	**0,7975**
$+f_3, f_4, f_5$	0,7000	0,7725	0,7800
$+f_2, f_3, f_4, f_5$	0,6675	0,7700	0,7800
$+f_2, f_3, f_4, f_5, f_6$	0,6675	0,7825	0,7750

In positive - negative classification, using combination of sentiment and lexical features (f_6) with unigram baseline results in the highest performance among all when either SVM or SVR is used. Similar to previous classification results, performance improvement of using SVM on discrete labels instead of using SVR is insignificant with a p-value of 0.46 whereas SVR provides a significant performance improvement over k-NN with a p-value of 5×10^{-4}.

6 Conclusion

In this study we conducted sentiment analysis on tweets about weather. We performed two types of experiments, one using confidence scores directly by regression and the other one by discreticising this information and using discrete classifiers. We expected that employing regression on confidence scores would better discriminate the sentiment classes of tweets than the classification on discrete labels since they consider the sentiment strength.

First, we extracted various types of features including lexical features, emoticons, sentiment scores and combination of lexical and sentiment features. Then, we created the feature vectors for these tweets. We trained a regressor for each class separately using continuous valued confidence scores. Then, a test tweet is assigned to the label, whose estimated confidence score is the highest among others. In our second experiment, we assigned class labels having the maximum confidence score to the tweets in the training set directly. Using the training data and discrete valued class labels, we trained a classifier. Then, a test tweet is assigned to a class label by the classifier.

Our results indicate that using classification on discrete valued class labels performs slightly better than using regression, which considers confidence scores during training. However, the performance improvement is shown to be insignificant. We would expect a significant performance improvement using SVR compared to SVM as in the case of k-NN vs. SVR. However, we explored that the effect of strength of sentiment is insignificant.

As future work, we will employ our methods on datasets including continuous scores rather than discrete class labels such as movie reviews including ratings. Moreover, we may enhance our approach on multi-aspect sentiment analysis problems where each aspect is given ratings.

References

Alec Go, Richa Bhayani and Lei Huang. 2009. Twitter sentiment classification using distant supervision. *Stanford Digital Library Technologies Project, NJ.*

Luciano Barbosa and Junlan Feng 2010. Robust Sentiment Detection on Twitter from Biased and Noisy Data. *Proceedings of COLING, Beijing China*, 36–44.

Efthymios Kouloumpis, Theresa Wilson and Johanna Moore 2011. Twitter Sentiment Analysis: The Good the Bad and the OMG! *Proceedings of the ICWSM, Barcelona, Spain.*

Hassan Saif, Yulan He, and Harith Alani 2012. Alleviating data sparsity for twitter. *2nd Workshop on Making Sense of Microposts, Lyon, France.*

Apoorv Agarwal, Boyi Xie, Ilia Vovsha, Owen Rambow and Rebecca Passonneau 2011. Sentiment analysis of twitter data. *Proceedings of the Workshop on Languages in Social Media, Portland, Oregon, USA*, 30–38

Siddharth Jain and Sushobhan Nayak 2012. Sentiment Analysis of Movie Reviews: A Study of Features and Classifiers. *CS221 Course Project: Artificial Intelligence , Stanford (Fall 2012) [Report].*

Bin Lu, Myle Ott, Claire Cardie, and Benjamin Tsou 2011. Multi-aspect sentiment analysis with topic models. *The ICDM2011 Workshop on Sentiment Elicitation from Natural Text for Information Retrieval and Extraction, Vancouver, Canada.*

Kristina Toutanova, Dan Klein, Christopher Manning, and Yoram Singer. 2003. Feature-Rich Part-of-Speech Tagging with a Cyclic Dependency Network. *Proceedings of HLT-NAACL 2003, Edmonton, Canada*, 252–259.

Stefano Baccianella, Andrea Esuli, and Fabrizio Sebastiani 2010. SentiWordNet 3.0: An Enhanced Lexical Resource for Sentiment Analysis and Opinion Mining *Proceedings of the Seventh International Conference on Language Resources and Evaluation (LREC'10), Valletta, Malta*

Peter S. Dodds, Kameron D.Harris, Isabel M. Kloumann, Catherine A. Bliss and Christopher M. Danforth 2011. Temporal Patterns of Happiness and Information in a Global Social Network: Hedonometrics and Twitter *PLoS ONE 6(12): e26752*

Chih-Chung Chang and Chih-Jen Lin 2011. LIBSVM: A Library for Support Vector Machines *ACM Transactions on Intelligent Systems and Technology*, 2:27:1–27:27

Kaggle "Partly Sunny with a Chance of Hashtags" competition dataset 2013 http://www.kaggle.com/c/crowdflower-weather-twitter

Quinn McNemar 1947 Note on the sampling error of the difference between correlated proportions or percentages *Psychometrika* 12(2):153-157

Bo Pang and Lillian Lee 2008 Opinion mining and sentiment analysis. *Foundations and Trends in Information Retrieval* 2(1-2): p. 1–135.

Bing Liu 2012 Sentiment Analysis and Opinion Mining *Morgan & Claypool Publishers*

A cognitive study of subjectivity extraction in sentiment annotation

Abhijit Mishra[1] **Aditya Joshi**[1,2,3] **Pushpak Bhattacharyya**[1]
[1]IIT Bombay, India
[2]Monash University, Australia
[3]IITB-Monash Research Academy, India
{abhijitmishra, adityaj, pb}@cse.iitb.ac.in

Abstract

Existing sentiment analysers are weak AI systems: they try to capture the *functionality* of human sentiment detection faculty, without worrying about how such faculty is realized in the *hardware* of the human. These analysers are agnostic of the actual cognitive processes involved. This, however, does not deliver when applications demand order of magnitude facelift in accuracy, as well as insight into characteristics of sentiment detection process.

In this paper, we present a cognitive study of sentiment detection from the perspective of strong AI. We study the sentiment detection process of a set of human "sentiment readers". Using eye-tracking, we show that on the way to sentiment detection, humans first extract subjectivity. They focus attention on a subset of sentences before arriving at the overall sentiment. This they do either through "anticipation" where sentences are skipped during the first pass of reading, or through "homing" where a subset of the sentences are read over multiple passes, or through both. "Homing" behaviour is also observed at the sub-sentence level in complex sentiment phenomena like sarcasm.

1 Introduction

Over the years, supervised approaches using polarity-annotated datasets have shown promise for SA (Pang and Lee, 2008). However, an alternate line of thought has co-existed. Pang and Lee (2004) showed that for SA, instead of a document in its entirety, an extract of the subjective sentences alone can be used. This process of generating a subjective extract is referred to as subjectivity extraction. Mukherjee and Bhattacharyya (2012) show that for sentiment prediction of movie reviews, subjectivity extraction may be used to discard the sentences describing movie plots since they do not contribute towards the speaker's view of the movie.

While subjectivity extraction helps sentiment classification, the reason has not been sufficiently examined from the perspective of strong AI. The classical definition of strong AI suggests that a machine must be perform sentiment analysis in a manner and accuracy similar to human beings. Our paper takes a step in this direction. We study the cognitive processes underlying sentiment annotation using eye-fixation data of the participants. Our work is novel in two ways:

- We view documents as a set of sentences through which sentiment changes. We show that the nature of these polarity oscillations leads to changes in the reading behavior.
- To the best of our knowledge, the idea of using eye-tracking to validate assumptions is novel in case of sentiment analysis and many NLP applications.

2 Sentiment oscillations & subjectivity extraction

We categorize subjective documents as *linear* and *oscillating*. A *linear* subjective document is the one where all or most sentences have the same polarity. On the other hand, an *oscillating* subjective document contains sentences of contrasting polarity (*viz.* positive and negative). Our discussions on two forms of subjectivity extraction use the concepts of linear and oscillating subjective documents.

Consider a situation where a human reader needs to annotate two documents with sentiment. Assume that the first document is linear subjective - with ten sentences, all of them positive. In

Proceedings of the 5th Workshop on Computational Approaches to Subjectivity, Sentiment and Social Media Analysis, pages 142–146,
Baltimore, Maryland, USA. June 27, 2014.

case of this document, when he/she reads a couple of sentences with the same polarity, he/she begins to assume that the next sentence will have the same sentiment and hence, skips through it. We refer to this behavior as *anticipation*. Now, let the second document be an oscillating subjective document with ten sentences, the first three positive, the next four negative and the last three positive. In this case, when a human annotator reads this document and sees the sentiment flip early on, the annotator begins to carefully read the document. After completing a first pass of reading, the annotator moves back to read certain crucial sentences. We refer to this behavior as *homing*.

The following sections describe our observations in detail. Based on our experiments, we observe these two kinds of subjectivity extraction in our participants: subjectivity extraction as a result of *anticipation* and subjectivity extraction as a result of *homing* - for linear and oscillating documents respectively.

3 Experiment Setup

This section describes the framework used for our eye-tracking experiment. A participant is given the task of annotating documents with one out of the following labels: positive, negative and objective. While she reads the document, her eye-fixations are recorded.

To log eye-fixation data, we use Tobii T120 remote eye-tracker with Translog(Carl, 2012). Translog is a freeware for recording eye movements and keystrokes during translation. We configure Translog for reading with the goal of sentiment.

3.1 Document description

We choose three movie reviews in English from IMDB (http://www.imdb.com) and indicate them as D0, D1 and D2. The lengths of D0, D1 and D2 are 10, 9 and 13 sentences respectively. Using the gold-standard rating given by the writer, we derive the polarity of D0, D1 and D2 as positive, negative and positive respectively. The three documents represent three different styles of reviews: D0 is positive throughout (linear subjective), D1 contains sarcastic statements (linear subjective but may be perceived as oscillating due to linguistic difficulty) while D2 consists of many *flips* in sentiment (oscillating subjective).

It may seem that the data set is small and may not lead to significant findings. However, we wished to capture the most natural form of sentiment-oriented reading. A larger data set would have weakened the experiment because: (i) Sentiment patterns (linear v/s subjective) begin to become predictable to a participant if she reads many documents one after the other. (ii) There is a possibility that fatigue introduces unexpected error. To ensure that our observations were significant despite the limited size of the data set, we increased the number of our participants to 12.

3.2 Participant description

Our participants are 24-30 year-old graduate students with English as the primary language of academic instruction. We represent them as P0, P1 and so on. The polarity for the documents as reported by the participants are shown in Table 1. All participants correctly identified the polarity of document D0. Participant P9 reported that D1 is confusing. 4 out of 12 participants were unable to detect correct opinion in D2.

3.3 Experiment Description

We obtain two kinds of annotation from our annotators: (a) sentiment (positive, negative and objective), (b) eye-movement as recorded by an eye-tracker. They are given a set of instructions beforehand and can seek clarifications. This experiment is conducted as follows:

1. A complete document is displayed on the screen. The font size and line separation are set to 17pt and 1.5 cm respectively to ensure clear visibility and minimize recording error.

2. The annotator verbally states the sentiment of this sentence, before (s)he can proceed to the next.

3. While the annotator is reading the sentence, a remote eye-tracker (Model: Tobii TX 300, Sampling rate: 300Hz) records the eye-movement data of the annotator. The eye-tracker is linked to Translog II software (Carl, 2012) in order to record the data. A snapshot of the software is shown in figure 1. The dots and circles represent position of eyes and fixations of the annotator respectively. Each eye-fixation that is recorded consists of: co-ordinates, timestamp and duration. These three parameters have been used to generate sentence progression graphs.

Document	Orig	P0	P1	P2	P3	P4	P5	P6	P7	P8	P9	P10	P11
D0	**+ve**	+ve	+ve	+ve	+ve	+ve	+ve	+ve	+ve	+ve	+ve	+ve	+ve
D1	**-ve**	-ve	+ve	-ve	-ve	-ve	-ve	-ve	-ve	-ve	Neu/-ve	-ve	-ve
D2	**+ve**	+ve	+ve	-ve	+ve	+ve	Neu	+ve	Neu	Neu	+ve	+ve	+ve

Table 1: Polarity of documents as perceived by the writer (original) and the participants *+ve*, *-ve* and *Neu* represent positive, negative and neutral polarities respectively.

Figure 1: Gaze-data recording using Translog-II

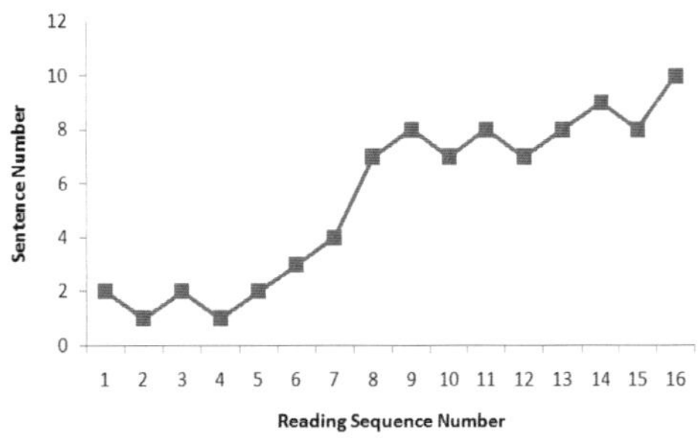

Figure 2: Sentence progression graph for participant P7 document D0

4 Observations: Subjectivity extraction through anticipation

In this section, we describe a case in which participants skip sentences. We show that anticipation of sentiment is linked with subjectivity extraction.

Table 2 shows the number of unique and non-unique sentences that participants read for each document. The numbers in the last column indicate average values. The table can be read as: participant P1 reads 8 unique sentences of document D0 (thus skipping two sentences) and including repetitions, reads 26 sentences. Participant P0 skips as many as six sentences in case of document D1.

The number of unique sentences read is lower than sentence count for four out of twelve participants in case of document D0. This skipping is negligible in case of document D1 and D2. Also, the average non-unique sentence fixations are 21 in case of D0 and 33.83 for D1 although the total number of sentences in D0 and D1 is almost the same. This verifies that participants tend to skip sentences while reading D0.

Figure 2 shows sentence progression graph for participant P7. The participant reads a series of sentences and then skips two sentences. This implies that anticipation behaviour was triggered after reading sentences of the same polarity. Similar traits are observed in other participants who skipped sentences while reading document D0.

5 Observations: Subjectivity extraction through homing

This section presents a contrasting case of subjectivity extraction. We refer to a reading pattern as *homing*[1] when a participant reads a document completely and returns to read a selected subset of sentences. We believe that during sentiment annotation, this subset is the subjective extract that the user has created in her mind. We observe this phenomenon in reading patterns of documents D1 and D2. The former contains sarcasm because of which parts of sentences may appear to be of contrasting polarity while the latter is an oscillating subjective document.

[1]The word is derived from missile guidance systems. The definition[2] of homing is "the process of determining the location of something, sometimes the source of a transmission, and going to it."

Document		P0	P1	P2	P3	P4	P5	P6	P7	P8	P9	P10	P11	Avg.
D0	Non-unique	9	26	23	17	18	18	35	16	33	19	15	23	21
	Unique	8	8	10	10	10	10	10	8	10	8	10	10	
D1	Non-unique	5	23	46	13	15	44	35	26	56	57	40	46	33.83
	Unique	3	9	9	9	9	9	8	9	9	9	9	9	
D2	Non-unique	36	29	67	21	23	51	64	48	54	59	73	80	50.42
	Unique	13	13	13	13	13	13	13	13	13	13	13	13	

Table 2: Number of unique and non-unique sentences read by each participant

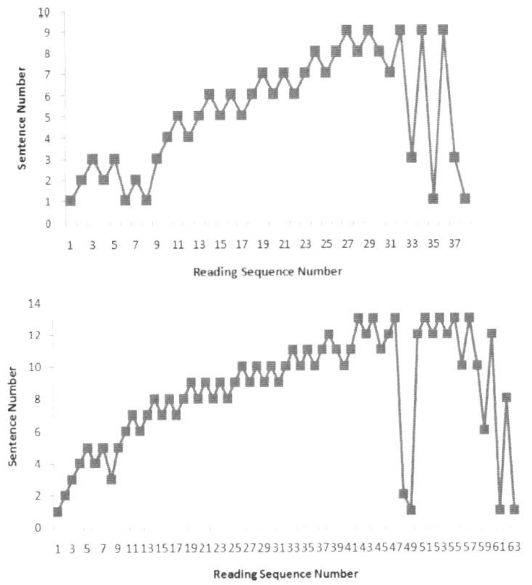

Figure 3: Sentence progression graph of participant P2 for document D1 (left) and document D2 (right)

Figure 3 shows sentence progression graphs of participant P2 for documents D1 and D2. For document D1, the participant performs one pass of reading until sequence number 30. A certain subset of sentences are re-visited in the second pass. On analyzing sentences in the second pass of reading, we observe a considerable overlap in case of our participants. We also confirm that all of these sentences are subjective. This means that the sentences that are read after sequence number 30 form the subjective extract of document D1.

Similar behaviour is observed in case of document D2. The difference in this case is that there is less overlap of sentences read in the second pass among participants. This implies , for oscillating subjective documents, the subjective extract is user/document-specific.

It may be argued that fixations corresponding

Participant	TFD-SE (secs)	PTFD (%)	TFC-SE
P5	7.3	8	21
P7	3.1	5	11
P9	51.94	10	26
P11	116.6	16	56

Table 3: Reading statistics for second pass reading for document D1; TFD: Total fixation duration for subjective extract; PTFD: Proportion of total fixation duration = (TFD)/(Total duration); TFC-SE: Total fixation count for subjective extract

to second pass reading are stray fixations and not subjective extracts. Hence, for the second pass reading of document D1, we tabulate fixation duration, fixation count and proportion of total duration in Table 3. The fixation duration and fixation count are both recorded by the eye-tracker. The fixation counts are substantial and the participants spend around 5-15% of the total reading time in the second pass reading. We also confirm that all of these sentences are subjective. This means that these portions indeed correspond to subjective extracts as a result of homing.

6 A note on linguistic challenges

Our claim is that regression after reading an entire document corresponds to the beginning of a subjective extract. However, we observe that some regressions may also happen due to sentiment changes at the sub-sentence level. Some of these are as follows.

1. **Sarcasm**: Sarcasm involves an implicit flip in the sentiment. Participant P9 does not correctly predict sentiment of Document D1. On analyzing her data, we observe multiple regressions on the sentence *'Add to this mess some of the cheesiest lines and concepts, and*

there you have it; I would call it a complete waste of time, but in some sense it is so bad it is almost worth seeing.' This sentence has some positive words but is negative towards the movie. Hence, the participant reads this portion back and forth.

2. **Thwarted expectations**: Thwarted expectations are expressions with a sentiment reversal within a sentence/snippet. Homing is observed in this case as well. Document D2 has a case of thwarted expectations from sentences 10-12 where there is an unexpected flip of sentiment. In case of some participants, we observe regression on these sentences multiple times.

7 Related Work

The work closest to ours is by Scott et al. (2011) who study the role of emotion words in reading using eye-tracking. They show that the eye-fixation duration for emotion words is consistently less than neutral words with the exception of high-frequency negative words. Eye-tracking[3] technology has also been used to study the cognitive aspects of language processing tasks like *translation* and *sense disambiguation*. Dragsted (2010) observe co-ordination between reading and writing during human *translation*. Similarly, Joshi et al. (2011) use eye-tracking to correlate fixation duration with polysemy of words during *word sense disambiguation*.

8 Conclusion & Future work

We studied sentiment annotation in the context of subjectivity extraction using eye-tracking. Based on how sentiment changes through a document, humans may perform subjectivity extraction as a result of either: (a) anticipation or (b) homing. These observations are in tandem with the past work that shows benefit of subjectivity extraction for automatic sentiment classification.

Our study is beneficial in three perspectives: (i) Sentiment classifiers may use interaction between sentiment of sentences. Specifically, this can be modeled using features like sentiment run length (i.e. maximal span of sentences bearing same sentiment) or sentiment flips (i.e. instances where consecutive sentences bear opposite polarity), (ii) Crowd-sourced sentiment annotation can devise variable pricing models based on our study. Based on anticipation and homing information about documents, documents can be grouped into difficulty categories and priced accordingly.

[3]**Related Terms**:
Eye-fixation: Long stay of visual gaze on a single location
Regression: Revisiting a previously read segment
Sentence Progression Graph: Graph showing reading sequence of sentences

Acknowledgment

We thank Tobii Corporation for lending us their eye-tracker for this study, and our annotators from CFILT, IIT Bombay. Aditya is funded by the TCS Research Fellowship Program.

References

Bo Pang and Lillian Lee. 2004. A Sentimental Education: Sentiment Analysis Using Subjectivity Summarization Based on Minimum Cuts In Proceedings of the *ACL*, 271-278.

Bo Pang and Lillian Lee. 2008. Opinion Mining and Sentiment Analysis *Foundations and Trends in Information Retrieval, 2008, vol. 2, nos.12* 1135.

B Dragsted. 2010. Co-ordination of reading and writing processes in translation. *Contribution to Translation and Cognition. Shreve, G. and Angelone, E.(eds.)Cognitive Science Society.*

Michael Carl. 2012. Translog-II: A Program for Recording User Activity Data for Empirical Reading and Writing Research. In Proceedings of the Eight International Conference on Language Resources and Evaluation, European Language Resources Association.

Scott G. , ODonnell P and Sereno S. 2012. Emotion Words Affect Eye Fixations During Reading. *Journal of Experimental Psychology:Learning, Memory, and Cognition 2012, Vol. 38, No. 3, 783792.*

Salil Joshi, Diptesh Kanojia and Pushpak Bhattacharyya. 2013. More than meets the eye: Study of Human Cognition in Sense Annotation. NAACL HLT 2013, Atlanta, USA.

Subhabrata Mukherjee and Pushpak Bhattacharyya. 2012. WikiSent : Weakly Supervised Sentiment Analysis Through Extractive Summarization With Wikipedia *European Conference on Machine Learning (ECML PKDD 2012), Bristol, U.K.*,

The Use of Text Similarity and Sentiment Analysis to Examine Rationales in the Large-Scale Online Deliberations

Wanting Mao
Department of Computer Science
The University of Western Ontario
London, ON, Canada
fiona.wt.mao@gmail.com

Lu Xiao
Faculty of Information & Media Studies
The University of Western Ontario
London, ON, Canada
lxiao24@uwo.ca

Robert Mercer
Department of Computer Science
The University of Western Ontario
London, ON, Canada
mercer@csd.uwo.ca

Abstract

To overcome the increasingly time consuming and potentially challenging identification of key points and the associated rationales in large-scale online deliberations, we propose a computational linguistics method that has the potential of facilitating this process of reading and evaluating the text. Our approach is novel in how we determine the sentiment of a rationale at the sentence level and in that it includes a text similarity measure and sentence-level sentiment analysis to achieve this goal.

1 Introduction

In an online deliberation situation where users join in and offer their opinions or suggestions, they are expected to provide the rationales that justify their standpoints in the deliberation. In the final decision making process, one expectedly needs to read through the content and weigh different key points and related rationales. Wikipedia Article for Deletion (AfD) deliberations represent one such example. In the Wikipedia community, any member can propose to delete an existing Wikipedia article. After an article is proposed to delete, a deliberation topic about the article is opened in the AfD forum. The community members can express their opinions (e.g., to keep or to delete the article) and provide their rationales within the specified time period. After that, a community member (often a Wikipedia administrator) closes the deliberation by making the final decision. Researchers have analyzed the Wikipedia AfD forum and have demonstrated that it presents a successful example of large-scale online deliberation by allowing many people to participate equally, encouraging people to deliberate, and producing rational and meaningful rationales (e.g., Schneider et al., 2012; Xiao & Askin, 2014). Wikipedia policy requires that the final decision about the article should be made based on the discussed rationales instead of the count of opinion votes. In practice many Wikipedia members who close the deliberations follow this policy, which implies the potential problem of representing the diverse rationales and identifying the influential ones in this context.

Generating the final decision of a large scale online deliberation can become a daunting task, as the amount of opinions and rationales in the deliberation content increases significantly. To facilitate this decision making process in large-scale online deliberations, we have developed a method that uses an existing text-to-text similarity measure and our developed sentence-level sentiment analysis algorithm to address this issue. Specifically, we first group participants' opinions according to the similarity measure, then we identify the positive, neutral, and negative sentiments suggested by the participants' rationales in each group, and finally we choose a representative rationale from each sentiment category in a group. With our method the diverse opinions and rationales are presented to the final decision maker through a representative set of the rationales, reducing the redundant information from the deliberation content so as to make the process of reading and evaluating the deliberation content more efficient.

Proceedings of the 5th Workshop on Computational Approaches to Subjectivity, Sentiment and Social Media Analysis, pages 147–153, Baltimore, Maryland, USA. June 27, 2014. ©2014 Association for Computational Linguistics

2 Related Work

2.1 Text Similarity

Recognizing the relation between texts (e.g., sentence to sentence, paragraph to paragraph) could help people better understand the context.

Text similarity can be interpreted as similarity between sentences, paragraphs, documents, etc. It has been used in various aspects in NLP such as information retrieval, text classification, and automatic evaluation. The most fundamental part is word similarity. We consider words to be similar in the following conditions: synonyms, antonyms, similar concept (e.g., red, green), similar context (e.g., doctor, hospital), and hyponym/hypernym relation (e.g., dog, pet).

WordNet, a word-to-word similarity library was developed by Pedersen et al. (2004), and has been widely used to compute the similarity at a coarser granularity (e.g., sentence-to-sentence similarity). Various methods to deal with text similarity have been proposed over the past decades. Mihalcea et al. (2006) proposed a greedy method to calculate the similarity score between two texts T1 and T2. Basically for each word in T1 (T2), the maximum similarity score to any word in T2 (T1) is used. The WordNet similarity can be used for assigning similarity scores between every pair of words in the two texts.

Rus and Lintean (2012) proposed an optimal method to compute text similarity based on word-to-word similarity. It is similar to the optimal assignment problem. Given a weighted complete bipartite graph (G = X È Y; X × Y), with weight w(xy) on edge xy, we need to find a matching from X to Y with a maximum total weight. Their results showed that the optimal method outperformed the greedy method in terms of accuracy and kappa statistics.

Other statistics-based algorithms are also developed to measure text similarity, e.g., the use of the Latent Dirichlet Allocation (LDA) model (Rus et al., 2013).

2.2 Sentiment Analysis

Sentiment analysis is meant to determine the polarity of a certain text, which can be positive, negative or neutral. Related academia and industries have been extensively investigating sentiment analysis methods over the last decade. While most of the early work in sentiment analysis is aimed at analyzing the polarity of customer reviews (e.g., Kim and Hovy, 2004; Hu and Liu, 2004; Turney, 2002), there is a proliferation in analyzing social media text (e.g., Balahur, 2013; Liebrecht et al., 2013; Bakliwal et al., 2012; Montejo-Raez et al., 2012) and online discussions (e.g., Sood et al., 2012a, 2012b).

Researchers have used a variety of approaches to detect the sentiment polarity of the given text. For example, in Kim and Hovy's system (2004) the sentiment region of the opinion is identified based on the extracted opinion holders and topics. The system combines the sentiments of the sentiment region and the polarity of the words to determine the polarity of the given text.

In Li and Wu's (2010) study, they interpreted the article as a sequence of key words and calculated the sentiment score of each key word based on the dictionary and its privative and modifier near it. In the analysis of the tweets, Balahur (2013) replaced the sentiment words and modifiers by sentiment labels (positive, negative, high positive and high negative) or modification labels (negator, intensifier or diminisher), and then applied Support Vector Machine Sequential Minimal Optimization (SVM SMO) to classify three different data sets.

Online discussions may have inappropriate use of language in some cases, which affects the online community management negatively. Sood et al. (2012a) proposed a multistep classifier by combining valence analysis and a SVM to detect insults and classify the insult object.

Researchers have also looked at the use of dependency tree-based method for sentiment classification. For instance, Nakagawa et al. (2010) used a probabilistic model of the information garnered from the dependency tree to determine the sentiment of a sentence. Rentoumi et al. (2010) combines word sense disambiguation, a rule-based system, and Hidden Markov Models (HMMs) to deal with figurative language (e.g. record-shattering day) in sentiment analysis. Moilanen and Pulman (2007) presented a compositional model for three-class (positive, negative, and neutral) phrase-level and sentence-level sentiment analysis. In their algorithm, each binary combination of a Head and Complement had a rule that determined which of the Head and Complement polarities dominated. In exceptional cases the rule inverts the polarity of the subordinate.

Socher et al. (2013) developed a Recursive Neural Tensor Network (RNTN) model. The authors showed that the accuracy obtained by RNTN outperformed a standard recursive neural network (RNN), matrix-vector RNN (MV-RNN), Naive Bayes (NB) and SVM. The advantage of

RNTN is especially evident when compared with the methods that only use bag of words (NB and SVM). This indicates the importance of using parse trees during sentiment analysis.

3 A Method for Identifying Representative Rationales in Online Deliberations

Our observation of the Wikipedia AfD forum suggests that one topic (e.g., notability) can appear multiple times in different rationales by different users. For example, two users' comments –"*Could be redirected to OpenXMA, the content of which isn't all that different from this article*" and "*Redirected to OpenXMA as suggested*"–are considered redundant.

The redundant information itself does not add a new perspective to final decision making. On the other hand, sometime the information about the same type of rationale represents different opinions about it. Here is one such example from an article's deletion discussion: "*redirecting the page to the lead actors future projects section will be cool*" and "*I don't think it is wise to redirect to the original film*".

To make the final decision making process more efficient, compared to human reading of all the deliberation content, we have developed a method that includes a text-to-text similarity measure and a sentence-level sentiment analysis algorithm. Specifically, we use text similarity to group the rationales according to the aspects they reflect so we can select some rationales from each aspect group instead of all of them. We note that although the rationales are redundant in showing the same aspect, the redundancy implies the importance of the aspect in the deliberation since they are used multiple times by users in justifying their opinions. So in our method, we record the number of members that proposed the same aspect assuming that this would indicate the level of importance of the aspect to some extent. .

With the rationales grouped according to the aspects that they involve (e.g., notability, credibility, etc), our method examines the sentiment polarity of each rationale in a group to further examine whether the rationale is positive or negative (e.g., the article is notable or not), or is neutral about the aspect. Then we can identify the representative rationales of an opinion by choosing those that have the highest similarity score in a group. In sum, the text-to-text similarity measure combined with our sentence-level sentiment analysis algorithm helps us identify the representative rationales of diverse opinions in an online deliberation. An overview of our method is shown in Figure 1.

We applied our method in analyzing Wikipedia Article for Deletion (AfD) deliberation content. Next we discuss how this method is used to analyze the content.

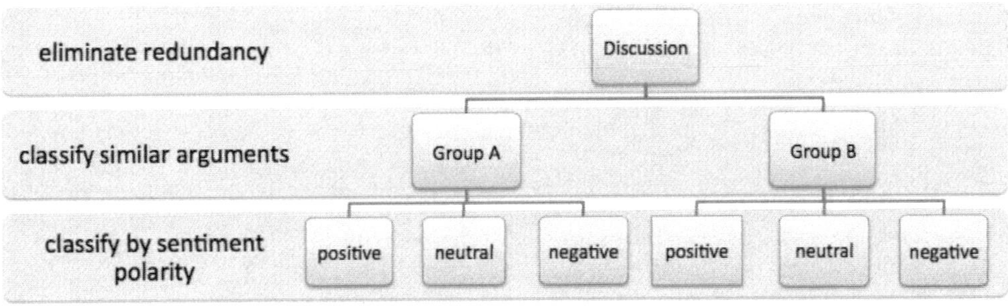

Figure 1. An overview of our method for identifying representative rationales from large-scale online deliberation

3.1 Text-to-Text Similarity Measure

In our study, we used SEMILAR, a semantic similarity toolkit (Rus et al., 2013), to measure We tested three similarity approaches provided in SEMILAR: optimum method based on WordNet, similarity based on Latent Semantic Analysis (LSA) and similarity based on Latent Dirichlet Analysis (LDA). We first extracted 80 pairs of sentences from the Wikipedia AfD forum and manually annotated them as similar or not. We then used these annotated results in measuring the accuracy of the three SEMILAR approaches. SEMILAR assigns a similarity score to each pair of sentences ranging from 0 to 1. To evaluate the accuracy of the three approaches, we identified a threshold to divide the result into two groups (i.e., similar and not similar). To do so, we computed the accuracy for 101 thresholds ranging from 0.00 to 1.00 with an interval of 0.01 to find the highest accuracy. Through this approach, we identified that the WordNet-based optimum method achieved the best accuracy of 76.3% at threshold 0.13. The other two methods achieved similar accuracy (76.3% and 75% respectively) but took more than double the time to process. Therefore, we chose the WordNet-based optimum method.

With this method, we have a similarity matrix that shows the similarity score between every pair of sentences in the discussion. We transform the similarity matrix to a dissimilarity matrix by transforming the similarity score x for two sentences to the distance between the sentences $1/x$. Then we used hierarchical clustering (Kaufman and Rousseeuw, 2009) to cluster the sentences into groups. To do so, we set the maximum allowed distance between two similar sentences to be 8 (i.e., the similarity score would be 0.125), and used the agglomerative approach to form the clusters. As a consequence, the sentences in the same group are related to a common theme.

3.2 Sentence-Level Sentiment Analysis

In our sentiment analysis algorithm, each word in a sentence is assigned a prior polarity based on an adapted MPQA Subjectivity Lexicon (Pedersen et al., 2004). Compared to the original Lexicon, this adapted one includes additional sentiment words that are important for the Wikipedia's AfD discussions (e.g., *notable).* Then, using the syntactic and dependency trees of the sentence, the algorithm calculates each word's current polarity score which can be affected by its children's polarity scores. Through this approach, the root's current polarity score becomes the sentence's polarity score.

The children's polarity scores can affect the parent's prior polarity score positively or negatively. The positive or neutral effect of the children's polarity scores is reflected through summing the children's polarity scores and then adding the sum to the parent's polarity score. The negative effect is reflected through summing the children's polarity scores and then multiplying the sum to the parent's polarity score. Because our algorithm only considers three sentiment situations: negative, positive, and neutral, it is the negation of the parent's prior polarity that affects the accuracy of our algorithm the most. Therefore, the core of our algorithm is a recursive method that examines different negation situations in the input sentence, starting from the leaf node of the sentence's dependency tree. We use this tree structure because it helps us detect the most of the negation situations:

1. I *agree* that the place is notable.
2. I *don't agree* that the place is notable. (Local Negation)
3. I *disagree* that the place is notable. (Predicate Negation)
4. *Neither* one of us agrees that the place is notable. (Subject Negation)
5. It is a *violation of* notability. (Preposition Negation)

However, there is one negation situation that cannot be detected from the syntactic structure of the sentence. For example, in the sentence "*the place is of indeterminable notability*", *notability* is a positive word, but as it is modified by a negative word *indeterminable* the phrase becomes negative. This negation case is called modifier negation. A negative modifier might also negate a negative word, such as *little damage*, *never fail.* However a negative modifier does not always negate the polarity of the phrase determined by the polarity of the related word. Instead, the phrase remains its prior polarity, e.g., *terribly allergic*.

It is also worth noticing that context affects the phrase polarity. Consider the phrase *original research* in our study context – the Wikipedia AfD forum. Because articles reporting original research violate Wikipedia's neutrality policy, the phrase *original research* in the deletion discussions should be considered to be negative.

As there is no straightforward way of determining whether or not a modifier negates the polarity of the word being modified, we decided to use machine learning methods to help classify the modifier negation cases. We considered the following modifier phrases in the study and at least one word in the phrase has to be a sentiment word:

- Noun modified by adjective
- Noun modified by noun
- Adjective modified by adverb
- Adverb modified by adverb
- Verb modified by adverb

We used six attributes to describe a two-word phrase: *first word token, second word token, first word polarity, second word polarity, first word part-of-speech (POS),* and *second word POS.* The machine learning algorithm is expected to predict the polarity of a word pair given these six attributes of the pair. To build our machine learning model, we obtained 961 two-word phrases from the AfD forum and annotated their polarities manually. They all follow the modifier negation combinations discussed earlier and at least one of the two words is a sentiment word. The selected phrases are balanced in terms of the number of positive, negative, and neutral cases represented in the data set. We then used Weka (Hall et al., 2009) to evaluate the performance of three machine learning algorithms with 10-fold cross validation: Naive Bayes, k-nearest neighbor (KNN) and decision tree. The results showed that the accuracy produced by KNN is the highest among the three methods. We further identified that when the k value is 1, the KNN performance is the best. Thus we selected the KNN method in detecting modifier negation in our method.

Figure 2 shows the calculated polarity score for the sentence "Neither one of us agrees that the place is notable".

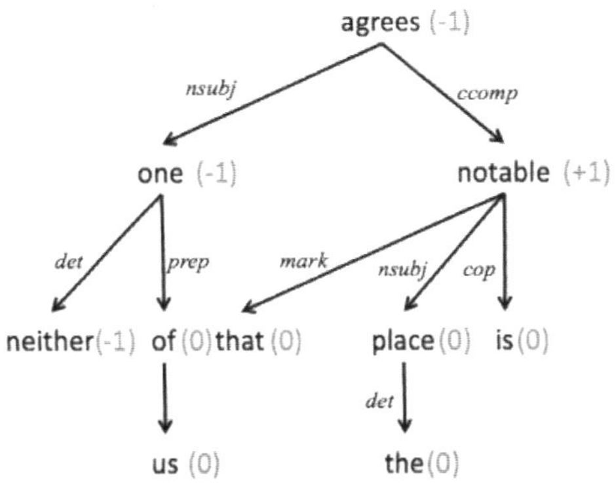

Figure 2. Polarity score on every node of the sentence' dependency structure

As shown in the figure, there are two positive words agree and notable and one negative word neither. If we simply use a bag of words approach and add the polarity scores together, we would get a result of positive. However, the negative word neither, being part of the subject, plays a dominant role in this sentence. Our algorithm is able to detect that negation influence: the root node is a verb and not neutral, so its current polarity score is the product of its prior polarity +1 multiplied by that of the node notable, which is also +1. Then because of the subject negation, the final polarity score of the root node is the multiplication of its current polarity score by the polarity score of the subject node, which is -1.

4 Evaluation and Discussion

To evaluate the performance of our sentiment polarity prediction algorithm, we randomly selected 236 sentences from the Wikipedia AfD forum and manually annotated their sentiment polarity. 83 sentences are annotated as positive, 102 as negative and 51 as neutral. With our algorithm that includes the machine learning process to detect modifier negations, the accuracy is 60.2%. In Socher et al.'s (2013) evaluation of their algorithm, 5-class (very negative, negative, neutral, positive, very positive) and 2-class (negative, positive) predictions of sentence-level sentiment analysis reached an accuracy of 45.7% and 85.4% respectively. We anticipate that the accuracy of their algorithm for 3-class prediction would be around 60%.

For sentence-level sentiment analysis, Moilanen and Pulman's algorithm obtained an accuracy of 65.6%. Our algorithm differs from Moilanen and Pulman in two ways: (1) the node-based computation is more general, i.e. for verbs, prepositions, and subjects it is a simple combination (multiplication or addition) of the subordinate nodes' polarities, and for local negation it is an inversion of the subordinate polarity; (2) a trained classifier serves two functions: it fulfills the role of determining the contextual information and it determines whether a modifier changes the polarity of what it modifies. .

5 Conclusion

Deliberation is a method of logical communication that rationalizes the process of reaching a decision. To reach the decision, people often need to weigh different opinions and rationales expressed in the deliberation. Given the proliferation of online platforms and communities for collective decision making and knowledge creation, online deliberation is becoming an increasingly important and common approach of engaging large numbers of people to participate in the decision making processes. One foreseen issue in such a context is the daunting tasks of reading through all the deliberation content, and identifying and evaluating diverse key points and related rationales.

Our study is interested in addressing the issue through a computational linguistic approach. We developed an approach that combines a text-to-text similarity technique with a sentence-level sentiment analysis method. The deliberation content is first divided into groups based on the similarity of texts, then within each group we use a recursive algorithm to examine the sentiment polarity of each sentence according to the identified similar topic to further classify the sentences into three groups: positive, neutral, and negative. Although not discussed in this paper, it is a simple step to identify the representative rationales of diverse opinions by choosing those that have the highest similarity score in each polarity group.

Acknowledgement

This project is partially supported by the Discovery program of The Natural Sciences and Engineering Research Council of Canada (NSERC).

References

Akshat Bakliwal, Piyush Arora, Senthil Madhappan-Nikhil Kapre, Mukesh Singh and Vasudeva Varma, Mining Sentiments from Tweets, Proceedings of the 3rd Workshop on Computational Approaches to Subjectivity and Sentiment Analysis. 11–18, Jeju, Republic of Korea, 2012

Alexandra Balahur. Sentiment Analysis in Social Media Texts. WASSA 2013, page 120. 2013.

Mark Hall, Eibe Frank, Geoffrey Holmes, Bernhard Pfahringer, Peter Reutemann, and Ian H Witten. The Weka data mining software: an Update. ACM SIGKDD Explorations Newsletter, 11(1):10–18, 2009.

Minqing Hu and Bing Liu. Mining and summarizing customer reviews. In Proceedings of the Tenth ACM SIGKDD International Conference on Knowledge discovery and data mining, pages 168–177. ACM, 2004.

Leonard Kaufman and Peter J Rousseeuw. Finding groups in data: an introduction to cluster analysis, volume 344. John Wiley & Sons, 2009.

Soo-Min Kim and Eduard Hovy. Determining the sentiment of opinions. In Proceedings of the 20th international conference on Computational Linguistics, page 1367. Association for Computational Linguistics, 2004.

Nan Li, and Desheng Dash Wu. Using text mining and sentiment analysis for online forums hotspot detection and forecast. Decision Support Systems 48(2):354-368. 2010.

Christine Liebrecht, Florian Kunneman, and Antal van den Bosch (2013). The perfect solution for detecting sarcasm in tweets# not, Proceedings of the 4th Workshop on Computational Approaches to Subjectivity, Sentiment and Social Media Analysis, 29–37, Atlanta, Georgia, 2013.

Rada Mihalcea, Courtney Corley, and Carlo Strapparava. Corpus-based and knowledge-based measures of text semantic similarity. In AAAI, volume 6, pages 775–780, 2006.

Karo Moilanen and Stephen Pulman. Sentiment composition. In In Proceedings of Recent Advances in Natural Language Processing, pages 378 – 382, 2007.

Arturo Montejo-Raez, Eugenio Martinez-Camara, M. Teresa Martin-Valdivia and L.Alfonso Urena-Lopez, Random Walk Weighting over SentiWordNet for Sentiment Polarity Detection on Twitter, Proceedings of the 3rd Workshop on Computational Approaches to Subjectivity and Sentiment Analysis. 11–18, Jeju, Republic of Korea, 2012.

Tetsuji Nakagawa, Kentaro Inui, and Sadao Kurohashi. Dependency tree-based sentiment classification using CRFs with hidden variables, In Human Language Technologies: The 2010 Annual Conference of the North American Chapter of the Association for Computational Linguistics, pages 786-794, 2010.

Ted Pedersen, Siddharth Patwardhan, and Jason Michelizzi. Wordnet:: Similarity: measuring the relatedness of concepts. In Demonstration Papers at HLT-NAACL 2004, pages 38–41. Association for Computational Linguistics, 2004.

Vassiliki Rentoumi, Stefanos Petrakis, Manfred Klenner, George A. Vouros, and Vangelis Karkaletsis. United we stand: Improving sentiment analysis by joining machine learning and rule based methods. In Proceedings of the Seventh conference on International Language Resources and Evaluation (LREC'10), Valletta, Malta. pages 1089 – 1094, 2010.

Vasile Rus and Mihai Lintean. A comparison of greedy and optimal assessment of natural language student input using word-to-word similarity metrics. In Proceedings of the Seventh Workshop on Building Educational Applications Using NLP, pages 157–162. Association for Computational Linguistics, 2012.

Vasile Rus, Mihai Lintean, Rajendra Banjade, Nobal Niraula, and Dan Stefanescu. Semilar: The semantic similarity toolkit. In Proceedings of the 51st Annual Meeting of the Association for Computational Linguistics: System Demonstrations, pages 163–168. 2013.

Jodi Schneider, Alexandre Passant, and Stefan Decker. Deletion discussions in Wikipedia: Decision factors and outcomes. In Proceedings of the Eighth Annual International Symposium on Wikis and Open Collaboration, page 17. ACM, 2012.

Richard Socher, Alex Perelygin, Jean Y Wu, Jason Chuang, Christopher D Manning, Andrew Y Ng, and Christopher Potts. Recursive deep models for semantic compositionality over a sentiment treebank. In Proceedings of the Conference on Empirical Methods in Natural Language Processing (EMNLP), pages 1631–1642, 2013.

Sara Owsley Sood, Elizabeth F. Churchill, and Judd Antin. Automatic identification of personal insults on social news sites. J. Am. Soc. Inf. Sci., 63: 270–285. 2012a.

Sara Sood, Judd Antin, and Elizabeth Churchill. 2012. Profanity use in online communities. In Proceedings of the SIGCHI Conference on Human Factors in Computing Systems (CHI '12). ACM, New York, NY, USA, 1481-1490, 2012b.

Peter D Turney. Thumbs up or thumbs down?: semantic orientation applied to unsupervised classification of reviews. In Proceedings of the 40th Annual Meeting of the Association for Computational Linguistics, pages 417–424. Association for Computational Linguistics, 2002.

Lu Xiao and Nicole Askin. What influences online deliberation? A Wikipedia study. Journal of the Association for Information Science and Technology, 65, pages 898–910, 2014

A Conceptual Framework for Inferring Implicatures

Janyce Wiebe
Department of Computer Science
University of Pittsburgh
wiebe@cs.pitt.edu

Lingjia Deng
Intelligent Systems Program
University of Pittsburgh
lid29@pitt.edu

Abstract

While previous sentiment analysis research has concentrated on the interpretation of explicitly stated opinions and attitudes, this work addresses a type of opinion implicature (i.e., opinion-oriented default inference) in real-world text. This work describes a rule-based conceptual framework for representing and analyzing opinion implicatures. In the course of understanding implicatures, the system recognizes implicit sentiments (and beliefs) toward various events and entities in the sentence, often of mixed polarities; thus, it produces a richer interpretation than is typical in opinion analysis.

1 Introduction

This paper is a brief introduction to a framework we have developed for sentiment inference (Wiebe and Deng, 2014). Overall, the goal of this work is to make progress toward a deeper automatic interpretation of opinionated language by developing computational models for the representation and interpretation of opinion implicature (i.e., opinion-oriented default inference) in language. In this paper, we feature a rule-based implementation of a conceptual framework for opinion implicatures, specifically implicatures that arise in the presence of explicit sentiments, and events that positively or negatively affect entities (*goodFor/badFor* events). To eliminate interference introduced by the noisy output of automatic NLP components, the system takes as input manually annotated explicit-sentiment and event information, and makes inferences based on that input information. Thus, the purpose of this work is to provide a conceptual understanding of (a type of) opinion implicature, to provide a blueprint for realizing fully automatic systems in the future.

Below, we give terminology, overview the rule-based system, and then present the rule schemas. Finally, via discussion of an example from the MPQA opinion-annotated corpus (Wiebe et al., 2005)[1], we illustrate the potential of the framework for recognizing implicit sentiments and writer-level sentiments that are not anchored on clear sentiment words, and for capturing interdependencies among explicit and implicit sentiments.

We have developed a graph-based computational model implementing some rules introduced below (Deng and Wiebe, 2014). Moreover, in ongoing work, we have proposed an optimization framework to jointly extract and resolve the input ambiguities.

2 Terminology

The building blocks of our opinion implicature framework are *subjectivity*, *inferred private states*, and *benefactive/malefactive* events and states.

Subjectivity. Following (Wiebe et al., 2005; Wiebe, 1994), *subjectivity* is defined as the expression of private states in language, where private states are mental and emotional states such as speculations, sentiments, and beliefs (Quirk et al., 1985). Subjective expressions (i.e., *opinions*) have *sources* (or *holders*): the entity or entities whose private states are being expressed. Again following (Wiebe et al., 2005; Wiebe, 1994), a **private state** is an attitude held by a source toward (optionally) a target. **Sentiment and belief are types of attitudes**. Subjectivity is the linguistic expression of private states. **Subjectivity is a pragmatic notion**: as the sentence is interpreted in context, a private state **is** attributed to a source in that context (Banfield, 1982). By **sentiment expression** or **explicit sentiment**, we mean a subjective expression where the attitude type of the expressed

[1] Available at http://mpqa.cs.pitt.edu

Proceedings of the 5th Workshop on Computational Approaches to Subjectivity, Sentiment and Social Media Analysis, pages 154–159,
Baltimore, Maryland, USA. June 27, 2014.

private state is sentiment.

There are many types of linguistic clues that contribute to recognizing subjective expressions (Wiebe, 1994). In the clearest case, some word **senses** give rise to subjectivity whenever they are used in discourse (Wiebe and Mihalcea, 2006). Other clues are not as definitive. For example, researchers in NLP have begun to develop lexicons of connotations (Feng et al., 2011), i.e., words associated with polarities out of context (e.g., *war* has negative connotation and *sunshine* has positive connotation (Feng et al., 2013)). However, words may be used in context with polarities opposite to their connotations, as in *Ghenghis Kan likes war*.

Inferred Private States and Opinion Implicatures. We address private states inferred from other private states, where the attitude type of both is *sentiment*. Inference is initiated by explicit sentiment subjectivity. We borrow the term *implicature* from linguistics, specifically *generalized conversational implicature*. Grice (1967; 1989) introduced the notion to account for how more can be pragmatically communicated than what is strictly said - what is implicated vs. what is said (Doran et al., 2012). Generalized conversational implicatures are cancellable, or defeasible.

Analogously, we can treat **subjectivity** as **part of what is said**,[2] and the **private-state inferences** we address to be **part of what is implicated**. Opinion implicatures are default inferences that may not go through in context.

Benefactive/Malefactive Events and States. This work addresses sentiments toward, in general, states and events which positively or negatively affect entities. Various lexical items and semantic roles evoke such situations. We adopt one clear case in this work (Deng et al., 2013): ⟨*agent, event, object*⟩ triples, where *event* negatively (*badFor*) or positively (*goodFor*) affects the *object*. An event that is goodFor or badFor is a *gfbf* event. Note that we have annotated a corpus with gfbf information and the speaker's sentiment toward the agents and objects of gfbf events (Deng et al., 2013).[3]

[2]While the focus in the literature on what is said is semantics, Grice and people later working on the topic acknowledge that what is said must include pragmatics such as co-reference and indexical resolution (Doran et al., 2012), and subjectivity arises from deixis (Bruder and Wiebe, 1995; Stein and Wright, 1995). However, as long as what is said is conceived of as only truth evaluable propositions, then it is not exactly the notion for our setting.

[3]Available at http://mpqa.cs.pitt.edu

3 Overview

In this section, we give an overview of the rule-based system to provide an intuitive big picture of what it can infer, instead of elaborating specific rules, which will be introduced in Section 4.

The system includes default inference rules which apply if there is no evidence to the contrary. It requires as input explicit sentiment and gfbf information (plus any evidence that is contrary to the inferences). The data structure of the input and the output are described in Section 3.1. The rules are applied repeatedly until no new conclusions can be drawn. If a rule matches a sentiment or event that is the target of a private state, the nesting structure is preserved when generating the conclusions. We say that inference is carried out in *private state spaces*, introduced in Section 3.2. Finally in Section 3.3, an example is provided to illustrate what the system is able to infer.

3.1 Data Structure

The system builds a graphical representation of what it knows and infers about the meaning of a sentence. A detailed knowledge representation scheme is presented in (Wiebe and Deng, 2014).

Below is an example from the MPQA corpus.

> Ex(1) [He] is therefore planning to **trigger** [wars] here and there to **revive** [the flagging arms industry].

There are two gfbf events in this sentence: ⟨He, trigger, wars⟩ and ⟨He, revive, arms industry⟩. The system builds these nodes as input (as printed by the system):

```
8 writer positive believesTrue
  4 He revive flagging arms industry
6 writer positive believesTrue
  1 He trigger wars
```

The system's printout does not show all the structure of a node. Consider node 8. It has a *source* edge to the node representing *the writer*, and a *target* edge to node 4, which in turn has an *agent* edge to the node representing *He* and a *object* edge to the node representing *flagging arms industry*. The nodes also have attributes which record, e.g., what type of node it is (node 8 is a privateState and node 4 is a gfbf), polarity (if relevant), etc.

The graph is directed. For example, node 4 is a child of 8. A specification for the input is that each root node must be a *sentiment* or *believesTrue* node whose source is *the writer*. Inference proceeds by matching rules to the graph built so far and, when a rule successfully fires, adding nodes to the graph.

3.2 Private State Spaces

The approach adopted here follows work on reasoning in belief spaces and belief ascription in natural language (Martins and Shapiro, 1983; Rapaport, 1986; Slator and Wilks, 1987). Other than private states of the writer, all propositions and events must be the target of *some* private state. In the simplest case, the writer believes the proposition or event he/she describes in the document, so the proposition or event is nested under a *writer positive believesTrue* node.

We want to carry out inferences within private state spaces so that, for example, from **S positive believesTrue P, & P $\Longrightarrow$ Q**, the system may infer **S positive believesTrue Q**. However, we are working with sentiment, not only belief as in earlier work, and we want to allow, as appropriate, these types of inferences: from **S sentiment toward P, & P $\Longrightarrow$ Q**, infer **S sentiment toward Q**. For example, if I'm upset my computer is infected with a virus, then I'm also upset with the consequences (e.g., that my files may be corrupted).

A *private state space* is defined by a path where the root is a *believesTrue* or *sentiment* node whose source is the writer, and each node on the path is a *believesTrue* or *sentiment* node. Two paths define the same private state space if, at each corresponding position, they have the same attitude type, polarity, and source. P is *in* a private state space if P is the *target* of the rightmost node on a path defining that space.

3.3 An Example

Now we have introduced the data structure and the private state spaces, let's see the potential conclusions which the system can infer before we go into the detailed rules in the next section.

> Ex(2) However, it appears as if [the international community (IC)] is *tolerating* [the Israeli] **campaign of suppression against** [the Palestinians].

The input nodes are the following.

```
writer negative sentiment
  IC positive sentiment
    Israeli suppression Palestinians
```

The gfbf event ⟨Israeli, suppression, Palestinians⟩ is a badFor event. According to the writer, the IC is positive toward the event in the sense that they tolerate (i.e., protect) it. *However* and *appears as if* are clues that the writer is negative toward IC's positive sentiment.

Given these input annotations, the following are the sentiments inferred by the system **just toward the entities** in the sentence; note that many of the sentiments are nested in private state spaces.

```
writer positive sentiment
  Palestinians
writer negative sentiment
  Israel
writer negative sentiment
  IC
writer positive believesTrue
  Israel negative sentiment
    Palestinians
writer positive believesTrue
  IC negative sentiment
    Palestinians
writer positive believesTrue
  IC positive sentiment
    Israel
writer positive believesTrue
  IC positive believesTrue
    Israel negative sentiment
      Palestinians
```

Note that for the sentiments between two entities other than the writer (e.g., Israel negative toward Palestinians), they are nested under a *writer positive believesTrue* node. This shows why we need private state spaces. The writer expresses his/her opinion that the sentiment from *Israel* toward *Palestinians* is negative, which may not be true outside the scope of this single document.

4 Rules

Rules include preconditions and conclusions. They may also include assumptions (Hobbs et al., 1993). For example, suppose a rule would successfully fire if an entity S believes P. If the entity S is not the writer but we know that the writer believes P, and there is no evidence to the contrary (i.e. there is no evidence showing that the entity S doesn't believe P), then we'll assume that S believes it as well, if a rule "asks us to".

Thus, our rules are conceptually of the form:

$$P1, ..., Pj : A1, .., Ak / Q1, ..., Qm$$

where the Ps are preconditions, the As are assumptions, and the Qs are conclusions. For the Qs to be concluded, the Ps must already hold; there must be a basis for assuming each A; and there must be no evidence against any of the As or Qs.

Assumptions are indicated using the term "Assume", as in rule 10, which infers sentiment from connotation:

```
rule10:
(Assume Writer positive ...
believesTrue) A gfbf T &
T's anchor is in connotation lexicon ⟹
                        Writer sentiment toward T
```

The first line contains an assumption, the second line contains a precondition, and the third contains a conclusion.

```
rule8:
S positive believesTrue A gfbf T &
S sentiment toward T ⟹
                    S sentiment toward A gfbf T
```

For example, applying rule 8 to "*The bill would curb skyrocketing health care costs*," from the writer's (S's) negative sentiment toward the *costs* (T) expressed by *skyrocketing*, we can infer the writer is positive toward the event ⟨bill, curb, costs⟩ (A gfbf T) because it would decrease the costs.

Note that, in rule 8, the inference is (sentiment toward object) ⟹ (sentiment toward event). Rules 1 and 2 infer in the opposite direction.

```
rule1:
S sentiment toward A gfbf T ⟹
     S sentiment toward idea of A gfbf T
rule2:
S sentiment toward idea of A gfbf T ⟹
                           S sentiment toward T
```

For rule 1, why "ideaOf A gfbf T"? Because the purview of this work is making inferences about attitudes, not about events themselves. Conceptually, *ideaOf* coerces an event into an idea, raising it into the realm of private-state spaces. Reasoning about the ideas of events avoids the classification of whether the events are realis (i.e., whether they did/will happen).

Rule 9 infers sentiment toward the agent in a gfbf event.

```
rule9:
S sentiment toward A gfbf T &
A is a thing &
(Assume S positive believesTrue ...
substantial) A gfbf T ⟹
                           S sentiment toward A
```

By default, the system infers the event is intentional and that the agent is positive toward the event; if there is evidence against either, the inference should be blocked.

```
rule6:
A gfbf T, where A is animate ⟹
                         A intended A gfbf T
rule7:
S intended S gfbf T ⟹
              S positive sentiment toward
                          ideaOf S gfbf T
```

So far, the preconditions have included only one sentiment. Rule 3 applies when there are nested sentiments, i.e., sentiments toward sentiments.

```
rule3.1:
S1 sentiment toward
   S2 sentiment toward Z ⟹
        S1 agrees/disagrees with S2 that
                       isGood/isBad Z &
                  S1 sentiment toward Z
rule3.2:
S1 sentiment toward
   S2 pos/neg believesTrue substantial Z
⟹
        S1 agrees/disagrees with S2 that
                       isTrue/isFalse Z &
   S1 pos/neg believesTrue substantial Z
rule3.3:
S1 sentiment toward
   S2 pos/neg believesShould Z ⟹
        S1 agrees/disagrees with S2 that
                    should/shouldNot Z &
             S1 pos/neg believesShould Z
```

Among the subcases of rule 3, one shared conclusion is *S1 agrees/disagrees with S2* *, which depends on the sentiment from $S1$ toward $S2$. The reason there are subcases is because the attitude types of $S2$ are various, which determine the inferred attitude type of $S1$.

By rule 3, given the sentiment between $S1$ and $S2$, we can infer whether $S1$ and $S2$ agree. Similarly, we can infer in the opposite direction, as rule 4 shows.

```
rule4:
S1 agrees/disagrees with S2 that * ⟹
                     S1 sentiment toward S2
```

Two other rules are given in (Wiebe and Deng, 2014).

5 Inferences for An Example from MPQA Corpus

This section returns to the example from the MPQA corpus in Section 3.1, illustrating some interesting inference chains and conclusions.

Recall that the input for Ex(1) in Section 3.1 is:

```
8 writer positive believesTrue
  4 He revive flagging arms industry
6 writer positive believesTrue
  1 He trigger wars
```

The first inference is from connotation to sentiment since the word *war* is in the connotation lexicon.

```
rule10:
(Assume Writer positive ...
believesTrue) A gfbf T &
T's anchor is in connotation lexicon ⟹
                    Writer sentiment toward T
Assumptions:
6 writer positive believesTrue
  1 He trigger wars
rule10 ⟹ Infer:
17 writer negative sentiment
  2 wars
```

From the writer's negative sentiment toward *wars*, the system infers a negative sentiment toward *trigger wars*, since triggering wars is good-For them:

```
rule8:
S positive believesTrue A gfbf T &
S sentiment toward T ⟹
                  S sentiment toward A gfbf T
Preconditions:
6 writer positive believesTrue
  1 He trigger wars
17 writer negative sentiment
  2 wars
rule8 ⟹ Infer:
28 writer negative sentiment
  1 He trigger wars
```

On the other hand, since the agent, *He*, is animate and there is no evidence to the contrary, the system infers that the triggering event is intentional, and that *He* is positive toward the idea of his performing the event:

```
rule6 ⟹ Infer:
38 writer negative sentiment
  20 He positive intends
    1 He trigger wars
rule7 ⟹ Infer:
41 writer negative sentiment
  25 He positive sentiment
    26 ideaOf
      1 He trigger wars
```

Continuing with inference, since the writer has a negative sentiment toward the agent's positive sentiment, the system infers that the writer disagrees with him (rule 3) and thus that the writer is negative toward him (rule 4):

```
rule3.1:
S1 sentiment toward
    S2 sentiment toward Z ⟹
          S1 agrees/disagrees with S2 that
                              isGood/isBad Z &
                       S1 sentiment toward Z
Preconditions:
41 writer negative sentiment
  25 He positive sentiment
    26 ideaOf
      1 He trigger wars
rule3.1 ⟹ Infer:
50 writer disagrees with He that
  49 isGood
    26 ideaOf
      1 He trigger wars
30 writer negative sentiment
  26 ideaOf
    1 He trigger wars
```

Then rule 4 works on node 50 and infers:

```
rule4 ⟹ Infer:
55 writer negative sentiment
  3 He
```

In addition to the sentiment related to the *wars*, we have also drawn several conclusions of sentiment toward the *arms industry*. For example, one of the output nodes related to the arms industry is:

```
32 writer positive believesTrue
  31 He positive sentiment
    5 flagging arms industry
```

The MPQA annotators marked the writer's negative sentiment, choosing the long spans *therefore . . . industry* and *therefore planning . . . here and there* as attitude and expressive subjective element spans, respectively. They were not able to pinpoint any clear sentiment phrases. A machine learning system trained on such examples would have difficulty recognizing the sentiments. The system, relying on the negative connotation of *war* and the gfbf information in the sentence, is ultimately able to infer several sentiments, including the writer's negative sentiment toward the *trigger* event.

6 Conclusions

While previous sentiment analysis research has concentrated on the interpretation of explicitly stated opinions and attitudes, this work addresses opinion implicature (i.e., opinion-oriented default inference) in real-world text. This paper described a rule-based framework for representing and analyzing opinion implicatures which we hope will contribute to deeper automatic interpretation of subjective language. In the course of understanding implicatures, the system recognizes implicit sentiments (and beliefs) toward various events and entities in the sentence, often of mixed polarities; thus, it produces a richer interpretation than is typical in opinion analysis.

Acknowledgements. This work was supported in part by DARPA-BAA-12-47 DEFT grant #12475008 and National Science Foundation grant #IIS-0916046. We would like to thank the anonymous reviewers for their feedback.

References

Ann Banfield. 1982. *Unspeakable Sentences*. Routledge and Kegan Paul, Boston.

G. Bruder and J. Wiebe. 1995. Recognizing subjectivity and identifying subjective characters in third-person fictional narrative. In Judy Duchan, Gail Bruder, and Lynne Hewitt, editors, *Deixis in Narrative: A Cognitive Science Perspective*. Lawrence Erlbaum Associates.

Lingjia Deng and Janyce Wiebe. 2014. Sentiment propagation via implicature constraints. In *Meeting of the European Chapter of the Association for Computational Linguistics (EACL-2014)*.

Lingjia Deng, Yoonjung Choi, and Janyce Wiebe. 2013. Benefactive/malefactive event and writer attitude annotation. In *Proceedings of the 51st Annual Meeting of the Association for Computational Linguistics (Volume 2: Short Papers)*, pages 120–125, Sofia, Bulgaria, August. Association for Computational Linguistics.

Ryan Doran, Gregory Ward, Meredith Larson, Yaron McNabb, and Rachel E. Baker. 2012. A novel experimental paradigm for distinguishing between 'what is said' and 'what is implicated'. *Language*, 88(1):124–154.

Song Feng, Ritwik Bose, and Yejin Choi. 2011. Learning general connotation of words using graph-based algorithms. In *Proceedings of the 2011 Conference on Empirical Methods in Natural Language Processing*, pages 1092–1103, Edinburgh, Scotland, UK., July. Association for Computational Linguistics.

Song Feng, Jun Seok Kang, Polina Kuznetsova, and Yejin Choi. 2013. Connotation lexicon: A dash of sentiment beneath the surface meaning. In *Proceedings of the 51st Annual Meeting of the Association for Computational Linguistics (Volume 1: Long Papers)*, pages 1774–1784, Sofia, Bulgaria, August. Association for Computational Linguistics.

Herbert Paul Grice. 1967. Logic and conversation. The William James lectures.

H Paul Grice. 1989. *Studies in the Way of Words*. Harvard University Press.

Jerry R. Hobbs, Mark E. Stickel, Douglas E. Appelt, and Paul Martin. 1993. Interpretation as abduction. *Artificial Intelligence*, 63(1-2):69–142, October.

João Martins and Stuart C. Shapiro. 1983. Reasoning in multiple belief spaces. In *IJCAI*.

Randolph Quirk, Sidney Greenbaum, Geoffry Leech, and Jan Svartvik. 1985. *A Comprehensive Grammar of the English Language*. Longman, New York.

William J. Rapaport. 1986. Logical foundations for belief representation. *Cognitive Science*, 10(4):371–422.

Brian M. Slator and Yorick Wilks. 1987. Towards semantic structures from dictionary entries. Technical Report MCCS-87-96, Computing Research Laboratory, NMSU.

Dieter Stein and Susan Wright, editors. 1995. *Subjectivity and Subjectivisation*. Cambridge University Press, Cambridge.

Janyce Wiebe and Lingjia Deng. 2014. An account of opinion implicatures. arXiv:1404.6491v1 [cs.CL].

Janyce Wiebe and Rada Mihalcea. 2006. Word sense and subjectivity. In *Proceedings of the 21st International Conference on Computational Linguistics and 44th Annual Meeting of the Association for Computational Linguistics*, pages 1065–1072, Sydney, Australia, July. Association for Computational Linguistics.

Janyce Wiebe, Theresa Wilson, and Claire Cardie. 2005. Annotating expressions of opinions and emotions in language. *Language Resources and Evaluation (formerly Computers and the Humanities)*, 39(2/3):164–210.

Janyce Wiebe. 1994. Tracking point of view in narrative. *Computational Linguistics*, 20(2):233–287.

Author Index

Association for Computational Linguistics
209 N. Eighth Street
Stroudsburg, Pennsylvania 18360